The Imperiled Economy

BOOK II

Through the Safety Net

THE IMPERILED ECONOMY

BOOK II

THROUGH THE SAFETY NET

Edited by

Robert Cherry
Christine D'Onofrio
Cigdem Kurdas
Thomas R. Michl
Fred Moseley
Michele I. Naples

The Union for Radical Political Economics
New York

Production Editor: Bill James
Design and Production: Lorraine Press, Salt Lake City, Utah
Cover Art: Linda Briggs

Library of Congress Cataloging-in-Publication Data

The Imperiled economy.
Bibliography: p.
Contents: bk. 1. Macroeconomics from a Left Perspective — bk. 2. Through the safety net.
1. Macroeconomics. 2. United States — Economic policy — 1981- . 3. Marxian economics. I. Cherry, Robert D., 1944-
HB172.5.154 1987 339.5'0973 87-34233

ISBN 0-933306-50-4

Published 1988 by The Union for Radical Political Economic, URPE
122 West 27th Street, 10th Floor, New York, NY 10001

Printed in the United States of America

Acknowledgements

Several people have helped to make this book a reality. A generous grant from an anonymous donor via the Capp St. Foundation financed the major portion of production costs. Thank you to Michael Jacobs of the URPE National Office, and the URPE Steering Committee for their patient assistance, and to Bill Tabb for his early help in getting this project off the ground. We are grateful to many authors in this book as well as Arlene Geiger, Peter Albin and Raymond Majewski for their comments on various manuscripts. The timely publication of these books would not have been possible without the unstinting efforts of our production editor, Bill James, and of Pat Albers. The advice and assistance offered by Lorraine Press was invaluable. We also thank the authors, who shared the burden of a time-consuming project with tight deadlines. The views presented herein remain those of the authors alone and do not necessarily represent those of the editors or of URPE.

The Editorial Collective

Table of Contents

PART FOUR: ORGANIZED LABOR

PART FIVE: SOCIAL POLICY ISSUES

The following essays are reprinted with permission of their original publishers:

Saskia Sassen, "Capital Mobility and Labor Migration," is taken from her "Introduction" to her book, *The Mobility of Labor and Capital,* New York: Monthly Review Press, 1987.

Diane Flaherty, "The Farm Crisis," is a revised version of chapter 7 of Center for Popular Economics, *The Economic Report of the People,* Boston: South End Press, 1986.

Michael Reich, "Black-White Income Differences," is an abbreviated version of his chapter, "Postwar Racial Income Differences: Trends and Theories," in Garth Mangum and Peter Philips, eds., *The Three Worlds of Labor Economics,* White Plains, New York: M. E. Sharpe, 1988.

Ruth Milkman, "Women Workers, Feminism and the Labor Movement," is a revised and updated version of her chapter, "Women Workers, Feminism, and the Labor Movement since the 1960s," in her edited collection, *Women, Work and Protest: A Century of US Women's Labor History,* Boston: Routledge and Kegan Paul, 1985.

Michael Fabricant and Michael Kelly, "No Haven for Homeless in a Heartless Economy," was originally published in *Resist,* No. 192, January 1987, pp. 1 ff.

Tom Riddell, "The Political Economy of Military Spending," was published in abbreviated form as "Military Buildup, Economic Decline? The Economy's Trillion-dollar Habit," *Dollars & Sense,* No. 129, September 1987, pp. 6–9.

PART ONE

INTRODUCTION

1

Introduction: Guide to Articles

ROBERT CHERRY
and
MICHELE NAPLES

Radical political economy recognizes that the health of a capitalist economy derives from a robust corporate profit rate, not the well-being of workers and citizens. David M. Gordon's introductory essay grounds this conflict of interest in the dynamics of capital-labor conflict and inter-capitalist competition. He emphasizes that the kinds of social, economic and political problems discussed in this volume are not accidential, but will likely persist and/or recur. Yet government policies consistently favor capital and protect profits against the needs and interests of the vast majority of the population.

This book situates recent social and economic changes in the context of declining profit rates. The first volume of the *Imperiled Economy* provided radical analyses of the causes of this profit-rate decline, assessed its impact on broad macroeconomic variables, and evaluated government macroeconomic policies to combat it. This volume addresses the impact of corporate actions to reverse declining profits along four dimensions: (1) efforts to restructure the labor market towards lower-wage employment; (2) the unequal experience of such particular groups as blacks, women, union members, farmers, immigrants, and the homeless; (3) organized labor's response; and (4) the targeted government policies which have resulted or could be pursued.

RESTRUCTURING LABOR MARKETS

In Part Two, the changing structure of labor markets which resulted from declining profitability is explored. This process has three dimensions: sectoral shifts out of manufacturing and into low-wage service jobs; secular increases in unemployment associated with depressed manufacturing and agricultural sectors; and general employer efforts to reduce wages in order to restore profitability.

Sam Rosenberg reviews the shifting employment distribution. He notes that the elimination of middle-wage manufacturing employment requires a painful restructuring of the labor market: displaced manufacturing workers must accept low-wage service employment, and new entrants, regardless of their educational qualifications, must accept lower entry-level positions than such entrants a decade earlier. Rosenberg surveys government policies attempting to increase the speed of workers' adaptation to the deteriorating employment distribution. He finds that beginning with the Carter Administration, the federal government has adjusted social legislation to make it more difficult for workers to withstand the decline in their living standard.

Marilyn Power assesses the extent to which labor-market restructuring has transformed women's traditional roles in the labor market and home. She discusses women's experiences in traditional male occupations as well as those in traditional female occupations, changes in household responsibilities, and the economic situation of women in poverty. Power finds that the majority of women are working more continuously and assuming more responsibility for support of their families. Except for a small elite working in traditionally male jobs, this has not meant increases in their standards of living.

Teresa Amott depicts the continuing "welfare crisis" and assesses the experimental reforms which have been an important part of the wage-reduction policies of the eighties. Current experiments with workfare are compared with the nineteenth century workhouse, and traced to employer efforts to draw on welfare recipients as a pool of low-wage workers. Amott draws a parallel between declining benefit levels and a falling real minimum wage, and explains the difficulty in accepting paid work given inadequate child care and health coverage. She then outlines suggestions for socially responsible welfare reforms.

Saskia Sassen explores how U.S. government policies and multinational economic activities have shaped immigration flows. The increased urban demand for low-wage workers combined with the macroeconomic move to deflate wages creates potential jobs for immigrants from depressed areas; by disrupting small-holder agriculture and local manufacturing, a potential for out-migration arises. This combination provides an opportunity for foreign firms to employ a low-wage labor force while investing in the United States. Her analysis suggests that an immigration law which targets individual immigrants rather than employers and larger economic forces misses the fundamental issues.

Rhon Baiman details the impact of changing jobs on workers' situation. He demonstrates that the growth of service-sector jobs resulted in a decline in middle-income jobs; they were then replaced overwhelmingly with low-wage rather than high-wage jobs. This has implications for the debate over appropriate full-employment policies among liberal and left economists.

INEQUALITY

While some analysts have vaunted the end of race discrimination, a post-feminist era, and the equalizing tendencies of declining relative wages in manufacturing, the essays in this section document that neither the rising tide of economic expansion nor the ebb tide lifts or lowers all boats equally. In some cases the structural shifts discussed in the last section have exacerbated inequality; in others continued inequality underlines the need for distinct structural policy solutions.

Chris Tilly documents the increasing income inequality which has occurred since 1978. He criticizes claims that this is due to the growth of single-parent families or government transfer programs. He argues that growing inequality is caused by the secular decrease in the share of middle-income jobs, and is not a transient cyclical phenomenon.

Diane Flaherty provides evidence that U.S. government agricultural policies created excess farm capacity in the 1980s. She discusses the subsequent increased concentration of agricultural production and distribution. Flaherty rejects the view that these changes simply reflect increased efficiency. She warns that free-market forces have the potential to create worse farm problems.

Michael Reich documents the end of progress in reducing racial income inequality during the 1970s. He finds that progress during the pre-1970 period was a result of the ability of rural black migrants to obtain expanding urban employment, as substantial pressure from the Civil Rights movement increased the relative demand for black labor in manufacturing. Reich demonstrates that there is little evidence of continued progress after 1975.

Robert Cherry surveys the extent of black youth employment problems, and explanations given for them. He summarizes conservative claims that black youth unemployment is neither a very serious problem nor a result of labor-market discrimination. Cherry shows liberal responses to conservatives to be inadequate because they do not take into account the changing needs of corporations. Cherry argues that young black men have increasingly become a reserve army and only militant actions can improve their situation.

Elaine Sorensen explores the possibilities presented by comparable worth as a government policy or union strategy for reducing wage inequality. She first explains what comparable worth involves. Sorensen then evaluates both conservative and radical critiques of comparable worth, in terms of its economic impacts, political viability, and social consequences.

Julie Matthaei surveys the crisis of the ''natural'' family system, traditionally interpreted as biologically based. She shows that the breakdown of its institutions has positive as well as negative aspects, insofar as the ''natural'' family system was unjust, inegalitarian, and unfree. She proposes an alternative, consciously social family-system. Her vision includes socializing parenting costs and pursuing policies which attack the sexual division of labor and better integrate economic and family life.

ORGANIZED LABOR

The decline in corporate profitability has in several sectors led to efforts to decertify unions, take back former gains, and to runaway shops. While about one-third of the labor force was unionized by the early fifties, that figure has declined to about one-sixth. Nevertheless, organized labor at the national and local levels has begun to pursue innovative responses to plant shutdowns and corporate demands for givebacks. Since women workers provide one of the largest potential pools of union members, the positive impacts of feminism on the labor movement provide some hope for future organizing successes.

Dan Swinney and Jack Metzgar explore the crisis of unionized manufacturing and organized labor's response. They provide examples of successful community-wide efforts to fight plant closings, and detail a procedure for identifying early warning signs that a company means to shut down a factory. They show that managers do not always ''know best'' which options a plant can profitably pursue to stay in business, and that unexpected coalitions can be pulled together when saving the plant means protecting the economic base of the local community.

Kim Moody assesses mainstream trade union leaders' failure to organize workers to resist the increasing attack made by corporations on workers' living standards. He discusses their capitulation to the givebacks demanded by corporations and their unwillingness to support groups of workers willing to fight back. Moody also details the breakdown of working-class unity when unions in support of "their" company undercut wages of workers in competing firms. He contends that this enterprise unionism, not concessions in and of themselves, poses the real threat to the labor movement.

Ruth Milkman gives an overview of the impact of the feminist movement on unions and organizing. She addresses what women and feminism can do for unions, for instance through separate locals like Local 925 of the Service Employees' International Union, which emphasizes worker participation and democracy. She reviews the part played by CLUW (the Coalition of Labor Union Women), and the importance of raising questions like sexual harassment or comparable worth for organizing and representing women workers.

SOCIAL POLICY ISSUES

The crisis of profitability and subsequent economic restructuring have produced new social needs and undercut historic policy solutions. In this section, the impact of efforts to cut social services related to housing and health while maintaining military spending are traced.

Peter Marcuse explains how the widely accepted "death" of cities during the 1970s was transformed into the "revitalization" of the 1980s. He develops an analytical framework for understanding the uses of space, based on the effects of changes in industrial structure on the profitability of certain land-use patterns (e.g., geographic proximity among producers or extensive land required for production). In this process some people benefit while others are hurt; for instance, gentrification and high rents help create homelessness. While certain economic classes have political advantages in shaping policies to facilitate such urban transformation, they nevertheless face coalitions of tenants and neighborhoods who can help constrain these trends and shape rental and housing alternatives.

Michael Fabricant and Michael Kelly describe the relationship between the political and economic landscape and homelessness. They focus on the response of the welfare state and the larger social order to the homeless, which they place in the context of the profitability crisis. Fabricant and Kelly link the dramatic decline in the social wage over the past decade to rising homelessness. They provide suggestions for developing actions and policies that can more effectively serve the interests of homeless people.

Meredith Turshen surveys the changing state of health and health care in the last ten to twenty years. The sources of ill-health are shown to extend beyond disease to occupational illness, poverty, stress, and the pollution and toxicities associated with petroleum bi-products. She identifies various strands of an emerging health movement based on coalitions across traditional "interest-group" boundaries. She cites the deleterious effect on health-care provision of reducing the government social-service budget. Turshen suggests that national health insurance or a nationalized health-care system would greatly improve health-care delivery and could provide political rallying points for progressive forces.

Peter Arno and Karyn Feiden present the dimensions of the AIDS epidemic. They document the slow federal response to funding research and expanding resources for caring for victims of AIDS, and suggest the magnitude of its ramifications for the spread of the disease. Arno and Feiden provide estimates of the economic impact of the rising epidemic, in particular when private insurers attempt to divest themselves of unprofitable AIDS-infected or high-risk clients. The epidemic highlights the absence of a coherent national policy to deal with catastrophic illness, and reinforces the need to consider less privatized health-care systems.

Tom Riddell addresses the functions of the United States' high level of military spending in the economy. He cites its role in sustaining aggregate demand, in preserving the postwar international economic order, and its relationship to the perceived Soviet threat and to the narrow interests of the military-industrial complex. Riddell argues that military spending can have adverse economic consequences, including interfering with investment, and contributing to the current government deficit. Recognition of these may help the effort to shift spending priorities to progressive social programs.

ACKNOWLEDGEMENT

Thanks to many of the authors, who helped draft summaries of their contributions.

2

Left, Right, and Center: An Introduction to Political Economy

DAVID M. GORDON

> The tradition of all the dead generations weighs like a nightmare on the brain of the living.
>
> — Karl Marx, 1852

What to do about the imperiled economy? Policy debates erupt sporadically about minimum wages and protectionism, about union rights and farm relief, about comparable worth and shelters for the homeless, about affirmative action and the defense budget.

These debates often seem like shotgun wars — quick to explode, thunderous noise, scattered buckshot. They come and they go, but they rarely seem to build in any kind of coherent way toward a more comprehensive vision of how to solve the urgent and widespread social and economic problems facing us.

One of the main reasons for the episodic and apparently arbitrary quality of such policy debates is that their protagonists rarely (if ever) make clear their basic policy perspectives. How do they believe the economy operates? What role do they think the government can and should play? What is their view of the kind of society they would like to create in the long run?

The essays in this volume of readings, *Through the Saftey Net,* focus on a number of the critical social and economic policy problems currently facing people in the United States. While they discuss a wide range of problems and embody diverse styles of exposition and argument, they share a common approach to the political economy.

For the purposes of this discussion, we can label that approach "radical political economy." This introduction to the volume outlines the basic premises of that approach and contrasts it with its two principal contending policy perspectives, liberalism and conservatism. We shall explore the basic elements of left, right, and center viewpoints, hoping to illuminate some of the reasons for and stakes involved in sharp differences toward policies for an economy and people in trouble.

The introduction begins with a brief outline of the principal tenets of each of these three perspectives.[1] It then briefly summarizes the principal differences among the perspectives. It concludes with some discussion of the implications of these basic differences for the critical policy debates of the coming decade.

ON THE LEFT: THE RADICAL PERSPECTIVE

The radical perspective proposes that current social and economic problems have their roots in the fundamental structures of our capitalist economic system. If we want to begin seriously addressing our current problems, this implies, we need to begin digging up those roots and moving toward a different kind of economic system. Unless we do, those same problems are likely to reappear, just as a tree's branches grow again after pruning — perhaps with a slightly different shape but still the same kinds of outgrowth from the same kind of tree.

Radicals build this perspective upon eight primary analytic propositions or areas of concern.

1. Modes of Production and Economic Structure

The structure and evolution of any society is likely to be shaped fundamentally by that society's dominant "mode of production," the way in which people join together to produce their basic means of livelihood and by which resulting surplus product is controlled and allocated. Operating through that system, people's lives are shaped by the structures surrounding them. The effects are widespread. "This mode of production must not be considered," Karl Marx and Friedrich Engels wrote in *The German Ideology* (1963:7), "simply as being the reproduction of the physical existence of the individuals."

> Rather it is a definite form of activity of these individuals, a definite part. As individuals express their life, so they are.... The nature of individuals thus depends on the material conditions determining their production.

Left feminists have extended this kind of analysis to suggest that "gender systems" constitute another kind of fundamental structural influence, analogous to modes of production — another kind of "definite form of activity" shaping people's lives. In modern societies, many suggest, people's lives are shaped by *patriarchal* gender systems in which adult male heads of households are able to exercise dominating power over women and children and enjoy disproportionate shares of the fruits of household life.

These introductory arguments provide the basis for a *materialist* view of history, a perspective suggesting that how we both live and think is fundamentally shaped by the prevailing *material* structures of production, distribution, and exchange. Some have historically responded to this perspective as a kind of rigid and relentless economic determinism, suggesting that people cannot ourselves have a decisive impact on our lives. But almost all materialists, even from the beginning, have argued explicitly against such reductive formulations. "[People] make their own history," Marx wrote in *The Eighteenth Brumaire*... (1963:15), "but they do not make it just as they please; they do not make it under circumstances chosen by themselves, but under circumstances directly encountered, given and transmitted from the past." To ignore those structural influences would be to ignore much of what matters in shaping our lives, to pretend that we can choose whatever fortunes and outcomes we prefer. But to treat these influences as straight-jackets would be to overlook the rich possibilities for action and transformation. " 'Society' is... never only the 'dead husk' which limits social and individual fulfillment," the English Marxist critic Raymond Williams has written (1977:87). "It is always also a constitutive process... an active and conscious as well as, by default, a passive and objectified historical experience."

2. The Defining Characteristics of Capitalism

Within this framework, it is useful to characterize the kind of economic system, or ''mode of production,'' which dominates our material lives in the United States at the end of the twentieth century. Radicals refer to this system as *capitalism* or as the *capitalist mode of production*.

From the radical perspective, capitalism has several distinctive features. In general, Samuel Bowles and Richard Edwards write in *Understanding Capitalism* (1985:68): ''Capitalism is an economic system in which commodities are produced for profit using privately owned capital goods and wage labor.'' This general definition in fact encompasses three basic aspects of capitalist systems. As Bowles and Edwards continue: ''First, the labor process produces commodities. Second, the capital goods used in production are privately owned. And third, the labor employed is primarily wage labor.''

We can look briefly at each of these three defining characteristics.

— *Commodities* are goods and services which are produced primarily for the purposes of selling them in order to earn money in exchange. They are different from goods and services produced for one's own use, for example, or for exchange in barter trade. Capitalist economies are not the only ones historically which have featured commodity production, of course, but this characteristic of capitalism has important interactions, as we shall see, with its other distinctive features.

— Capitalism features *private ownership of capital goods* — the plants, offices and machines which help make us productive. Capital goods are not, or need not always be, privately owned. In the United States, for example, many highly-efficient utility plants are publicly-owned and a fair number of factories and offices are jointly owned as worker cooperatives.

One of the most important features of the private ownership of capital goods is that it sanctions owners' rights to allocate the use of the capital goods among potential workers. This provides the basis, among many consequences, for the owners' essentially unbridled prerogatives in hiring and firing their employees.

— Capitalism also features *wage labor*. Wage laborers are people who must earn their living by working for a wage or salary income. If they find a job, they can get some income on which (at least partly) to support themselves. If they can't find work, they run the risk of poverty, malnutrition, or worse. In commodity economies in which consumers must have income in order to acquire commodities — since they are able to produce so little for their own use — the risks of loss of wage-and-salary income are particularly acute.

In order to survive, in short, wage-and-salary earners must sell themselves — their time and their capacities — to an employer in return for employment income. In exchange for that wage-or-salary payment, they must agree to work under someone else's direction and to surrender all title to the products of their labor. If we make bread and shirts at home, we can do whatever we like with those products. If we work for Wonder Bread or Arrow Shirts, hands off the final fruits of the loom!

3. *The Structural Contradictions of Capitalism*

These characteristic features result in two basic driving forces in capitalist economies.

Capital-Labor Conflict. The owners of capital goods in capitalist economies will not put those means of production to work unless they can earn a profit from their investment. The most reliable potential source of profits comes from whatever surplus they can earn by getting workers to produce more than is necessary to cover the costs of their own wages. Once the wage is covered, as a result, owners always have an interest in their employees' working longer and harder than the workers are themselves likely to want to work. More work, more for the owners. Less work, less strain on the workers.

This establishes the basis for an underlying and persistent conflict of interest in capitalist economies — between employers and employees, bosses and workers, capital and labor. It can erupt or moderate, provoke strikes or subside in occasional truce. But the roots of the conflict lie in the essential structural logic of capitalism as a system: those who own the means of production and those who perform wage labor are bound together but have significantly different needs about the intensity of production and the distribution of its proceeds.

Competitive Instability. If one capitalist firm captures the market for cars or coffee-makers, it can potentially drive its competitors out of business. Relentless competition among firms is therefore an inescapable and uncompromising force in capitalist economies, driving firms to cut costs, to invest in anticipation of innovations their competitors may initiate,. . . to compete, compete, compete in order to survive and expand.

One of the positive contributions of this pressure to innovate is that capitalist economies are dynamic and often produce significant improvements in social productivity. But inter-firm competition is more like warfare than contemplative research and development: there is no higher authority which can manage or regulate the intensity of competition. The warfare can thus lead to waves of mergers and speculation, to wildly fluctuating roller-coaster rides of boom and bust, to unpredictably alternating episodes of growth and stagnation. The competition drives us forward. But it also takes us for a very bumpy ride.

4. *Classes and Power*

Driven by this dynamic of conflict and competition, the long-term development of capitalism has tended to push larger and larger proportions of people into wage labor and therefore to concentrate the means of production into the hands of fewer and fewer, increasingly large corporations. Capitalism has tended to create an increasingly important division, as a result, between a small group who effectively control the means of production and a huge mass of people who survive through wage-and-salary labor. Radicals refer to this as the basic and most fundamental *class division* in capitalist societies, the division between capital and labor. (This does not preclude, of course, significant divisions arising *within* each of these two constituent classes.)

The logic of this class division is neither omnipresent nor fixed in time. It interacts with many other social forces and changes constantly. As the English historian E.P. Thompson has put it (1967:9; emphasis in the original):

> the notion of class entails the notion of historical relationship. . . . We can see a *logic* in the responses of similar experiences, but we cannot predicate any laws. Consciousness of class arises in the same way in different times and places, but never in just the same way.

What is constant about this relationship is that the balance and dynamic of class divisions in capitalist economies is fundamentally mediated by *power*. The control and resilience of those on top depends on their ability to push, cajole, and intimidate the vast majority of citizens. And the counter-responses of workers — their ability to organize, bargain and strike — depends equally on their ability to counter-push, counter-cajole, and counter-intimidate. Not all relationships in capitalist economies are conducted under the point of a gun, to be sure, but basic economic and political transactions are constantly shadowed by the relative power of those who own and those who don't own the means of production.

One of the main regulators of relative class power in capitalist economies is the relative size of what radicals call the *reserve army of labor,* that portion of the labor force which is unemployed. Capitalist economies tend repeatedly to generate high levels of unemployment. (See Book I of *The Imperiled Economy* for analyses of this tendency.) High unemployment can have a chilling effect on employed workers, since the costs of losing their jobs — and not being able to find an alternative — are a direct function of the probability of remaining unemployed after dismissal. The greater the size of the reserve army, the more likely it becomes that employers can, indeed, intimidate their employees.

The balance of power is also affected by the extent of divisions among workers, such as racial or gender divisions. Employers can benefit from such inequalities or discrimination in two important ways. They can benefit directly if they are able to pay relatively lower wages, at a given skill level, to workers who suffer discrimination. And they can benefit somewhat more indirectly if such inequalities create divisions and competition among workers. The more unified are workers, presumably, the greater their bargaining power with employers. In unity is strength and in division lies weakness in the never-ending contest of power between classes (see Michael Reich [1981] for a useful analysis of these effects).

5. *Accumulation, Crises, and Stages of Capitalist Development*

Capitalism is driven forward by the pace of capital accumulation. If the owners of capital mobilize their wealth for productive investments, the economy can grow. If they abstain from those investments, the economy will sputter.

The accumulation process is itself governed by the logic and dynamics of capitalist relations. But the contradictions of class conflict and competition, as well as the continuing contest for power, do not and cannot operate in a vacuum. When workers and corporations negotiate over wages in modern capitalist economies, for example, they do so under a particular structured relationship — among workers, unions and firms; under the watch of labor laws and government agencies; working with relatively determinate expectations about how corporations, banks, and the government will interact to generate future movements in prices, output, investment, and interest rates, . . . and so on.

Capitalist economies are thus located in and mediated by specific institutional forms — the rules of the game which shape and govern its dynamics and contradictions. Without such regulating institutional structures, indeed, the short- and long-term weather prospects would be so unpredictable and uncertain that capitalist firms would never dare invest and produce for fear that they could never forecast the conditions under which they would eventually produce and sell their products.

Many radicals now think that there are successive stages of such institutional configurations, leading capitalism through a sequence of what several call *social structures of accumulation* (SSAs) (see Gordon, Edwards, and Reich [1982: Ch. 2] for an introduction). The social structure of accumulation refers to those institutions whose strength and stability make rapid accumulation possible. The institutions of any given SSA are likely to last for a while but are also likely eventually to experience stresses and strains. As those tensions develop, the prospects are bound to cloud over and the process of accumulation is itself likely to become more and more problematic and unstable.

What radicals call *crisis* may then result, a self-reinforcing process of instability and stagnation (see Book I of *The Imperiled Economy* for full discussions of the wide variety of possible origins and dynamics of crises). As some firms begin to experience trouble, they stop investing. Their problems then spread: workers lose their jobs and the loss of that purchasing power then infects other firms. A downward spiral can result.

How does a crisis stop? According to this analytic perspective, a new set of institutions — a new social structure of accumulation — is necessary if capitalism is to revive. As Bowles and Edwards remark (1985:97): "Such reconstruction is by no means inevitable, since it depends on the outcome of many specific conflicts and deals. Nonetheless, the crisis creates a situation in which the inadequacies of the old social structure of accumulation become visible, the problems more pressing, and the demand for action urgent."

If and when a new SSA begins to emerge and a vigorous pace of capital accumulation is restored, we may say that a new *stage* of capitalist development has commenced. It is useful, indeed, to view the last roughly 150 years of capitalism in a country like the United States as having passed through several stages of development:

— From the 1840s through the 1890s, we experienced a stage of "competitive industrial capitalism."

— From the 1890s through the 1930s, we passed through a stage of "oligopolistic corporate capitalism."

— From World War II to the present, we have been digesting a stage of "state corporate capitalism."

Table 1, drawn from Bowles and Edwards (1985: 98), reviews some of the main characteristics of these three stages.

6. The "Capitalist State"

Because the mode of production in any society is viewed as playing such an important role in shaping social and political life, the role of the government in a capitalist society is considered to be fundamentally shaped and delimited by the structure and power relations of the capitalist economy. This leads many radicals to refer conceptually to the *capitalist state*.

This economic influence on the state can occur in either of two principal ways.

The first is called an "instrumental" influence because representatives of the interests of capital are often able actually to hold the levers — the "instruments" — of power. Corporations and the wealthy are better able to shape elections and lobby for their special interests than others because of their money and connections. Their representatives often gain, hold or control positions of influence and power in the government. And their representatives can therefore gain special privileges like cozy defense contracts, subsidies for research and development, tax breaks, or advantageous labor laws.

The second path of influence is called "structural." Whoever holds positions of government power, they are continually forced to confront some of the basic rules of the game in capitalist economies: Investment will not take place unless capital can secure a "healthy" profit on those investments. And jobs and income will not be provided unless those investments occur.

Table 1
The Stages of American Capitalist Development

Key relations in the social structure of accumulation	**Social structure of accumulation I:** Competitive Industrial Capitalism (1840s–1890s)	**Social structure of accumulation II:** Oligopolistic Corporate Capitalism (1890s–1930s)	**Social structure of accumulation III:** State Corporate Capitalism (1940s–present)
Capital-capital relations	Small business, local, competitive capitalism	National monopolistic competition, large corporations (trusts)	Monopolistic competition on a world scale, U.S. corporations dominant
Capital-labor relations	Strong craft-based unions in some industries, extensive workplace control exercised by skilled workers	Capitalists are dominant, unions weak, not recognized	Labor accord, unions recognized with legal rights
Labor-labor relations	Craft-based distinctions between skilled and unskilled workers	Homogenized labor, semiskilled factory, operatives become important	Segmented labor markets, unions among mass production workers
Government-economy relations	Limited government	Limited government (some regulation, e.g., Federal Reserve)	Keynesian regulation of macroeconomy, United States as world policeman for capitalism

Government policies therefore constantly confront the threat of what radicals call "capital strike." If government policies, however motivated, hit too hard at the bottom line, capital may go on strike, withdrawing its means of production, and the whole economy may suffer. Private ownership of capital goods and wage labor's dependence on capital, in short, provides capitalist corporations with a kind of veto power over government policies. If those policies step over certain boundaries established by the structures of the economic system, they are likely to run into brick walls.

But these two kinds of influence are neither certain nor uncontested in societies with democratic political structures. Citizens can vote for and seek to influence governments as well. State policies in democratic capitalist societies constitute a kind of contested terrain, a venue for continual tussle and struggle over directions and priorities. While capital's monopoly ownership of the means of production provides them with both advantages and an ultimate veto power, the numbers, energy, and commitment of workers and citizens provides them with considerable (at least potential) power as well.[2]

7. Beyond Capitalism?

If we have problems we would like to solve.... And if the structure and dynamics of our capitalist economic system contributes significantly to the creation and reproduction of those problems. . . . Then it makes sense to think about the longer-term possibilities of moving beyond capitalism. But where and how?

Many radicals suggest four standards for charting a course beyond capitalism.

Fairness. Many agree that people should be treated fairly: we should not be penalized because of our family of birth or skin color or gender. The notion of fairness in both process and outcome reaches back over several centuries in the development of modern societies.

Radicals argue that capitalism undermines social fairness in at least one fundamental respect. The owners of capital goods have a kind of power and control which is denied the rest of us. Have they earned these advantages? The average net wealth of the wealthiest 400,000 households in the United States was roughly $9 million in 1983, while the average net wealth of the bottom 90 percent of households, accounting for about 76 million households, was roughly $40,000 (U.S. Congress 1986:Table 3). The top 400,000 were 225 times as wealthy, on average, as the bottom 76 million. Were they 225 times smarter? Did they work 225 times as hard? These huge wealth differentials derive in large part, radicals argue, because capitalism accords and protects the concentration of capital goods ownership in a few hands.

We could achieve a much greater degree of economic fairness, therefore, if we moved toward an economic system in which there was much more shared and common ownership of capital goods.

Efficiency. No one wants to work harder than necessary to achieve a comfortable life. It makes no sense at all to invest heavily in social structures or economic systems which are inefficient. But, for all the advertisements touting the vaunted efficiency of the capitalist machine, capitalism is a remarkably wasteful kind of economic operation — with its untapped resources, its armies of managerial and supervisory personnel, its continuing labor conflicts, and its ever-present overproduction of dangerous or wasteful products (see Bowles, Gordon and Weisskopf [1983:Ch. 7] for a detailed review of the hundreds of billions of dollars of economic waste generated by the U.S. economy in the 1980s).

It is reasonable to argue that we could construct a much more efficient economic system if we moved toward greater worker participation and control in the organization of production and greater social participation and control in the planning and allocation of economic resources.

Democracy. The basic ideal of democracy is that people should be able to shape decisions affecting them. We have a substantial amount of political democracy in the United States. But we have almost no economic democracy. Workers cannot shape decisions about investment and the organization of production. Even worse, as many union organizers put it, they have to check their bill of rights at the plant gates and office elevators. In the late 1970s, for example, roughly two-thirds of union contracts provided for the suspension or dismissal of employees who were "disrespectful" of their supervisors (*New York Times,* July 1, 1979:F-3).

This lack of economic democracy, as we saw above in discussing the state, can spill over into the political arena. We could much better pursue democracy, radicals argue, if we began to apply democratic principles to the organization of our economy as well as our government.

Community. Capitalism operates to promote profits, not to develop people. If someone has skills which need re-tooling, capitalism is just as likely to toss that worker aside as to provide for retraining. If a community's capital stock or infrastructure is aging, capital may decide to pack its bags and move away without concern for the lives of community workers and residents left behind. People are expendable in capitalism and communities are ignored. Relationships are destroyed while commodities are produced and worshipped.

It would make sense, radicals argue, to move toward an economic system which placed a much higher priority on developing people and promoting strong communities.

8. Power and Struggle

None of that comes easily, radicals agree. But we must begin to argue, debate, protest, and mobilize in order to move beyond capitalism. If we tinker with stop-gap solutions to our problems, they will recur or reappear in new forms. Our serious social problems cannot themselves be eradicated or more than marginally resolved without fundamental changes in our dominant economic forces and institutions.

We have a choice, in short, betweeen racing on a treadmill or building a more decent society. The choice is ours.

ON THE RIGHT AND IN THE CENTER: CONSERVATIVE AND LIBERAL PERSPECTIVES

Most conservative and liberal policy perspectives share a common view of the economy embodied in what is generally called *neoclassical* analysis. They depart in their view of how markets and the state interact and in their approaches to policy. We can begin this section, therefore, with a very brief review of the principal tenets of their shared economic perspective and then turn to their respective and differing policy approaches.

The Best of All Possible Worlds

Neoclassical economics builds on some basic postulates about the behavior of individual decision-making units, such as households, workers, and firms, and the ways in which they make choices within an existing institutional environment.

The analysis begins with a view of individual decision-making units as rational actors, seeking to maximize their welfare subject to certain constraints. Consumers choose their purchases, for example, in such a way as to maximize their "utility" subject to the budget constraint of their available net income and wealth.

Neoclassical economics places a great emphasis on the *freedom* of choice experienced by these actors. What this actually means, given the notion of rational choice *subject to constraints,* is that neoclassical economists place paramount emphasis on the range of choices which households, workers, and firms enjoy, placing much less weight on explaining why so many face such *limited* choices. The analysis does not explore the ways in which structured institutions predetermine the range of goods from which individuals can choose, shaping the constraints within which choices are made. Neoclassicals primarily study choice, in short, and leave the study of politics, power, and conflict to the rest of us.

The aggregate economy is made up of the composite of all these millions of individual actors' choices. Neoclassical economists place great emphasis on the desirability of those aggregate outcomes. This builds on three basic presuppositions.

Equilibrium. Neoclassical economists argue first of all that the "invisible hand" of market interactions will generate outcomes which tend to reproduce themselves. Since people have chosen according to their preferences, and since preferences are unlikely to change very rapidly, then economic outcomes are themselves likely to remain relatively stable.

This idea is commonly applied, for example, to outcomes at work. If wage inequalities persist over time, neoclassical economists argue that they must be persisting because of market interactions and, therefore, because people have chosen the best jobs available, paying the best wages they can secure. (If there were better jobs available, they would take them!) This kind of analysis ignores all the other possible influences on relative wages — including firm power, union power, differential productivities in different firms and jobs, the effects of government regulation. . . . The invisible hand, though unseen, rules throughout.

Harmony. Neoclassical economists also stress the harmony and mutuality of interests promoted by market economies. If people didn't like the terms of their market exchanges, after all, they wouldn't participate. The parties on both sides of the exchange benefit mutually. As market economies operate, therefore, they promote a condition of harmony among its participants because of the reciprocity of its transactions. "The role of the market. . . ," conservative economist Milton Friedman argues (1962: 23), "is that it permits unanimity without conformity. . . ."

This emphasis on harmony spills over into analyses of many different social problems. One might think, for example, that the poor would be unhappy with their plight. Not really, according to many neoclassical analyses. We earn what we're worth in the market, they suggest. What we're worth depends largely on how much we've invested in ourselves. The poor have freely chosen to invest relatively little in their own skills and capacities. They deserve what they earn and earn what they deserve. Everyone should remain content with their conditions, by this logic, because everyone has chosen the paths to their present locations.

Optimality. Neoclassical economists conclude by arguing that market economies work better than any other kind of economic arrangement. The freer people are to choose in the marketplace, the more satisfied they will become. Participants in market economies would never choose to adopt another mode of economic organization, as a result, because they would not be able to enjoy as high a level of utility as they do in market economies.

We can see an example of this kind of reasoning, again, in the workplace and labor market. Suppose there are recurring work accidents in some firms and industries. Should the government impose safety regulations? Neoclassical economists tend to argue, on balance, that there is no need for such regulation. Why? Workers in unsafe jobs must be getting paid extra to compensate them for their exposure to risk, because if they weren't earning safety or hazard pay, they would simply grab their lunch pails and march over to some other job in which the relationship between pay and safety was more to their liking. Since the market works, jobs are assumed to be plentiful, and since workers — like other economic actors — are free to choose, the current configuration of pay and safety must be optimal.

With these postulates as a basic platform, both conservatives and liberals nonetheless admit that the outcomes of market economies may be a little rough around the edges. Both agree that some remedial actions might be undertaken to help smooth the edges. But their differences then emerge as they consider what kinds of actions might be appropriate or effective.

Policy from the Right

Conservatives tend to argue that imperfect outcomes emerge in market economies for either of two main reasons. First, some actors may not have enough information about or access to market opportunities. Second, institutions like the state or unions may interfere with market operations in ways which undermine their effectiveness.

Conservatives therefore place the highest possible priority on promoting market competition and avoiding interference with competitive market outcomes. They believe that the state in modern market societies should play an extremely limited role, confined to promotion of more efficient markets and to protection of individual liberties and physical well-being.

Many accuse conservatives of ruthless disregard for the lives and well-being of the disadvantaged, of those who fare least well in the rough and tumble of the capitalist marketplace. But conservatives defend their policy views on at least three grounds.

First, they stick to their guns about the glories of market competition. That economy works best, they insist, whose market encounters the least interference.

Second, because they have such faith in the market's capacity to serve the interests of the vast, nearly overwhelming majority of citizens, they fear that the only ones who remain disgruntled, pushing for remedial government action, are small pockets of "special interests." The majority should resist, they insist, the imposition of the will of these special interests on everybody else.

Third, and crucially, they argue that even the most well-intended government policies are likely to fail even on their own terms. They may produce unintended reverberations which undermine their original intent. They may cause market dislocations which swamp their short-term benefits. And the complexity of the operations of market economies will simply defy the capacities of government planners to moderate their behavior (see Edward C. Banfield [1974] for a vigorous presentation of this view).

Policy from the Center

While sharing a basic faith in market economies, liberals believe that market economies are somewhat more likely to run into problems than conservatives think they are. Liberals therefore believe that the "general interest" can often be served through government action. This leads to two somewhat more specific policy differences with conservatives.

Government Support for Capital. Liberals generally believe that the government *can* provide a wide variety of critical aids to private business and that private business often needs it. Markets may fail for a wide variety of reasons: lack of information, too short a time horizon, market imperfections, inadequate scale of available investment capital. . . . When the market fails, the government should step in to help.

Redistributive Policies. Many liberals also advocate policies to help the disadvantaged and the poor — through broadened education and training programs, more effective income supports, and reduced discrimination.

Some advocate these policies because they care about equality and fairness. Others, somewhat tougher-minded, push for such policies rather more because they fear that spreading and destabilizing unrest may result from a continuation of poverty, discrimination, and widening inequality.

Liberals face their toughest problem when these two policy concerns tend to conflict. Redistributive policies may help prompt movement toward full employment, for example, but tight labor markets also tend to squeeze corporate profits. Faced with such incursions on the private sector, liberals typically back off their concern for job programs and greater equality, placing higher priority on "help for capital" than "help for the disadvantaged." When the going gets tough in capitalist economies, it appears, liberals tend to look the other way. Liberals' enthusiasm for full employment, as a result, always seems to fade.

A SUMMARY OF DIFFERENCES

These differences in viewpoint among the three perspectives result in significantly different approaches to the role of the state and the possibilities for effective government policy. It seems useful to summarize those differences in four main areas.

Basic Economic Structure

Radicals view the basic structure of capitalist economies as fundamentally flawed, arguing that we could move toward alternative systems which would much better promote fairness, efficiency, democracy, and community. Liberals and conservatives tend to share a view, by contrast, that the basic structure of capitalist economies is fundamentally sound.

These differences lead to sharply contrasting views of the character of economic and social problems. Radicals tend to view the social and economic problems arising in capitalist economies as having deep roots in the logic and dynamics of that economic system; this suggests that problems are likely to be both serious and recurring. Conservatives have a much more sanguine view, believing that social and economic problems are relatively unlikely to occur and, if and when they occur, are bound to be relatively superficial and short-lived. Liberals are more likely than conservatives to expect problems and treat them seriously, but since these problems reflect imperfections rather than structural faults in the economic structure, they should be viewed as remediable (without having to consider or countenance structural changes in the underlying economic system).

Actual Role of the Government

There are also important differences about the role the government plays in capitalist democracies and the interests it either seeks or is able to serve.

Radicals argue that the state in capitalist societies, however much it may be an arena for contest among a wide variety of competing interests, tends disproportionately to serve the interests of capital — whether intentionally through the instrumental actions of actual governmental representatives or more structurally through respect for and constraint by the power of capital's ownership of the means of production.

Liberals believe that the outcomes of market economies are sufficiently balanced and sufficiently fair that they do not fundamentally distort the political process. And yet, since they believe that many citizens may feel the need to redress market imperfections, they view the state as an arena in which a full range of interest groups, representing most of the citizenry, seeks to address its needs. Because the state is democratic (in capitalist democracies), it is further capable of representing and balancing all those interests, achieving policies which tend to reflect the ''general interest.''

With their much greater respect for the optimality of market outcomes, conservatives are inclined to believe that few people will feel the need for government redress. Those who do seek such government help, consequently, are likely to reflect relatively narrow and therefore ''special'' interests, stamping government policies with their particular needs.

Desired Role for Government Policy toward the Economy

Because radicals believe that the basic structure of capitalist economies is flawed, they would hope that workers and citizens would demand government policy aimed increasingly at economic transformation, promoting structural changes in the rules of the game and the distribution of economic power so that the interests of the vast majority of citizens could be better served. In seeking such transformation, government policies should aim, wherever and however possible, to promote fairness, efficiency, democracy, and community.

Conservatives have a simple normative view about the government: do as little as possible! More specifically, they argue that governments should seek to promote market competition and otherwise protect against its own or others' interference with the actions of the ''invisible hand.''

Liberals believe that the government should act to address market imperfections, helping to support capital accumulation and to redistribute to the needy. But it should also take care to avoid interfering with the underlying structure of market economies.

What If Capital Goes on Strike?

Suppose that governments purposefully or inadvertently step on capital's toes. What then?

Radicals believe that governments should keep on stepping. If capital refuses to mobilize its capital goods because it views its own profits as more important than social needs, then government actors should consider policies to mobilize those capital goods on behalf of those social needs.

Since conservatives believe that the government should never get itself into such situations, they also believe that the government should back off as quickly as possible, respecting the sanctity of private ownership of and control over capital goods as one of the fundamental pillars of the structure of market economies.

Liberals are caught in the middle. And so they propose a compromise; negotiation. They tend to suggest that in such situations tri-partite councils representing business, labor and the government should seek to resolve differences and strike a balance among competing interests.

Table 2
Principal Differences among Left, Center and Right Perspectives

Issue	Left	Center	Right
1. Basic Structure of Economy	Flawed Structure	Sound Structure	Sound Structure
Social & Economic Problems	Problems serious, recurring	Problems serious but remediable	Problems superficial
2. Actual Role of Government	Serves capital; Reproduces economic structure	Serves "general interest"	Serves "special interests"
3. Desired Role of Government	Transform economic structure; Promote efficiency, fairness, democracy & community	Address market imperfections; Help capital; Promote redistribution	Do little: Promote market competition; Prevent market interference
4. What about Capital Strike?	Counter it	Negotiate	Capitulate

Table 2 digests these general differences about the political economy, summarizing the principal contrasts among the three perspectives in their approach to the economy and government policy about the economy.

THE WEATHER FORECAST FOR THE REST OF THE CENTURY

Outlining these differences is hardly an academic exercise. Significant political forces are mobilized in the United States to advance these different perspectives. If anything, it is likely that such contests over government policy will grow sharper and more intense through the 1990s.

From the right, conservatives have enjoyed considerable success during the 1980s in promoting their views. Government regulation of business in certain key social and economic areas has been cut back substantially. Taking advantage of high unemployment rates and the threat posed by international competition, forces on the right have helped erode the base and strength of organized labor, exposing workers to stagnating income and shaky job security.

And yet, as many essays in the first volume of *The Imperiled Economy* show, corporations have still not recovered from the profit doldrums of the 1970s. It is likely, therefore, that conservatives will continue to push their agenda vigorously during the 1990s. We can expect more attacks both on unions as obstacles to market competition and on safety net policies and the minimum wage as interference with efficient labor market operations (at the low end of the wage distribution).

In the center, liberals have been on the defensive over the past several years and are trying to regroup. Under the banner of "neo liberalism," they are tending to concentrate more and more on only one of their two standard objectives for economic policy.

On the one side, intimidated by conservative assaults and worried about low-wage competition from abroad, they have become skittish about promoting "too much" redistribution. They believe, along with conservatives, that profits and saving are the key to restoring the economy's vigor. And so, along with conservatives, they have placed a high priority on encouraging savings and protecting profits through tax breaks for corporations and the wealthy. In an environment of frenetic concern about government deficits, this has left little in the budget for pursuit of redistributive policy objectives.

On the other side, in contrast with conservatives, liberals have been arguing for even more vigorous government programs to help provide for business what it can't or doesn't provide for itself. There is an important role for the government in promoting productivity and investment, they argue. We need merely look at the supportive role played by government planning and finance agencies in Japan, they suggest, to appreciate the critical importance of such government support. If spending for these government programs tends to displace programs with redistributive objectives, they counsel, the needy and disadvantaged will nonetheless benefit in the long run from the "trickle-down" benefits of sustained economic growth.

Where is the left? Relatively few politicians advocate the radical perspective. It does not capture the headlines. But there are growing numbers of groups organizing in various constituencies around the United States who have begun to raise questions about economic policy for which the kinds of radical analyses presented in this volume could potentially provide some useful answers.

In particular, it appears that the experience of the 1980s has prompted many different groups to question the premises and promises of the "trickle-down" approach to economic policy upon which both liberals and conservatives build their policy prescriptions. The radical analysis provides a direct and strong alternative to that approach. We could even call it a "bottom-up" approach to economic policy. It argues that economic policies which both serve the needs of the vast majority of people *and* provide much greater democratic control over production and distribution can promote a more decent *and* a more efficient economy.

In short, radicals argue, it is not necessary to sacrifice the interests of the vast majority of U.S. citizens in order to achieve economic prosperity. We do not need to cater to the interests and power of the rich. We can build a decent, working economy for the many, not merely the few.

NOTES

1. Since this volume itself concentrates on radical analyses, and since the conservative and liberal perspectives are represented in countless other volumes, I devote more space here to outlining the radical perspective than to reviewing the other two.
2. Some radicals argue that capitalist control over the state is so tight — relying ultimately on the courts and the cops if necessary — that there is almost no room for discretionary citizen influence over the state. If gains benefitting the vast majority are realized, according to this view, they are *granted* by the ruling elites, not *won* by the citizenry.

RESOURCES

The following references can provide additional introduction to the three perspectives reviewed in this essay.

The Radical Perspective

Samuel Bowles and Richard Edwards. 1985. *Understanding Capitalism: Competition, Command, and Change in the U.S. Economy*. New York: Harper & Row.

Richard Edwards, Michael Reich, and Thomas E. Weisskopf (eds.). 1986. *The Capitalist System*. 3rd ed. Englewood Cliffs, NJ: Prentice-Hall.

Robert Cherry *et al.* (eds.). 1987. *Macroeconomics from a Left Perspective,* Book I of *The Imperiled Economy*. New York: Union for Radical Political Economics.

Martin Carnoy. 1984. *The State and Political Theory*. Princeton, NJ: Princeton University Press.

The Conservative Perspective

Milton Friedman and Rose Friedman. 1981. *Free to Choose*. New York: Avon Books.

Jude Wanniski. 1983. *The Way the World Works: How Economies Fail and Succeed*. Rev. ed. New York: Touchstone Books.

The Liberal Perspective

Arthur Okun. 1975. *Equality and Efficiency: The Big Trade-Off*. Washington, D.C.: The Brookings Institution.

Lester Thurow. 1986. *The Zero-Sum Solution*. New York: Touchstone Books.

REFERENCES

Banfield, Edward C. 1974. *The Unheavenly City Revisited*. Boston: Little, Brown and Co.

Bowles, Samuel and Richard Edwards. 1985. *Understanding Capitalism: Competition, Command, and Change in the U.S. Economy*. New York: Harper & Row.

Bowles, Samuel, David M. Gordon, and Thomas E. Weisskopf. 1983. *Beyond the Waste Land: A Democratic Alternative to Economic Decline*. New York: Anchor Press/Doubleday Books.

Friedman, Milton. 1962. *Capitalism and Freedom*. Chicago: University of Chicago Press.

Gordon, David M., Richard Edwards, and Michael Reich. 1982. *Segmented Work, Divided Workers: The Historical Transformation of Labor in the United States*. New York: Cambridge University Press.

Marx, Karl. 1963. *The Eighteenth Brumaire of Louis Bonaparte*. New York: International Publishers. [Originally published in 1852.]

_____ and Friedrich Engels. 1963. *The German Ideology*. New York: International Publishers. [Originally published in 1846.]

Reich, Michael. 1981. *Racial Inequality: A Political-Economic Approach*. Princeton, NJ: Princeton University Press.

Thompson, Edward P. 1967. *The Making of the English Working Class*. New York: Vintage Books.

U.S. Congress, Report of the Democratic Staff of the Joint Economic Committee. 1986. *The Concentration of Wealth in the United States: Trends in the Distribution of Wealth among American Families*. Washington, D.C.: Joint Economic Committee, United States Congress.

Williams, Raymond. 1977. *Marxism and Literature*. Oxford: Oxford University Press.

PART TWO

RESTRUCTURING LABOR MARKETS

3

Restructuring the Labor Force: The Role of Government Policies

SAM ROSENBERG

During the post-World War II period, the American economy has undergone an important transition. There has been a relative expansion of non-goods producing industries and a relative decline of goods-producing ones. Employment growth has occurred at the top and bottom of the occupational hierarchy but not in the middle.

Workers are forced to respond, eventually, to changes in the structure of employment. But their speed of adjustment can be influenced by government policy. Such policies can either cushion them from the blows of structural change or make them respond quicker to shifts in the nature of the demand for labor in the private sector.

The Reagan Administration has taken the latter policy direction. It wants to "knock the props" out from under workers, leaving them with little choice but to accept what employers provide. This is done by limiting such non-wage sources of income as unemployment compensation, trade adjustment assistance, and Aid to Families with Dependent Children, eliminating public service employment as a potential substitute for private sector work, and making higher education more difficult to get. In addition, the government has set a union-busting tone.

The stated objective of some of the government initiatives is to improve labor market efficiency. The unstated effect of the agenda has been to restructure the labor force. The reserve army has grown in size and its impact on employed workers has become more severe. The policies have likely increased the pliability of many semi-skilled blue-collar and white-collar workers, augmented the supply of labor to the low-wage segment of the labor market and increased the flexibility of these workers, and limited the potential supply of educated labor to professional, technical, and managerial positions.

STRUCTURAL CHANGE: JOBS AND WORKERS

Employment in manufacturing as a proportion of total employment declined from 28.2 percent in 1960 to 19.1 percent in 1986. The relative decline began during the 1960s and quickened in the 1970s and 1980s. In fact, during the 1980s there was an absolute decrease in the number of manufacturing workers. In addition, as corporations have shifted production components abroad, there has been a shift in jobs within manufacturing to non-production workers, including managers, engineers, scientists, clerical workers and sales personnel.

Taken together, the share of employment accounted for by trade, FIRE (finance, insurance and real estate) and services increased from 45.4 percent in 1960 to 58.7 percent in 1986. Professional services including health and education, and trade were major gainers in employment.

Table 1
Occupational Distribution of Employment, 1960–80

Major Occupation Group	1960		1980	
	No.	%	No.	%
Professional, technical	6986	11.37	15613	16.05
Managers, administrators	5626	9.15	10919	11.23
Sales	4637	7.55	6172	6.35
Clerical	9126	14.85	18105	18.61
Craft	8945	14.55	12529	12.88
Operatives	11348	18.47	13814	14.20
Laborers, non-farm	3322	5.41	4456	4.58
Service, except private household	5754	9.36	11918	12.25
Private household workers	1718	2.80	1041	1.10
Farmers, farm managers	2507	4.08	1485	1.53
Farm laborers, foremen	1486	2.42	1218	1.25
Occupation not reported	3184	—	0	—
Total	64639	100.0	97270	100.0

Sources: 1960 figures are from U.S. Bureau of the Census, Census of Population: 1970, Vol. 1, *Characteristics of the Population*, Part 1, United States Summary-Section 2 (Washington, D.C.: U.S. Government Printing Office, 1973), Table 221, pp. 718–724. 1980 data are from *Employment and Earnings*, January 1981, Table 21, p. 178.

Note: The numbers are in thousands.

The shifts in industrial employment have important implications for the occupational structure because job tasks vary across industries. Table 1 presents data on the distribution of employment by broad occupational group from 1960 to 1980.[1] The relative decline of craftworkers and laborers is slight but operatives who were 18.5 percent of the work force in 1960 were only 14.2 percent of total workers in 1980. Professional and technical workers, non-household service workers, clerical workers and the managerial group gained in relative importance.

A more bipolar job distribution developed from 1960 to 1980, with employment growth occurring at the top and bottom of the wage structure and occupational hierarchy. Table 2 presents 1980 data on median usual weekly earnings of full-time non-agricultural wage and salary workers. The median weekly earnings of managers and administrators were $380; for professional and technical workers they were $341. But for clerical workers they were only $215 and for service workers they were $180. Earnings in between these two extremes were for craft, sales, operative and laborer occupations, just those occupations which were growing the slowest.

While the American occupational structure became more bifurcated from 1960 to 1980, the story for the 1980s is somewhat different. During the 1980s, there has been a proliferation of low-wage jobs. Bluestone and Harrison (1986) have found that 60 percent of the new jobs created between 1979 and 1984 paid less than $7000 in 1984 dollars. This is in contrast to the 1970s when about one out of every five jobs paid below this level. All regions of the country experienced the trend toward low-wage employment. But it was most pronounced in the Midwest, reeling from deindustrialization and the farm crisis. Though part time schedules have become more prevalent and temporary work has been increasing, the trend to lower wages also held for year-round, full-time workers.[2]

Table 2
Median Usual Weekly Earnings of Full-Time Wage and Salary Earners, 1980

Major Occupation Group	Median Weekly Earnings
Managers, administrators	$380
Professional, technical	341
Craft	328
Sales	279
Operatives	240
Laborers, non-farm	220
Clerical	215
Service, except private household	180

Source: U.S. Bureau of the Census, *Statistical Abstract of the United States: 1981*. 102nd edition, (Washington, D.C.: U.S. Government Printing Office, 1981), Table 681, p. 407.

THE POLICY AGENDA

The restructuring of the labor force requires many former middle-income blue-collar manufacturing workers to shift to the lower end of the wage distribution and for new entrants to fill the growing demand for low-wage labor rather than compete for the higher-wage jobs. Government policy initiatives have attempted to facilitate this restructuring.

The policies of the Reagan Administration have resulted in a weakened, restructured labor force with lowered expectations.[3] In some respects, its actions are an extension of those of the Carter Administration. However, on balance, a more conservative direction in social policy has taken hold, both in terms of the debate and the policies being instituted.

Growing Reserve Army of Labor

A large reserve army of labor attacks the bargaining power of employed workers. With substantial unemployment, workers fear for their jobs and know they can easily be replaced if they strike. They are aware that if they are fired they will be unlikely to find equivalent positions. In such an atmosphere, employees are more responsive to the demands of their employers.

After the 1975 recession, unemployment remained at relatively high levels. When Reagan took office in 1981, serious inflation and extensive unemployment were occurring simultaneously. Priority was placed on reducing inflation. Restrictive monetary policy, together with falling world prices for food and energy, resulted in the rate of inflation dropping from 13.5 percent in 1980 to 3.2 percent in 1983.

But American workers paid dearly for this as the unemployment rate reached heights not experienced since the Great Depression. The trough of the 1981–82 recession occurred at the end of 1982. In December 1982, the unemployment rate was 10.7 percent, and for the entire year it was 9.5 percent. In that year 26.5 million people encountered some unemployment, 22 percent of those in the labor force for all or part of the year.[4]

While unemployment rose throughout the economy, it was centered in mining, construction, and manufacturing, those areas where unions have traditionally been the strongest. For example, within manufacturing, by December 1982 the unemployment rate had reached 23.2 percent in the motor vehicle industry and 29.2 percent in the primary metals industry. Reflecting these sectoral trends, the unemployment rates of operatives and nonfarm laborers were distinctly higher than those of workers in other occupations.[5]

After December 1982, conditions began to improve. The unemployment rate began to drop though it still averaged 9.5 percent for 1983. Even now (December 1987), after a lengthy economic expansion, the unemployment rate is hovering around 6 percent, quite high by historical standards. The number of involuntarily part-time workers is also high by historical standards.

Weakening and Busting Unions

The large reserve army has hurt unions. Government policy, setting a union-busting tone, has done the same. In its first year in office, the Reagan Administration fired the striking air traffic controllers and had the Professional Air Traffic Controllers Organization decertified. That action sent a clear message to employers; they should feel free to bash unions.

The Reagan Administration's appointments to the National Labor Relations Board (NLRB) have been designed to create a majority who would roll back many of the gains made by the labor movement. Donald Dotson, the chair of the NLRB from 1983 through 1987, has said that "collective bargaining frequently means... the destruction of the marketplace," and that "the price we have paid is the loss of entire industries and the crippling of others" (AFL-CIO Committee on the Evolution of Work 1985:11). Robert Hunter, another Reagan appointee, played an important role in the defeat of the Labor Law Reform Bill of 1978. Hugh Reilly, appointed solicitor of the NLRB — who oversees the filing of court papers by lawyers for the agency — spent eight years with the Right to Work Foundation, which specializes in attacking unions in court (Owens 1983).

With such a line-up, it is not surprising that the NLRB rulings have made it more difficult for union organizing drives to succeed and for unionists to achieve their goals at the bargaining table. Employers are now more able to engage in unfair labor practices designed to stop a union victory in a representation election without suffering negative consequences (e.g. the Gourmet Foods case in 1984). Previously, the NLRB could certify a union at a company that egregiously violated labor law even though the union had not won a representation election. Now, a company is not required to bargain with a union unless the labor organization has received a majority of the votes in a representation election.

In addition, employer rights during a union organizing drive have been expanded. Employers may now lawfully question employees about a union organizing drive in progress (the Rossmore House case in 1985). In doing so, they cannot threaten workers. Yet, there is a fine line between an actual threat and implied intimidation.

Recent NLRB decisions have also made it more difficult for unions to gain their demands at the bargaining table. It is now easier for employers to move union jobs to nonunion locations. Previously, the NLRB had found that as long as a collective bargaining agreement was in effect, an employer was prohibited from moving work to a nonunion facility. A company may now move work during the life of a contract unless there is a clause in the contract explicitly prohibiting such action. All the company need do, if the move is designed to lower labor costs, is bargain over the decision and its effects (the Milwaukee Spring case in 1984). Yet, there is no requirement that an agreement be reached or that the work remain at the unionized plant. And if the movement of work hinges on factors other than cutting labor costs, there is no requirement to bargain at all (the Otis Elevator case in 1984).

It is now more difficult for unions to wage successful strikes. Unions can no longer fine workers who resign their union membership during a strike and return to work in violation of union rules. In upholding an earlier NLRB decision, the U.S. Supreme Court suggested that any union rules limiting the freedom of workers to resign during or just prior to a strike may be illegal (the pattern makers case in 1985).

It is now easier for an employer to succeed with a lockout. In a lockout, the employer bars unions workers from the workplace in order to gain concessions in bargaining. The NLRB ruled that management is allowed to hire "temporary replacements" during a lockout (the Harter case in 1986).

For a time it had been easier for a company to declare bankruptcy in order to void a labor contract. This tactic was successfully used by several firms including Continental Airlines and Wilson Foods. In 1984, the U.S. Supreme Court ruled that a company may use bankruptcy proceedings to rid itself of a collective bargaining agreement (NLRB vs. Bildisco case). The company could void its collective bargaining contract as soon as it filed a bankruptcy petition, even before the bankruptcy had been approved by the Bankruptcy Court. As a result of this decision, the U.S. Congress passed legislation limiting the use of bankruptcy as a tactic in labor relations.[6]

Unemployment Insurance

Not only have unions been weakened and the reserve army grown, there has also been an increase in the potential impact of the reserve army on employed workers. While the number of unemployed workers was rising, the government began cutting back on unemployment insurance (UI). UI provides a cushion for workers as they search for work. That cushion is being withdrawn.

When UI was first established by the Social Security Act of 1935, it was designed to provide support for workers with a history of stable employment. It would enable them to search for and find jobs virtually equivalent to the ones they had lost. Also, it was seen as supporting aggregate purchasing power during slack periods.

As time went on, UI came to be viewed in a different light. The Carter Administration claimed to support the initial rationale for UI. However, its actions proved otherwise. Implicitly, it took the position that UI, rather than enabling people to search for appropriate jobs, unnecessarily lengthened the duration of a spell of unemployment, thus increasing the overall level of unemployment. Policies were implemented, either by action or inaction, lowering these benefits, limiting their duration, and making it more difficult to collect them.

As a basis for understanding the initiatives of the Carter Administration, and of the Reagan Administration to follow, some institutional information on the operation of the UI system will be provided. Depending on the length of previous employment, all workers who lose their jobs for acceptable cause can receive benefits for up to 26 weeks.

While collecting, they must show they have searched for work and have not declined a "suitable work" offer. There is no nationwide definition of "suitable work" but it is often defined by states as a job equivalent to the previous one.

In specific instances, 13 additional weeks of "extended benefits" may be granted. The U.S. Congress has occassionally created temporary programs providing for additional UI beyond the "extended benefits." For example, during the Ford Administration, the maximum duration of benefits was temporarily extended to 65 weeks.

Under President Carter, the tax-exempt status of UI was ended. Legislation was passed to tax the unemployment benefits of individuals who receive a combination of income and benefits exceeding a base amount ($20,000 for single persons, $25,000 for married persons filing joint returns). The program enabling benefits to be paid for up to 65 weeks was allowed to expire in January, 1978. A regulation was implemented making it more difficult for workers to collect "extended benefits." "Suitable work" for such workers was defined as a job paying at least the weekly benefit or the minimum wage whichever was higher. Those refusing such work would lose their benefits.

The Reagan Administration has further weakened the UI system.[7] It wants to eliminate what it calls "excess unintended benefits." It has tried to accomplish this by limiting the provision of "extended benefits" and increasing the taxation of UI.

The Reagan Administration, with the approval of the U.S. Congress, redefined the conditions under which "extended benefits" are to be paid. The unemployment rate required to trigger "extended benefits" increased. This made it more difficult for states to provide this assistance.[8]

In August 1982, legislation was passed increasing the taxation of UI. Single persons with a combination of income and uenmployment benefits of at least $12,000, rather than the $20,000, and married persons filing joint returns, having a combination of income and unemployment benefits of at least $18,000, rather than $25,000, would have to pay tax on their UI. The widely heralded tax revisions of 1986 further increased the taxation of UI. Now everyone receiving UI regardlesss of their annual income are taxed on their benefits.

As a result of the Reagan reforms, relatively fewer people received UI during the 1981–82 recession than in any post-World War II recession. In 1975, when the unemployment rate was 8.5 percent, approximately 78 percent of the unemployed received UI. This is in contrast to 1982, with a higher unemployment rate, when only 45 percent received compensation (Burtless 1983:226).

The reasons given by the Reagan Administration for these changes reflect its desire to create more flexibility in the labor market, by limiting non-wage sources of income. More specifically, it argues that structural shifts have occurred in the nature and location of jobs, though it does not specify these trends in great detail. It claims explicitly, while the Carter Administration did so implicitly, that overly generous unemployment insurance lengthens the duration of a spell of unemployment. These payments discourage workers from relocating or from seeking employment in new industries which may initially pay lower wages than workers are used to but which hold out the promise of higher wages in the future. Through its changes in UI, the Reagan Administration hopes to force workers to lower their job expectations and to adapt more quickly to labor market conditions.

The cutbacks in UI potentially affect all workers. But those most likely to be hurt are former operatives, non-farm laborers, and service workers. They are the ones most likely to suffer long-term unemployment. The new developments in the UI system have probably increased, to some degree, the flexibility of these workers as well as the labor supply to low-wage positions.[9]

While the government claims that its initiatives will reduce structural unemployment, this is unlikely to be the case. The primary problem is an inadequate number of jobs. Abraham (1983) has found that the number of people looking for work has exceeded the number of vacancies whenever the unemployment rate has been greater than 3 percent. During the latter part of the 1970s, when the unemployment rate was lower than during the 1980s, there was an average of four–five job seekers for every vacant job.

Trade-adjustment Assistance

While the UI system is being eroded, the trade-adjustment assistance (TAA) program has been eliminated. TAA was instituted as part of the Trade Expansion Act of 1962 and was the price set by the AFL-CIO for its support of the trade expansion measure.

TAA was received by workers whose unemployment was deemed to be in part due to imports. The payments were for more per week and for longer periods than people received from UI. In addition, training opportunities, and relocation and job search allowances were also provided.

Most of the TAA payments went to unionized industrial workers, mainly steel, automobile, and clothing and textile workers, in the mid-Atlantic and North Central regions. During the Carter years, many workers were certified to receive TAA.

The TAA program ended during Reagan's second term in office. Some money for training and other employment assistance for workers who have lost their jobs due to imports remains available through the Job Training Partnership Act (JTPA). (All displaced workers, not merely those affected by imports, are eligible for JTPA funds.)

Initially, in 1981, the Reagan Administration developed, and the U.S. Congress passed, legislation increasing the difficulty of qualifying for TAA, limiting the size of the benefit and shortening its duration.[10] The government argued that it was eliminating "excess unintended benefits." These benefits, rather than helping workers adjust to industrial decline brought on by international competition, enabled them to avoid doing so. Too many received such benefits. Few were interested in retraining, job search or relocation assistance. After receiving TAA, many returned to their original jobs. Also, as payments were retroactive, workers had sometimes returned to their original jobs before payment of compensation.[11] Labor market rigidity, rather than labor market flexibility was, it was argued, the result of this program.

Eventually the government decided to request the elimination of TAA. On equity grounds, the Reagan Administration claimed all workers who lose their jobs should be treated the same. Thus, no workers should receive benefits other than UI.

The effects of ending TAA are apparent. The majority of workers who received TAA were blue-collar manufacturing workers. The impact on them will be similar to that caused by the changes in the UI system.

Public Service Employment

Not only have alternative sources of income to private sector wages been scaled down, but alternative sources of jobs outside of the private sector have been eliminated. Public service employment programs (PSE), funded by the federal government, providing for positions in state and local governments and in non-profit making organizations, have been ended. The positions had been funded under the Comprehensive Employment and Training Act of 1973.

The basic reasoning behind PSE is that it could quickly increase the employment of selected workers. The Carter Administration made PSE a central component of its employment strategy.

When Reagan entered office in 1981, 309,000 PSE positions existed, approximately 85 percent of which were held by people officially considered to be living at or below the poverty line. None remained by the end of the year as the funding was eliminated.

Despite the fact that much of the research on PSE was favorable toward it as a means to lessen cyclical and structural unemployment (Briggs 1982), the Reagan Administration developed arguments to eliminate it. At the time when it ended PSE, officials in the Administration were making the case that an expanding private economy was a necessary — and in most cases, sufficient — condition for reducing long-term unemployment (Moran 1982:402). The private sector was where long-term, career employment opportunities do and should exist. PSE jobs had not, it was argued, provided experience easily transferable to private sector employment.

The ending of PSE hurt the unskilled, less-educated and unemployed, especially among minority groups. It likely increased the supply of labor to low wage jobs, causing increased competition for such positions and increased unemployment. Also, it probably resulted in low-wage workers becoming, of necessity, more responsive to the demands of the employers.

Welfare

While voluntary PSE programs have ended, mandatory public employment programs for welfare recipients are being developed. Criticisms concerning the ineffectiveness of PSE are conveniently forgotten by federal policymakers responsible for "welfare reform." Mandatory "workfare" plans complement welfare changes which limit the number of people eligible for assistance and the amounts they receive.

Since 1973, there has been no growth in the number of households receiving welfare. Thus, politicians must have reasons other than growing welfare rolls for placing increasing importance on welfare reform legislation in the 1980s.

The American welfare system is a complex array of many uncoordinated programs. Aid to Families with Dependent Children (AFDC), the most controversial, is emphasized here. AFDC has its roots in the Aid to Dependent Children program established under the Social Security Act of 1935.

Initially welfare was viewed as primarily for "deserving" white widows and their children. Eventually more and more recipients were black and an increasing proportion of cases involved families with divorced or unmarried mothers. As the welfare population changed from the "deserving poor" to the "undeserving poor," work requirements were instituted. In 1967, a mandatory work-training program for all adult recipients was begun (Lynn 1977).

Welfare reform ideas percolated during the 1970s. During the Carter Administration, AFDC and food stamp benefits did not keep pace with inflation. After adjusting for inflation, real benefits in 1980 were 20 percent lower than a decade earlier. At the end of its term in office, the Carter Administration began proposing cuts in AFDC outlays. The Reagan Administration accepted these cuts and added some of its own.

The means test for eligibility for welfare has been tightened.[12] To guarantee that AFDC recipients work, the Reagan Administration has proposed legislation requiring states to develop mandatory ''workfare'' programs for AFDC recipients. States now have the option to do so. Public jobs would be provided if private sector positions were unavailable. Recipients would do enough work each month, calculated at the minimum wage, to earn their payments. Those unwilling to work would lose their assistance.

On balance, it is likely that the implemented and suggested policy changes will help to increase the labor supply to the low-wage segment of the labor market. Those deemed ineligible for AFDC or receiving lessened benefits will be more readily available for such employment.[13] Those forced to work in the private sector at the minimum wage under ''workfare'' programs will also be available to be called on if needed by employers. This will guarantee that wage levels and employment conditions will not improve, with employers having little or no incentive to respond to worker demands. An existing worker could always be replaced by a participant in a ''workfare'' program.

Aid to Students in Higher Education

Federal aid is designed to increase the college attendance of students from low-income and middle-income families. It is provided principally through grants, loan subsidies and loan guarantees. National Direct Student Loans (NDSL) were created by the National Defense Educational Act of 1958. The Higher Education Act of 1965 added three new programs: (1) Equal Opportunity Grants, now named Supplemental Educational Grants (SEOG), which provide funds to schools for scholarships based on student financial need; (2) federally insured Guaranteed Student Loans (GSL) for middle- and low-income students; and (3) the Work Study program which subsidizes jobs for needy students. In 1972, the Nixon Administration established Pell Grants for low-income students. The Carter Administration increased the access of middle-income families to grants and loans. But, toward the end of its term in office, it suggested several reforms designed to limit the growth of the GSL program.

The Reagan Administration has built on and gone well beyond the cuts suggested by Carter. It believes that student aid programs are too expensive and provide funds to many who do not need them to attend school. It wants students and their families to pay a larger share of the costs of higher education.

These are the explicit reasons given by the government for restricting aid. But there is another factor to consider, which likely lies behind the government's actions. Even when there was strong employment growth at the top of the occupational hierarchy, it did not keep pace with the increase in the supply of educated labor. Rumberger has found that the incidence of overeducation — workers employed at jobs requiring substantially fewer educational skills than they actually have — increased dramatically from 1960 to 1976. By 1976, about 40 percent of all college-educated workers were overeducated for their jobs (Rumberger 1981:75–78).

Since that time it is likely that there has been a growth in overeducation. Younger, more-educated workers have been replacing, older less-educated ones who have retired. In addition, many adult workers have been returning to school to both improve their education and gain educational credentials providing them with the potential for upward occupational mobility. This has been occurring at the same time as there has been substantial relative growth in low-wage employment. Given this overeducation, it is likely that the government wishes to limit the supply of educated labor.

In 1981, the Reagan Administration convinced the U.S. Congress to restrict the terms of GSLs and reduce support for Pell Grants. The real value of individual Pell Grants declined, as did the proportion of college costs covered by Pell Grants. No further aid cuts were legislated after 1981 (*Focus* 1987).

In fact, in 1986, in response to the concern over the quality of higher education, legislation was passed expanding the GSL, Pell Grant, and Work Study programs. The Administration did not support these measures. In its budget proposals for fiscal year 1988, it has called for doing away with SEOG's, work study, and NDSL's. It wants funding reduced for Pell Grants, claiming that better targeting of the awards would result in no reduction of awards to the truly needy.

With cutbacks in educational aid, those least able to finance their education would find themselves unable to attend school. Family income plays a role in determining college attendance (*Focus* 1987). Pell Grants increase the likelihood of low-income students going to college (Baum and Schwartz 1985). During the 1980s, minority enrollment in colleges has been declining.

CONCLUSION

Since 1980, the federal government has implemented many, and proposed even more, changes in employment, income security and education policies. Its actions foster the labor market restructuring that employers desire. Workers have been forced to become more responsive to competitive forces in the economy.

Unions have been weakened. The reserve army has grown in size and its impact on employed workers has become more severe. As the share of low-wage employment has grown, cutbacks in unemployment insurance, the elimination of trade-adjustment assistance and public service employment, and changes in welfare programs have likely increased the supply of labor available to take such work. Many people have little choice but to do so. They have become more flexible, more willing to accept what employers have to offer.

NOTES

1. Figures are only provided through 1980 because changes in the Census Bureau's occupational definitions make comparisons with earlier years extremely difficult.
2. Danziger and Gottschalk (1986) find a growth of low-wage earners who head households, especially male heads of households, from 1979 to 1984. These household heads could not keep a

family of four out of poverty even if they worked all year at their current weekly earnings. McMahon and Tschetter (1986) argue that from 1973–85 there has not been a growth of low-wage occupations. Rather, they find a growth of lower-wage tracts within occupations. For a further discussion of employment trends, see the articles by Rhon Baiman and Chris Tilly in this volume.
3. A weakened, restructured labor force, while necessary, is not sufficient for increasing the average rate of profit. Weakening and restructuring the labor force is designed to lower unit labor costs and thus increase the average rate of profit. However, to the extent that this strategy is successful, problems of underconsumption may emerge.
4. The official unemployment rate undercounts the number of unemployed. It does not include discouraged and involuntarily part-time workers. If they were counted the jobless rate would be even higher. For an interesting discussion of the limitations of the official unemployment rate as a measure of unemployment, see *Dollars and Sense* (1986).
5. The unemployment data are elaborated upon in Rosenberg (1986).
6. For additional information on the rulings of the NLRB and the courts, see *Business Week* (1984), Diamond (1985), Lewiston and Wise (1987), and Taub and Needleman (1984).
7. The major sources for information on the Reagan policy agenda include *America's New Beginning: A Program for Economic Recovery* (1981), *Economic Report of the President* (1983), Office of Management and Budget (1981a), Office of Management and Budget (1981b), Office of Management and Budget (1982a), Office of Management and Budget (1982b), Office of Management and Budget (1983), Office of Management and Budget (1984), Office of Management and Budget (1986), Office of Management and Budget (1987).
8. The specifics of this policy change are discussed in Rosenberg (1983).
9. Though not directly related to the UI changes, a U.S. Department of Labor study of displaced workers from January 1979 to January 1984 found that by January 1984 less than 25 percent of the 5.1 million workers were holding positions paying in nominal terms more than or equal to the jobs they had lost (Flaim and Sehgal 1985).
10. The specifics of this policy change are discussed in Rosenberg (1983).
11. These criticisms, while valid, do not necessarily justify the steps taken by the Reagan Administration.
12. The specifics of this policy change are discussed in Rosenberg (1983).
13. On balance, this is likely to occur. But some of the policy changes may have reduced the incentives to work of some of the recipients. For a discussion of the work incentive effects of the AFDC reforms, see Haveman (1984).

REFERENCES

Abraham, K. G. 1983. Structural/Frictional vs. Deficit Demand Unemployment. *American Economic Review* 73(4):708–724.

AFL-CIO Committee on the Evolution of Work. 1985. *The Changing Situation of Workers and Their Unions*. Washington, D.C.: AFL-CIO.

America's New Beginning: A Program for Economic Recovery. 1981. Washington, D.C.: U.S. Government Printing Office.

Baum, S.R. and S. Schwartz. 1985. The Fairness Test for Student-Aid Cuts. *Challenge* (May/June):39–46.

Bluestone, B. and B. Harrison. 1986. *The Great American Job Machine: The Proliferation of Low Wage Employment in the U.S. Economy*. Joint Economic Committee of the U.S. Congress. Washington, D.C.

Briggs, V.M. 1982. *The Revival of Job Creation Programs in the 1970s: Lessons for the 1980s*. In, *Proceedings of the Thirty-Fourth Annual Meeting*. pp. 258–265. Industrial Relations Research Association.

Burtless, G. 1983. Why is Insured Unemployment So Low? *Brookings Papers on Economic Activity* 1: 225–249.

Business Week. 1984. NLRB Rulings That Are Inflaming Labor Relations. June 11.

Danziger, S. and P. Gottschalk. 1986. Work, Poverty, and the Working Poor: A Multifaceted Problem. *Monthly Labor Review* 109(9):17–27.

Diamond, S.F. 1985. No Friends in Labor's Court. *The Nation* (December 14).

Dollars and Sense. 1986. Undercounting the Unemployed: What the Unemployment Rate Doesn't Show. (October).

Economic Report of the President. 1983. Washington, D.C.: U.S. Government Printing Office.

Flaim, P.O. and E. Sehgal. 1985. Displaced Workers of 1979–83: How Well Have They Fared? *Monthly Labor Review* 108(6):3–16.

Focus. 1987. Vol. 10, No. 3, (Fall). Institute for Research on Poverty, University of Wisconsin.

Haveman, R.H. 1984. How Much Have the Reagan Administration's Tax and Spending Policies Increased Work Effort? In, *The Legacy of Reaganomics: Prospects for Long-Term Growth*, C.R. Hulten and I.V. Sawhill (eds.). Washington, D.C.: The Urban Institute Press.

Lewiston, T. and T. Wise. 1987. Locked Out by Lockheed: Seattle Workers Stand Firm. *Dollars and Sense* (December).

Lynn, L.E. Jr. 1977. A Decade of Policy Developments in the Income Maintenance System. In, *A Decade of Federal Antipoverty Programs*, R.H. Haveman (ed.). New York: Academic Press.

McMahon, P.J. and J.H. Tschetter. 1986. The Declining Middle Class: A Further Analysis. *Monthly Labor Review* 109(9):22–27.

Moran, D.W. 1982. Human Resource Implications of the Budget Cuts. In, *Proceedings of the Thirty-Fourth Annual Meeting*, Industrial Relations Research Association.

Office of Management and Budget. 1981a. *Additional Details on Budget Savings, Fiscal Year 1982*. Washington, D.C.: U.S. Government Printing Office.

———. 1981b. *Budget of the United States Government, Fiscal Year 1982*. Washington, D.C.: U.S. Government Printing Office.

———. 1982a. *Budget of the United States Government, Fiscal Year 1983*. Washington, D.C.: U.S. Government Printing Office.

———. 1982b. *Major Themes and Additional Budget Details, Fiscal Year 1983*. Washington, D.C.: U.S. Government Printing Office.

———. 1983. *Budget of the United States Government, Fiscal Year 1984*, Washington, D.C.: U.S. Government Printing Office.

———. 1984. *Major Themes and Additional Budget Details, Fiscal Year 1985*. Washington, D.C.: U.S. Government Printing Office.

———. 1986. *Major Policy Initiatives, Fiscal Year 1987*. Washington, D.C., U.S. Government Printing Office.

———. 1987. *Budget of the United States Government, Fiscal Year 1988*, Washington, D.C.: U.S. Government Printing Office.

Owens, P. 1983. Unionbuster at the N.L.R.B. *The Nation* (July 23–30).

Rosenberg, S. 1983. Reagan Social Policy and Labour Force Restructuring. *Cambridge Journal of Economics* 7(2):179–196.

———. 1986. The State and Employers Versus Trade Unions: Minimal Cooperation Amidst Conflict. In, *The State, the Trade Unions and the Labour Market: Possibilities of and Limitations to Intervention*, G. Sziraczky (ed.), Vol. I. Budapest: Hungarian Academy of Sciences, Institute of Economics.

Rumberger, R.W. 1981. *Overeducation in the U.S. Labor Market*. New York: Praeger.

Taub, E. and R. Needleman. 1984. *Introduction to Labor Law Update*. Division of Labor Studies, Indiana University Northwest.

4

Labor Market Restructuring and Women's Economic Experience Since 1970

MARILYN POWER

INTRODUCTION

After experiencing unprecedented growth in the post-World War II period, the American economy has entered a period of instability in the 1970s and 1980s, characterized by poor economic growth, severe recessions, and chronically high unemployment rates. One response to this economic instability has been the gradual transformation of the U.S. economy, including a restructuring of labor markets which has weakened labor unions, decreased real wages, and worsened job insecurity. Women have been affected by this restructuring in many of the same ways men have been affected, as workers and members of households. But it is also important to examine the effects of crisis on wage earning women as a separate category because women have historically had a different relationship to the economy than men. At the same time, there are differences among women as well, by race and by class, which have been exacerbated in this period.

The 1970s and 1980s have been a period of dramatic change for women in the United States. Economic instability has influenced this change in important ways, but it is not the sole influence on women's experience. Powerful secular trends have been important in determining how, exactly, labor market restructuring is played out in the lives of working women. In addition, the 1970s and 1980s have witnessed political and cultural changes which affect working women, in particular, the growth of the women's movement and the enforcement (however inadequately) of the anti-discrimination and affirmative action legislation of the 1960s.

Three distinct theoretical arguments have been made about the role of women's employment in the economic cycles of a capitalist economy (for a more detailed discussion, see Rubery 1988). First, women could function as a *buffer,* cushioning male unemployment during the economic downturn, and providing a convenient pool of labor during the economic upswing. In this case their employment should vary procyclically Second, women could serve as cheap labor *substitutes* for male labor. In this case their employment should vary countercyclically, as employers seek to restore profits by restructuring employment and depressing wages (Rosenberg 1983; Power 1984). Third, women's employment could be determined by secular trends, separate from cyclical factors. That is, because women's employment has historically remained concentrated in separate occupations from men's, women in many cases cannot serve as either a buffer or as substitutes for male labor. Although these arguments may seem mutually exclusive, an examination of the effects of economic crisis on women workers in any given advanced capitalist country is likely to provide evidence for all three theoretical positions, as different groups of women workers are affected differently by economic fluctuations.

To understand the effects of the current economic instability on women's experience in the wage labor force, we must first locate this experience in terms of four broader historic trends which affect women workers. First, capitalism has a long-term tendency to incorporate women into wage labor. Throughout the nineteenth and early twentieth centuries, women in the United States were most likely to work outside the sphere of capitalist production, engaging in production for use and exchange at home. Over the course of the twentieth century, however, women have been progressively incorporated into the wage labor force, a process which will almost certainly not reverse itself. In the postwar period this movement into wage labor has been especially rapid, as the female labor force participation rate increased from 31.4 percent in 1950 to 55.3 percent in 1986.

Second, there has been a persistent sexual division of labor in wage work. This tendency toward occupational segregation by sex has been a feature of U.S. capitalism since its inception, and continues to be firmly entrenched despite rising female participation and federal laws outlawing discrimination. Although there has been a slight decline in occupational segregation by sex in recent years, in 1981 still over 60 percent of women workers would have to change jobs to be proportionally represented in all detailed occupational categories (Beller 1984:14). On the level of the individual firm, segregation is much greater. In a study of 200 establishments, Bielby and Baron (1984) found that 51.4 percent were *completely* segregated, with men and women sharing no job categories. Among the rest of the firms, the mean segregation index was 84.1 percent, meaning that over 84 percent of women workers would have to change jobs to be proportionally represented (Bielby and Baron 1984:35). The traditionally female jobs in which most women work tend to be relatively low paid, with limited possibilities for advancement; in 1984 clerical work and service work accounted for nearly one-half of all working women.

Third, women of color have historically been confined to the most disadvantaged of the female occupations, largely in unskilled blue collar and service occupations. In 1940, 60 percent of all employed black women were domestic servants; as late as 1960, 36 percent were in this extremely low-paid occupation (Wallace 1980:7). In recent decades there has been a change for the better, as black women have moved rapidly out of domestic work and into clerical occupations which, while not lucrative, at least pay better and offer more steady employment than the manual occupations.[1] Despite this improvement, there is still a substantial difference in occupational distribution by race: in 1986, 42.0 percent of black women, compared to only 25.2 percent of white women were service workers or factory operatives. In addition, there is evidence that within the clerical occupations black women have more difficulty than white women in moving above the lower ranks (Power and Rosenberg 1987).

Finally, whether or not they work for wages, women still face primary responsibility for housework and child care. Despite rapidly rising rates of female labor force participation in the 1960s and 1970s, studies of household time use indicated that women performed about 70 percent of their families' housework; male allocation of time to housework was completely unresponsive to the hours of wage work performed by their wives (Sanik 1981:177). A recent time use study has indicated a small improvement in the distribution of housework time, as husbands' weekly contribution increased by one hour while their wives' declined by one and one-half hours (Juster 1985, cited in Blau and Ferber 1987), but this change still leaves women with the bulk of housework time. This responsibility becomes particularly onerous in times of economic crisis, as women face the difficult task of keeping their families fed and clothed within the constraints of a dwindling family budget.

Women's experience in the economic instability of the 1970s and 1980s must be seen in light of these four broad historic trends, but this is not to imply that all women have been affected equally. Indeed, for some women, the past two decades have been a period of continuous and dramatic improvement in their economic position, while for others the period has been nothing short of disasterous. To understand the effects of economic crisis on wage-earning women, then, I will divide women into three groups: women in traditionally-male professional and managerial occupations, women in traditionally-female occupations, and women in poverty, most of whom work sporadically in jobs at the lowest pay and skill categories.

WOMEN IN TRADITIONALLY-MALE PROFESSIONS AND MANAGEMENT

Women remain highly concentrated in female professions: 85 percent of elementary school teachers were women in 1986, as were 86 percent of librarians and 94 percent of registered nurses. High-paid, high-prestige professional and managerial occupations remain male-dominated: for example, 82 percent of lawyers and judges were male, as were 82 percent of physicians and 94 percent of engineers. However, for a small group of highly-educated women, the 1970s and 1980s witnessed a marked improvement in their economic prospects, as female participation in these elite, traditionally-male professional and managerial positions has expanded extremely rapidly. Between 1972 and 1982, women accounted for one-fourth of the increase in the number of physicians and lawyers, one-third of the increase in computer specialists, and two-thirds of the increase in accountants. These proportions are likely to increase further as, for example, about one-third of first-year students in law and medicine in the early 1980s were women (Parrish 1986).[2]

There are undoubtedly a number of reasons for this marked improvement in women's representation in traditonally-male high powered occupations. First, over 60 percent of all new entrants into the labor force during the period were women. Second, government enforcement of anti-discrimination laws and affirmative action has made professional and graduate programs, and the jobs that require those degrees, far more available to women than they have been in the past. Third, the rise of the women's movement in the 1960s and 1970s changed many women's attitudes toward careers, encouraging young middle-class women in particular to seek nontraditional occupations. The effects of both government policy and changing attitudes are evident in the marked increase in advanced academic and professional degrees awarded to women: between 1971 and 1981 the percentage of masters degrees awarded to women increased from 40.1 percent to 50.3 percent and the percentage of professional degrees increased from 6.3 percent to 26.6 percent (Blau and Ferber 1986).

In the 1980s the Reagan Administration has cut back on enforcement of the civil rights laws and has been actively working to dismantle affirmative action. The effect these changes will have on women in traditionally-male professions is unclear, but many of the discriminatory apparatuses limiting access to the fields (e.g. quotas for women in professional school admissions) have been dismantled and would be extremely difficult to reestablish. This is not to say that women do not face discrimination in professional and managerial occupations, which may in fact worsen in the face of governmental indifference, but their representation in these fields is not likely to decrease (in fact, given the high number of women currently seeking advanced degrees, it is likely to increase).

WOMEN IN TRADITIONALLY-FEMALE OCCUPATIONS

The majority of women workers remain in traditionally-female occupations. The major change affecting women in this category has been an increase in labor force participation, particularly among women with young children. Historically, labor force participation by women with pre-school children has been extremely low. The pattern of labor force participation in the 1950s and 1960s suggested that many women dropped out of the labor force in their child bearing years, returning to work some years later. In the 1970s and 1980s, this decline in participation in the middle years has gradually disappeared: the cross-sectional data for 1984 indicate uniform (and high) participation rates between the ages of 20 and 44. Thus by 1980, 45.1 percent of married women with pre-school children were in the labor force, and by 1985 53.4 percent. Among women without husbands, participation rates were even higher: for example, 67.5 percent of divorced mothers of pre-schoolers were in the labor force in 1985.

Despite this striking growth in labor force participation and continuity, there has been no dramatic change in the occupational distribution of women workers in nonprofessional and nonmanagerial occupations. The majority of nonprofessional women continue to work in traditionally-female clerical and service occupations, which tend to be characterized by low pay and little opportunity for advancement. Indeed, it would have been surprising to find much movement of women into more lucrative traditionally-male nonprofessional occupations, since deindustrialization has severely curtailed the availability of such jobs (Bluestone and Harrison 1986; Tilly, in this volume).

In fact, one reason for the increased presence of married women with pre-school children in the labor force may have been the stagnation or decline in real wages for male workers.[3] Despite stagnant or declining real wages in female occupations as well, and the fact that women consistently earn less than men in *every* occupational category, wives' earnings have been a crucial factor in preserving family income. By the 1980s, in families where both husband and wife worked full time, wives provided an average of nearly 40 percent of family earnings (U.S. Bureau of the Census 1986).

An additional reason for the increase in labor force participation of women with small children may have been rising male unemployment and underemployment (Maloney 1987). Because the economic instability has affected production workers, who are predominately male, most severely, unemployment rates for male workers tend in many cases to be higher than in predominately female occupations. For example, male factory operatives in 1982, at the height of the 1980–82 recession, had an unemployment rate of 17.3 percent, while female clerical workers faced 7.0 percent unemployment (female factory operatives, however, experienced 18.3 percent unemployment). Many households may have found themselves more reliant on wives' earnings than in the past because of this greater stability.

Another trend which affected women's economic experience was the growth of female-headed households. In 1970, 10.8 percent of families had a female householder; by 1984, 15.9 percent did. Among black families the growth in female householder families was even greater, rising from 28.3 percent of black families in 1970 to 43.1 percent in 1984. The rising number of female-headed families has contributed to growing poverty among women, as will be discussed in the next section. But even when the family's income is above poverty, it is frequently quite low, as many women struggle to support their families through work in low-paid traditionally-female occupations.

This growing incidence of female-headed families has affected the labor force behavior not only of the women in such families, but of other women as well. Increasingly women recognize that they must plan for the possibility of single-parenthood through greater continuity in the work force. The women's movement has also undoubtedly had an effect in encouraging women to seek the independence and self-development that can come from sustained work outside the home. Additionally, sustained work for pay may improve a woman's position in her family, especially if her pay is necessary to the maintenance of the household (Ferree 1984).

In sum, women in traditionally-female occupations have experienced rising labor force participation without any significant change in the degree of occupational segregation by sex. To some extent, this increased participation may be seen as simply the continuation of a long-term secular trend. However, the acceleration of this trend in the 1970s suggests cyclical factors were important as well. Increased participation has been coerced by declining real wages, rising male unemployment rates, and the growth of female-headed households; but it also has been encouraged by a change in ideology, fostered by the women's movement, which has made sustained wage work for women more acceptable. The increased labor force participation has created a considerable amount of stress, particularly for women with small children who face heavy burdens of work at home, and difficulties in finding good care for their children, with little assistance from society or spouses. At the same time, women have expressed satisfaction with working, with the independence of their own paychecks, and with the opportunity to move outside the sphere of the home.

Some economists have argued that women in traditionally-female occupations could be seen as cheap *substitutes* for male labor in the restructuring of the labor market, in that their participation has grown while male unemployment has risen and male participation rates have fallen. However, for women to be seen as substitutes, it would be necessary to argue that the occupations which were expanding during the 1970s and 1980s were accessible to male workers. In fact, many of the most rapidly expanding occupational categories were traditionally-female clerical and service occupations. For example, secretarial employment increased by 39.5 percent between 1970 and 1980; this occupational category was 98.8 percent female in 1980. Health service occupations, 88.1 percent female, increased 54.3 percent, while precision production occupations, 81.7 percent male, increased only 5.8 percent (U.S. Bureau of the Census 1984). Between 1972 and 1980, absolute increases in employment were greatest among secretaries, cashiers, and registered nurses, three occupations that are highly female-dominated (Leon 1982).

While, in theory, men displaced from traditionally-male blue-collar jobs could have competed for jobs in these female-dominated occupations, in practice, both employer bias and male reluctance to enter occupations identified as female made this option untenable. In addition, occupations such as secretary and nurse require considerable training, making them difficult for displaced male blue-collar workers to enter. Finally, since traditionally-female occupations are relatively low-paid, they are likely to be avoided by male workers. In short, while the continuing decline in blue-collar employment may eventually spur a movement of men into traditionally-female occupations, at present there is little evidence that women in these occupations are serving to any great extent as substitutes for male labor. In the process of deindustrialization, women who have been hired in traditionally-male blue-collar occupations, often as the result of affirmative action pressure, may fill a *buffer* role, cushioning the rise in male unemployment, since the low seniority of women in these occupations makes them disproportionately vulnerable to lay-offs. However, their numbers remain extremely small.

WOMEN IN POVERTY

The percentage of the population below the government poverty line fell from 22.4 percent in 1959 to 12.1 percent in 1969, in response to economic growth, the Civil Rights movement, and the government war on poverty program. During the 1970s the percentage stagnated at around 12 percent, and in the 1980s rose again, reaching 15.3 percent in 1983, declining somewhat to 14.4 percent in 1984. Black poverty has been consistently more than three times as great, proportionately, as white poverty, and rose more rapidly in the 1980s. Female-headed households have also experienced poverty rates consistently higher than the population as a whole. Their rate of poverty fell somewhat during the 1970s, from 38.0 percent in 1969 to 32.0 percent in 1979, and has since risen, to 34.0 percent in 1984. At the same time, because female-headed families constitute a rising proportion of the population as a whole, they also account for a growing proportion of the poor: in 1959 around one-fourth of the poor were in female-headed families; by 1984, the percentage had risen to one-half. These trends, together with those discussed above, indicate that the period has seen increased class polarization among women workers, with an increasing number of women in elite occupations on one end, women in poverty on the other.

Many poor female-headed families receive government assistance in the form of Aid to Families with Dependent Children (AFDC). However, since 1970 there has been no federal act requiring AFDC payments to be indexed for inflation (individual states have made adjustments of varying, but always inadequate, magnitudes). As a result, between 1972 and 1981, the purchasing power of the average AFDC check fell 28 percent (Harrington 1984:35). Thus, as the number of female-headed families was rising in the 1970s, government support for poor women and their families dropped sharply.

It is important to include poor women in a discussion of women's labor force experience because, despite the popular image of the ''indolent'' welfare mother, the majority of women on welfare engage in wage work (Harrison 1979). The problem is that they frequently can only find work that is temporary or part time, and extremely poorly paid, at the bottom level of traditionally-female service, clerical, and blue-collar occupations. Many cycle between periods of total self-support, periods of supplemental welfare, and periods of full dependence on welfare, depending on such factors as the state of the economy, the seasonality of jobs, and their own and their children's health (Duncan 1984).

When Ronald Reagan took office in 1981, he brought with him a conservative strategy to restructure the economy in response to economic crisis. This strategy involved restoring profits through tax cuts and increased military spending, weakening unions, and slashing social welfare benefits (Rosenberg 1983; Power 1984). Reagan was especially hostile to AFDC, which he viewed as interfering with the free play of labor markets, as well as threatening to the patriarchal structure of the family. His budget for fiscal year 1982, in which he implemented most of his budget-cutting program, took particular aim at supplemental welfare for working mothers.

The effect of this cut in AFDC, coupled with cuts in food stamps and other welfare programs, has been increased misery for poor single mothers and their children. A study of women in Georgia, Michigan, and New York City, who had been terminated from AFDC because of the Reagan cuts found that between one-third and one-half had run out of food at least once since losing their welfare benefits, and large numbers could not afford medical care for themselves or their children. In addition, the loss of welfare benefits forced many of the women to work longer hours or seek an additional job (Center for the Study of Social Policy 1984; Zinn and Sarri 1986).

To the extent that the Reagan cuts force low-income women into seeking more wage labor, these women can be seen as serving a *substitute* role. Women forced off welfare compete with others (mostly other women) for low-wage, low-skilled work, possibly lowering relative wages in these occupations even further. Depression of wages at the bottom can potentially affect the entire wage structure. Cutting welfare benefits, then, can be seen as one part of the Reagan Administrations's strategy to restore profits by weakening labor. Recently proposed legislation, supported both by the Administration and by the state governors, would make working compulsory for all women on welfare with children age three or older; this legislation would be likely to exacerbate the substitution effect.

CONCLUSION

It is apparent, then, that the labor market restructuring of the 1970s and 1980s has affected women differently according to their class positions, increasing segmentation among women workers. Elite women entering traditionally-male occupations have experienced virtually uninterrupted improvement in their economic position, despite continuing discrimination. The majority of women, working in traditionally-female occupations, have found themselves working more continuously, and assuming more responsibility for the support of their families. Many experience greater stress and, in the case of the growing number of women raising families alone, declining incomes; but greater attachment to the work force has also had its benefits in greater financial independence and in the intrinsic rewards of working. For women in poverty the period brought worsening economic conditions, first as inflation ate away at social welfare benefits, and later as the Reagan Administration's drastic cuts in programs for the poor created further immiseration and increased competition for jobs at the bottom of the economic ladder.

There is considerable debate about whether and how U.S. capitalism can generate a genuine economic recovery. There is no room here to enter this debate; however, three observations are likely to be true for women over the decade ahead. First, women will continue to increase their labor force participation. Second, labor force segregation by sex will be a persistent source of economic inequality. And third, women in poverty and their children will continue to constitute a major social and economic emergency.

NOTES

1. The movement into clerical work and female-dominated professions has dramatically improved relative income for black women full-time workers. Their median income increased from 51 percent of white women's income in 1955 to 91 percent in 1982 (Blau and Ferber 1986). However, the ratio seems to have peaked in 1975, at 98 percent. Further, the ratio overstates the improvement in black women's economic position, because it includes only full-time full-year workers. Black women are more than twice as likely to be unemployed as white women, and are considerably more likely to be involuntary part-time workers. Although only 21 percent of black employed women worked part time in 1986, compared to 28 percent of employed white women, 45 percent of the black part timers wanted full-time work, compared to only 21 percent of the white women working part time (U.S. Dept. of Labor 1987). Finally, black women tend to work more continuously than white women, so even near parity in median incomes may represent a lower return to experience for black women workers.
2. The movement of women into traditionally-male professional and managerial positions may be less impressive than it first appears, for two reasons. First, women are entering some professions — e.g. academics, law, and medicine — at a time when over-supply and structural changes are downgrading their pay, prestige, and autonomy (Carter and Carter 1981). Second, within the male-dominated professions, women tend to be concentrated in a limited number of specialties, which are lower status and less lucrative. Within management, women are frequently relegated to positions with little or no access to promotion to top management (Fox and Hesse-Biber 1984).
3. For the working population as a whole, real weekly earnings for full-time workers peaked around 1973, then declined during the 1974–75 recession. From 1975 to 1980 earnings stagnated, then fell further during the 1980–82 recession period. Since 1983 real earnings have increased very slightly, but remain considerably below their peak in the early 1970s (Hedges and Mellor 1979; U.S. Bureau of the Census 1985). Actual earning trends varied among groups, with young workers (age 16–24) faring the worst, and adult men faring somewhat better than adult women (Hedges and Mellor 1979). Trends varied markedly by industry as well, with manufacturing (67 percent male) maintaining earnings growth until 1978, while services (61 percent female) peaked before 1975 (U.S. Bureau of the Census 1985; earnings in services were lower over the entire period, declining from 72 percent of manufacturing earnings in 1970 to 68 percent in June, 1985). While adult males seem to have fared the best, they were still confronted, in many cases, with stagnating or declining real wages. Further, there appears to be growing polarization among adult male workers, with substantial growth in the proportion with low earnings (Dooley and Gottschalk 1985).

REFERENCES

Amott, Teresa. 1985. Race, Class and the Feminization of Poverty. *Socialist Politics* 3:5-11.

Beller, Andrea H. 1984. Trends in Occupational Segregation by Sex and Race, 1960–1981. In, *Sex Segregation in the Workplace*, Barbara F. Reskin (ed.). pp. 11–26. Washington, D.C.: National Academy Press.

Bielby, William T. and James N. Baron. 1984. A Woman's Place Is With Other Women: Sex Segregation Within Organizations. In, *Sex Segregation in the Workplace*, Barbara F. Reskin (ed.). pp. 27–55. Washington, D.C.: National Academy Press.

Blau, Francine D. and Marianne A. Ferber. 1986. *The Economics of Women, Men, and Work*. New Jersey: Prentice-Hall.

_____. n.d. Women's Progress in the Labor Market: Should We Rest on Our Laurels?. IRRA Papers and Proceedings. (Forthcoming).

Bluestone, Barry and Bennett Harrison. 1986. *The Great American Job Machine: The Proliferation of Low Wage Employment in the U.S. Economy*. Washington, D.C.: Joint Economic Committee of Congress.

Carter, Michael J. and Susan Boslego Carter. 1981. Women's Recent Progress in the Professions or, Women Get a Ticket to Ride after the Gravy Train Has Left the Station. *Feminist Studies* 7(3):477–503.

The Center for the Study of Social Policy. 1984. *Working Female-Headed Families in Poverty*. Washington, D.C.

Dooley, Martin and Peter Gottschalk. 1985. The Increasing Proportion of Men with Low Earnings in the United States. *Demography* 22(1):25–34.

Duncan, Greg J. 1984. *Years of Poverty, Years of Plenty*. Ann Arbor, MI: Institute for Social Research, University of Michigan.

Fox, Mary Frank and Sharlene Hesse-Biber. 1978. *Women at Work*. Palo Alto, CA: Mayfield.

Ferree, Myra Marx. 1984. Sacrifice, Satisfaction, and Social Change: Employment and the Family. In, *My Troubles Are Going to Have Trouble With Me,* Karen Brodkin Sacks and Dorothy Remy (eds.).pp. 61–79. New Jersey: Rutgers University Press.

Harrington, Michael. 1984. *The New American Poverty*. New York: Penguin Books.

Harrison, Bennett. 1979. Welfare Payments and the Reproduction of Low-Wage Workers and Secondary Jobs. *Review of Radical Political Economics* 11(2):1–16.

Hedges, Janice Neipert and Earl F. Mellor. 1979. Weekly and Hourly Earnings of U.S. Workers, 1967–78. *Monthly Labor Review* 102(8):31–41.

Juster, F. Thomas. 1985. A Note on Recent Changes in Time Use. In, *Time, Goods and Well-Being,* Thomas Juster and Frank P. Stafford (eds.). Ann Arbor: Institute for Social and Policy Research, University of Michigan.

Leon, Carol Boyd. 1982. Occupational Winners and Losers: Who Were They During 1972–80? *Monthly Labor Review* 105(6):18–28.

Maloney, Tim. 1987. Employment Constraints and the Labor Supply of Married Women. *The Journal of Human Resources* 22(1):51–61.

Parrish, John B. 1986. Are Women Taking Over the Professions? *Challenge* 28(6):54–58.

Power, Marilyn. 1984. Falling Through the 'Safety-net'. Women, Economic Crisis, and Reaganomics. *Feminist Studies* 10(1):31–57.

Power, Marilyn and Sam Rosenberg. 1987. Black Women Clerical Workers: Movement Toward Equality With White Women? Unpublished paper.

Rosenberg, Sam. 1983. Reagan Social Policy and Labour Force Restructuring. *Cambridge Journal of Economics* 7:179–196.

Rubery, Jill (ed.). 1988. *Women and Recession*. London: Routledge and Kegan Paul.

Sanik, Margaret Mietus. 1981. Division of Household Work: A Decade Comparison, 1967–1977. *Home Economics Research Journal* 10(2):175–180.

U.S. Bureau of the Census. 1984. *Detailed Occupation of the Experienced Civilian Labor Force by Sex for the U.S. and Regions: 1980 and 1970*. Supplementary Report PC 80-S1-15. Washington, D.C.

——. 1986. *Statistical Abstract of the United States,* 106th edition. Washington, D.C.

U.S. Dept. of Labor. 1987. *Employment and Earnings* 34(1).

Wallace, Phyllis. 1980. *Black Women in the Labor Force*. Cambridge: MIT Press.

Zinn Deborah K. and Rosemary Sarri. 1986. Turning Back the Clock on Public Welfare. In, *Women and Poverty,* Barbara C. Gelpi, Nancy C. M. Hartsock, Clare C. Novak, and Myra H. Strober (eds.). pp. 25–40. Chicago: University of Chicago Press.

5

Welfare Reform: A Workhouse Without Walls

TERESA L. AMOTT

Periodically, policymakers in Washington and across the country decide that it is time for a major overhaul of the nation's welfare system. Pressure for the most recent round of welfare reform began building early in the 1980s, when Ronald Reagan was elected President on a conservative platform that included a broad assault on social programs. The prime target of this assault has been Aid to Families with Dependent Children (AFDC), the main welfare program for poor families (see Appendix). Charging that welfare causes a range of social problems from family breakup to drug abuse, conservatives have sparked a nationwide interest in welfare reform (Piven and Cloward 1987:45).

Politicians, academics, and government bureaucrats across the country began developing a host of proposals for revamping the system. Marketed to the public as solutions to a "welfare crisis," the proposals came packaged with slick, Madison Avenue names. Massachusetts offered ET as well as JEDI. REACH and GAIN came from New Jersey and California, respectively, while Illinois sold Project Chance and Missouri marketed Learnfare.

The National Governors' Association meeting in 1986 generated the unifying theme for these proposals: "Making America Work" (Herbers 1987). As the slogan suggests, welfare reform in the 1980s comes down to one thing: forcing those on public assistance into the labor market. Nearly all the new programs seek to change the welfare system from an income support program into a jobs program through a mix of carrots and sticks which are designed to compel welfare recipients to take low-paying jobs.

None of the proposals speaks adequately to the real reasons most adult welfare recipients don't take paying work: they are already working — raising children. Rather than recognizing the value of this unpaid work, reformers want those on welfare to "get a job." Unfortunately, the reforms under consideration in the 1980s offer minimal training, poor job placements with inadequate health coverage, and too-small subsidies for childcare.

But what is bad for welfare recipients is good for local employers. In the nineteenth century, welfare reform meant the establishment of workhouses in which the poor, many of them men, split wood or farmed in exchange for room and board. Welfare reform in the 1980s is more subtle: it's a workhouse without walls, and most of the workers are women.

WELFARE: AN "ENABLER"

According to the new strain of reformers, including both conservatives and liberals, welfare must be overhauled because it breeds illegitimate children and dependency and erodes the work ethic. In his 1986 State of the Union Address, President Reagan blamed welfare for "the breakdown of the family," and said the "welfare culture" was responsible for "female and child poverty, child abandonment, horrible crimes, and deteriorating schools."

A White House report on welfare reform gave a sense of why conservatives are so bent on changing the welfare system. The report called AFDC an enabler — a program which enables women to live without a husband or a job (U.S. Executive Office of the President 1986). In other words, conservatives' recent rush to reform welfare reflects their agenda for the labor market and the family. If welfare enables women to survive without paid employment, that's a problem for employers, particularly employers who depend on women's cheap labor. Similarly, if welfare enables women to survive without being married, that means major changes in the balance of power between men and women.

The American family has changed a great deal from the "Father Knows Best" ideal of 1950s television shows. The number of single-parent families in the United States has doubled over the past 15 years. The reasons for this change are complex, but include the impact of the women's movement, the gay rights movement, easier divorce laws, and growing labor force participation by married women with children. As a result of these changes, different lifestyles are tolerated more today and women have greater economic independence from men. The outcome of this changing family structure is dramatic: one in four families with children is now headed by a single parent, compared to one in eight in 1970. Today, three in five black children and one in five white children are being raised by a single parent, the vast majority of whom are women (Children's Defense Fund 1987).

These changes are deeply threatening to conservative proponents of the nuclear family. But prayer and sermons have not been enough to halt the growth of single-parent families, and conservatives have made welfare the scapegoat. Unfortunately for the conservative case, there is no conclusive evidence that AFDC promotes the formation of single-parent families through divorce, separation, or out-of-wedlock births. High benefit states, for instance, don't have a greater share of single-parent families than low benefit states (Wilson and Neckerman 1986: 249).

The availability of welfare also doesn't seem to have much impact on the child-bearing rates of unmarried women. There has been a rise in the share of births to unmarried women over the past 15 years. But this is mainly due to the fact that married women have been having fewer babies. As a result, the *share* of out-of-wedlock births has risen. And despite the media hype about teenage pregnancy, teen birth rates (births per 1000 women aged 15–19) have been declining steadily since the 1970s (Wilson and Neckerman 1986:236).

Despite the lack of evidence for their position, conservatives have steadfastly pursued their agenda of eliminating income support payments to poor families. The main element of conservative welfare reform is workfare: forcing welfare recipients to work off their benefits or lose them. In practice, this means that a family receiving $335 in monthly cash benefits would have to spend up to 100 hours per month performing unpaid work in a government or nonprofit agency (the number of hours may not exceed the grant divided by the minimum wage).

Liberals add a few carrots like training and childcare subsidies to the work requirement stick. But nearly all of the state projects, liberal and conservative alike, make the job programs mandatory, requiring recipients with children over a certain age to participate or lose some or all of their benefits. The experience at the state level in the early 1980s shows that the threat of losing benefits (known as "sanctioning") is very real. In New York City's misnamed "Employment Opportunity" program, over 8,000 families were sanctioned in one six-month period alone (Statewide Youth Advocacy 1987).

THE REAL WELFARE CRISIS

Most poor people would probably agree that there is a welfare crisis, but of a different sort. The real welfare crisis is that tightened eligibility requirements since the early 1970s have squeezed many of the poor off the rolls, while inflation has eaten away at the purchasing power of welfare benefits.

Welfare rights groups which organized among the poor in the early 1970s demonstrated that more people were in need than were receiving benefits. As a result of their organizing, welfare rolls expanded dramatically (Piven and Cloward 1971). Between 1970 and 1973, the average number of recipients rose nearly 50 percent. But since 1973, the number of people on AFDC has stayed constant at roughly 10.7 million (U.S. Senate Committee on Finance 1987:18).

The stability of the caseload level masks increasing need. Between 1970 and 1985, the number of people living in families below the federal poverty line rose by 41 percent — from 18.3 million to 25.7 million (U.S. Bureau of the Census 1986:3). But caseloads didn't grow because increasingly restrictive eligibility requirements held down the number of recipients so that only half of poor families could qualify.

Not surprisingly, combined federal, state, and local spending on AFDC has fallen in real terms since the mid-1970s. In 1975, net outlays on AFDC were nearly $17 billion (in 1985 dollars). By 1986, outlays had fallen to $14.7 billion (U.S. Senate Committee on Finance 1987:25).

Outlays have fallen because the real value of AFDC benefits has dropped. AFDC benefit levels are set by state legislatures, and no state automatically raises AFDC benefits when prices rise. As a result, the purchasing power of AFDC benefits fell by one-third between 1970 and 1986. (Some states were slightly less stingy. For instance, Wisconsin raised benefits by 10 percent over the rate of inflation in that period. But other states, like Illinois and New Jersey, permitted real benefits to fall by over 50 percent.) Even if we add in the value of food stamps, which are received by most AFDC families, the combined value of AFDC and food stamp benefits still fell an average of 26 percent between 1971 and 1984 (U.S. House of Representatives, Committee on Ways and Means 1986:378-379).

WELFARE REFORM REALITY

Historically, welfare has played an important role within capitalism. Public assistance has appeased dissent when protest by the poor threatened to disrupt society. It is no accident that the periods of greatest expansion of the welfare system have been those following the unrest of the Great Depression and the urban riots of the late 1960s (Piven and Cloward 1971).

In addition to regulating the poor, the welfare system has been used to regulate the supply of workers to employers paying low wages. When there is a shortage of workers willing to take low-paying work, government historically tightens eligibility requirements to force more recipients into the work force. For instance, the Work Incentive Program (WIN), which created workfare and training programs that compelled welfare recipients to find jobs, was established in the full-employment years of the late 1960s.

Over the past 15 years, the number of low-paid jobs in the United States has been rising. In a study prepared for the Joint Economic Committee of the U.S. Congress, economists Barry Bluestone and Bennett Harrison examined net employment growth between 1963 and 1985. Between 1963 and 1973, only 20 percent of the new jobs created paid low wages (categorized in their study as less than $7400 per year in constant 1986 dollars). But between 1979 and 1985, the share of low-wage jobs had risen to 44 percent (Bluestone and Harrison 1986).

Despite chronically high unemployment rates, the mid-1980s saw a developing shortage of workers willing to take these low-wage jobs. The labor shortage is particularly acute in urban areas where many welfare recipients reside. Employers have responded with minor incentives, but still have difficulty attracting workers. (For instance, McDonald's franchises in Boston now lure workers with scholarship programs and wages near $6 an hour, but there are still help wanted signs below the golden arches.) The immigration reform bill passed by Congress in 1986 also has employers worried as it is expected to reduce the supply of undocumented workers who do much of the low-wage work in the United States (*Business Week* 1987).

Welfare mothers represent a labor pool to be tapped by these low-wage employers. Some welfare reform proposals, such as New Jersey's REACH, require employment or training for mothers of children as young as two. New Jersey's plan even provides the jobs: new casinos in the Atlantic City area have agreed to employ 1500 graduates of the state's AFDC work and training program. Just in case there's any doubt as to whose interests welfare reform is serving in New Jersey, REACH is administered by Private Industry Councils dominated by local employers.

One of the reasons economic compulsion is no longer sufficient to generate enough low-wage workers is that the real value of the minimum wage has fallen even faster than the value of welfare benefits. (The minimum wage lost approximately 30 percent of its purchasing power to inflation between 1981 and 1987.) In 1981 — the last time the minimum wage was raised — monthly earnings from a full-time minimum wage job were levelled at $558 (U.S. Congressional Budget Office 1986). At that time, average AFDC benefits per family were $277, 50 percent of earnings from minimum wage work. Since then, benefits have fallen in real terms but risen in relation to the minimum wage. By 1985, AFDC benefits were worth 61 percent of minimum wage earnings.

So despite the falling value of benefits, the financial advantage to taking a job has been declining for welfare recipients. This is particularly true when the value of other benefits is taken into account. For instance, increased cash income reduces the amount of food stamps a family can collect, so what they gain through wages, they lose in food stamps. When families leave the welfare rolls to take paid employment, they also lose Medicaid benefits, but few low-wage jobs provide company-paid health care. Many low-wage jobs are in the service sector, which provides health insurance to roughly one-third of its employees. In contrast, 80 percent of manufacturing sector employees have employer-provided health plans (U.S. Bureau of the Census 1986:421). Welfare recipients are thus faced with a choice between providing health insurance for their families and taking paid jobs.

Another problem for welfare recipients is the high price of childcare. Childcare costs vary widely, depending on the age of the child and the type of facility, but most estimates of the costs of one year's care for a preschool child are in the range of $1500 to $4000 (National Commission on Working Women 1987). By way of comparison, the average after-tax income of women heads of households was a meager $10,309 in 1985 (U.S. Bureau of the Census 1987).

Squeezed between low wages and high costs, there is often little economic gain — if any — for a welfare mother who takes a paid job. If she does, she is usually forced to endure poor working conditions in a dead-end job at the expense of time spent with her children.

Welfare reform proposals fail to adequately address these welfare realities. Most states offer only short-term training programs, and usually prepare recipients for sex-stereotyped jobs such as nurses' aide or file clerks. The childcare benefits allowed to recipients while they attend training programs are far below the cost of enrolling a child in a daycare center. Finally, the most any of the state plans offer for health coverage is a grace period during which the recipient can continue to receive Medicaid. In Massachusetts, whose program has been considered one of the most successful, a recent survey of recipients placed in jobs showed that only 55 percent had any health coverage where they worked and only 14 percent received benefits paid in full by the employer (Commonwealth of Massachusetts 1986).

WELFARE AND POLITICS

Despite all the deficiencies of the proposed programs, welfare reform is a perennially appealing topic for politicians. To Republicans, an attack on welfare is an attack on the role of government in redistributing income to the poor. To Democrats, welfare reform is an opportunity to demonstrate that they are efficient state managers. They emphasize the cost-saving aspects of proposals to show that they can do more than just throw money at problems.

But neither Republicans nor Democrats will associate themselves with real welfare reform — proposals which address the basic problems that generate poverty: unemployment, low-paying jobs without benefits, inequitable wages for women, women's continuing responsibility for childrearing, and an inadequate supply of affordable childcare.

A more progressive welfare reform would recognize that a job is not an automatic ticket out of poverty for single-parent families. A meaningful system of income supplements for low-income families, such as the European family allowance system, comes closer to what is required. In this system, the government pays a uniform subsidy to all families with children. In Western Europe as a whole, between 1 percent and 2 percent of Gross National Product is devoted to family allowances (Kuttner 1984:244). Devoting the same share of GNP to alleviating family poverty in the United States would require between $40 billion and $80 billion, roughly twice what we are currently spending on AFDC and food stamps. In the short run, AFDC benefits should be made more uniform across states, and raised, at a minimum, up to the federal poverty level. Eligibility should be expanded to include two-parent families and families with low earnings.

If the policy goal is to expand the labor market options available to welfare recipients, the most important consideration should not be welfare reform, but rather raising the effective wages of the work that is available. Such a change, which workers have as much interest in demanding as those on public assistance, would begin with the important first step of raising the minimum wage. Expanding the number of workers in the service sector who are covered by union agreements would also go a long way toward raising women's wages. In 1985, for instance, union women earned on average $4,000 per year more than non-union women (National Commission on Working Women 1987). Publically provided health insurance and childcare are also needed if women are to support themselves and their families through participating in the labor market. And lastly, payment of equal wages to men and women doing work of comparable worth would help the 80 percent of women workers trapped in traditional women's jobs (see Sorensen in this volume).

Meaningful welfare reform would expand the opportunities and the income available to women with children — both from the labor market and from the state. There are many obstacles to such reform, including the power of low-wage employers, Congressional reluctance to expand social programs in an era of federal budget deficits, and the conservative pro-nuclear-family lobby. Only sustained organizing by the poor and their allies can overcome these obstacles. The early 1970s saw such a period of sustained organizing. Perhaps the latest round of welfare reform will spark another mobilization by the poor.

APPENDIX

What is AFDC?

Aid to Families with Dependent Children (AFDC) is the largest income support program for poor families in the United States. Eligibility requirements and benefit levels are set by each individual state, and the federal government provides half the funds.

The vast majority of AFDC recipients are children. Of the 10.7 million people receiving AFDC in 1986, 7 million were dependent children. Almost 90 percent of families receiving AFDC are headed by single women. In theory, 26 states permit a two-parent family to qualify for AFDC benefits if the father is unemployed, but in practice other requirements limit the number of two-parent families who are eligible.

In order to collect AFDC benefits, a recipient whose youngest child is at least six years old must also register for work or job training. In many states, such as North Carolina and West Virginia, this means the recipient must work an average of 20 hours per week in a public sector job in order to collect her benefit check.

Families must be very poor to qualify for AFDC, since states set limits on recipients' income and assets. The limit on assets means that families have to spend most of their savings before they become eligible. If a family has savings over $1000, it cannot collect benefits. Under the asset limits, a family with a car valued over $1500 is also ineligible.

There are also stringent limits on the amount of other income a family can receive while collecting AFDC. In Kentucky, for instance, a three-person family with total income over $364 per month is ineligible for AFDC. In fact, nearly all states set eligibility standards so strictly that many families which have earnings below the poverty line cannot qualify. At present, only about half of all poor children live in families which receive AFDC.

In no state are AFDC benefits high enough to bring a family out of poverty. Thirty states pay less than 50 percent of the poverty level for a three-person family. Like eligibility, benefit levels vary widely across states. In 1987, the lowest payment for a family of three was $118 in Alabama; the highest payment was $833 in Alaska. Even when we add in the value of food stamps, the average state provides benefits equal to $533 per month — only 73 percent of the federal poverty line. Nationwide, 80 percent of AFDC families also receive food stamps (U.S. Senate Committee on Finance 1986).

States are required to provide Medicaid — a program which provides free health care — for all families who qualify for AFDC. For many women who might otherwise take jobs which don't provide health insurance, this is the most important reason for collecting welfare.

The common perception of AFDC is that a large number of recipients stay on AFDC for many years at a stretch. This perception is incorrect: in fact, while roughly one-quarter of U.S. households rely on public assistance *at some point* in any 10 year period, very few are dependent upon assistance for the full 10 years. The average stay on AFDC is less than 2 years. Most welfare recipients apply for assistance because of a major family event such as divorce, separation, or the birth of a child. Once their life circumstances have stabilized, they leave the caseload. Only one in five of all women beginning a stay on AFDC will remain on it for more than 8 years (Duncan and Hoffman 1986).

REFERENCES

Bluestone, Barry and Bennett Harrison. 1986. The Great American Job Machine. Washington, D.C.: Joint Economic Committee, U.S. Congress.

Business Week.1987. Help Wanted. (August 10):48–53.

Children's Defense Fund. 1987. *A Children's Defense Budget FY 1988: An Analysis of Our Nation's Investment in Children*. Washington, D.C.

Commonwealth of Massachusetts, Department of Public Welfare. 1986. An Analysis of the First 25,000 ET Placements. Boston, MA.

Duncan, Greg J. and Saul D. Hoffman. 1986. Welfare Dynamics and the Nature of Need. Institute for Social Research, Mimeo. University of Michigan, Ann Arbor.

Herbers, John. 1987. Governors Ask Work Plan for Welfare Recipients. *New York Times* (February 22):30.

Kuttner, Robert. 1984. *The Economic Illusion: False Choices Between Prosperity and Social Justice*. Boston: Houghton Mifflin Company.

National Commission on Working Women. 1987. Fact Sheets on Women in the Work Force and Childcare. Washington, D.C.

Piven, Frances Fox and Richard A. Cloward. 1971. *Regulating the Poor*. New York: Pantheon Books.

_____. 1987. The Contemporary Relief Debate. In, *The Mean Season*. pp. 45–108. New York: Random House.

Statewide Youth Advocacy. 1987. Hope or Hassle: New York City's AFDC Employment Initiatives. Albany, New York.

U.S. Bureau of the Census. 1986a. *Money Income and Poverty Status of Families and Persons in the United States: 1985*. Series P-60, No. 154. Washington, D.C.

_____. 1986b. *Statistical Abstract of the United States*. Washington, D.C.

_____. 1987. *Household After Tax Income: 1985*. Series P-23, No. 151. Washington, D.C.

U.S. Congressional Budget Office. 1986. *The Growth in Poverty: 1979–1985. Economic and Demographic Factors*. Washington, D.C.

U.S. Executive Office of the President, Domestic Policy Council Working Group on the Family. 1986. *Up From Dependency*. Washington, D.C.

U.S. Senate, Committee on Finance. 1987. *Data and Materials Related to Welfare Programs for Families with Children*. S. Prt. 100-20. Washington, D.C.: U.S. Government Printing Office.

U.S. House of Representatives, Committee on Ways and Means. 1986. *Background Material and Data on Programs within the Jurisdiction of the Committee on Ways and Means.* WMCP. 99-14. Washington, D.C.: U.S. Government Printing Office.

Wilson, William Julius and Kathryn M. Neckerman. 1986. Poverty and Family Structure: The Widening Gap between Evidence and Public Policy Issues. In, *Fighting Poverty: What Works and What Doesn't,* Sheldon H. Danziger and Daniel H. Weinberg (eds.). pp. 232-282. Cambridge: Harvard University Press.

6

Capital Mobility and Labor Migration

SASKIA SASSEN

INTRODUCTION

Capital mobility has created new conditions for the mobility of labor. Economic practices and technology have contributed to the formation of a transnational space for the circulation of capital. Policies, many originating in the United States, delimit, regulate, and make this space viable. What economic theory as well as governments define as movement between countries is also movement within one single entity encompassing those countries. One important question for understanding U.S. immigration today concerns the impact of such a transnational space for the circulation of capital on the formation and directionality of international labor migrations.

The current migration to the United States shares a number of general traits with earlier migration phases. But it is also predicated on specific conditions that arise out of the reorganization of the world economy over the last two decades. Emphasizing the latter is not a denial of the weight of the general conditions at work in most migrations. It is, rather, an attempt to identify the particular historical and political context of the current migration phase. It means, for example, viewing the 1965 liberalization of U.S. immigration policy as but one instance of a whole series of policies, from the lifting of import-export restrictions to the implementation of the Eurodollar market, that had the effect of internationalizing the country's economy. The overall result was the formation of a transnational space within which the circulation of workers can be regarded as one of several flows, including capital, goods, services, and information.

However, the fact that not all countries became large-scale senders of immigrants to the United States points to the need for specifying the manner in which countries are incorporated into this transnational space. A key assumption in much thinking about immigration in the United States is that poverty, overpopulation and a stagnant economy are the central causes for emigration. Most countries in the Third World have one or more of these conditions; yet most do not have significant emigration flows. We need to understand whether there are specific kinds of linkages between the United States and those countries that do become major senders of immigrants to the United States. It may well be that particular forms of incorporation into the internationalization of production coalesce with basic conditions, such as poverty or unemployment to promote a migration-inducing situation.

In what follows I will briefly discuss how these conventional variables fail to explain the current migration phase adequately and hence the need to recognize the migration impact of other conditions. In the second half I will present the main outline of an alternative way of analyzing the current phase of U.S. immigration. (An appendix contains tables describing the basic characteristics of immigration in the United States today.)

THE CONVENTIONAL VIEW: OVERPOPULATION, POVERTY, STAGNATION

Population growth in Third World countries cannot be disregarded, as it signals the possibility of increased emigration. However, there is considerable evidence that not all countries with high population growth have high emigration. A second consideration that needs to be incorporated into the analysis of population growth and migration is the relation between population growth and population density. Some of the countries with high population growth in the Third World do not necessarily have high density, certainly not compared with countries such as France, the Netherlands, or Luxembourg. But the assumption that migrants come from countries with very high population growth, where there is simply no room left for them, requires careful examination. Excessive population density may not necessarily be the main reason for migration.

While it would be very useful to have a criterion as simple and quantifiable as population growth to predict what countries will be emigration countries, the migration reality is less tidy and more elusive. It then becomes clear that we need to introduce a number of other factors into the analysis. This need to introduce additional factors is evident and generally accepted in the case of war refugees. Few, if any, would insist that refugee flows are generated by high population growth and density, even though refugees may come from countries with those characteristics, and even though these may lead to war. Yet an insistence on demographic explanations is common in the analysis of labor migrations. Further, refugee policies acknowledge indirectly that U.S. military activities abroad make the United States accountable, at least to some degree, for the fate of an ally's displaced people. Refugee entitlements carry such an acknowledgment. One might ask whether people displaced because of commercial developments by U.S. corporations abroad, e.g. large-scale export crops, are entitled to certain indemnities for being forced to become emigrants. This kind of formulation in never introduced into the immigration debate.

There is a similar need for a critical examination of the relation between emigration and poverty. Poverty is held to be a basic migration push factor. This raises two questions. First, why are not all countries with extensive poverty emigration countries? Secondly, why is it that large-scale emigration in what are today the main sending countries started when it did and not earlier, since many of these countries were poor long before emigration commenced? Haiti was poor long before massive emigration began in the early 1970s. The Dominican Republic had considerable unemployment, underemployment, and poverty long before large-scale emigration began in the middle 1960s.

Finally, it becomes necessary to examine the relation between emigration and economic growth. Again, one key assumption has been that emigration is a consequence of stagnant economic growth. Yet growth rates in employment and domestic product in the main migrant-sending countries were relatively high during the 1970s, certainly compared with those of developed market economies. These high growth rates do not preclude the existence of unemployment insofar as job creation, even if high, may not be able to keep up with labor force growth or with unemployment in sectors other than those experiencing high growth. But what does need to be emphasized is that these growth rates were considerably higher than rates in other countries which did not have high emigration. That is to say, the long-held assumption that a stagnant economy generates emigration is not necessarily borne out by the facts in the current migration phase. To cite one of the most blatant examples: South Korea, with one of the highest growth rates in GDP, in general employment, and particularly, in manufacturing employment, also was one of the countries with the highest growth rate in migration to the United States. Similarly, Taiwan and the Philippines had very high rates of economic growth and emigration.

The possibility of migration pressures under conditions of poverty, unemployment, and overpopulation cannot be denied. Yet is has become evident that by themselves these conditions will not promote large-scale emigration. It is necessary to identify processes that transform these conditions into a migration-inducing situation. This distinction may carry significant implications for policy. Given U.S. attempts to regulate immigration, what may be needed is a recognition of such intervening processes. Thinking and policies stemming from this recognition may carry a rather different focus from current U.S. policies aimed at controlling the border or (until recently) reducing population growth and promoting certain types of economic growth in Third World countries (e.g. the Caribbean Basin Initiative). Recognition of intervening processes may move the focus away from conditions in emigration countries and invite an examination of *processes that link* the United States to those countries and may contribute to the initiation of new migration flows to the United States. And it would invite an examination of labor demand conditions in the United States that may contribute to the *continuation* of such flows. Policies stemming from such a recognition may have to address issues not usually considered relevant to immigration.

A DOMESTIC OR AN INTERNATIONAL ISSUE?

A focus on high population growth, poverty, and economic stagnation easily leads one to view emigration as a domestic matter, and the inadequacy of socioeconomic conditions and policies in countries of origin as promoting emigration. Immigration, in turn, becomes a domestic matter (or "problem") for the receiving country. For humanitarian or more pragmatic reasons, the receiving country, such as the United States, commits itself to accept immigrants under certain conditions. The acceptance of immigrants is based ultimately on factors internal to the United States, including a tradition of immigration. If international factors are brought to bear on immigration policies or decisions concerning immigrants they are typically not viewed as pertaining to migration but rather to other economic or diplomatic ties between the countries involved. Migration simply becomes an obvious, handy or unavoidable arena within which these other issues can also be played out. A classic example is the use of the migration situation in oil negotiations between Mexico and the United States.

International factors must be introduced into the analysis of migration, specifically the effects of U.S. foreign policies and activities in migrant sending countries and in the U.S. domestic economy. It then becomes evident that U.S. immigration policies and practices address, wittingly or not, both domestic and international issues that have to be dealt with in the domestic arena, i.e., inside the territory of the United States. In its most extreme version, the current phase of U.S. immigration could be seen as representing, in addition to its other dimensions, a *domestic* consequence of U.S. activities *abroad*. One can point to the active role of U.S. firms in the disruption of ''traditional'' economies due to large-scale development of commercial agriculture with its associated displacement of small-holders and subsistence growers, or due to massive recruitment of young women into wage labor for export manufacturing. By ''traditional'' economies I refer to a whole range of activities, from subsistence and semi-waged types of work to industrial activity geared to the local or national market, with no, or little, foreign investment and typically less mechanized than would be the case in highly developed countries. The disruption of these forms of work need not be an inevitable consequence of the development of agriculture and manufacturing for export. Yet historically that has tended to be the case. Furthermore, this disruption does not necessarily generate emigration. Other objective and ideological linkages need to be established between the sending and receiving countries. It is here that the facts of foreign investment and general cultural westernization acquire weight, as do a liberal immigration policy and a tradition of immigration.

In each of the major countries sending immigrants to the United States today, we can find a specific set of conditions which, together with poverty and unemployment, induce outmigration. Here I briefly touch upon items that have not received sufficient attention in the debate on immigration to show the importance of introducing international factors into the analysis.

Emigration from the Dominican Republic began in the middle of the 1960s. Subsequent to the election victory of Bosch in the Dominican Republic, the U.S. government sent marines to Santo Domingo. This occupation had, among others, two effects that directly bear on emigration: (1) it created a stream of middle-class political refugees who came to the United States and (2) it created objective linkages with the United States. Both of these eventually evolved into conditions that facilitated further emigration of Dominicans to the United States and, very importantly, the emergence of emigration to the United States as an option actually perceived by individuals as available to them. Additional linkages were consolidated via direct foreign investment in agriculture and manufacturing for export.

In the case of Haiti, insufficient attention has been given to the change in economic development strategy and the types of upheaval these brought about. The transition from the older Duvalier to his son was also a transition from one type of economic regime to another. There was an opening to foreign investment and large-scale development of commercial agriculture and manufacturing for export. The United States was the key partner in this new strategy. The development of commercial agriculture, export processing zones, and manufacturing for export outside the zones, had one thing in common: they required securing a labor supply. We observe, indeed, large-scale displacements of small-holders who become laborers on plantations or in the cities. There is some evidence that the intensification of police violence in the countryside may be in part explained by the need to secure wage-labor in the context of a tradition of subsistence farming and the associated resistance to becoming wage-laborers.

An aspect of Mexican immigration that is not sufficiently emphasized is that a number of studies show the large-scale emergence of illegal Mexican flows to be associated with a *legal* program. The development of the ''bracero'' program created objective linkages between the United States and Mexico and promoted the whole notion of migrating to the United States. Thus an arrangement made by the United States with Mexico had unanticipated consequences. The initiation of guest worker programs with various countries may emerge as a mechanism promoting emigration to the United States outside the bounds of such programs. This is particularly significant if such treaties were to be signed with a country that has not had a history of migration to the United States. It could set the stage for the occurrence of new migration flows.

In the case of Southeast and East Asian migration to the United States, we cannot disregard the fact that after World War II and the Korean War, U.S. strategy sought to build up U.S. business in the region and promote economic development as a means to "stabilize" the region politically. U.S. business and military interests coalesced to create a vast array of linkages with the Asian countries sending immigrants to the United States over the last decade. The massive increase of direct foreign investment during that same period reinforces these patterns.

All the above examples accentuate first, the fact that U.S. business, military, or diplomatic activities were a strong presence in countries that have significant migration to the United States. Secondly, it is the *combination* of poverty, unemployment, or underemployment *with* the emergence of objective and ideological linkages which probably operates as a migration-inducing factor. It then becomes necessary to make distinctions: what kind of U.S. military, political, and economic policies abroad have the potential in conjunction with unemployment, or underemployment and poverty, to create a migration-inducing situation. In this context, the image of the United States as a country of immigrants with opportunities for all, and the 1965 liberalization of immigration policy, become significant. In combination with objective conditions and linkages, the existence of such an open migration policy becomes truly consequential. Without this context of linkages it is difficult to see how such a policy could have generated massive immigration to the United States. Thus, the 1965 Act should be seen in combination with military and economic policies facilitating a wide range of U.S. activities abroad. This would explain not only the massive increase in immigration but also why the countries that sent most of the new migrants are not necessarily the ones that should have done so according to the stipulations of the Act. And it would explain why most countries in the world are far from using their quota of immigrant visas to the United States.

THE GLOBALIZATION OF PRODUCTION AND LABOR MIGRATIONS

Displacing the locus of explanation away from poverty or economic stagnation in sending countries and onto the processes that link sending and receiving country introduces a set of variables into the analysis not usually thought of as pertaining to immigration. Such linkages are constituted through processes that are historically specific. In the current period, the internationalization of production is central in the constitution of such linkages, even when there may be purely political objectives associated with aspects of that internationalization. A wide array of countries are incorporated as production sites into a single encompassing system or, more tentatively, a transnational space. The question then becomes what are the specific forms under which the internationalization of production contributes to the formation of labor migrations, and the related question, what are the specific forms under which international labor migrations become incorporated into the internationalization of production?

My recent book (1988) addresses these questions by focusing on processes that contain pronounced forms of this transnationalization. Three stand out. One, beginning in the middle 1960s, is the development of production for export in several Third World countries through a massive increase of direct foreign investment and international subcontracting by industrialized countries. We are seeing the development of an offshore production sector for these countries, especially in agriculture and manufacturing, but now increasingly also in clerical work. Export Processing Zones[1] are the most formalized instance. These are concentrated in Southeast Asia, Eastern Asia and the Caribbean Basin, including Mexico. Central to the analysis is the rapid and massive mobilization of young women into wage labor, a movement that would not have happened on this scale and at this speed without the large influx of direct foreign investment for the development of export manufacturing.

A second process is the rapid growth of major cities into global centers for the regulation and servicing of the global production system, international financial markets and other components of the world economy. These cities and their metropolitan areas are also the main destinations of the new migration from the Caribbean Basin and Southeast and East Asia. The analysis seeks to establish whether there is any articulation between the two processes. To that end it examines the economic base, and particularly the job supply, in these cities to see whether the absorption of immigrant workers is associated with the expanding growth sectors linked to internationalization, rather than merely with declining economic sectors in need of cheap labor for survival. Does the economic base, often thought of as post-industrial, resulting from these cities' role in the global economy generate a demand for the kinds of workers that immigrants represent?

A third process is the recent emergence of the United States as the major recipient of direct foreign investment in the world, after being the main exporter of capital for thirty years. The major recipient areas are California and the New York-New Jersey region. The magnitude of direct foreign investment in the United States since 1981 and the fact that it represents almost half of global direct foreign investment makes this a new development. One can posit that these areas are emerging as new investment zones in a global marketplace; changes in the organization of production alongside a large supply of immigrant workers may make these areas competitive with locations in the Third World.

In these three locations we can posit an intersection between the internationalization of production and international labor migrations. The major task of empirical analysis is to document and explain the concrete forms of this intersection.

CONCLUSION

This type of analysis shifts a good deal of the burden of immigration away from the individual migrant and onto the U.S. government and economy. First, U.S. government and private sector activities abroad build bridges between the United States and countries with heavy U.S. involvement. Such involvement may range from military interventions which cause refugee and migrant streams into the United States, through significant levels and concentrations of direct foreign investment of the sort that affects the lives of many people directly (notably Export Processing Zones) to the negotiation of temporary contract-labor programs that create vehicles for large-scale undocumented migrations alongside the regulated labor migration. These activities by governments and firms can be seen as building bridges to the United States, and immigrants can then be seen as those who decide to make use of these bridges.

Secondly, these government and private sector activities can contribute to the formation of a potential supply of migrants through various processes, particularly the disruption of small-holder agriculture and small-scale agriculture and small-scale regional or locally oriented manufacturing by replacing these with large-scale export-oriented agriculture and manufacturing through direct foreign investment and international subcontracting. This displacement under conditions of un- or under-employment and given the existence of linkages with the United States makes emigration into an option. It also explains why emigration is not an option for most people in the world: it takes a specific (and historically variable) combination of conditions for emigration to emerge as a feasible option.

Thirdly, this type of analysis brings to the fore certain aspects of labor demand in the United States which contribute to explaining the continuation of immigration at ever higher levels throughout the 1970s, a time of slow growth and high unemployment in the United States. Alongside the overall effort to lower wages and undermine unions, we see a restructuring of labor demand in major cities during this period. These cities emerge as strategic centers in the world economy and they engender a large demand not only for highly specialized workers but also for low-wage workers. In these strategic centers the low-wage question becomes strategic as well. The need is for a highly disciplinable low-wage work force. Immigrants have filled that role, besides being cheap labor for marginal firms struggling for survival. Forty percent of immigrants live in the ten largest cities which account for only 10 percent of the U.S. population. The occupational distribution of immigrants has become notably less advantaged over the last 15 years. This is particularly the case for women. About 70 percent of Hispanic women are in operative and service jobs, compared with 29 percent of all women. The figure for Asian women arriving in the 1970s was 40 pecent. These 1980 census figures are underestimates in that they probably exclude significant numbers of undocumented who are likely to have a high incidence of low-wage operative and service jobs.

Fourthly, this type of analysis suggests that once a significant immigrant work force is available this in itself creates new conditions for accumulation or profitable economic operation. Thus, the recent massive influx of direct foreign investment into the United States finds here a combination of resources that includes a vast and disciplinable low-wage work force and has weakened labor unions. The recently approved new immigration law is of interest here.

Three key provisions in this new law will have the effect of contributing to the low-wage labor input of immigration. These provisions are: (1) an extended contract-labor program; (2) a limited regularization program for undocumented aliens, specifically those who can prove continuous residence as of January 1982; and (3) sanctions against employers who knowingly hire undocumented workers. It is especially the combination of the last two that will have this effect. By being partial and putting a severe burden of proof on residents who have lived for years trying to leave no traces of their existence, the regularization program is likely to exclude a large number of undocumented, including many who are in fact entitled to regularization. In combination with the employer-sanctions program it will restrict the work opportunities of these undocumented workers even further. They will become a supply of absolutely disenfranchised workers confined to homework or employment by the most unscrupulous employers. By itself, employer sanctions could be a vehicle for enfranchising workers.

In combination with the new regularization program, it will not only contribute to discrimination on the basis of color and presumed nationality, but also to the formation of an underclass.

The new law clearly and explicitly puts the burden of immigration on the immigrants themselves. There is no recognition of broader forces, many U.S. generated, as contributed to this process. The terms of the debate, the language of the law, preclude the possibility of asking whether immigration begins not at the border, but in the corporate board rooms where U.S. transnationals make their decisions.

APPENDIX

THE NEW IMMIGRATION

Immigration to the United States has changed from a preponderance of high wage countries of origin in the 1950s to one of low-wage countries of origin in the 1970s. This recomposition cannot be taken for granted, especially since the family reunion emphasis of the 1965 Immigration Act was expected to bring in the relatives of those already here, i.e. mostly Europeans. Second, the data show that there has been a massive increase in annual entries, even excluding undocumented immigrants. From 265,000 in 1960, annual entries reached 570,000 in 1985. If we include undocumented, the level would approach that of the peak period at the turn of the century. Third, the data show a tendency toward concentration in a limited number of large metropolitan areas: New York City is the major recipient of immigrants from the Caribbean Basin, including several South American countries, while Los Angeles, San Francisco and, again, New York City are the major recipients of Asians.

Thus, the new Caribbean and Asian immigration can be seen as, (1) backing up two earlier low-wage immigrations — Mexicans to Los Angeles and other West Coast cities and Puerto Ricans to New York City; and (2) complementing the large and continuing flow of Mexicans to the Sunbelt.

The tables which follow provide the most current data available on immigrant characteristics. Because most data derive from the census, they are not available after 1980.

Table 1
Immigrants Admitted by Selected Origin, 1960, 1980, 1985.

Selected Origins	1960	1980	1985
Europe	138,426	72,121	63,043
Asia	24,956	236,097	264,691
Africa	2,319	13,981	17,117
Latin America and the Caribbean	66,440	186,077	209,718
Mexico	32,684	52,096	61,077
Caribbean	14,047	73,296	83,281
Central America	6,661	20,968	26,302
South America	13,048	39,717	39,058
Total Immigrants Admitted[1]	265,398	530,639	570,009

[1]Also includes origins not listed here.

Sources: Immigration and Naturalization Service, "Tabulation of Immigrants Admitted by Country of Birth" (1981 and 1985, unpublished; 1984 Statistical Yearbook of the INS).

Table 2
Top Immigration Flows from Asia, Latin America & Caribbean by Sex, 1972–79*

	Percent Female	Total both sexes
Mexico	49.0	530,378
Philippines	59.9	289,429
Korea (South)	60.8	225,339
China (Taiwan and People's Republic)	52.8	160,454
India	48.1	139,834
Dominican Rep.	52.5	118,147
Jamaica	51.8	108,454
Colombia	56.2	59,829
Trinidad and Tobago	52.7	49,492
Haiti	52.3	44,721
Hong Kong	52.0	40,438

*Includes only flows with over 40,000 immigrants admitted in 1972–1979. Excludes Vietnam and Cuba because most of them came as refugees, often years before their status was changed to immigrant, but are counted in year in which that change took place.

Source: Immigration and Naturalization Service, Unpublished Tabulations.

Table 3
Residential Distribution of Immigrants: Leading States, 1972-79

	All Immigrants		Females	
	n	%	n	%
California	812,928	22.6	430,596	22.6
New York	751,519	20.9	384,431	20.2
Florida	236,680	6.6	129,773	6.8
Texas	232,322	6.5	120,115	6.3
New Jersey	223,559	6.2	118,964	6.2
Illinois	213,479	5.9	108,936	5.7
Massachusetts	107,744	3.0	55,732	2.9
Pennsylvania	80,141	2.2	42,891	2.3
Michigan	81,829	2.3	42,204	2.2
Total	2,740,201	76.2	1,433,642	75.2
Other States	752,003	23.7	471,781	24.8
TOTAL	3,492,204	99.9	1,905,423	100.0

Source: Immigration and Naturalization Service, Unpublished Tabulations.

Table 4
Foreign Born in the U.S., 1970 and 1980

	1970	1980
U.S. Total Population (a)	203,302,031	226,504,825
Foreign Born (b)	9,619,302	13,956,077
(b)/(a)	4.7%	6.2%

Source: U.S. Bureau of the Census, 1980 Census of Population and Housing: Advance Report (Washington, D.C.: U.S.G.P.O., 1981).
U.S. Bureau of the Census, 1980 Census of Population and Housing: Provisional Estimates of Social, Economic, and Housing Characteristics (Supplement Report); States and Selected Standard Metropolitan Statistical Areas (Washington, D.C.: U.S.G.P.O., 1982).

Table 5
Occupational Distribution of the Foreign Born 1950–1979 (Percentage)

Year of Entry	Professional Managerial	Clerical Sales	Craft Workers	Other Blue-Collar	Service Workers	Farm Workers
1975–79	18.1	11.2	6.6	35.4	21.3	7.2
1970–74	20.3	15.6	11.6	31.0	17.8	3.7
1965–69	24.0	24.0	12.9	24.7	18.3	3.1
1960–64	30.4	20.9	12.0	21.4	13.0	2.3
1950–59	29.0	19.2	13.8	23.3	13.0	1.8
Pre-1950	27.1	25.4	13.5	16.6	15.4	2.0

Sources: Current Population Survey, November, 1979; April, 1983.

Table 6
Economic Characteristics by Race and Spanish Origin, 1980

	White	Black	Asian and Pacific Islander	Spanish Origin
Total Labor Force	**89,339,672**	**10,573,445**	**1,751,484**	**5,944,156**
Employed	84,134,204	9,300,661	1,665,706	5,421,433
Unemployed	5,205,468	1,272,784	85,788	522,723
Female Labor Force	**37,458,881**	**5,210,640**	**801,792**	**2,366,949**
Employed	35,297,665	4,625,693	758,397	2,127,752
Unemployed	2,161,216	584,947	43,395	239,197
Median Income ($)	20,840	12,618	22,075	14,711
Mean Income ($)	24,279	15,721	25,681	17,360
Persons, Poverty Status Determined	184,431,365	25,661,955	3,610,970	14,343,741
Income in 1979 below Poverty Level	17,301,567 (9.3%)	7,752,010 (30.2%)	503,089 (13.9%)	3,409,754 (23.8%)

Source: U.S. Bureau of the Census, *1980 Census of Population and Housing: Provisional Estimates of Social, Economic, and Housing Characteristics* (March) 1982.

NOTE

1. These are free zones where foreign firms receive special treatment: tax holidays, land, energy and other infrastructure at no or reduced cost, and import-export tariff exemptions.

REFERENCES

Bach, Robert L. 1978. Mexican Immigration and the American State. *International Migration Review* 12(Winter):536–558.

Borjas, G. and M. Tienda. 1983. *Hispanics in the U.S. Economy*. New York: Academic Press.

Bryce-Laporte, Roy S. and Delores M. Mortimer (eds.). 1981. *Female Immigrants to the United States: Caribbean, Latin American and African Experiences*. RIIES Occasional Papers No. 2. Washington, D.C.: Smithsonian Institution. Research Institute on Immigration and Ethnic Studies.

Bustamante, Jorge A. 1972. The Historical Context of the Undocumented Immigration from Mexico to the United States. *Aztlan* 3(Fall).257–282.

Centro de Estudios Puertorriqueños. 1979. *Labour Migration Under Capitalism: The Puerto Rican Experience*. History Task Force. New York: Monthly Review Press.

Chaney, Elsa. 1980. *Women in International Migration: Issues in Development Planning*. Washington, D.C.: Office for Women in Development, U.S. Agency for International Development.

Chaney, Elsa and Constance Sutton (eds.). 1979. Caribbean Migration to New York. *International Migration Review* Special Issue, 13(Summer).
Cornelius, Wayne A. 1981. *Mexican Migration to the U.S.: The Limits of Government Intervention. Working Papers,* No. 5. Center for U.S.-Mexican Studies, University of California, San Diego.
DAWN (Development Alternatives with Women for a New Era). 1985. *Development, Crises, and Alternative Visions: Third World Women's Perspectives.* New Delhi: DAWN.
Fernandez Kelly, Maria Patricia. 1983. *For We Are Sold, I and My People: Women and Industry in Mexico's Frontier.* Albany: SUNY Press.
INS (Immigration and Naturalization Service). *Annual Report.* Washington, D.C.: U.S. Government Printing Office.
Keely, Charles B. 1979. *U.S. Immigration: A Policy Analysis.* New York: The Population Council.
Kritz, Mary M. with Douglas T. Gurak (eds.). 1979. International Migration in Latin America. *International Migration Review* 13(Fall):Special Issue.
Morokvasic, Mirjana (ed.). 1984. *Women in Migration. International Migration Review,* Special Issue, 18(4), Winter.
NACLA (North American Congress on Latin America). 1979. Undocumented Immigrant Workers in New York City. Special issue, *Latin America and Empire Report* 12:6.
Nash, June and M. P. Fernandez Kelly. 1983. *Women, Men and the International Division of Labor.* Albany, NY: SUNY Press.
Pessar, Patricia. 1982. *The Role of Households in International Migration.* Center for Latin American and Caribbean Studies, New York University: *Occasional Papers,* No. 34.
Petras, Elizabeth McLean. 1980. The Role of National Boundaries in a Cross-National Labor Market. *The International Journal of Urban and Regional Research* 4(2):157–195.
Piore, Michael. 1979. *Birds of Passage: Migrant Labor and Industrial Societies.* Cambridge University Press.
Portes, Alejandro and John Walton. 1981. *Labor, Class and the International System.* New York: Academic Press.
Portes, Alejandro and Robert L. Bach. 1985. *Latin Journey.* Berkeley, CA: California University Press.
Reimers, David M. 1983. An Unintended Reform: The 1965 Immigration Act and Third World Immigration to the U.S. *Journal of American Ethnic History* 3(Fall):9–28.
Ricketts, Erol R. 1983. Periphery to Core Migration: Specifying a Model. Unpublished Ph.D. dissertation, University of Chicago, Department of Sociology.
Samora, Julian with Jorge A. Bustamente and Gilberto Gardenas. 1971. *Los Mojados: The Wetback Story.* Notre Dame: University of Notre Dame Press.
SOPEMI [Systeme d'observation permanente pour les migrations]. Annual report. Paris: OECD, Directorate for Social Affairs, Manpower and Education.
Sassen, Saskia. 1988. *The Mobility of Labor and Capital: A Study in International Investment and Labor Flow.* Cambridge: Cambridge University Press.
Teitelbaum, Michael S. 1985. *Latin Migration North: The Problem for U.S. Foreign Policy.* New York: Council on Foreign Relations.
Thomas, Brinley. 1973. *Migration and Economic Growth: A Study of Great Britain and the Atlantic Economy,* 2nd edition. Cambridge University Press.
Waldinger, Roger. 1986. *Through the Eye of the Needle.* NY: New York University Press.
Zolberg, Aristide R. 1978. International Migration Policies in a Changing World System. In, *Human Migration: Patterns and Policies,* W.H. McNeill and R.S. Adams (eds.). pp. 241–286. Bloomington: Indiana University Press.

7

Structural Subemployment in the U.S. and the Full Employment Debate

RHON BAIMAN

INTRODUCTION

Data from the Bureau of Labor Statistics indicate that average and median real wages have been generally declining in the United States since 1973 (BLS 1986:79–81). Bennett Harrison and Barry Bluestone (1986), in a study commissioned by the Joint Economic Committee of the U.S. Congress, reveal that the rate of low-wage job creation in the U.S. economy more than doubled during the 1979–85 period compared to the 1973–79 or 1963–73 periods.[1] As would be expected, these results have raised considerable controversy which will be discussed below.

Assuming, for the moment, that the data is accurate, the obvious question is: Why is the U.S. economy, long noted for its high wages, now generating so many low-wage jobs? In an earlier book, Harrison and Bluestone estimate that a policy of "deindustrializing" disinvestment by U.S. management can be directly linked to the loss of at least 38 million jobs during the decade of the 70s alone (Bluestone and Harrison 1982). In their view, in the face of increasing international competition, rising raw materials costs, declining profits, and general macroeconomic crisis, U.S. management opted for a strategy of unproductive speculation, mergers and acquisitions, foreign investment and direct political confrontation over labor and other social costs. A stepped up domestic investment and labor-management cooperation strategy designed to meet the competition head on was not pursued.

Bluestone and Harrison contend that new transportation and telecommunications technologies have profoundly altered the postwar capital-labor balance of power by making capital much more mobile both domestically and internationally. Management has been successfully using the threat, if not the actuality, of capital flight to reduce wages, taxes, and labor standards when not directly eliminating jobs. In this view, management's elimination, particularly of high-wage manufacturing jobs, and fixation with wage concessions, part-time work, two-tier wage contracts, and subcontracting is undermining U.S. real wages.

Samuel Bowles, David Gordon, and Thomas Weisskopf (1984) present a similar analysis of the breakdown of the (exclusive) postwar labor-capital accord and the direct big-business assault on labor and social costs, emphasizing the increasing cost to capital of maintaining the corporate system of production rather than corporate disinvestment.

This paper will focus on structural and technological transformations of the forces of production of advanced capitalism which are not primarily a result of capital's recent social and political offensive. These "post-industrial" structural changes have, until recently, been given much more serious consideration in western Europe where virtually *zero* net new jobs have been created since 1979 (Bluestone and Harrison 1986:1). An unfounded neglect or dismissal of the importance of this structural transformation of the economy could result in an overly optimistic view of the effectiveness of traditional left Keynesian demand stimulation and "radical industrial policy" programs even if these are coupled with extensive unionization, flexible wage-price controls, plant closing legislation, and capital and international trade flow restrictions.

The recent so-called "full employment debate" within the U.S. left, directly addresses the possible political implications of the "post-industrialization" of the U.S. economy. Some of the questions raised in this debate are: "Can advanced capitalism continue to rely almost exclusively on paid employment outside the household for widespread income generation, or are direct income distribution and work time reduction policies becoming increasingly necessary to reverse economic and class polarization?" and "Should the *type* of jobs become as important on a national level for the U.S. left as the *number* of jobs has been traditionally?"

This paper will include: a) an outline of major structural, institutional, and technological changes taking place in the U.S. economy, b) a review of recent empirical studies relevant to the question of whether a trend towards "structural subemployment," or low wage employment caused in large part by structural economic transformations, exists in the United States and c) a summary of the implications of the above within the context of the "full employment debate."

THE MODERN STRUCTURAL TRANSFORMATION OF THE U.S. ECONOMY

Major structural transformations have occurred both in the technology and institutional framework of production, and in the amount, composition and type of products produced in the U.S. economy in the last thirty years. Stanback, Bearse, Noyelle, and Karasek (1981) characterize these changes as involving primarily a dramatic growth in the service sector of the economy, or the development of a new "Service Economy" because of:

(1) Changing patterns of consumption involving increasing product differentiation with an increasing linking of services (design, packaging, advertisement, maintenance, finance, training, etc.) with goods and a recent rapid growth in demand for specific kinds of retail and consumer services.

(2) A growth in the size and differentiation of markets reflecting technological advances, increasing concentration and growth and development of producers, and increased national and international cultural integration.

(3) Rising firm size and complexity which along with technological advances have resulted in increased managerial attention to planning, product development, marketing and administration and a relative decline in the share of labor involved in direct production.

Clearly these developments are closely linked to the increasing concentration, centralization, and mobility of U.S. capital, aided and abetted by U.S. government policy which is extensively documented in Bluestone and Harrison (1982). They report, for example, that the mining and manufacturing share of *employment, profits* and *assets* held by the Fortune 500 in the United States increased by between 40–70 percent between 1955 and 1970 (Bluestone and Harrison 1982:122). This paper, however, will focus on these structural and technological changes as reflecting general and often irreversible long-term trends of advanced capitalist production.

These changes have led to a large increase in demand for "producer" (for example software, advertisement, and financial consulting) and "non-profit" (education and health care) services — the latter probably more closely related to the specific structure of the U.S. health care industry, and to a recent rapid growth in specific kinds of "retail" and "mostly consumer" (for example food, drinking and hotel) multiplant franchises.[2] Franchising allows for *firm* economies of scale in development, administration and distribution rather than the traditionally emphasized *plant* economies of scale in production.

The most recent major technological changes in the U.S. economy are generally associated with what has come to be called "the microelectronic technological revolution." The microelectronic revolution is based on the use of integrated microelectronic circuits printed on silicon "chips" which can replace virtually any (earlier) electric, manual, mechanical, electromechanical, pneumatic, or hydrolic control system. These extremely inexpensive and highly efficient "microprocessors" can be linked with modern computers and telecommunications equipment in addition to serving as their building blocks. The microelectronic revolution has received widespread attention, particularly in western Europe.

Some major and historically distinctive economic characteristics of the microelectronic revolution are:

(1) The potential applicability of microelectronic technology across industrial sectors may be more pervasive than any other technology in history. Unlike previous technological revolutions which had major impacts on a fairly narrow range of products and/or processes, all of which were generally confined to the primary (agriculture and mining) or secondary (construction and manufacturing) sectors, the extreme versatility and low cost of micro-processors, especially when linked to computers and telecommunications systems, enables their application in all three major sectors of the economy and particularly in the tertiary (service) sector which is the last remaining holdout from previous technological revolutions. A wide range of advanced capitalist country government, academic, and union sponsored reports provide extensive documentation of this (Rothwell and Zegveld 1979; ETUI 1980; Nora and Minc 1980; Norman 1980).

(2) Microelectronic based goods or components require significantly less labor and raw materials input than the capital or consumer goods and services that they replace. The microelectronic technological revolution has a *negative multiplier* effect on employment because it hollows out the traditional production pyramid by eliminating multiple stages of component production and product assembly. This means that the microelectronic revolution has its greatest labor saving effects on precisely the low skill, labor intensive but relatively well paid kind of work that has traditionally comprised the largest share of industrial and service sector employment (Barrow and Curnow 1979:196–197). The elimination of these jobs, particularly in manufacturing, has directly resulted in wage loss or unemployment for many workers. A digital watch, for example, is assembled from five basic components, compared with the one thousand operations required to assemble mechanical watches.

(3) The new microelectronic technology is expected to proliferate much faster than the technologies of preceding technological revolutions. Whereas earlier technological revolutions took at least fifty and sometimes one hundred years to disseminate throughout the economy, many observers expect the major effects of the microelectronic revolution to be over in twenty years (ETUI 1980; Norman 1980).

In conclusion, both the long-term structural-technological and the more recent microelectronics based technological changes may be important factors behind the low-wage employment trend. Is this conclusion substantiated by empirical research?

RECENT EVIDENCE OF STRUCTURAL SUBEMPLOYMENT IN THE U.S.

The most obvious direct effect of these structural changes in the economy has been a long-term post-WWII shift of employment out of the primary and secondary economic sectors, and into the tertiary sector (see Table 1).

Table 1
Distribution of Full-Time Equivalent Employees Among Sectors, 1948 and 1985

	1948		1985	
	Number	Employee Share (%)	Number	Employee Share (%)
Primary (Agriculture and Mining)	3,040	6.37	2,370	2.53
Secondary (Construction and Manufacturing)	17,799	37.01	23,373	24.96
Tertiary (Services)	27,226	56.61	67,910	72.51
Total	48,090	99.99	93,653	100.00

Source: Stanback et al. (1981: Table 1.2, p. 12–13) and *Survey of Current Business* (July 1986). Slight errors due to adjustments are neglected in comparing these series.

The shift of employment out of manufacturing and into services has accelerated since 1969. In fact, the *absolute,* and not just relative or proportional, number of workers employed in U.S. manufacturing has fallen since 1979 in spite of very rapid overall employment growth in the economy. A recent Data Resources Inc. report concludes that productivity improvements have been the major factor restraining employment growth in U.S. manufacturing (Chinitz 1986). A Sussex University report summarizing the findings of representatives of the ministries of industry of Canada, France, West Germany, the Netherlands, Ireland, and the U.K. notes that OECD data for all of the EEC-9 countries reveals a general pattern of "jobless growth" (1965–73) and then "job displacing growth" (1974–78) in manufacturing (Rothwell and Zegveld 1979).

The reduction in manufacturing employment in western Europe and the United States would not have occurred if worldwide demand for industrial product had expanded more rapidly than industrial productivity increased, as occurred in the 1960s. Unfortunately the recent technological and organizational restructuring has tended to be of a rationalization, replacement, and labor cost reduction variety unlike the employment expanding technological transition of the 1960s. Many of what were the fastest growing industrial sectors in the postwar period (like chemicals, steel, ship-building, and automobiles), are now suffering from increased international competition and relative demand saturation (OECD 1980).

In fact, the few countries in western Europe like Sweden and Norway who are maintaining full-employment are often using the kind of extensive direct labor market intervention policies which will be discussed in the conclusion to this paper. Even Sweden has not relied *exclusively* on public sector expansion to maintain full employment.[3]

A calculation of annual rates of growth by industry indicates that the fastest growing service sector employers are, as has been previously noted: "Producer," "Non-profit," "Retail," "Mostly Consumer" (excluding private household domestic services), and in an earlier period "Government" services (see Table 2). These trends appear to confirm much of the Stanback et al. analysis of the economy.

Table 2
Annual Rate of Growth of Full-Time Equivalent Employees by Industry, 1948 to 1985

Industry Classifications	1948–59	1959–69	1969–77	1977–85
Domestic industries	1.3	2.5	1.3	2.0
Agricultural, extractive and transformative	0.1	1.6	0.1	.3
Agricultural	-1.2	-2.5	2.5	-.3
Extractive and transformative	0.3	2.0	-0.1	.3
Manufacturing	0.3	2.1	-0.3	-.2
Services	2.0	3.0	2.0	2.8
Distributive services	0.3	1.5	1.8	1.8
Transportation, Communication and Utilities	0.5	0.9	0.6	1.2
Wholesale	1.6	2.1	3.0	2.4
Retail services	1.4	2.8	2.4	3.1
Nonprofit services	4.1	5.5	5.2	4.4
Health	4.6	5.6	7.1	4.3
Education	2.9	5.0	-0.6	4.6
Producer services	4.1	4.5	3.6	5.1
Mainly consumer services	-0.2	1.3	-0.4	2.6
Private household	0.1	-0.7	-3.3	-3.3
Government	3.8	3.5	0.7	.9
Public Education	4.6	5.6	2.9	1.0

Source: Stanback et al. (1981: Table 1.3, p. 15) and *Survey of Current Business* (July 1986). Decimals have been omitted without rounding.

Evidence of increasing low-wage employment in the economy is provided in Bluestone and Harrison (1986, 1987a). Table 3 shows their results for all U.S. workers over 16 with non-zero wage and salary incomes. "Low stratum" refers to real incomes which are below 50 percent of the 1973 median nominal income of $6,000 in 1973 dollars, or $14,024 in 1984 dollars. "Middle stratum" refers to real incomes which are between 50 percent and 200 percent of the 1973 median. "High stratum" is reserved for real incomes which are over 200 percent of the 1973 median.

Table 3
Employment Levels and Employment Shares, All U.S. Workers (000's)

	Number of Employees						Shares of Net New Employment	
	1973	**1979**	**1985**	**1973**	**1979**	**1985**	**'73–79**	**'79–85**
Low Stratum	29648	32063	36158	31.8%	30.4%	31.5%	19.9%	43.9%
Middle Stratum	48107	55908	60175	51.6	53.1	52.5	64.2	45.7
High Stratum	15441	17374	18339	16.6	16.5	16.0	15.9	10.3
Total	93196	105345	114673	100%	100%	100%	100%	100%

Source: Bluestone and Harrison (1986: Table 2, p. 17), updated in Bluestone and Harrison (1987a).

After breaking down their data into broad age, education, gender, race, region, industry, and full-time/part-time categories, Bluestone and Harrison are able to show that the low-wage trend is extremely pervasive as it is common *to all* categories of workers, although, of course, some subgroups have been affected more than others. White males show the most dramatic low-wage trend of all race and gender groups.

This evidence has been disputed. Some of the criticism, i.e. that Bluestone and Harrison deliberately distorted the data by including 2,000,000 armed forces members, or by refusing to use the PCE (Personal Consumption Expenditures) price deflator is without basis (Brooks 1987a, 1987b). The Bureau of Labor Statistics (BLS), and not Bluestone and Harrison, decided from January 1983, to include resident armed services personnel in the Current Population Survey (CPS) data which the Bluestone and Harrison study is based on, as are most other labor studies. Similarly, using the Personal Consumption Expenditures (PCE) price deflator, rather than the standard Consumer Price Index (CPI), would make little sense as almost no other labor economists use the PCE. Moreover, using the PCE would give less dramatic but *not* qualitatively different results.

The most serious objection is one raised by BLS commissioner Janet Norwood and others concerning the business cycle dependency of the data (Norwood 1987; Samuelson 1987). However, the possibility that the increase in low-wage jobs is a temporary cyclical rather than a long-term phenomena is directly refuted by a more recent Bluestone and Harrison study which statistically demonstrates that there has been a secular trend toward low-wage employment *after* taking into account the effect of the business cycle (Bluestone and Harrison 1987b). The secular low-wage employment trend starts in 1972 when data going back to 1963 is reviewed.

Most studies in fact confirm a "declining middle" or directly low-wage trend in the economy (see Lawrence 1984; Thurow 1987; McMahon and Tschetter 1986). Only one major study, by BLS economist Neal Rosenthal (1985), referred to by Norwood and Brooks, appears to provide contrary evidence as it shows that there has been an employment shift to traditionally high-wage occupations. However, a more recent investigation co-authored by another BLS economist, John Tschetter, concludes that a low-wage trend indeed exists but is not revealed in the Rosenthal study because of a substantial decline in wage levels *within* occupations (McMahon and Tschetter 1986).

Other studies by Harrison, Tilly and Bluestone (1986a, 1986b) investigate the *causes* of an increase in *inequality* among annual wages and salaries for all workers in the United States which has occurred since the late 1970s, reversing a previous postwar trend toward equality. Since increasing inequality combined with the trend towards decreasing average and medium wages, noted above, can only reflect increasing low-wage employment these investigations may also be regarded, in part, as inquiries into the causes of U.S. subemployment.

Harrison et al. (1986a) first note that increasing wage and salary inequality *cannot* be completely attributed to public policy, i.e. to "Reaganomics" or even to the "great (monetarist) repression" of 1979–82, as the trend clearly started before the commencement of these regimes. Focusing on inequality among *individual* wage and salary workers also eliminates the impact of changes in family structure resulting in a significant increase in the number of female single-parent headed families which has often been cited as a major cause of the widely publicized increasing income inequality between *households*.

Moreover, through statistical regression techniques, Harrison et al. are able to show that temporary macroeconomic and demographic phenomena, which are the preferred explanations of mainstream and neoclassical economists; like the mid 1970s and early 1980s recessions, the postwar "baby-boom" demographic bulge of younger workers, and the (until recently) overvalued dollar can account for at most one-third of the year to year variation in inequality between 1969 and 1983.[4]

Further statistical analysis demonstrates that other *"supply-side"* factors captured in an augmented human capital model which takes into account changes in the interpersonal variance of education and work experience, as well as the increasing labor force participation of women and people of color, also cannot explain increasing inequality (Harrison et al. 1986b).

However, *"demand-side"* factors, which include the effects of "deindustrialization" and the growth of involuntary part-time work, *can* statistically account for a large share of the 1978 to 1984 increase in inequality. "Deindustrialization" refers to the employment shift out of the higher and relatively more equitable salary structure of the manufacturing sector into the service sector with its lower and more unequally distributed wages and salaries. This may be a result of disinvestment or "post-industrialization" as discussed above, as well as the temporarily overvalued dollar. Since low-wage service sector growth and industrial subcontracting is also strongly correlated with involuntary part-time employment growth, the latter may also be seen as a partial proxy for deindusrialization.

It is important to note, however, that Harrison et al. find that 78 percent of the total increase in inequality from 1978 to 1984 is explained by increasing inequality *within* thirteen industrial subgroups rather than by shifts of employment between them (Harrison et al. 1986b:13, Table 5). This would appear to indicate that much of the increase in inequality, and low-wage employment in the U.S. economy is caused either by "institutional mechanisms," such as domestic outsourcing or two-tiered or pay-for-performance wage systems as Harrison, Tilly, and Bluestone suggest, or by the internal structural and technological transformation of the economy discussed above.

Earlier studies by Bennett Harrison reveal that the fastest growing high tech industrial sectors (office machines and computer and electronic components) and service sectors (department stores, supermarkets, and hotels and motels) in New England during the region's 1957 to 1975 period of renewed economic growth are also the sectors with the fastest growing wage and salary inequality for year-around employees. This would appear to provide direct regional support for structural explanatory factors or ''structural subemployment'' (see Bluestone and Harrison 1982:92–98).

THE SO-CALLED "FULL EMPLOYMENT DEBATE"

To the extent that the subemployment trend in the United States is structural and pervasive it may not be subject to traditional ''point of production'' struggles. To the extent that it is internal, it will not be affected by restrictions on imports and capital outflows. To the extent that increases in demand *alone* cannot reverse it, it will require direct political confrontation. Finally, to the extent that paticularly women and people of color cannot attain paid-employment, or can only find low-wage employment, the traditional left emphasis of ''full employment politics'' is fundamentally lacking. Policies of the kind proposed by Bluestone and Harrison, such as plant closing legislation and ''radical industrial policy,'' would certainly help the United States regain, or retain, a critical manufacturing base *in production* but would not reverse the low-wage service sector *employment* trend.

This is the starting point of the so-called ''full employment debate'' (Block 1985, 1984a; Schor 1985; Block, Cloward, Ehrenreich, Fox Piven 1987; Gorz 1983, 1985, 1987; Baiman 1986). Unfortunately, I cannot do justice to this debate in this paper because of space limitations. The following principally reflects my own point of view. (For more extensive and wide-ranging discussions the reader is strongly encouraged to consult the references cited above.)

A number of prominent left ''post-industrialists'' and feminists have criticized the traditional left emphasis on ''full-employment'' as a unifying and universally beneficial political demand, as being out of touch with current economic reality in the United States where *the type* of jobs generated by the economy is as important as their number. This reformulated full-employment position would include an *increased emphasis* on social and institutional change directly addressing structural subemployment through: (1) increased income and resource distribution not tied to obligatory paid employment, and (2) across the board working hours reductions. Both of these kinds of measures would reduce unemployment and *tighten* labor markets so that the issue in question is *not* really the relative desirability of full employment but rather what kind of policies can best lead to full employment and to what kind of ''full employment'' will they lead.

Critical to this reformulated full-employment position is the question of whether service sector unionization alone would be sufficient to raise overall wage levels within a full-employment economy. The fact the *low-wage* service sector jobs often are decentralized, unskilled, part-time, and of relatively low productivity suggests that low-wage service sector unionization may be much more difficult and, even if successful, less powerful a strategy than industrial unionization. Also, the increased mobility of capital leading to ''multiple sourcing'' and ''parallel production'' which has often succeeded in circumventing local and national union power in manufacturing, as is extensively documented in Harrison and Bluestone's book, may increasingly be applied through computerized telecommunications systems to the service sector.

The inability, or great difficulty, that unions have been having in promoting *"comparable worth,"* or comparable pay for jobs typically held by women with educational and experiential requirements equal to those of other more highly paid "men's jobs," may be viewed as an important counter-example to the "full-employment" position. It is widely recognized that "comparable worth" must be pursued through the courts and general political system, as well as through direct union job actions.

One of the central questions with regard to the full-employment debate is: "Why are low-wage jobs low wage?" The western European experience suggests that even if a large share of the service sector is unionized, as in Sweden, structural *sub*employment would be transformed to structural *un*employment without general work hours reductions, early retirement, extensive maternity/paternity leaves, education/retraining breaks, longer vacations and other policies which directly reduce labor supply. The more socialized and thus centralized, rationalized, and unionized western European health care, social security, and insurance sectors have not experienced dramatic employment growth as their U.S. counterparts have, as Fred Block (1984b) has pointed out.

Unions themselves are, of course, central to any progressive struggle within capitalism. To confront structural subemployment, however, coordinated national, or at least state level, direct income redistribution and labor supply restriction initiatives would appear to be required, and unions will have to play a central role in these efforts. It is worth remembering that Mitterrand's extension of worker's vacation time to five weeks from four weeks was one of the French socialist's more successful policy achievements.[5] This should remind us again of our extreme backwardness among advanced countries with regard to our "social wage" and average work time (Bowles et al. 1984:292–295).

General economic policy measures designed to alleviate subemployment *without* directly raising the cost of production through redistribution from progressive income taxes, or through profit sharing not proportionate to wages, may also be preferable to direct union demands for higher wages and benefits as these policies would not effect international price competitiveness and would not be an employment disincentive.[6] The resulting squeeze on the after-tax profits and income of the wealthy would, of course, have to be dealt with as has apparently been done in Sweden which has a very low profit rate. There is abundant evidence that progressive income distribution and other policies which promote social equity *help* long-term economic growth in spite of the pervasive neoclassical view to the contrary (Kuttner 1984).

In any case, in order to reverse "structural subemployment" the focus of left politics may have to increasingly be directed towards the state and the basic socially and culturally determined system of income, resource, and power distribution. In its latest incarnation capitalism is undergoing a fundamental internal restructuring which will require direct political confrontation. Policies which address "structural subemployment" may be critical to the success of any modern left political program.

ACKNOWLEDGEMENTS

I would like to thank Chris Tilly, the URPE Crisis Reader collective and Sandy Malman for their comments on earlier drafts of this paper and Barry Bluestone and Thomas Stanback for the use of their tables and data. All errors are, of course, my own.

NOTES

1. See Barry Bluestone and Bennett Harrison (1986). The figures in this study have been updated to 1985 in (Bluestone and Harrison (1987a).
2. See Stanback et al. (1981:11) for exact definitions of these categories in terms of SIC codes.
3. See Goren Therborn (1986) and Block (1987). Therborn convincingly demonstrates that *politics* can have a much more direct effect on the unemployment rate, and without adverse economic consequences, than is commonly recognized or acknowledged. Block agrees with Therborn's major conclusion but critiques some of his other points along lines similar to those advanced in this paper.

With even more radical public sector expansion Sweden probably could employ everyone forty hours a week. Shortened work hours are in this sense a public policy choice. There clearly has to be an economic and political balance between public sector expansion and shortened work hours. The traditional full employment view in the United States (see last section of article) tends to emphasize the former at the expense of the latter. There is also widespread recognition of the fact that most of the world's most serious problems are *political* and are *not* a result of lack of global productive output. More leisure time and associated grants for public policy research, education, political participation, and general cultural activities might be particularly effective in stimulating democratic, socialist, feminist and humanist politics.
4. See, for example, Lawrence (1984) and other references in the Harrison, Tilly and Bluestone (1986) paper.
5. Harrington (1987) also discusses other labor supply restriction attempts by the French socialists which were less successful but does not dispute the overall importance of such policies. He points out that these kinds of policy initiatives should be carefully adapted to the unique political economic characteristics of the country in which they are to be implemented.
6. According to Harrington (1987) these reflect some of the conclusions drawn by French economist Serge-Christophe Kolm from the French experience.

REFERENCES

Baiman, Rhon. 1986. Technological Subemployment in the U.S.: An Economic and Political Analysis of Current Trends. Unpublished paper presented at the Union for Radical Political Economics (URPE) summer conference.

Barrow, Iann and Ray Curnow. 1979. *The Future with Microelectronics*. London: Frances Pinter Ltd.

Block, Fred. 1984a. The Political Perils of Full Employment. *Socialist Review*.

_____. 1984b. Technical Change and Employment: New Perspectives on an Old Controversy. *Economia & Lavoro*.

_____. 1985. Full Employment as False Necessity. *Socialist Review* (Nov./Dec.).

_____. 1987. Unemployment in Advanced Capitalism. *Dissent* (Summer).

_____. R. Cloward, B. Ehrenreich and F. Fox Piven. 1987. The Trouble with Full Employment. *The Nation* (May 17).

Bluestone, Barry and Bennett Harrison. 1982. *The Deindustrialization of America*. New York: Basic Books.

_____. 1986. *The Great American Job Machine*. Washington, D.C.: Joint Economic Committee.

_____. 1987a. The Grim Truth About the Job Miracle. *New York Times* (Feb. 1).

_____. 1987b. The Increasing Incidence of Low-Wage Employment in the U.S. Submitted to the *Monthly Labor Review*.

Bowles, Samuel, David M. Gordon and Thomas E. Weisskopf. 1984. *Beyond the Waste Land*. New York: Basic Books.

Brooks, Warren. 1987a. Low-pay Jobs: The Big Lie. *Wall Street Journal* (March 25).

_____. 1987b. Sorry Wrong Numbers on Jobs. *Washington Times* (April 20).

Bureau of Labor Statistics (BLS). 1986. *Employment and Earnings* 33(3) March.

Chinitz, Benjamin. 1986. Employment in the U.S. Manufacturing Sectors: Prospects for Revival in the 1990's. Data Resources Inc.

European Trade Union Institute (ETUI). 1980. *The Impact of Microelectronics on Employment in Western Europe in the 80's*. Brussels: ETUI.

Gorz, Andre. 1983. *Paths to Paradise: On the Liberation from Work*. Boston: South End Press.

_____. 1985. The American Model and the Future of the French Left. Socialist Review (Nov./Dec.).

_____. 1987. (S)He Who Doesn't Work Shall Eat All the Same. *Dissent* (Spring).

Harrington, Michael. 1987. Miterrand's Term: A Balance Sheet. *Dissent* (Winter).

Harrison, Bennett, Chris Tilly and Barry Bluestone. 1986a. Wage Inequality Takes a Great U-Turn. *Challenge* (March-April).

_____. 1986b. What Is Making American Wages More Unequal. Paper presented to the 1986 Meetings of the Industrial Relations Research Association.

Kuttner, Robert. 1984. *The Economic Illusion: False Choices Between Prosperity and Social Justice*. Boston: Houghton Mifflin.

Lawrence, Robert. 1984. Sectoral Shifts and the Size of the Middle Class. *Brookings Review* (Fall).

McMahon, Patrick and John Tschetter. 1986. The Declining Middle Class: A Further Analysis. *Monthly Labor Review* (Sept.).

Nora, Simon and Alin Minc. 1980. *The Computerization of Society*. Cambridge, MA: MIT.

Norman, Colin. 1980. *Microelectronics at Work: Productivity and Jobs in the World Economy*. Washingont, D.C.: Worldwatch Paper 39.

Norwood, Janet. 1987. A Cyclical Rebound: The Job Machine Has Not Broken Down. *New York Times* (Feb. 22).

Organization for Economic Cooperation and Development (OECD). 1980. *Technical Change and Economic Policy*. Paris: OECD.

Rosenthal, Neal. 1985. The Shrinking Middle Class: Myth or Reality? *Monthly Labor Review* (March).

Rothwell, R, and W. Zegveld. 1979. *Technical Change and Employment*. New York: St. Martin's Press.

Samuelson, Robert. 1987. The American Job Machine. *Newsweek*(Feb. 23).

Stanback, Thomas M. Jr., Peter J. Bearse, Thierry J. Noyelle and Robert A. Karasek. 1981. *Services/The New Economy*. Totowa, NJ: Allanheld and Osmun.

Therborn, Goren. 1986. *Why Some People Are More Unemployed Than Others*. London: Verso Books.

Thurow, Lester. 1987. A Surge in Inequality. *Scientific American* (May).

PART THREE

INEQUALITY

8

Regenerating Inequality: The Distribution of U.S. Family Income and Individual Earnings in the 1980s

CHRIS TILLY

INTRODUCTION

The United States is experiencing a rising tide of inequality in the distribution of income and earnings. Put simply, the rich are getting richer while the poor are getting poorer and more numerous. The rising tide of inequality is a new development. Tracing change in the Gini coefficient of family income — one standard measure of inequality — over time shows that a dramatic increase in inequality began in the late 1970s (Figure 1).

How much should we worry about increasing income inequality? What has caused the turn toward more unequal income distribution? What can be done about it? This paper offers several conclusions:

1) Inequality in the distribution of total income (including earnings, capital income such as profits or interest, and transfer income such as AFDC payments) among families and inequality in the distribution of earnings among persons are only two types of inequality among many. Although this paper will focus on these two forms of inequality, the others are also important.

2) The recent growing dispersion in family income has resulted largely from worsening earnings inequality.

3) Growing earnings inequality, in turn, has resulted in large part from increasing inequality of the wage-earning opportunities open to workers — rather than from increasing dispersion in the skills and qualities that workers bring to the labor market.

4) Several factors seem to help account for the widening inequality in job opportunities: prolonged macroeconomic stagnation, changes in the mix of employment among industries, changes in working hours.

5) Only a sharp change in economic, industrial, and social welfare policy — or a sharp shift in class power — is likely to reverse the trend toward inequality.

TYPES OF INEQUALITY

Interfamily income inequality and interpersonal earnings inequality summarize *overall* inequality in the U.S. population, rather than disparities between particular groups such as blacks and whites or men and women. Perfect equality in family income would denote a situation where every family received exactly the same income; pure inequality would occur if one family received all the income. The reality, of course, lies somewhere in between.

Why should we care about differences in family income and individual earnings? A neoclassical economist would argue that such inequalities play an essential role in the market system by giving economic actors the cues that will lead them to allocate resources efficiently. But equality is a value in its own right. We worry about family income if we believe that a growing gulf in the standard of living between rich and poor is destructive. We worry about widening individual earnings inequality if we believe that there should be some parity in the rewards to human labor.

It's also important to keep in mind what interfamily or interpersonal income inequality is *not*, and what's happening along other dimensions of inequality:

— Interfamily and interpersonal inequality are *not* direct measures of racial inequality. The income gap between black and white families is growing wider in the 1980s, although wages for employed black males and employed white males have become more similar.

— They also are *not* direct measures of gender inequality. As in the case of racial inequality, the income disparity between female-headed and male-headed households is widening in the 1980s (a trend summarized as the "feminization of poverty"), even though the wage differential between individual male and female full-time, year round workers is shrinking slowly.

Interfamily and interpersonal inequality express the *cumulative* effects of both of these forms of inequality, and others.

MEASUREMENT PROBLEMS

Measuring overall inequality raises a host of technical issues. For example, in order to analyze an income distribution, one must make some choices about what to measure. Three poverty analysts at the University of Wisconsin's Institute for Research on Poverty (Danziger, Haveman, and Plotnick 1984) identify the key choices as the income concept (cash income only? what about in-kind income such as food stamps or executive perks? what about capital gains?), the income unit (person? family?), and the income accounting period (month? year? lifetime?). They conclude that:

> Although few principles guide the choice of these constructs, there is agreement that an ideal study should measure inequality in command over resources, among income-sharing units, over some specified time period, adjusting for 'needs' and life-cycle differences (1984:13).

As a practical matter, the data for this "ideal study" are unavailable in the United States. Most income distribution studies use data gathered by the Census Bureau, which have a number of shortcomings:

— Property income (interest, rent, profits) is grossly understated. The rich are actually richer than they appear in U.S. income figures.

— Only cash income is measured. It is recorded after transfers (such as AFDC) but before taxes. Thus, for example, the regressive effects of Reagan-era tax "reform" remain invisible in these income statistics.

— The Census Bureau gathers some information about needs (for example, number of children) but not other information (for example, amount of assets a family has to draw on). Most analysts ignore needs and simply compare unadjusted incomes.

— Census Bureau data provide one-year snapshots rather than lifetime portraits of income. Since most people move from lower to higher incomes over their working lives, current differences among families and among earners are considerably greater than differences in lifetime standard of living.

In addition, measurements of inequality depend crucially on the definition of the population within which income distribution is measured. Some studies of family income distribution include only families with children, some include any family of two or more, and some count persons living alone as families. Some studies of interpersonal earnings distribution include only men, some look only at full-time workers, while some include workers who earned as little as a dollar in a year. There is no "correct" population for the study of inequality; each population offers insights into different aspects of inequality. This paper emphasizes what's happening in the most broadly-defined populations, in order to offer a look at the "big picture."

FAMILY INCOME INEQUALITY

Setting measurement problems aside for the moment, what can we say about the trends in the distribution of income among families? Figure 1 summarizes one disturbing trend. The fall and rise of the Gini coefficient reflects the fact that the share of total income

Figure 1
Family Income Inequality
(Gini coefficients, 1947–1984)

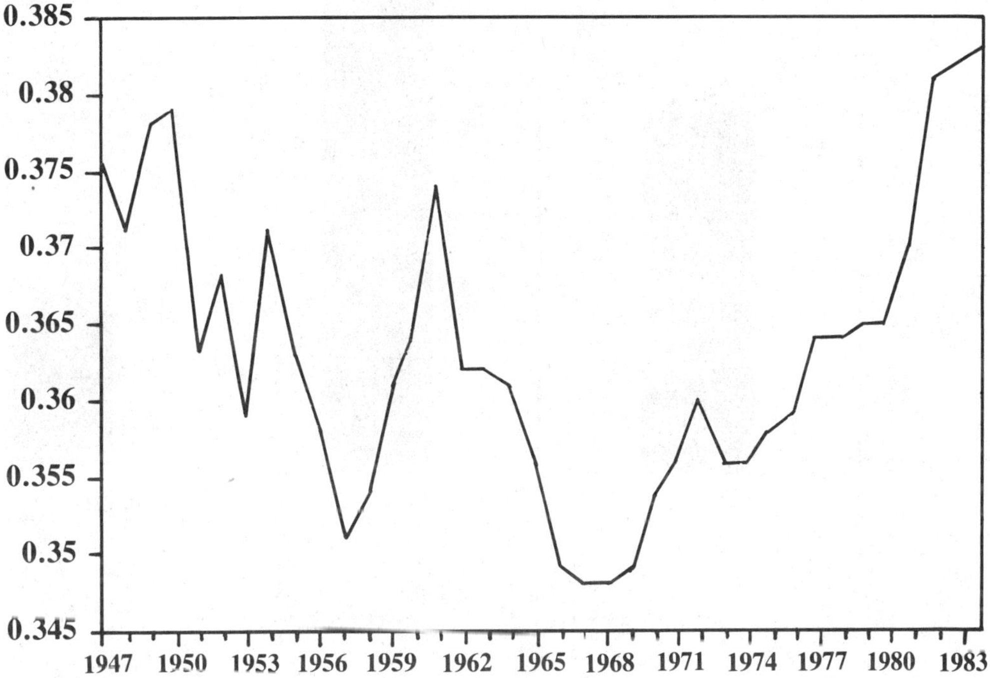

Note: The Gini coefficient measures inequality in family income: a higher Gini coefficient corresponds to a more unequal distribution of family income. The Gini coefficient began increasing in the late 1960s, and increased even more rapidly in the later 1970s and early 1980s. The 1984 Gini coefficient showed the most unequal distribution of income since the government began keeping these statistics in 1947 (Source: U.S Bureau of the Census, 1985).

received by the poorest fifth of all families grew by 12 percent between 1947 and 1969, only to drop by 16 percent between 1969 and 1984; over the same period, the share of income received by the richest fifth dipped only to rise again (U.S. Bureau of the Census 1985).

Other changes confirm this trend. The percentage of American families falling within a middle income range has fallen, while the percentages in the high and low ranges have grown, as shown in Figure 2 (Bradbury 1986). The richest receive a larger share of total income, while the majority — the bottom 6 percent — receive a smaller share (Thurow 1987). And the fraction of families whose income lies below the poverty line is climbing, after one decade of declining poverty and another decade of stability in the poverty rate (Ellwood and Summers 1986).

Figure 2
Percentage of Families by Income Group
(1973 and 1984)

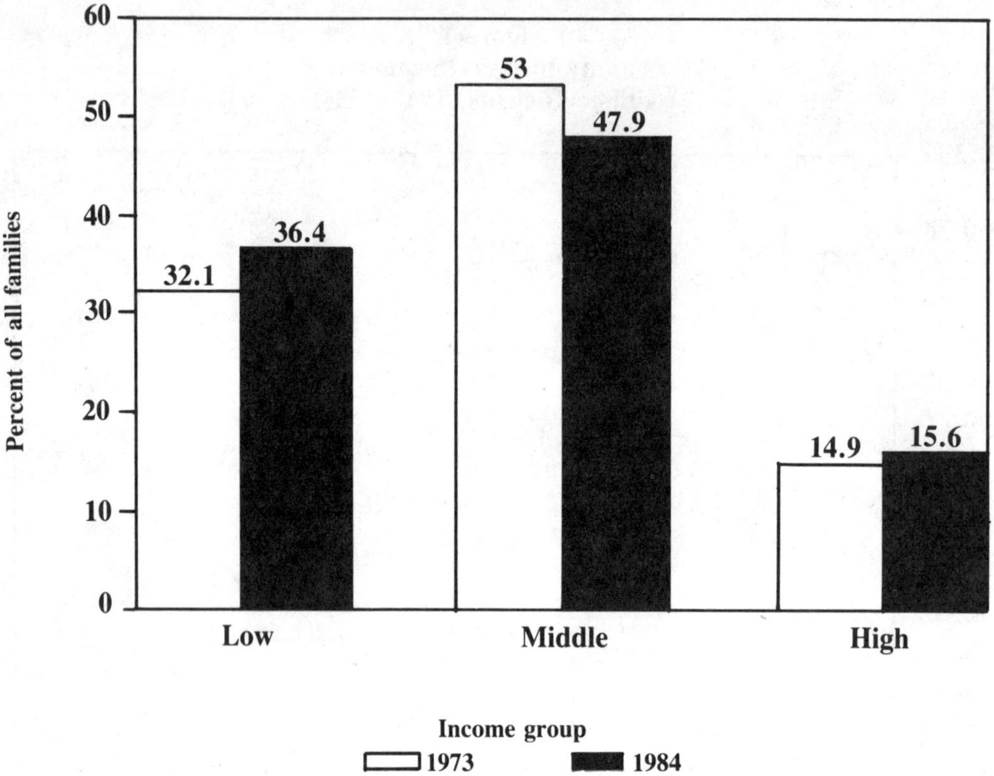

Note: The middle income group has shrunk, while low and high income groups have grown. (Low income is defined at $0–$20,000 in 1984 dollars; middle income is $20,000–$50,000; high income is $50,000 and over. Source: Bradbury (1986).

Why are family incomes becoming more unequal? Three main explanations have been advanced. First, some analysts argue that changes in family structure lie at the root of the new trend toward inequality. There are more female-headed families at the low-income end, and more two-earner families at the top end. The low end of the income distribution is also weighted down by increasing numbers of young people and old people living alone; previously these individuals were more likely to live in and pool their income with an extended family.

A second theory, espoused by neo- and not-so-neo-conservatives like Charles Murray (1984), is that anti-poverty policy has actually led to increases in poverty. By setting the poor apart and cutting them off from the labor market, these analysts argue, our system of public assistance has spawned a growing underclass that is unwilling or unable to seek employment.

A third explanation, favored by myself and many others, points to the economy as the culprit. Inequality could be worsening because the sputtering, recession-prone business cycle has hit those on the bottom harder than those on top, or because deep structural changes are taking place in the type of jobs that the economy generates. Either way, it's *earnings* inequality that's driving up income inequality.

Each explanation leads to different policy consequences. If family income appears more unequal simply because extended families are living in separate units but still sharing incomes, there may be little cause for concern. If single-parent and two-earner families are stretching apart the income distribution, then perhaps the government should provide family allowances for the families with fewer parents and more children. If the welfare state is causing poverty, the natural solution is a conservative one: pare back the welfare state. And if changes in macroeconomic performance or microeconomic structure are generating increased inequality, then economic responses are called for.

Which of the three processes are actually contributing to growing inequality? Let's start with family structure. Harvard economists Blackburn and Bloom (1986) found that when they took family size into account in comparing family incomes, the striking swing toward inequality — as measured by the Gini coefficient — became even more pronounced. In other words, the increase in inequality does *not* result from greater variation in family size, such as the increased variation due to more individuals living alone.

There is also little evidence that the proliferation of two-earner families and single-parent families has contributed much to overall inequality. Blackburn and Bloom performed the hypothetical "experiment" of calculating the Gini coefficients that would have resulted each year if working wives' earnings had been zero. They found that this adjustment made almost no difference. The income provided by working wives has the equalizing effect of raising very low family incomes, as well as the disequalizing effect of augmenting high family incomes; apparently, the two effects roughly canceled out over time.

Nobody has done a comparable analysis of the impact on income inequality of the increasing numbers of single parents. But Bane (1984), another Harvard economist, discovered a related fact: very few families enter poverty through family breakup. While 60 percent of the poor in 1979 were people living alone or members of female-headed families, almost two-thirds of these people either were poor before the split-up (divorce, child leaving home, etc.) that resulted in the single person or female-headed family, became poor some time after the split-up, or were children born into a family that was already poor. It was not the immediate loss of a husband's income that plunged these people below the poverty line.

So changes in family structure seem to account for little, if any, of the growing inequality. What about the effects of the welfare system? A number of pieces of evidence cast doubt on policy-generated poverty as an explanation for worsening inequality. First, there are changes at the top of the income distribution as well as the bottom. The rich got richer and their numbers grew (see Figure 2). The welfare state doesn't help to explain this.

Second, the ups and downs of the poverty rate seem above all to reflect the ups and downs of the economy rather than changes in welfare policy. The non-elderly poverty rate almost exactly tracks the poverty line divided by median family income — in other words, the fraction of people in poverty depends on the level of overall economic prosperity (Ellwood and Summers 1986). So the long-term growth in the poverty rate can best be attributed to long-term stagnation in the economy.

In addition, most families who use AFDC do not get "trapped" in welfare dependency. At least 50 percent leave welfare in two years or less, and 85 percent are off welfare within eight years. And decreasing welfare benefits over time has not led to less participation in AFDC; nor do states with lower benefits have less AFDC participation (Ellwood and Summers 1986). Thus, those on AFDC seem to be people who have no other choice, not "free riders" who could work but choose not to. In fact, over half of the families living in poverty have at least one worker, and over one-fifth have two or more workers (*Business Week* 1986).

Since changing family structure and antipoverty policy do not explain growing income inequality, it seems that changes in the economy must hold the explanation. Economic changes could push family incomes apart via two channels. First, if capital income — such as dividends and capital gains — goes to a smaller, more concentrated group of families, the rich become richer while some of the middle-income families lose out. And in fact, the percentage of families owning at least one share of stock fell from 25 percent of the population in 1977 to 19 percent in 1983, even though the share of total GNP going to capital increased over that period (Thurow 1985). Economic crisis led to a concentration of ownership and to a shift in resources from labor to capital. However, changes in the distribution of capital income cannot account for the big changes in the Gini coefficient or other inequality measures based on Census data, because 95 percent of income reported to the Census is *earned* income.

The second way that economic changes can affect income distribution is through the distribution of labor income. Indeed, the distribution of earnings among individuals — like the distribution of income among families — became much more unequal starting in the late 1970s. The puzzle, then, becomes one of explaining why earnings became more unequal.

EARNINGS IN THE U.S.: LOWER AND MORE UNEQUALLY DISTRIBUTED

Earnings are becoming both lower on average *and* more maldistributed. Average weekly earnings of private nonfarm workers, which rose from 1947 (the first year they were measured) until 1972, fell 14 percent (in real terms) between 1972 and 1986 (U.S.

Bureau of the Census). Figure 3 demonstrates that one measure of interpersonal earnings inequality — the variance in the logarithm of annual wages and salaries — moved toward equality through most of the 1960s and 1970s, but then took a sharp "U-turn" toward inequality in 1978, although it has dipped back down from the extreme inequality of 1983 (Tilly, Bluestone, and Harrison 1986).

Figure 3
Inequality in Annual Wages and Salaries
(1963–1984)

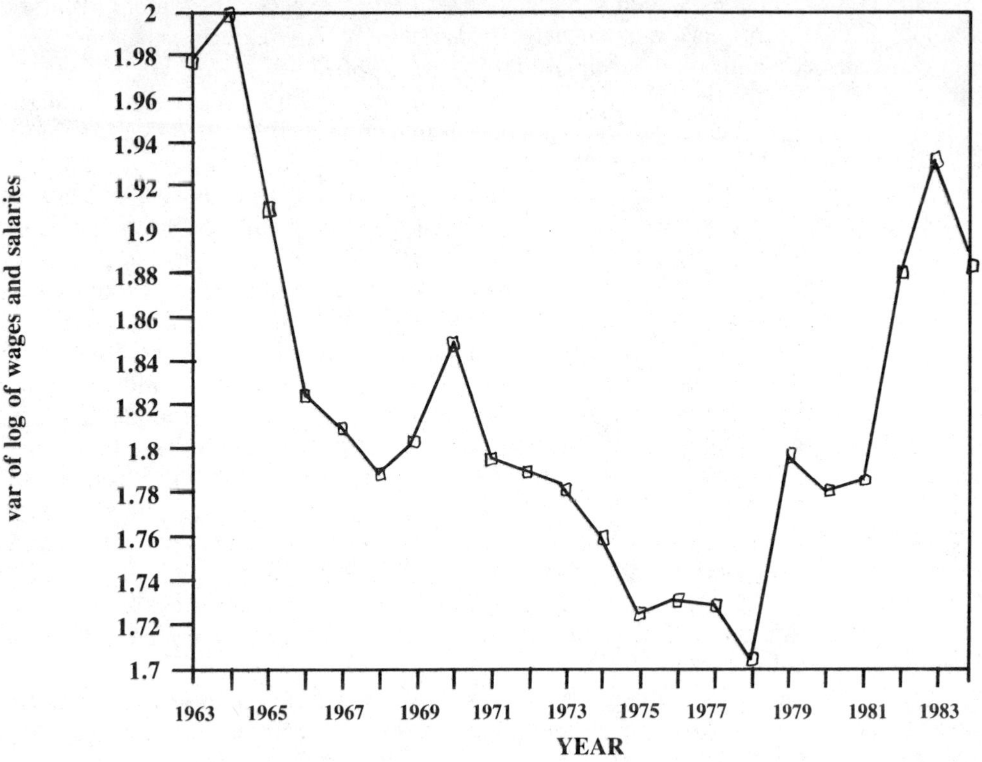

Note: Earnings inequality declined through most of the 1960s and 1970s, but began to increase in 1978. (Inequality is measured by the variance in the logarithm of annual wages and salaries. Higher variance corresponds to greater inequality.) Source: Tilly *et al.* (1986).

There are two important questions to answer about increasing earnings inequality. First, does growing wage dispersion result from changes in the mix of labor supplied — for example, a flood of young and female workers, both groups with below-average wages — or from changes in the mix of jobs created by employers? Second, does increasing inequality and low-wage job growth since the late 1970s represent a blip caused by an unkind business cycle, or a long-term structural change?

Some economists have suggested that earnings inequality has increased because different kinds of workers — particularly the young "baby boomers" and women —

have entered the labor market in large numbers. Since these workers have less earning power, the economists reason, they have expanded the low end of the wage distribution. It's true that young people and women — and, for that matter, people of color — have made up a higher and higher proportion of the work force since the 1960s. But essentially *all* of the rise in earnings inequality is due to growing wage dispersion *within* age, sex, and race subgroups, rather than to growth in the size of certain subgroups. For example, the distribution of income among men became more unequal, and so did the distribution of income among women. It is these changes, not the fact that there are more women in the work force, that explain growing overall inequality. Furthermore, the distribution of "human capital" attributes such as education and work experience, which are often assumed to determine earnings, actually became more *equal* during the time that earnings were becoming more unequal (Tilly *et al.* 1986).

In short, changes in the type of labor supplied do not account for growing earnings inequality. However, changes in the types of jobs that employers create *do* seem to have had an important impact. One change is the creation of more part-time jobs. Employers have created part-time jobs as part of a search for a low-cost, high-turnover, "flexible" work force. About 40 percent of the increase in earnings inequality between 1978 and 1984 can be explained by the growth of the part-time work force and the decline of annual wages of part-time workers relative to those of full-timers* (Tilly *et al.* 1986).

Another change in the job mix is the decline in traditional manufacturing and the rise of the service industries, a trend termed "deindustrialization." Deindustrialization is taking place because America has lost its dominant position in the world capitalist economy, and because American-owned industry has itself grown more footloose, while the business coordination and control functions provided by service work are becoming more important. Changes in industry mix account for a little over one-fifth of the increase in inequality between 1978 and 1984. Most of this effect is due to the growth of sectors with very unequal wage profiles, such as insurance with its high-paid executives and low-paid clerks (Tilly *et al.* 1986). Some of the increase in earnings inequality can be tracked down to the fact that exporting and import-competing industries, which have relatively equal earnings distributions, lost employment, while non-traded industries gained employment (Thurow 1987).

While the types of jobs are changing, the ways families use these jobs to piece together a total family income are also changing. A disproportionate number of new jobs are part-time, part-year, and/or pay very low hourly wages. For the most part, these are not "breadwinner" jobs; they are jobs that are used to supplement income from other sources (which may include a second low-wage job held by another family member).

The second question about growing earnings inequality and falling real wages is whether the business cycle is responsible for these distributional changes. We certainly would expect recession, with high unemployment and excess capacity, to lead firms to offer lower real wages and put workers on shorter schedules. Recessions also curtail manufacturing employment. And wage differentials *do* widen during recessions and

---

*This 40 percent figure, as well as the figure for the percentage of the increase in inequality explained by changes in industry mix, cited in the next paragraph, are derived from partial, univariate analyses. For example, this particular analysis looks only at the difference between part-time, full-time, and more-than-full-time workers. If other explanatory variables were included, the fraction of the increase explained by part-time schedules (or industry mix) would surely decrease.

narrow during expansions. Higher wages tend to be institutionally fixed (by union agreements or more implicit arrangements), while low wages tend to be flexible and to respond to the ups and downs of the economy. The long slump of 1979–82, which included the deepest recession since the 1930s, might have widened pay differentials to an extent that has not yet been reversed. If so, then cyclical recovery should bring with it a move back toward equality and better-paying jobs.

Part of the change in income distribution does seem to be a result of the business cycle, but there is also a long-term, structural change taking place. The dramatic leap in inequality between the late 1970s and mid-1980s is probably largely the outcome of the extra-deep recession; the long-term trend is a more modest increase. Inequality seems to be following a pattern something like the pattern unemployment has followed since 1969: increasing during recessions, decreasing during recoveries, but starting from a higher baseline each time through the business cycle.

INEQUALITY AND POLICY

It is tempting to blame the Reagan Administration and its policies for the rising tide of inequality in the United States. But the increase in inequality began years before Reagan took office, and its roots lie in an economic crisis that has been brewing much longer. Prolonged economic stagnation and heightened competition on a national and international level have led employers to restructure America's jobs.

Nonetheless, the federal government has done almost everything it possibly can to *worsen* the trend toward inequality, by assisting employers in shifting the burden of the crisis onto working and poor people. Presidents Carter and Reagan have pursued a low-wage, high-unemployment economic policy aimed at "wringing out" inflation and defending the position of the U.S. dollar. This policy includes tolerance for corporate union-busting, the lowest real minimum wage on record, plus fiscal and monetary policies that have dragged us through the deepest recession of the postwar era. And the substance of the nation's current industrial policy is to pour money into military production and R&D while doing little to revitalize declining sectors and regions.

Reagan and Congress have cut taxes on the wealthy and cut transfers to the poor. A Congressional Budget Office study (1984) showed that as a *direct* result of tax and budget policies, families with income below $10,000 would lose a total of $23 billion between 1983 and 1985, while the 1.4 percent of families with incomes above $80,000 would gain $35 billion.

To reverse the trend toward inequality and move us in the direction of an equitable distribution of income, we need a virtually opposite set of policies. Tax and welfare policy should be used to redistribute income — as well as in-kind goods such as health care — downward, not upward. Union organizing of non-unionized workers, targeted particularly to low-wage service and clerical workers, should be facilitated. After all, the biggest transformation of low-wage jobs into high-wage jobs in this century was the transformation wrought upon mass production manufacturing jobs by the C.I.O. during the 1930s and 1940s. The minimum wage should be raised, not lowered. Fiscal and monetary policy should be oriented to full employment and growth; unemployment takes a much greater toll on the poor than inflation. Industrial policy should be developed to assure job security (e.g., through plant closing restrictions) and job quality (e.g., through assistance to businesses conditioned on guaranteed pay levels for jobs created). Finally, the government should adopt an active role in overcoming other forms of inequality, such as disparities in pay by race and sex — a role that the federal government under Reagan has abdicated.

In the current political climate, most of these changes are not likely to be carried out "from above," regardless of who succeeds Reagan in office. Instead, the best prospect for moving toward greater equity lies in working "from below," using community and labor organizing along with local and state legislative strategies. We may not be able to stop the rising tide of inequality, but at least we can start piling up the sandbags.

ACKNOWLEDGEMENTS

I would like to thank Bennett Harrison, Barry Bluestone, Michael Piore, Lester Thurow, the *Dollars and Sense* editorial collective, William J. Wilson, Robert Aponte, the University of Chicago Urban Poverty Seminar, Rhon Baiman, and my editor, Robert Cherry, for comments on this paper and earlier formulations. All errors remain my own.

REFERENCES

Bane, Mary Jo. 1984. Household Composition and Poverty. Institute for Research on Poverty Conference Paper. University of Wisconsin, Madison.

Blackburn, McKinley and David Bloom. 1986. Family Income Inequality in the United States: 1967–1984. *Proceedings* of the 39th annual meetings of the Industrial Relations Research Association.

Bradbury, Katharine L. 1986. The Shrinking Middle Class. *New England Economic Review* (September/October):41–55.

Business Week. 1986. Poking Holes in Some Myths about the Poor. (May 5):16.

Congressional Budget Office. 1984. The Combined Effects of Major Changes in Federal Taxes and Spending Programs Since 1981. Staff memorandum.

Danziger, Sheldon, Robert Haveman, and Robert Plotnick. 1984. Antipoverty Policy: Effects on the Poor and the Nonpoor. Institute for Research on Poverty Conference Paper. University of Wisconsin, Madison.

Ellwood, David T. and Lawrence N. Summers. 1986. Is Welfare Really the Problem? *The Public Interest*. No.83:57–78.

Murray, Charles. 1984. *Losing Ground: American Social Policy, 1950–1980*. New York: Basic Books.

Thurow, Lester C. 1987. A Surge in Inequality. *Scientific American* (May):30–37.

Tilly, Chris, Barry Bluestone, and Bennett Harrison. 1986. What Is Making American Wages More Unequal? *Proceedings* of the Industrial Relations Research Association 39th annual meeting.

U.S. Bureau of the Census. 1985. *Current Population Reports*, Series P-60, No.151. Washington, D.C.: Government Printing Office.

9

The Farm Crisis

DIANE FLAHERTY

RURAL AMERICA IN DECLINE

A front page report in the *New York Times* of September 29, 1987 makes official what farmers and their supporters have known for at least five years now: poverty is widespread in America's heartland (Schneider 1987:B4). Once limited to migrant agricultural workers and poor black southern farmers and hence ignored, rural misery has spread so far that it has become news.

How did farms and rural communities fall into such pervasive crisis? The Reagan Administration argues that the fault lies with farmers who during the good years in the 1970s expanded production beyond what the market could bear. Many farmers blame the government or bankers, claiming they were encouraged to expand and become more mechanized to support the government's foreign policy objectives or the profits of bankers. Government policies and the overexpansion they promoted in the 1970s do explain part of the crisis in agriculture. But the decline of American farming is rooted in deep structural changes in the U.S. economy since the 1950s which are more powerful than any short-term farm policy. The most important of these changes are: (1) the "technology treadmill," which prompts increased mechanization, as well as chemical and biological innovation; (2) the increasing control of large agribusiness corporations over food production and distribution; and (3) changes in the farm sectors' relations with the international economy.

TROUBLE DOWN ON THE FARM

American agriculture, despite rosy reports from the Reagan Administration, continues to suffer a severe crisis (see Table 1). Record numbers of family farms face a crippling combination of overproduction, depressed prices, rising debt, and falling land values. As a result, farmers in the Midwest and elsewhere have not only failed to make a profit; increasingly, they cannot even make payments on their debts. In 1986, farm debt amounted to $225 billion, or 25 percent of assets, a historical high (Council of Economic Advisors 1987:356). In the same year, 80 banks in Iowa alone had more insecure loans than capital (McCoy 1986:6). The Farm Credit System, the major supplier of credit to distressed farmers, has lost $4.8 billion since 1985 and expects $3 billion in losses over the next three years to put it $1.8 billion in debt by 1990 (Nash 1987:8).

Table 1
Indicators of the Farm Crisis

1. In 11 midwestern farm states, land values dropped by an average of 17 percent from 1981 to 1984. The decline was 12 percent in 1984, the largest one-year decline since the Depression.

2. In 1987, 40 percent of the 70,000 farmers in Kansas are in danger of losing their farms.

3. Agricultural bank failures are running at 10 times the annual rate for the past 30 years. In 1984, agricultural banks accounted for 32 percent of the total of 78 bank failures in the United States, up from 13 percent of total failures in 1983.

4. Interest on farm liabilities in 1985 was $18.7 billion, but farm income was only $30 billion.

5. More than 25 percent of all U.S. cropland, much of it highly productive, is eroding at rates exceeding the soil's regenerative capacity. This is an erosion rate greater than 5 tons per acre.

6. The United States farm equipment sector has shrunk by 50 percent since 1982.

7. The share of American farm products in the world market has fallen from 16.8 percent in 1980 to 12.0 percent in 1985.

8. In 1980, the average export price per ton for Argentine wheat was $25 more than the United States export price. By March 1985, the Argentine price was about $30 less than the United States.

9. Wharton Econometrics estimates that the cost of the high dollar to American farmers through loss of export markets was $4.42 billion between January 1983 and February 1985 for just corn, wheat and soybean producers.

10. Net farm income in 1986 was only 75 percent of 1985 income for the same period (Jan–Sept.).

Sources: 1. "The Current Financial Condition of Farmers and Farm Lenders," USDA Economic Research Service, Agriculture Information Bulletin No. 490, p. 6; "Farmland Values Dropped 12% in '84," *The Boston Sunday Globe,* June 9, 1985, p. 15.
2. Keith Schneider (1987:B24).
3. USDA *Bulletin* No. 492:7; Robert Pear, "Farm Banks' Troubles Are Worsening," *The New York Times,* March 6, 1985, p. B11.
4. USDA (1985d:12, 75).
5. USDA (1985b:2).
6. Jean Marie Brown, "Deere Doesn't See Profitable 3rd Period," *Wall Street Journal,* August 26, 1987, p. 8.
7. USDA, *Foreign Agricultural Statistics of the U.S.,* May–June, 1987, p. 140.
8. Wendy Wall, "Sudden Worsening of Nation's $37 Billion Farm-Export Market," *Wall Street Journal,* March 25, 1985, p. 6.
9. William Robbins, "Surging Value of Dollar Spurs Chaos on Farms, *Wall Street Journal,* February 1, 1985, p. 1.
10. *Economic Report of the President,* 1987, p. 352.

Finding the way out of the crisis is not possible without a convincing explanation of how we got into it. David Stockman, former Director of the Office of Budget and Management, expressed in February 1985 the consistent position of the Reagan Administration: farmers brought on their own problems by borrowing too much. Their growing debts, declared Stockman, were "willingly incurred by consenting adults" (Stockman 1985:6). For this comment he got into trouble with his mother, who is a farmer, but he won favor with the conservative economists whose proposed solution to the farm problem is a good dose of market discipline.

Another administration response has been that farm problems are not really so bad. Paul Volcker, Chairman of the Federal Reserve Board, argued in testimony to the Joint Economic Committee in February 1985 that the credit problem was only regional, not national (Easterbrook 1985:6). Only particular commodities and areas of the country have been hit, he claimed, proving that only those farmers who are bad financial managers or inefficient producers are in trouble — and they deserve to be. According to

Volcker, farm foreclosures signal a "shakeout" of inefficient producers, making the farm economy as a whole more healthy.

Populist farmers offer an alternative to simplistic conservative economic explanations which focus on "too much" government involvement or bad farm management. Instead, the populists blame the collapse of farms on particular policies of the Reagan Administration, the control and pricing policies of big grain dealers and food processors, and/or greedy bankers. Populist spokesman and former Texas Agriculture Secretary Jim Hightower emphasizes: "It comes down to one key question: Are we going to have a system of hard-working, efficient, independent, family farms in this country, or are we going to turn control of our food supply over to a handful of conglomerates and superfarm combines"? (Lanner 1985:19).

It is true that the farm sector has been pushed over the brink by both direct and indirect effects of Reaganomics. The anti-inflation package introduced in Reagan's first two years had a significant impact upon farmers. Relying mainly on contractionary monetary policy to keep prices down, the monetarist approach forced up interest rates, triggering the deep, worldwide recession of 1981–1982. As a result, high interest rates added millions of dollars to farm debt. In addition, the world recession reduced demand by poor countries for United States grain. In fact, some of these countries, like Argentina and Brazil, are now forced to sell their grain on the world market at very low prices because they are desperate to earn foreign exchange to pay off their huge international debts. A second side-effect of conservative economic policies is the strong dollar, which has exacerbated the loss of exports. Between 1980 and 1986, the value of total farm exports fell almost by half, from $51.9 billion to $23.5 billion. Loss of export markets cost American farmers over $4 billion, between January 1983 and February, 1985 just for corn, wheat, and soybean production (Robbins 1985:1).

Table 2
Changes in Ten Farm Characteristics:
1950–84

Farm Characteristic	1950	1980	1984
Population in agriculture as percent of total population	15%	3%	2.2%
Number of farms (millions)	5.4	2.4	2.4
Average size of farms (acres)	216	429	436
Percent of farm labor that is hired	23%	35%	39%
Value of machinery per worker (1984 dollars)	5303	32934	31263
Crop production per acre (1984 = 100)	52.7	88.4	100
Ratio of prices received to prices paid by farmers (1984 = 1.0)	1.45	1.06	1.0
Farm debt as a percent of assets	9.3	16.5	20.8
Farm exports (billions of 1983 dollars)	12.5	51.9	36.6
Number of people fed by one farmer	15	76	75**

Sources: Rows 1–3, USDA, *Agricultural Statistics*.
Rows 4–9: *Economic Report of the President,* 1985; 1987.
Row 10: USDA, Economic Indicators of the Farm Sector, Productivity and Efficiency Statistics, 1985.

**1985 data

Banks also played a part in farm troubles, offering farmers loans based on unrealistic expectations about future land values. When loans were made in the 1970s, the average value of land was increasing at a rate which would have doubled land values in a decade (Figure 1). This inflated the value of farm collateral, allowing farmers to assume more debt without excessively high debt/asset ratios. But between 1974 and 1978, a time of peak borrowing, net income per farm fell by 22 percent in real terms. By 1986, it had fallen another 50 percent, dramatically reducing farmers' capacity to service their higher debts. When land prices started falling, the debt-to-asset ratios deteriorated rapidly. While farmers themselves paid insufficient attention to price and income trends, both they and the banks argue that their practices were sound at the time, given expected international demand for United States food exports. Neither farmers nor banks could have been expected to anticipate the collapse in land prices which resulted from falling exports and rising interest rates.

Figure 1
Land Value
($ per Acre)

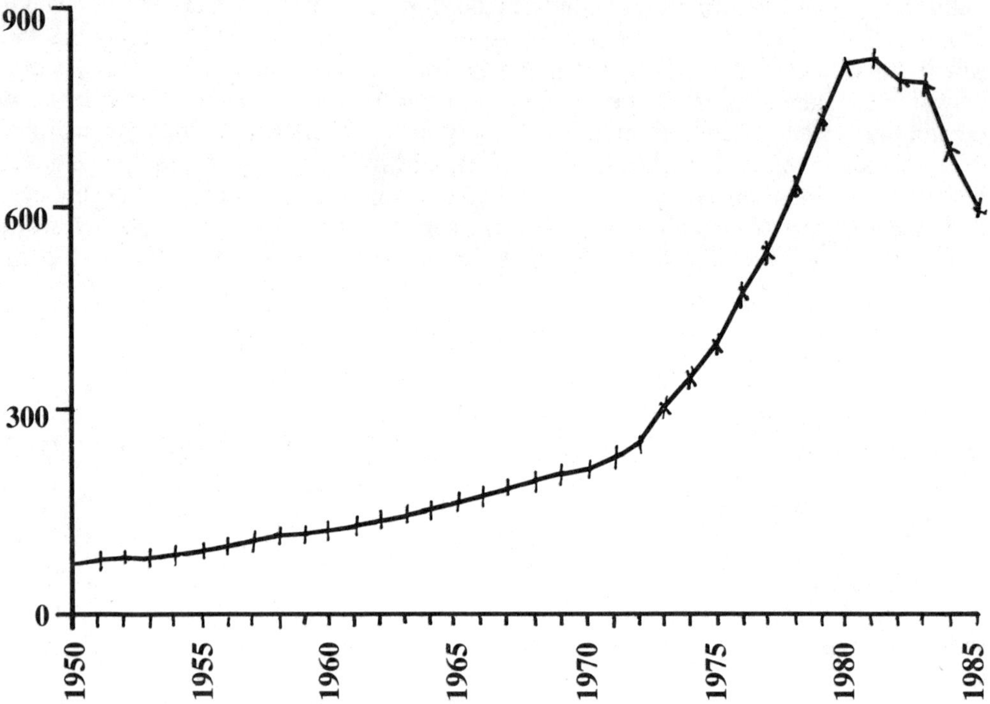

Source: USDA (1985d:61).

Conservative economic policies thus certainly brought the current crisis to a head. As *The Nation* (1985:260) editorialized in 1985: "Reagan's do-nothing farm policies will, in fact, do nothing to revitalize agriculture." However, a much more important focus than the effects of specific policies is the issue of agriculture's underlying vulnerability to the vagaries of Reaganomics. The analysis presented here is that the farm crisis is a product of an explosive interaction of recent farm policy with long-term structural change throughout the United States economy since 1950.

STRUCTURAL CHANGE AND POSTWAR FARM POLICY

The farm sector of the American economy looked quite different in the first years of the crisis than it did in 1950 (see Table 2). A small farm which relied on family labor and relatively little capital in the 1950s has likely switched to large-scale, mechanized and "chemicalized" production using more hired labor in the 1980s. Farms are also more dependent on exports: in 1950, exports accounted for only 8.8 percent of farm sales; by 1980, 27.4 percent of farm sales came from exports (Economic Report of the President 1985). These changes have been fostered by United States government policy throughout the agricultural economy. Since 1950, policy has focused on four major areas: developing water resources; supporting research and development of seeds, fertilizers and pesticides; supporting research and development of mechanization and technological innovation; and protecting farmers' incomes from swings in market prices. Policies aimed at these objectives have directly or indirectly favored large farms over small and hence concentration of farms into fewer and fewer hands, reduction in diversity of crops, mechanization with dependence on borrowed finance and greater reliance on purchased rather than home-produced inputs.

The benefits of water resources in the postwar period have gone disproportionately to large farms. For example, two recent reports by the Natural Resources Defense Council and the California Rural Legal Assistance Foundation estimated that the Interior Department illegally provided nearly $1.5 billion in subsidies to irrigate farms in California's Central Valley, many of which are owned by large corporations (Peterson 1985:A8). Distribution of benefits of research and development are harder to evaluate. However, while researchers argue that new technologies are adaptable to all size farms, most also believe that large farms are in a significantly better position to use the new technology (Schertz 1979; Dorow 1985).

The fourth area of government policy, protecting farmers' incomes through direct subsidies and credit, has also benefitted large farmers disproportionately. In 1978, farms with more than 500 acres — which comprised only 10 percent of all farms participating in commodity programs — received 46 percent of all commodity support payments. Direct government payments also go mainly to large producers. In 1970, the largest producers received an average payment of $31,000 each, middle size farms (those likely to be big family farms rather than corporate farms) received $7,400, and the smallest family farms received only $4,300. This distribution did not change significantly with the deepening crisis on family farms: in 1985, the direct payments to these three kinds of farms were $38,000, $13,000 and $5,000 (USDA 1985:46). A 1981 government report on agriculture concluded that ". . . of the participants, the largest farmers receive most of whatever benefits the programs offer (USDA 1981:103).

Credit policies, too, now tend to favor large producers. According to the U.S. Department of Agriculture, government-sponsored credit agencies (Farm Credit System) and insured loan programs (Farmers' Home Administration) gradually shifted their priorities during the 1950s and 1960s. Originally these programs were designed to maintain low-income, self-sufficient farms. Now the emphasis is on "bringing about commercially-viable enterprises'' (USDA 1984c). In 1978, in response to cash-flow and credit problems in the farm sector, the emphasis shifted again and legislation was enacted to provide emergency loans. Emergency credit has been a major emphasis of USDA programs during the past five crisis years. These loans have higher ceilings than other forms of government assistance ($400,000) and corporate farms are now eligible (USDA 1984c; *Small Farm Advocate* 1984–1985).

Government encouragement of agricultural exports began in the 1960s with Public Law 480, which allowed the government to buy up surpluses for export. This was followed by the ''Food for Peace'' program and by the Berg Commission of 1966, convened by President Johnson, which called for restructuring agricultural production around export crops. Reduction of support prices to meet world market prices meant that farmers would be encouraged to grow more corn, wheat, soybeans and cotton for export.

This was an important role for farm exports to play, because exports relieved pressure on the farm price floor held up by government price supports. But by the beginning of the 1970s, agriculture was playing a second important role: it was the key to keeping the U.S. balance of payments deficit under control. Accelerating decline of markets for the products of U.S. industry and the end of the dollar as the world currency marked a fundamental structural change in the U.S. economy at the beginning of the 1970s. In 1973, a further shock happened when OPEC organized and raised oil prices.

In response to severe balance of payments deficits generated in part by the skyrocketing value of oil imports, the Nixon Administration looked to agriculture to save the day. It was ''Food for Crude,'' as farmers were encouraged to plant ''fence row to fence row.'' Rather than address the root causes of the international trade deficit, successive administrations seized on agriculture (and other exports, such as arms and military equipment) as a quick fix. As a result, farmers were dragged into the chaos of the international trade and financial systems of the 1970s. Since then, any time the dollar rises or falls, farmers' fortunes swing in the opposite direction.

CONCENTRATION IN FARMING

The push to export has had far-reaching effects on the structure of United States agriculture. One of the most important is the change in the mix of crops produced. Between 1969 and 1980, the share of the major export crops — corn, wheat, soybeans and cotton — rose from 58 percent to 70 percent of total acres of cropland (Wessel 1983:55). According to agricultural economist Philip Raup, this land use shift is ''. . . creating a pattern of one-crop, export-based agricultural activity [in the grain belt]. . . that is very similar to the type of monocultural dependence formerly associated with colonialism (Raup 1979:103). This dependence makes farmers in general more susceptible to changing prices, and small and medium-size farms are much more vulnerable to bad years than large ones, who have superior ability to generate precautionary savings.

Tax policy has also changed the structure of agriculture. A serious consequence is the effect of taxes on absentee ownership of farms and land speculation. The most important of these policies are a cash method of accounting, capital gains provisions, deductions for interest payments and tax write-offs.

Under cash accounting, farms offer big tax advantages because expenses are deducted in the year they are paid and income is recognized in the year it is received. As a result, an investor with a tax problem can buy feed for cattle to be sold next year, thereby reducing this year's taxable income and in effect obtaining an interest-free loan from the federal government (Schertz 1979:179; USDA 1985a:247–251; USDA 1981:92–94; *Small Farm Advocate* 1984-1985). This has been one factor in taking cattle feeding off middle-sized family farms and into large feedlots, shares in which are bought by absentee owners of the cattle. This artificial advantage to large-scale competitors deprives middle-sized family farms of a potential source of income, making them more dependent on a few crops.

Capital gains taxes, tax write-offs, and deductions for interest payments encourage absentee ownership and speculation. This added demand for land helps bid up land prices and prevents promising entry-level farmers from starting up their operations. In addition, these tax provisions are expensive in lost tax revenues. The Congressional Budget Office has estimated that the combined cost of cash accounting and capital gains in farming produced a loss of $815 million in 1980 and $970 million in 1982 in tax revenues (Boehlje 1985:3).

Since 1976, farm land has also offered estate tax breaks designed to permit family farms to survive from one generation to the next. The overall impact of these tax provisions has been, in the words of agricultural economist Michael Boehlje, that "tax policy has exerted upward pressure on the price of farmland. . . , encouraged the expansion of individual farm firms. . . , encouraged incorporation of farm and agribusiness firms. . . , and stimulated the production of tax-shelted crops" (Boehlje 1985:6). Indeed, another agricultural economist, Harold Breimyer, has argued that "the income tax code virtually confines new capital to that coming in under shelters" (Breimyer 1985:53).

Government research reports agree (USDA 1981:76; 1985a:247). These advantages are most attractive in times of inflation, when they provide an unusually powerful tax shelter. But this means that when general inflation leads to increases in land values and fuels speculation, tax policy further pushes up land prices, intensifying a vicious circle of rising land values and increased ownership of land for tax advantages and speculative gain, rather than for production. As an agricultural economist at Nebraska's Center for Rural Affairs has noted: "Under these conditions, simply owning land comes to be rewarded more highly than producing food on it — and unearned wealth becomes a bigger factor in farm expansion than is earned income from farming" (Wessel 1983:52).

All of these policies and the impact they have had in the farm sector have helped create a system of concentrated ownership and large farms. In 1978, the largest 5 percent of landowners owned 75 percent of the land (Geisler 1984:8). The average farm acreage in 1980 was double that of 1950 (see Table 2). The percentage of farms in the largest size category (measured by value of sales in constant dollars) quadrupled between 1960 and 1980, from less than 1 percent of all farms to 4.4 percent. One force behind this structural shift is increased mechanization, reflected in the fact that large farms (sales of $200,000 or more) use more than twice the amount of machinery per acre as middle-sized farms (those with sales of $40,000 to $199,000).

The character of the farm has changed as its size has increased. In 1949, less than 1 percent of all farms were classified as larger than single family farms. In 1980, 49 percent of farms were larger than a single family could run without substantial wage labor.[1] Although we know from these data that the traditional family farm is dying out, its opposite, corporate farming, is difficult to measure. Corporate farms accounted for roughly 2.5 percent of farms in 1982, 14 percent of land and 24 percent of sales. But most of these corporate farms have only ten or fewer stockholders and are typically family-owned and operated (USDA 1984c:23). Less than 1 percent of all farms are corporations whose income comes mostly from non-farm activities.

Farming, in short, is still nominally a family business in most places. But the largest family farms are more like the family-owned oil companies on the soap operas "Dallas" and "Dynasty," rather than mom and pop stores. In California, for example, only 45 corporations owned nearly half of the state's crop land in 1980, but most of these owners were family companies, not corporations like Del Monte and United Brands. In fact, industrial corporations may find the prospect of becoming farmers themselves unattractive, because profit margins are small and prices very variable. Large industrial corporations can do better by pushing the risks of farming off on to smaller producers, whose products the corporations can then contract to buy (Burbach and Flynn 1980). This contract farming, like tenant farming, has expanded significantly during the 1980s in response to the farm crisis, since so many independent farmers are now faced with a choice between leaving the farm or farming for someone else.

The fact that ownership of farms still rests with families, in other words, should not obscure the fact of concentration of land ownership. To keep these various kinds of farms straight, is used here the term family farm to mean only middle-sized farms (sales between $40,000 and $200,000) or those that can be run by a single family. Larger farms which are family-owned are not counted as family farms, but as corporate farms.

CONCENTRATION IN FOOD PROCESSING AND DISTRIBUTION

Concentration in processing has been expensive for both farmers and consumers. Today, over 90 percent of food is processed, and agricultural processing and distribution are characterized by large-scale corporations with fewer and fewer firms (Connor and Marion 1985). The largest 100 food corporations increased their share of total industry assets from 46 percent in 1950 to 75 percent in 1981, largely as a result of conglomerate mergers. The share of industry sales made by the top four food manufacturers rose by about 10 percentage points between 1958 and 1977, to about 50 percent of total industry sales. However, if we look only at those food manufacturers that produce differentiated products, for example, brand name products, the share of industry sales going to the top four rose by 18 percentage points, to almost 70 percent of total industry sales in 1977. This has led one study to conclude that advertising, and in particular television advertising, "appears to be the major force behind the upward pressure on sales concentration" (Connor and Marion 1985:4).

Competition among food outlets has followed the pattern for production and processing of food. Using census data, a recent study of food retailing found that, in 1958, the top four supermarket chains captured more than half of all sales in about 40 percent of local markets. By 1977, the top four firms accounted for more than half of food sales in 67 percent of local markets. This has happened largely because of national concentration in retailing. The share of sales going to chains with more than 11 stores rose from about 42 percent in 1958 to almost 60 percent in 1982. The growth of chains was most rapid after 1975, apparently because of the relaxation of enforcement by the Federal Trade

Commission of enforcement of laws regulating "horizontal mergers" of chain stores (Marion 1985:45).

The last important change in the structure of agricultural production is expansion in vertical integration. This is the incorporation within one firm of many or all stages in the production of a product, from providing seed to growing crops or feeding animals to processing and marketing the product. A closely related arrangement is vertical coordination, in which agreements are made for farmers to sell their products to one processor.

These arrangements mean that even middle-sized family farms, those that seem to fit most closely the image of the rugged, independent farm family, may not be what they seem. When farmers enter into such arrangements, they lose the freedom to choose where and at what time to sell their product. They get some protection from sudden collapses in prices, but they lose their autonomy — what the USDA calls "loss of entrepreneurial independence" — and end up being in effect divisions of large food processing corporations. To accurately measure the degree of corporate control over farming, the integration arrangements between the family farm and the companies that buy their farm products must be taken into account.

Today, virtually all the chickens we buy at the supermarket fall under these two arrangements, as do products made of sugar from sugar beets and sugar-cane. Overall, the percent of agricultural output vertically integrated or coordinated has risen from 19 percent in 1960 to a little over 30 percent in 1980 (Manchester 1983:7; Stanton 1983:6). According to a government report on the state of agriculture in 1981, vertical integration and contract arrangements are one more force pushing family-sized farms to grow or die. Contract arrangements also limit the role of the open market in agriculture (USDA 1981:62).

These trends toward concentration have shifted the distribution of the consumers' food dollar and made food prices more dependent on marketing costs than on prices paid to farmers. In 1950, farmers' share of the food dollar was 47 percent; by 1980 it was only 27 percent. Although farmers have never completely captured the gains of food price increases, their share is lower than ever now. Between 1980 and 1983, most of the increase in food prices came after the food left the farm, in what is called the farm-to-retail price spread, or the retail spread. Of the almost 8 percent increase in food prices in 1981, for example, less than 1 percent went to farmers while almost 6 percent went to wholesalers and retailers (USDA 1963:161; 1984b:33). Consumers, as well as farmers, have been losers from increasing concentration of market power in the food system. A recent study suggests that if food distributors were forced to cut prices to a level that brought them a "normal rate of profit," American households would enjoy an increase of 1.1 percent in purchasing power. Poor people would gain even more, since they tend to spend a larger fraction of their income on staples like food (Connor and Marion 1985:297). A report by the Federal Trade Commission found that if the food distribution industry were more competitive — that is, the top four firms accounted for only 40 percent or less of the industry's sales — retail prices would fall at least 25 percent.

But monopoly is good profits in agribusiness. Rates of profit in major food companies show that concentration leads to relatively stable and high profit rates. In 1980, for example, Kellogg's after-tax return on equity was 26 percent; for General Foods it was

21 percent. These profit rates are as high as those of big oil companies (Wessel 1983:120).

ECONOMIES OR DISECONOMIES OF SCALE IN FARMING?

Important shifts have occurred in the structure of the farm and of those industries which dominate and shape farming. But why should economists be concerned about these changes? After all, output per acre grew by 70 percent over the years between 1950 and 1980. Moreover, in 1950 one farm worker could feed only 15 people; in 1985 s/he could feed 75 people (USDA 1983b:56). And isn't size associated with efficiency? Aren't large farms more efficient because they capture the cost advantage of economies of scale?

Because farms differ so much by crop and by region, it is difficult to talk about national averages for the best size of farm. Government studies have found, however, that United States farms today are larger than the size needed to gain the potential cost advantages associated with size. A detailed USDA study which takes these differences into account found that wheat farms could capture 90 percent of potential cost advantages with a size ranging from 14 percent of average size in Oklahoma to 46 percent of average size in Oklahoma. A small wheat farm in North Dakota, in other words, could be just as efficient as its twice-as-big neighbor. For corn, the figures were somewhat higher and very similar across states: the size necessary to get 90 percent of the benefits of large scale was only approximately 60 percent of the average size (USDA 1981:58–59). These and similar findings in other studies have led the USDA to conclude that the problems of middle-sized farms cannot be blamed on their lack of "efficiency" (USDA 1979:112).

Private cost advantages of larger-than-single family farms, in short, are not very large and it seems that the costs of concentration outweigh any benefits. But middle-sized farms may be less profitable, even if they typically operate at comparable levels of cost with large firms. As the markets for farm inputs and crops become more concentrated, the large farmers have advantages that come from the sheer volume of their purchases and sales, not from superior production efficiency. For example, a large farmer in a small midwestern town can get preferred credit terms and bulk discounts from local suppliers of machines, seed and money. The suppliers of credit and inputs have lower transactions costs in dealing with fewer, bigger farmers. Similarly, USDA studies show that large farms tend to get better deals in vertically-integrated selling arrangements because of their whole truckload or traincar deliveries to processors. Being large has advantages, but they do not necessarily have anything to do with production efficiency. In an industry of low profit margins, like farming, these advantages can be the difference between survival and foreclosure.

The conclusion that size has little to do with efficiency is even stronger if we take into account social as well as private costs. Social costs include both the private costs borne by producers and the costs of polluted water, dirty air and depletion of soil and water resources, which raises their cost to future generations. The structural changes in agriculture have raised the social costs substantially. But because these costs are not measured in private "efficiency" calculations, looking only at private costs gives a false reading of how farms are doing today.

THE SOCIAL COSTS OF THE TECHNOLOGY TREADMILL

The first problem for social costs with a mechanized and chemicalized agricultural system based on a few crops that are easy to export is high rates of soil erosion. Corn and soybeans are row crops that leave more land surface exposed to wind and water. Wheat is grown close together, but it too is erosive because it leaves land exposed for part of the year. It is just these crops that the government encouraged farmers to plant on newly-cleared and highly-erosive land during days of "food weapon" diplomacy in the 1970s. As a result, on 9 percent of United States cropland the rate of erosion is 15 or more tons per acre — three times higher than the rate at which the soil can regenerate; on 17 percent of cropland, the rate is 10 tons per acre or more (USDA 1985b:1–4; 1981:81–82).

The situation is even worse if we consider the off-farm consequences of erosion for water quality, lakes and reservoirs and plant and animal life. A recent USDA study has found that "costs of off-farm erosion may be substantially greater than the costs of productivity loss [on farms]." Citing research by government and non-government sources, this study estimates on-farm losses to have been $1.3 billion in 1980 and off-farm losses at $3 billion annually (USDA 1985c:10–12).

The total costs of an export-led strategy for getting rid of agricultural surpluses should then include some $4.3 billion to account for soil problems. Water resources, too, have been affected by the trend toward export crops and monoculture, because these changes necessitate increased use of pesticides and fertilizers compared to more mixed cropping. Farmland is now the major source of off-point pollution, or pollution which does not come from a well-defined source like a smokestack. Fertilizers, pesticides and sediment from soil erosion are all "pervasive" sources of pollution.

Another problem is the decline in water tables. Until recently, agriculture accounted for 86 percent of all the water used in the United States. In 1958, 37 million acres of land were irrigated; by 1977, 63 million acres got their water from ground sources. In some areas, water tables are dropping 3 to 5 feet a year. A USDA study concludes that "decreasing availability and increasing cost of ground water" may cause the loss of $2.5 billion (in 1980 dollars) of crop production and 6.6 million acres (USDA 1985c:16–17).

Excessive use of water has been promoted by technological innovations such as center pivot irrigation, as well as price structures. The relative price of corn and beef, for example, have given farmers the incentive to grow corn rather than graze cattle on semi-arid land. The price of water itself is distorted, often through federal or state subsidy. One 1985 study of California's Central Valley, for example, found that farmers paid $6.15 per acre-foot of water, while the cost of supplying the federally-subsidized water was $72.99 an acre-foot (Peterson 1985:A8).

In summary, the structural evolution of the farm and food industry since World War II has not minimized either private or social costs. And *all* farmers contribute to the social costs, not just the biggest. A hard look at the family farm, a sentimental favorite, shows that these farms also deplete the soil and pollute ground water supplies. This isn't surprising, because these farms right now are being squeezed so hard that conservation is a luxury they can't afford.

Another serious consequence of the "modern" farm is potential instability in costs. Farms are using a much larger percentage of purchased inputs. From 1950 to 1960, purchased inputs rose by about 15 percent and non-purchased fell by 20 percent (USDA 1963:38). This trend has continued, and as a result farms are also more vulnerable to changes in the input prices of fertilizers, pesticides and farm equipment. Since production of these inputs is now highly concentrated, it means that the success or failure of farms depends on the pricing strategies of oligopolistic firms, and farms increasingly are squeezed between non-competitive suppliers and non-competitive processors and distributors.

Furthermore, the increased capital-intensity of production in agriculture means that farmers rely increasingly on heavy borrowing to finance machinery purchases. Increasing debt makes farmers highly vulnerable to fluctuations in interest rates. The more that farms borrow, the more the value of their asset base — land — becomes critical to farm survival. Between 1950 and 1960, land values changed by only about 4 percent per year in real value, increasing slowly and steadily. Between 1975 and 1980, the real change was almost 7 percent per year, reflecting a speculative land boom. But then the bottom dropped out, and real land value fell by almost 4 percent per year between 1980 and 1983 (see Figure 1).

DEMOCRATIZING ACCESS TO LAND

All of these features of the farm system indicate that farms can be seriously threatened by forces completely beyond their control. Inflation, the government's monetary policy, the value of the dollar, the size of the federal deficit, growth of foreign competition in agricultural products, bad weather, and decisions by monopolistic suppliers and processors all affect the ability of a family farm to earn a decent income.

Conservative economic policies, however, have speeded up the farm crisis by exacerbating a long-term trend toward concentration of control over the land into fewer and fewer hands. A "solution" to the farm crisis which offers more of the same is bound to fail, at least in the long run. Agricultural surpluses and soil and water depletion will likely continue to get worse if the farm sector is left to "free market" forces. Increasing concentration of land ownership forecloses an economic and cultural option to ordinary people. Solving the farm crisis requires a reorientation of policies and programs toward expanding, rather than contracting, popular access to land. Amidst all the statistics and claims and counterclaims, greater access to the land is the fundamental issue.

NOTE

1. Terminology for describing farms is confusing because different terms are used to describe the same farms. For these classifications, single family or middle-sized family farms are those with sales between $40,000 and $200,000 in real terms (1980 dollars) and larger-than-single family farms as those with sales in real terms over $200,000 (USDA 1984d).

REFERENCES

Boehlje, Michael D. 1985. *An Assessment of Alternative Policy Responses to Financial Stress in Agriculture*. Washington, D.C.: U.S. Government Printing Office.

Breimyer, Harold F. 1985. Agriculture's Problem is Rooted in Washington. *Challenge* (May–June):53–54.

Burbach, Roger and Patricia Flynn. 1980. *Agribusiness in the Americas*. New York: Monthly Review Press.

Connor, John M. and Bruce W. Marion. 1985. Food Manufacturing in the Farm and Food System. In, *The Farm and Food System in Transition*. Ann Arbor: University of Michigan Extension Cooperative Service (43).

Council of Economic Advisors. 1987. *Economic Report of the President*. Washington, D.C.: U.S. Government Printing Office.

Dorow, Norbert A. 1985. The Farm Structure of the Future: Trends and Issues. In, *The Farm and Food System in Transition*. Ann Arbor: University of Michigan Extension Cooperative Service (45).

Easterbrook, Gregg. 1985. Making Sense of Agriculture. *Atlantic* (July):551–562.

Geisler, Charles G. and Frank J. Popper. 1984. *Land Reform, American Style*. Totowa, NJ: Roman & Allanheld.

Lanner, Deborah. 1985. A Farm Bill by and for Farmers. *The Nation* (July 6):19–20.

Manchester, Alden. 1983. The Farm and Food System: Major Characteristics and Trends. In, *The Farm and Food System in Transition*. Ann Arbor: University of Michigan Extension Cooperative Service (1).

Marion, Bruce W. 1985. Food Retailing and Wholesaling: Trends in Competition. In, *The Farm and Food System in Transition*. Ann Arbor: University of Michigan Extension Cooperative Service (41).

McCoy, Charles. 1986. Many Farmers May Face Loan Cutoffs. *Wall Street Journal* (February 24).

Nash, Nathaniel. 1987. Farm Loan Aid Pushed by House. *New York Times* (September 22).

Peterson, Cass. 1985. Hidden Subsidies Alleged in California Irrigation. *Washington Post* (August 22).

Robbins, William. 1985. Surging Value of Dollar Spurs Chaos on Farms. *New York Times* (February).

Schertz, Lyle. 1979. *Another Revolution in U.S. Farming?* Washington, D.C.: U.S. Government Printing Office.

Schneider, Keith. 1987. New Product on Mid-West Farms: Hunger. *New York Times* (Sept. 29):1, 1324.

The Nation. 1985. (March 9):259.

Raup, Phillip M. 1979. Some Questions of Value and Scale in American Agriculture. *American Journal of Agricultural Economics* 61(May):303–308.

Small Farm Advocate. 1984–1985. (Winter).

Stanton, B. F. 1983. What Forces Shape the Farm and Food System? In, *The Farm and Food System in Transition*. Ann Arbor: University of Michigan Extension Cooperative Service (2).

USDA. 1963. *Agricultural Handbook* (258). Washington, D.C.: U.S. Government Printing Office.

_____. 1976. *Agricultural Economic Research Report* (438). Washington, D.C.: U.S. Government Printing Office.

_____. 1981. *A Time To Choose*. Washington, D.C.: U.S. Government Printing Office.

_____. 1983a. *Agricultural Handbook* (258). Washington, D.C.: U.S. Government Printing Office.

_____. 1983b. *Economic Indicators of the Farm Sector: Productivity and Efficiency Statistics*. Washington, D.C.: U.S. Government Printing Office.

_____. 1984a. *Agricultural Economics Research Report* (441). Washington, D.C.: U.S. Government Printing Office.

_____. 1984b. *Agricultural Handbook* (637). Washington, D.C.: U.S. Government Printing Office.

———. 1984c. *Agricultural Information Bulletin* (483). Washington, D.C.: U.S. Government Printing Office.

———. 1984d. *Statistical Reporting Service*. Washington, D.C.: U.S. Government Printing Office.

———. 1985a. *Agricultural Economic Report* (530). Washington, D.C.: U.S. Government Printing Office.

———. 1985b. *Agricultural Economic Report* (534). Washington, D.C.: U.S. Government Printing Office.

———. 1985c. *Agricultural Information Bulletin* (486). Washington, D.C.: U.S. Government Printing Office.

———. 1985d. *Economic Indicators of the Farm Sector, National Financial Summary*. Washington, D.C.: U.S. Government Printing Office.

Wessel, James with Mort Hantman. 1983. *Trading the Future*. San Francisco, CA: Institute for Food and Development Policy.

10

Black-White Income Differences

MICHAEL REICH

Progress in race relations in the United States historically has occurred in concentrated bursts, rather than through a gradual and continuous evolution. These concentrated bursts of progress often have been followed by periods of regress that diminished but did not totally erase the previous advances. The abolition of slavery in 1861 and the Reconstruction Era of the post-bellum years offer the most dramatic cases of concentrated bursts of progress. The Reaction Era that began in 1877 and the subsequent rise of Jim Crow offer an equally dramatic illustration of a period of regress. More recently, the Second World War and the Civil Rights era of the 1960s provide important examples of concentrated bursts of progress, each followed by some reaction.

This pattern of concentrated bursts of progress followed by regress invites explanation. Through an analysis of black-white income differences in the post-World War II era, I attempt such an explanation here for the postwar period. Conventional wisdom notwithstanding, I show that black-white income ratios exhibit a long-swing pattern, with a period of upward trends followed by one of declines. I suggest that neither the supply-based nor the demand-based analyses of conventional economics provides an adequate explanation of the postwar patterns of black-white income differences. I argue that an account that stresses the rise and fall of socio-political movements pressing for institutional change provides a superior explanation.

To preview my approach, consider first the concentrated burst of progress that occurred during World War II. Weaver writes (1948:78): "[The] changes in a period of four years [1940 to 1944] represented more industrial and occupational diversification for Negroes than had occurred in the seventy-five preceding years."

Income data from the 1940 and 1950 censuses indeed indicate the dramatic extent of this progress. During the 1940s the median income of urban black males relative to that of urban white males rose by a fifth, nearly twice the increase recorded during the 1960s. Comparable increases were recorded for black females (Reich 1981:Chap. 2).

Sitkoff's (1978) explanation of these advances is of interest. He does not refer to the gains in educational attainment of blacks in this period, for these were modest; nor to equalizing effects of increasing competitiveness in labor or product markets, for wartime labor and procurement policies make it arguable whether these occurred; nor to the great wartime expansion of demand for labor, for blacks at first did not share in increased employment; nor to government intervention, for President Roosevelt at first opposed equal employment policies.

Instead, Sitkoff assigns the credit to a solidaristic socio-political movement, led by blacks but encompassing a coalition with organized labor, white liberals and white radicals. Constructed painstakingly during the 1930s, this coalition successfully pressured the government in 1941 to open wartime production employment to blacks and to establish, for the first time in U.S. history, nondiscriminatory hiring as official government policy.

Many accounts of the implementation of this new policy (Meier and Rudwick 1979) document employers' resistance to altering the color line. Even under the pressure of wartime the government's antidiscrimination efforts proved effective only when the civil rights and labor movements joined with the Federal government to press employers to hire blacks. Sitkoff's choice of explanatory variables for this important episode thus seems persuasive.

The postwar era constitutes the period of main interest here. Sitkoff's account, I shall suggest, is instructive for economists attempting to understand the racial dynamics of the postwar era. In this period the major political and civil upheavals of the late 1950s, 1960s and early 1970s demolished the separatist and unequal practices that had characterized race relations in the United States since Reconstruction ended in Reaction in 1877. With its major progress toward racial justice and equality in political and civil affairs, this period deserves to be called the Second Era of Reconstruction in U.S. history.

Progress toward racial justice and equality in the economic dimensions of employment and income has not followed such a dramatic trajectory. Blacks no longer are concentrated in the sharecropping agrarian South, which has virtually disappeared, nor in the very lowest paid industrial and domestic employment that had comprised their northern job ghetto before World War II. A much larger proportion of blacks are employed in either the capitalist or government sectors of the economy, many in professional and managerial occupations.

On the other hand, and contrary to much popular and scholarly opinion, progress toward racial equality within the capitalist and government sectors has been severely uneven. Increasing unemployment, declining labor force participation rates and increasing inequality among blacks constitute one set of indicators of unevenness. Changes in the black-white income ratio over the period constitute another. Among men, most of the increase in black-white income ratios was concentrated in the 1960s and early 1970s, with no visible improvement since 1975. Among women, racial progress looks more dramatic: since the early 1970s black and white female incomes have come close to equality. This apparent improvement, however, must be weighed against the continuing inequality between women and men and the considerable postwar divergence in black and white family patterns.

How are these contradictory developments to be understood? Why are the outcomes of the 1980s so different from those of the 1940s and 1960s? In this paper I take up these questions by examining postwar trends and theories concerning male racial economic inequality. The discussion is limited to the case of males both because racial inquality among men has proven more intractable and because the analysis of female racial inequality would require (to an extent that the male racial case does not) an analysis of male-female relations and family structure that is beyond the scope of one paper.

I first show how sectorally-disaggregated data on racial inequality revise popular images of continued racial progress. I then consider alternative theories of racial inequality in capitalist societies characterized by free markets and liberal-democratic governments. The main theories, in my view, break down not into neoclassical, institutional and radical, but into conservative neoclassical, liberal neoclassical and radical-institutional. Against neoclassicals I argue that racial inequality need not disappear even under conditions of perfectly competitive markets. Changes come about not because of economic development or political freedom per se, but because socio-political movements arise that undermine and then restructure the existing institutions and norms of economic and political relations. A radical-institutional conception of the capitalist economic and political process is better equipped to explain recent patterns of change and continuity in race relations.

RACIAL INCOME TRENDS: WHAT IS TO BE EXPLAINED?

Census data show that in the postwar period the median annual income of black males has risen from a level averaging about 55 percent that of whites in the late 1940s to 63 percent in the early 1980s (see Table 1). The annual aggregate figures show considerable short-run cyclical fluctuation. But they also seem to suggest an inescapable conclusion: modest but permanent relative improvement since the war for black men.

This optimistic conclusion is not so inescapable, however. Table 1 also reveals that most of the improvement occurred during the late 1960s and that no improvement has occurred since 1975. Equally important, the familiar aggregate figures of Table 1 obscure as much as they reveal. The published median and mean income statistics, for example, exclude those with zero incomes who have dropped out of the labor force during the year; estimates (Darity 1980; Brown 1981; Hoffman and Link 1984) suggest that about half of the observed improvement in Table 1 may just reflect the declining labor force participation of blacks relative to whites.

Economists of the supply-side, human capital school frequently have argued that racial income data, when disaggregated by age, schooling attainment level and gender of family "head," show even *more* progress than the aggregate figures of Table 1 and that advances in racial equity in schooling in recent decades best explain this racial economic progress (Smith and Welch 1977; Smith 1984; Cain 1985). Many demand-side oriented economists agree that much racial progress has been made, but suggest that growth in the demand for black labor, assisted by governmental anti-discrimination efforts, is primarily responsible. The demand-side view accepts the importance of increased schooling of blacks, but suggests that schooling gains represent a response to improved opportunities (Freeman 1973, 1978; Brown 1981).

Whether the ultimate cause falls on the demand or the supply side, gains attributable to improvements in black schooling undoubtedly are significant. But how much black economic progress is really shown in data disaggregated by schooling and age? And how much of the gains can be attributed to human capital variables? Smith and Welch (1986) represent perhaps the most impressive attempt to measure the importance of schooling variables. However, the evidence marshalled in their article is not conclusive.

One important question simply involves choice of income measures. Smith and Welch (1986) use usual weekly wage figures and exclude individuals who worked less than 26 weeks in the previous year. This reduces the impact of declining black male labor force participation rates and higher black unemployment rates which became significant during the 1970s. I (Reich 1988) have made the same calculations using yearly data, which includes all male workers with nonzero income regardless of the number of weeks worked in the previous year.

Table 1
Ratio of Nonwhite to White Median Income
Postwar United States

Year	Nonwhite Families	Black Families	Nonwhite Males	Nonwhite Females
1945	.56		n.a.	n.a.
1946	.59		.61	n.a.
1947	.51		.54	n.a.
1948	.53		.54	.49
1949	.51		.49	.51
1950	.54		.54	.49
1951	.53		.55	.46
1952	.57		.55	n.a.
1953	.56		.55	.59
1954	.56		.50	.55
1955	.55		.53	.54
1956	.53		.52	.58
1957	.54		.53	.58
1958	.51		.50	.59
1959	.52		.47	.62
1960	.55		.53	.70
1961	.53		.52	.67
1962	.53		.49	.67
1963	.53		.52	.67
1964	.56	.54	.57	.70
1965	.55	.54	.54	.73
1966	.60	.58	.55	.76
1967	.62	.59	.59	.78
1968	.63	.60	.61	.79
1969	.63	.61	.59	.85
1970	.64	.61	.60	.92
1971	.63	.60	.61	.90
1972	.62	.59	.62	.95
1973	.60	.58	.63	.93
1974	.64	.60	.63	.92
1975	.65	.61	.63	.92
1976	.63	.59	.63	.95
1977	.61	.57	.61	.88
1978	.64	.59	.64	.92
1979	.61	.57	.65	.93
1980	.63	.58	.63	.96
1981	.62	.56	.63	.92
1982	.62	.55	.64	.92
1983	.62	.56	.63	.90
1984	.62	.56	n.a.	n.a.

Sources: U.S. Bureau of the Census, "Income of Families and Persons in the United States," *Current Population Reports,* P-60 Series (Washington, D.C.: U.S. Government Printing Office, various years).

Smith and Welch's figures show dramatic improvements in racial equality over the period 1940 to 1980. My figures, however, show a much more modest gain. Both sets of data indicate that much improvement occurred during the war decade of the 1940s and little improvement in the 1950s. But the patterns from 1960 to 1980 look quite different. For example, in these years my estimates indicate that the black-white income ratio among college graduates rose only one-third as much as Smith and Welch's.[1]

The Persistence of Racial Inequality

Disaggregations of black-white male income data, by the characteristics of economic sectors rather than the human capital attributes of individuals, reveals not more but substantially *less* progress than is shown in the postwar aggregate data. This sectoral analysis disaggregates the national black-white male income data by urban-rural differences, regions, metropolitan areas, and detailed industries.[2]

Within each of these sectors black-white differences in traditional supply-side variables, such as years and quality of schooling, age and experience, diminished over this period. The substantial pressure from the civil rights movement and from governmental efforts to reduce discrimination at the same time increased the relative demand for black labor within these sectors. Consequently, a traditional supply-and-demand framework would predict improvements in the relative incomes of blacks within sectors, as well as in the nation as a whole.

For the urban United States, the urban South and the urban nonSouth median income ratios can be calculated from each of the decennial censuses since 1940. During the 1940s the relative income of black males increased substantially in both the urban South and the urban nonSouth. Decreases throughout the urban United States occurred during the 1950s. Between the 1960 and 1970 censuses the relative income of black men improved in the urban South. It deteriorated, however, in the urban nonSouth. Between 1970 and 1980 the black-white income ratio declined in both the urban South and the urban nonSouth. Progress in the urban South ended sometime after 1969, while regress in the urban nonSouth has been continuous since 1949.

A further disaggregation into four regions reinforces these findings. Income data by race and region (but not by urban-rural) are available for each year since 1953. In the Northeast, the Midwest and the West no trend is visible between the mid-1950s and the late 1970s. In two of these regions, the Northeast and the Midwest, black men have fallen farther behind white men since 1979; in the West, a small gain is registered in these years. The biggest gains since the mid-1950s again occurred in the South. However, improvement in this region seems to have ended by 1972.

Racial income data on particular metropolitan areas exhibited a similar pattern. Black-white male income ratios rose slightly between 1949 and 1979 in southern metropolitan areas, but fell considerably more in nonsouthern metropolitan areas. A more detailed tabulation of the 48 largest metropolitan areas in the United States further generalizes this finding.

A final disaggregation examines trends for detailed industries, covering 49 private-sector industries for which consistent decennial census data for the period could be obtained. In 1979 the average black-white male earnings ratio among these detailed industrial sectors was exactly the same as in 1949. Some gains occurred during the 1960s and small declines in the 1950s and 1970s.

Taken together, the findings suggest that some of the national improvement for black males registered in Table 1 occurred because of declines in inequality within economic sectors. But most of the improvement resulted from shifts in the sectoral composition of the economy rather than because of declining inequality within sectors. The national data obscure the continuities in racial inequality within the major urban areas where blacks are now concentrated.

The collapse of the low-income sharecropping South and the associated black outmigration play a major role in these sectoral shifts. Contrary to conventional wisdom, outmigration from the *rural* South did not end in the early 1960s. As late as 1970, 17.3 percent of all blacks and 10.3 percent of all whites still resided in the rural South (Reich 1981:63). The growth of government employment, which paid blacks higher salaries than the private sector, also generated significant intersectoral shifts and raised the observed national ratios.

Within economic sectors, both public and private, the relative position of black males has displayed a modest upward curve, followed by a modest downward one, with little permanent improvement. This pattern suggests that a long-swing mechanism may be at work in the capitalist and government sectors of the economy.

In short, these postwar trends in black-white income differences among blacks raise many interesting questions, and not just for supply or demand theorists. The human capital approach may not explain the limited progress evident in these trends. But can other theoretical approaches do any better? With the trends in the above table in mind, let us turn next to the discussion of alternative theories of racial inequality.

THEORIES OF RACIAL INEQUALITY

How can we understand the persistence of racial inequality in a society such as the modern United States? Unlike the eras of southern slavery or debt peonage and unlike contemporary South Africa, blacks and whites today work in a capitalist economy that is premised upon free labor mobility. Unlike the era of Jim Crow, blacks and whites today live in a liberal democratic policy that is premised upon one-person, one-vote principles. Government policy, moreover, explicitly prohibits discimination based upon race and attempts, through affirmative action programs, to remedy past racial inequities. Schooling, moreover, is supposed to be equally available to all, and racial differences in schooling have narrowed dramatically. With such liberal economic and political institutions, the continuing reality of racial inequality demands explanation.

Among economists the discussion of racial inequality can be categorized into three major approaches. A conservative neoclassical approach regards competitive capitalism as the best cure for racism and attributes the persistence of racial inequality to noncompetitive market structures and to extra-market phenomena, notably the family and the state (including the educational and welfare apparatus). A liberal neoclassical approach takes a less sanguine view of the effects of competitive markets upon racial inequality, has been mainly silent with regard to the family, and has been more sanguine with regard to the efficacy of liberal government interventions. The third approach, which shall be my main concern in this paper, is constituted by both the institutional and radical "worlds" of economics. It emerges from a radical approach to economics that has been developed in the past 15 years, in which, in my view, the similarities between radical and institutional approaches dominate the differences.

In recent years radical economists have developed theoretical tools and analyses to study capitalist economies: for the first time, a Marxist microeconomics has been developed that is distinct from, rather than a subset of the neoclassical approach. And a Marxist-Institutional approach to macroeconomics has been created that is distinctive from both traditional and Marxist macroeconomic theory. These efforts have contributed significantly to our understanding of capitalist economies.[3]

I draw upon these recent innovations in radical economics to develop further a political-economic analysis of racial inequality. In order to contrast the contending positions clearly, I first review the conservative and liberal neoclassical approaches. I then outline the approach to capitalist economies that forms the core of the radical theory.

The Conservative and Liberal Neoclassical Approaches

On the subject of race, neoclassical economics speaks not with one voice, but two. The conservative neoclassical approach sees competitive markets as the great dissolver of racial discrimination, eliminating all differences in factor returns that are not related to differences in individual productivity or preference (for leisure, hazardous work, present vs. future consumption, risk aversion and so forth). The persistence of racial inequality is then attributed either to imperfections in market competition (in which case "pure" discrimination can persist) or to extra-market phenomena, particularly government and family structures and policies that may disadvantage blacks. According to this view, if competitive markets are operating, governmental efforts can only hurt blacks, whether by intention as in the era of Jim Crow, or despite benevolent intentions, as in the current conservative view of governmental anti-poverty, welfare and affirmative action policies as constituting in effect a "government plantation" analogous to the plantations of the cotton era.

The liberal neoclassical view, by contrast, takes a less sanguine view of markets and a more sanguine view of government policy. Markets do not eliminate discrimination because of difficult-to-eradicate imperfections — such as information and personnel costs — and feedback effects. Alternatively, markets might eliminate discrimination but the time period involved is so great as to constitute effective market failure and justify governmental policies.

Since I (1981: Chap. 3) have elsewhere presented a detailed discussion and critique of these two neoclassical approaches I confine myself here to a single summary comment: both conservative and liberal neoclassical approaches ignore conflict and power and consequently contain inadequate accounts of markets and governments. (I leave aside here their treatments of the family.) Alternative approaches to markets and governments, that build upon the institutional and radical traditions to examine changing structures of power in both markets and governments can better aid our understanding of the dynamics of racial inequality.

The Radical Approach to Racial Inequality

The radical view of the capitalist economy builds upon two institutional specifications. First, the distribution of property in the means of production is highly concentrated, so that most households are dependent upon labor incomes. The second institutional specification, related to the first but not reducible to it, states that the labor market is of necessity a market of incomplete contracts. Employers cannot purchase workers with a definite flow of labor services in the way that they can purchase a capital good with a technologically specified flow of capital services. The purchase of labor time does not determine the flow of labor services because workers are conscious human agents who pursue goals that differ at least in part from those of their employers.

These goals are not limited to the pace of work or the extent of compensation; they also include the desire to obtain meaning and identity through work and through social relationships at the workplace. These goals are pursued through both individualistic and solidaristic practices, the mix varying greatly in degree. Such practices, which can coexist with competition among workers, are inherent in workplace relationships. Consequently, for capitalist production to be profitable, a set of managerial practices must be adopted by employers to extract work from workers at an average product wage less than the average product of labor. This specification of the problem of extracting work from workers distinguishes radical theory from traditional neoclassical theory.[4]

The above two institutional specifications can be combined with assumptions of competitive market conditions with flexible wages and no information, monitoring or personnel costs to generate surprising results: involuntary unemployment and wage inequality between black and white workers (of equal productivity and preference characteristics) can persist in competitive equilibrium. The presence of unemployed workers outside the workplace and the presence of wage differences among black and white workers inside the workplace (as well as out) constitute sources of employer power over individual and collective action by employees (Reich 1981:204–215). It is through this power that employers are able to profitably extract work from workers.

The theory thus states that racial wage differentials are profitable to individual employers and will not be competed away, even if employers are not the direct agents of racial discimination. The theory also predicts that inter-racially solidaristic practices by workers will be associated with less racial inequality, higher wages for all workers and lower profits for employers.

Such a theory is difficult to test empirically. Nonetheless, the empirical work that has been performed is consistent with the theory, but not with neoclassical approaches to discrimination. I have already reviewed the persistence of racial income differentials in the face of equalizing pressures in the capitalist sector of the economy. My previous econometric research using detailed industry data also supports the radical theory. I found that black-white wage ratios are positively associated with greater unionism, higher white wages and lower profit rates (Reich 1981:300–303). Similar research across metropolitan areas using size distribution of income data comes to similar conclusions (Reich 1981:Chaps. 4 and 7).

Institutional Variation

This view of the capitalist economic process rejects the conservative neoclassical view that competitive capitalism provides the best cure for racism, or that capitalists constitute a progressive historical force opposing racism. At the same time, the opposite slogan, that capitalism needs racism, seems to me also inadequate. Capitalists can benefit, both individually and in the aggregate, from racial inequality. But there is a complex set of possible relationships among capitalism, government policy and racial inequality. In both the economic and the political realms, progressive coalitions can alter structures of power and, in fact, race relations vary considerably among the advanced capitalist nations. The range on racial issues goes from the more egalitarian, such as Sweden,

Denmark and the Netherlands, to the most brutal, such as South Africa, with the United States and the rest of Western Europe somewhere in between.

To comprehend this particular variation we must see it as part of a more general historical reality. There are many different kinds of actually-existing capitalisms, with no single path of development discernable among them. A satisfactory theory of capitalism needs to be able to encompass and explain these differences.

Elsewhere, Gordon, Edwards and Reich (1982) have sketched an institutional theory of the sources of historical variations in capitalist countries. This theory emphasizes the importance of the institutional environment that surrounds the capitalist accumulation process. The institutions that form this environment together constitute what we call the social structure of accumulation. The rise and decline of a social structure of accumulation is correlated with long swings in economic activity and delineates succesive stages of capitalist development. A new social structure of accumulation emerges when a complex and lengthy struggle among classes and groups is resolved and a new governing coalition is able to institute its reform program.

I cannot in this paper develop a full analysis of the relationship between race relations and the social structure of accumulation. Instead, I present some schematic remarks concerning the dynamics of postwar race relations and their connection to the rise and decline of the postwar social structure of accumulation. These remarks illustrate how I would use the social structure of accumulation framework.

To begin, consider the role of racial issues in the construction of the postwar limited capital-labor accord, which constitutes a central element of the liberal postwar social structure of accumulation. The limited accord between organized labor and capital emerged from the 1940s resolutions of labor struggles that had been waged since the 1930s. A relatively egalitarian approach to race relations by the industrial union proved to be a critical variable in these struggles (Meier and Rudwick 1979; Reich 1981: Chap. 5). Earlier attempts to organize industrial workers had foundered largely on the divisive factor of race, as many employers of blacks, such as Henry Ford, well knew.

The formation of a multi-racial coalition among industrial workers therefore constituted a key innovation in the early successes of the CIO. Had this breakthrough in race relations not occurred, the CIO's strength certainly would have been much diminished. Despite all its well-known limitations, this proved to be the first durable multiracial coalition among U.S. workers in the nation's history. The CIO's experience contrasts especially with the record of other New Deal era reforms, none of which significantly changed the lives of blacks for the better.

Both black and white workers in the industrial unions gained enormously from the CIO's efforts. Blacks particularly benefited from the CIO opposition to racial segregation and the policy of disproportionately raising the wages of unskilled workers. The experiences of this period show that race and class issues can be brought together in struggles without sacrificing the integrity of either issue. Bringing them together resulted not in divisive splits or a longer list of demands, but in a progressive coalition whose whole was greater than the sum of its parts.

The changes of the 1930s were contained by the late 1940s as the limited capital-labor accord became solidified. A key turning point occurred in 1948 when the labor movement's campaign to extend unionization to the largely unorganized South failed dismally. The major reason for this debacle involved a decision not to challenge the pattern of southern race relations. The labor movement's failure to challenge race relations in the South defined the point beyond which labor could make no further gains. Progress in race relations proved critical in the formation of the CIO, and regress in race relations proved critical in its containment.

Under the capital-labor accord, blacks inside the industrial sector had made some gains. But the majority of blacks remained outside, either in what we now call the secondary sector of the labor market or outside the wage-labor sector altogether, trapped in the sharecropping economy of the agrarian South. The exclusion of most blacks from the limited capital-labor accord soon generated pressures upon it. From 1957 on, a mass civil rights movement gathered steam, initially in the South. The early attention of the civil rights movement was centered entirely upon the dismantling of legal segregation and disfranchisement in the South.

At first the movement had little impact upon the capitalist sector, where blacks still mainly provided a supply of low-wage labor to employers. By the late 1960s this structure began to change, as the combined effects of the civil rights movements and the booming demand for labor succeeded in opening many primary sector jobs, blue-collar and white-collar, to black workers. Blacks became much more heavily represented in the traditional working class than ever before, and at a rate of change much greater than in any period since the Second World War. Equally important, the black consciousness movements of the period transformed the expectations of black workers, who no longer formed a docile low-wage labor supply.

The civil rights movement also ignited other movements in the 1960s and 1970s, including feminist, anti-war, environmental and labor struggles. Collectively, and in conjunction with other contemporary developments, these movements contributed to the decay of the capital-labor accord and other key elements of the postwar social structure of accumulation. By the early 1970s the collective strength of coalitions of the labor movement joined with various social movements had grown considerably. The concomitant decline in the strength and power of capital was equally advanced. The decline in the power of capital first became highly visible in the aftermath of the 1973 oil crisis, when much of the burden of adjustment for higher energy prices fell upon capital, and in the deep 1974–75 recession, when labor, minorities and women were able to maintain their relative position and again capital proved surprisingly weak.

By the mid-1970s economic pressure — inflation and slower growth in real wages — were beginning to be felt by many whites as well as blacks, placing strains upon interracial alliances. At about the same time capital began a systematic counter-offensive to restore its former power. In this counter-offensive two racial factors played an important part. Each contributed to the end of the period of black advancement and disproportionately benefited capital.

First, visions of a greater social good and of greater racial equality to be jointly brought about through multiracial coalitions acting collectively were repeatedly challenged and defeated. The process by which this occurred was complex. Challenges were frequently organized by capital, as could be seen in the furor over the very limited affirmative action employment programs in place in the 1970s (recall the hysteria over the Bakke case). Many whites also participated actively in these challenges. Many white conservative, liberal and radical elements in all layers of American society at the time saw further racial progress as a zero-sum game, played at white expense.

The econometric evidence in *Racial Inequality* established that a nonzero-sum game, based on class rather than race conflict, could have been played. But by the 1970s the 1930s conception of the integration of race and class issues through a broader reform process was largely absent from existing understandings and programs. As a result whites and blacks lost an opportunity for progressive reform that would have benefited both.

A second racial element of the capitalist counter-offensive also contributed both to the end of the period of advancement for blacks and the re-establishment of capitalist power in the labor market. By the late 1960s employers began to recognize that blacks were no longer a source of docile and cheap labor. This shift in the character of the black labor supply should be understood primarily in terms of the heightened consciousness of blacks developed by the civil rights movement and only secondarily as resulting from the growth of transfer payments (in part also a result of the civil rights movement). In any case, employers began actively to recruit and to switch to new labor supplies, mainly Latinos already in the United States and new immigrants from Latin America, the Carribean, Asia, the Pacific Islands and elsewhere. These groups became a major source of new labor supplies for the private sector. At the same time, the growth of government, which had been the fastest growing employment sector for blacks, slowed substantially. The two-fold reduction in the demand for black labor explains declining black employment to population ratios in this period. (No expansion in black labor supply occurred when transfer payments were reduced in the 1980s.) Employers succeeded in re-establishing low-wage employment, which grew rapidly, but a remarkably small percentage of these jobs were filled by blacks.

The reconstruction of race relations proved to be an important part of the capitalist counter-offensive. The result of this counter-offensive is clear: the rise of a vision and reality dominated by competition among all and social meanness toward disadvantaged groups. Was this not a preview, or rather, the first act of the drama that we now know as the broader conservative political shift of the past decade?

CONCLUSIONS

I conclude that progress and regress in race relations do not depend in a simple manner upon traditional labor economic variables unmediated by considerations of power and conflict. In the prewar and the postwar eras progress in race relations has depended upon the development of inter-racial class and multiclass coalitions and the ability of such coalitions to conceptualize and effect progressive reform programs that would transform black-white relations from perceived zero-sum games into nonzero-sum games. High rates of economic growth can create permissive conditions for such coalitions and nonzero-sum games to develop. But the extent to which they are effective depends upon power relations that are not themselves reducible to traditional economic variables.

The improvement in the relative position of black men in the 1960s was not just the product of high rates of economic growth, as James Tobin argued at the time. It was also directly connected to the socio-political movements pressuring for change in that decade.

These movements did not succeed in creating a nonzero-sum game based upon class rather than race conflict. As a result, little was left of these movements by the early 1970s. As a further consequence, existing pressure upon the capitalist and government sectors to maintain affirmative action and other such programs soon further eroded, ushering in the current era of reaction.[5]

NOTES

1. I would also question the completeness of the human capital explanations. Cross-sectional data usually show that black-white income ratios for particular schooling groups decline with increasing age. Some have interpreted this decline as the result of on-going discimination, particularly in career promotions; others as the result of segmented labor markets. Human capital theorists see this pattern as the result of the lower relative quality of black schooling in earlier decades — the so-called vintage effect. One cannot doubt the improved relative quality of black schooling since the 1930s and earlier. However, Smith and Welch's contention that the quantity, quality and vintage of human capital accounts for much of the variation in black-white income ratios over time is not so persuasive.

First, the results seem to hold mainly for college-educated blacks; much smaller improvements in income are found for lower schooling groups. Since improvements in quality occurred at all schooling levels, the divergent trends in earnings seem to confound the human capital explanation. Second, as I have already mentioned, the extent of improvement is not clear, and even Smith and Welch's data show continuing unexplained black-white income differences. Third, cohort data show that black-white income ratios rose over time well after the cohorts completed their schooling. Since blacks in these cohorts are not likely to have received more on-the-job training or experience over their careers than whites, the continuing increases in relative incomes must have been due to other than human capital-related explanations. Fourth, several researchers have used longitudinal data sets to obtain more appealing tests of the vintage hypothesis than is possible from moving cross-sectional data. Their results often contradict the vintage hypothesis and support the segmented labor market or promotion discrimination hypotheses (Hoffman 1979; Lazear 1979; Duncan 1981). Fifth, historical research in progress by Gavin Wright (1984) has shown that prewar trends in racial wage differentials were often related not to human capital variables but to institutional variables such as the extent and type of labor union power. Finally, changes in the extent of schooling and the returns to schooling themselves reflect institutional variables not analyzed by human capital theories. (Levin 1979 provides a cogent alternative account emphasizing the role of the civil rights movement.) For all these reasons, human capital approaches seem incomplete as explanations of either past or present trends of racial inequality.

2. For detailed data, see Reich (1988).

3. Gintis (1976); Reich (1981); Reich and Devine (1981); Gordon, Edwards and Reich (1982); Bowles, Gordon and Weisskopf (1983); Bowles and Edwards (1984); Bowles (1985); Bowles and Edwards (1985).

4. Recent neoclassical literature on the employment relationships shows greater signs of similarity, but substantial differences remain. See Reich and Devine (1981) and Bowles (1985).

5. For qualifications of this conclusion, see Reich (1988).

REFERENCES

Bowles, Samuel. 1985. The Production Process in a Competitive Economy: Walrasian, Neo-Hobbesian and Marxian Approaches. *American Economic Review* 75(1):16–36.

_____ and Richard Edwards. 1984. Theoretical Developments in Radical Political Economy. Paper presented at the American Economic Association meetings. Dallas, Texas.

_____. 1985. *Understanding Capitalism*. New York: Harper and Row.

_____, David M. Gordon and Thomas E. Weisskopf. 1983. *Beyond the Waste Land*. New York: Anchor Doubleday.

Brown, Charles. 1981. Black/White Earnings Ratios Since the Civil Rights Act of 1964: The Importance of Labor Market Dropouts. Working Paper 617, National Bureau of Economic Research.

Cain, Glen G. 1985. The Economic Analysis of Labor Market Discrimination: A Survey. Special Report No. 37. Institute for Research on Poverty. University of Wisconsin. Madison.

Darity, William G. 1980. Illusions of Black Economic Progress. *Review of Black Political Economy* 10:153–168.

Duncan, Greg. 1981. Recent Trends in the Relative Earnings of Black Men. Survey Research Center, University of Michigan.

Edwards, Richard. 1979. *Contested Terrain: The Transformation of the Workplace in the Twentieth Century*. New York: Basic.

_____, Michael Reich and Thomas E. Weisskopf. 1986. *The Capitalist System*. Third edition. Englewood Cliffs, NJ: Prentice-Hall.

Freeman, Richard B. 1973. The Changing Labor Market for Black Americans, 1948–72. *Brookings Papers on Economic Activity*:67–120.

_____. 1978. Time Series Evidence on Black Economic Progress: Shifts in Demand or in Supply. Discussion paper 632, Harvard Institute of Economic Research.

Fusfeld, Daniel R. and Timothy Bates. 1984. *The Political Economy of the Urban Ghetto*. Carbondale IL: Southern Illinois University Press.

Gintis, Herbert M. 1976. The Nature of the Labor Exchange and the Theory of Capitalist Production. *Review of Radical Political Economics* 8:36–54.

Gordon, David M., Richard Edwards and Michael Reich. 1982. *Segmented Work, Divided Workers*. New York: Cambridge University Press.

Hoffman, Saul D. 1979. Black-White Life Cycle Earnings Differences and the Vintage Hypothesis: A Longitudinal Analysis. *American Economic Review* 69:855–867.

_____ and Charles R. Link. 1984. Selectivity Bias in Male Wage Equations: Black-White Comparisons. *Review of Economics and Statistics* 66:320–324.

Lazear, Edward. 1979. The Narrowing of the Black-White Wage Gap is Illusory. *American Economic Review* 69:553–564.

Levin, Henry M. 1979. Education and Earnings of Blacks and the Brown Decision. Report 79-B13. Institute for Research on Educational Finance and Governance, Stanford University.

Meier, August and Elliott Rudwick. 1979. *Black Detroit and the Rise of the UAW*. New York: Oxford University Press.

Reich, Michael. 1981. *Racial Inequality: A Political-Economic Analysis*. Princeton: Princeton University Press.

_____. 1988. Postwar Racial Income Differences: Trends and Theories. In, *The Three Worlds of Labor Economics,* Garth Mangum and Peter Philips (eds.). White Plains: M.E. Sharpe, Inc.

_____ and James Devine. 1981. The Microeconomics of Conflict and Hierarchy in Capitalist Production. *Review of Radical Political Economics* 12:27–35.

Sitkoff, Harvard. 1978. *A New Deal for Blacks*. New York: Oxford University Press.

Smith, James P. and Finis Welch. 1986. *Forty Years of Progress*. Santa Monica: Rand.

Weaver, Robert. 1948. *Negro Labor: A National Problem*. New York: Harcourt and Brace.

Wright, Gavin. 1984. Race and the Labor Market in Virginia, 1900–1926. Department of Economics, Stanford University.

11

Black Youth Employment Problems

ROBERT CHERRY

Despite extensive Civil Rights legislation, unemployment rates for black males aged 16–19 and 20–24 years old have remained over 30 percent and over 20 percent, respectively. These rates are more than double those of comparably-aged white males. Between 1969 and 1977, black male labor force participation rates fell dramatically and continued to decline afterwards. In contrast, the labor force participation rates for white male youths increased between 1969 and 1977 and fell only modestly thereafter. As a result, since 1969 there has been a striking change in black but not white youth *employment* rates — the percentage of youth employed. Table 1 indicates that employment rates for black male teenagers are only one-half those of white male teenagers; for youth aged 20–24 years old, the black employment rate is only three-quarters the white rate.

Table 1
Black and White Male Employment Rates, 1969–86

Age	Black Employment Rate				White Employment Rate				Black–White Ratio			
	1969	1977	1984	1986	1969	1977	1984	1986	1969	1977	1984	1986
16–17	28.4	18.9	15.1	17.6	42.7	44.3	37.7	39.7	0.67	0.43	0.40	0.44
18–19	51.1	36.9	32.5	36.2	61.8	65.2	60.2	60.1	0.83	0.57	0.58	0.61
20–24	77.3	61.2	58.1	61.3	78.8	80.5	78.0	79.3	0.98	0.76	0.75	0.77

Source: U.S. Bureau of Census, *Employment and Earnings* (various years).

Economists have varied interpretations of this data. They disagree as to the seriousness of the employment problems, the role government policies have played, and the reasons for the black–white employment differential. Conservatives tend to believe that more accurate measures would indicate that black youth employment problems are not very serious, affecting only a small percentage of the black youth population. Moreover, conservatives contend that to the extent problems exist, they reflect the internal inadequacies of black youth, compounded by the adverse effects of government anti-poverty policies: welfare and minimum wage legislation.

Liberals reject conservative beliefs that internal inadequacies of black youths or problems created by government policies are responsible for the persistence of high unemployment and low employment rates among young black males. Instead, liberals emphasize external factors: declining employment opportunities due to a weakening of economic growth and increasing labor market imbalances. They also note that discrimination continues to effect black workers adversely.

Radicals believe more strongly than liberals that discrimination has a decisive influence on black youth employment rates. Liberals tend to believe that capitalists have no financial stake in the perpetuation of discriminatory hiring practices and thus do not believe they can remain once affirmative action programs are instituted. In contrast, radicals believe capitalists have a strong economic stake in their perpetuation and thus believe that affirmative action has had only a modest impact on discriminatory hiring practices. Moreover, radicals contend that changes in labor markets during the post-World War II period have led firms to rely *increasingly* on racial discrimination, worsening the position of black youth. This paper summarizes these contrasting viewpoints.

EMPLOYMENT PROBLEMS

Many economists do not believe the official unemployment rate is an accurate measure of the labor market difficulties experienced by youth. Wachter and Kim (1982) construct an adjusted unemployment rate by assuming military service or school attendance are equivalent to employment. In this case, the only unemployment counted would be out-of-school youth who are engaged in active search. We would also adjust the "labor" force to include individuals if they are either in school or the military. These adjustments dramatically lower measured unemployment rates. Whereas the official unemployment rate (1978) for black youths aged 16–17, 18–19, and 20–24 years old was 40.7 percent, 30.9 percent, and 20.1 percent respectively, the adjusted rate was only 7.8 percent, 14.2 percent, and 13.6 percent respectively.

Not only does it appear that rates are quite low once they are adjusted for military enlistment and schooling but problems may be serious for only a small percentage of youths. Martin Feldstein and David Ellwood (1982) document that for youth as a whole, unemployment is a momentary occurrence if it occurs at all. They find that sustained unemployment — more than twenty-six weeks — is experienced by only 8 percent of the youth population; a group of 250,000 youths.

Feldstein and Ellwood also minimize the seriousness of the high percentage of youths who are neither in school nor in the labor force. They reject the notion that these youths are "discouraged" workers — individuals who do not seek employment due to a lack of available jobs. They cite the doubling of youth employment during summer months as an indication of the large demand for youth employment. Moreover, surveys indicate that the vast majority of the out-of-school, out-of-work population live with parents and thus, according to Feldstein and Ellwood, have little pressure to seek employment.

Feldstein and Ellwood contend that much of the youth racial unemployment differential is due to education and family income differences rather than racial discrimination. Black youth tend to have less income and live in poorer households than white youth. If black youth had the same education and came from households with the same family income as white youths, more than 50 percent of the racial unemployment differential would be eliminated.

Liberal and radical economists do not agree with Feldstein and Ellwood that employment problems are severe only for a small percentage of black youth. Using the same data set, Freeman and Medoff (1982:44) point out that 21 percent of 20–24 year-old, out-of-school black men had no work experience in the previous year. This was more than double the white rate (7.2 percent) and almost double the black rate seven years earlier (12.8 percent).

Feldstein and Ellwood (1982) emphasize that unemployment is concentrated among high school dropouts who live in poor households. Though they minimize the significance of the large out-of-school, out-of-the-labor force youth population, their data indicates otherwise. Almost 30 percent of black high school graduates aged 20–24 years old, are out of the labor force. Also, unemployment and labor force participation rates are the same for black youths living in low-income and middle-income households. Thus, for black youth, gaining a high school degree or being fortunate enough to live in a middle-income household does not eliminate severe employment problems.

The shortness of spells of youth unemployment Feldstein and Ellwood document reflects their measurement technique: they consider an unemployment spell to end if either the individual finds employment or drops out of the labor force. Since more than one-half of the unemployment spells of in-school youth end within a month due to exit from the labor force it is not surprising that measured unemployment spells are short. Clark and Summers (1982) contend that these movements out of the labor force reflect an inability to find employment. Thus for them, the appropriate measure is the duration of "joblessness" — how long do youth spend *between* jobs. They find that for high school graduates, the average duration of joblessness is over six months and for high school dropouts almost ten months.

Clark and Summers also contend that black youth have much more difficulty finding employment than white youth; they have a lower probability of gaining employment whether they are officially unemployed or not in the labor force. Ballen and Freeman (1986:99) believe this is a result of the hiring criteria used by firms; firms are sensitive to spotty work records in their black but not white youth applicants. Again, we find the high proportion of black youths who are outside of the labor force is a serious problem not to be trivialized.

INTERNAL INADEQUACIES

Conservatives contend that black labor market failures reflect internal inadequacies. Summarizing this perspective, Glen Loury (1985:14) claims: "The next frontier for the black community is to grapple with the internal problems which lower class blacks now face." As evidence that cultural factors strongly influence labor market outcomes, Datcher-Loury and Loury (1986) and Freeman (1986a) cite evidence that there is a significant positive correlation between church attendance and productive time (school, work, or household activities). Freeman also finds that family environment played a significant role in determining the productive activity of young black males; the more parents work, the more time youth will spend at productive activities. These studies yield results consistent with the culture of poverty thesis: growing up in poor households, black youth develop dysfunctional attitudes which increase their likelihood of remaining poor.

Many conservatives claim that black nonemployment reflects voluntary choice rather than a lack of jobs. They contend that black youth set too high a reservation wage — the lowest wage at which they would be willing to work. Varied explanations are given.

Kip Viscusi (1986) has found that for a large proportion of black innercity youth, criminal activity is a quite acceptable alternative to legal employment. Basing his assessment on Viscusi's findings, Harry Holzer (1986:51) contends: "[O]utside income generated by illegal activities (and other sources) for young blacks with low skill levels may be an important source of their relatively high reservation wage."

Christopher Jencks (1987) associates it with rising expectations. He claims that blacks believed that their inability to attain good jobs in the 1960s was due solely to discrimination. As a result they thought that once discrimination was illegal they would be able to obtain these jobs so that they were unwilling to take lower paying traditional jobs. Similarly, Elijah Anderson (1980) suggests that current youth, having developed a new consciousness and set of expectations as a result of the civil rights movement, shun low status jobs; jobs which in the past had been associated with racial degradation.

Data consistently indicates that black youth are much more likely to be fired or laid off than white youth. According to liberals, black youth tend to have higher termination rates as a result of discrimination or their lack of seniority. In contrast, conservatives believe that the source must be internal inadequacies which undermine work ethics. Sometimes conservatives cite government data which indicate that black youth have a higher rate of absenteeism than white youth. Walter Williams (1985:50) claims that as a result of these inadequacies, black youth are much less productive than white youth; hence, they are more likely to be laid off.

Conservatives believe black youth have severe internal inadequacies: poor work ethics, high reservation wage, and high absenteeism. Liberals believe that to the extent black youth exhibit behavioral problems, they are due to a maladaption to discriminatory barriers and do not significantly affect racial employment differentials. More importantly, liberals question the validity of conservative assertions that black youth have more behavioral problems than white youth.

Even if black youth have a higher reservation wage, it is likely an outgrowth of the migration process. Michael Piore (1979) argues that rural migrants to urban areas have willingly accepted the lowest rung jobs because they still represented upward mobility. For their children, however, these jobs do not represent mobility, so will be rejected. Thus, independent of race, Piore conjectures that all second-generation migrants will reject low-wage dead-end employment. It is only because black youth have not had the opportunity for upward mobility that this has resulted in black youth employment problems.

Even if criminal activity adversely affects black youth, its importance is overstated by conservatives. Data tabulated by Richard Freeman (1986b) indicates that the employment rate differential between those who did and those who did not commit crime was entirely the result of the lack of employment of a small hardcore — those who had spent time in jail the previous year. The legal employment record of the other 84 percent who committed crimes was virtually the same as that of youths who reported they did not commit crimes in the previous year. Second, even if there was no crimes committed, the unemployment rate among innercity black youth would have declined from 50 percent to 37 percent, leaving it still far above that of white youth.

Critics also question conservative claims that black youth have dysfunctional behavioral traits compared to white youth. Studies (Wachter and Kim 1982; Culp and Dunson 1986) find that the wage rates at which black innercity youths will accept employment are virtually the same as white youths. However, since the actual wages paid to black youths are below those paid to white youths, researchers characterize this as blacks having a higher reservation wage *relative* to earnings. While black youth may be "unrealistic" in attempting to earn wages similar to white youths, this hardly supports conservative claims that blacks reject job offers which white youth are willing to accept.

While black youths have higher rates of absenteeism than white youths, Allen (1981) and Ferguson and Filer (1986) found that the differences could be accounted for by differences in job characteristics. Black youth have a disproportionate share of the dead-end jobs everyone quits. If black and white youths were employed at jobs with the same characteristics, there would be no difference between their rates of absenteeism. Jackson and Montgomery (1986) found that even among youth, black workers have less job tenure than white workers and this has a significant impact on job-loss rates. They (1986:131) contend, "[I]ndustry and occupation may explain part of the black-white difference in job-loss rates." These studies indicate that black youth are not very different than white youth: give them decent jobs and they will behave just as responsibly.

WELFARE PROGRAMS

Conservatives generally believe that welfare programs have had an adverse impact on black youth employment rates. As already mentioned, Freeman (1986a) and Lerman (1986) found that black youth growing up in a welfare household were much more likely to have employment difficulties than comparably-educated black youth growing up in a working family even after holding income and family structure constant. Wachter and Kim (1982) suggest that availability of welfare raises the reservation wage of black youth, resulting in their having higher nonemployment rates.

Charles Murray (1984) also believes that welfare generates significant work disincentives. He reviews federally-funded negative income tax (NIT) studies to determine the impact on labor supplies (hours of work) if the government increased guaranteed welfare payments. He takes as representative the Seattle-Denver NIT results, which estimated a 40 percent decline in the youth labor supply. Murray (1984:151) considers this most damaging because this was a "critical age in their lives: about to enter into responsibilities of marriage and just establishing themselves in the labor force."

Even if living in welfare households is associated with less employment, Samuel Myers (1986) claims that the relationship is far more complex than conservatives believe. Myers notes that the percentage of black youth 18–24 years old living at home is double that of comparably-aged white youth. For Myers, this suggests that black youth, unable to find employment, are forced to remain at home, often in a welfare household. Thus, he believes that the correlation between nonemployment and living in a welfare household reflects deficient job opportunities rather than cultural deficiencies of welfare households.

Critics believe conservatives overstate the impact of welfare on work ethics. John Cogan (1982) found that between 1950 and 1970, the black teenage employment rate rose from 26 percent to 27 percent in the North but declined from 55 percent to 27 percent in the South. This occurred despite the fact that the growth in AFDC participation rates was three times faster in the North than in the South.

Critics contend that the large impact in NIT studies which Murray emphasizes are questionable to generalize from: the NIT transfers were far more generous than the actual welfare system and the vast majority of the labor supply withdrawals were by youth in school who presumably were now able to spend more time on their education. Myers (1986:440) also finds that an increase in welfare recipiency has little effect on black-white earnings ratios, causing him to claim: "These results . . . dim any hopes of finding major new explanations for wage inequality in the phenomenon of welfare participation."

MINIMUM WAGE LEGISLATION

Minimum wage legislation is the most widely accepted explanation for high youth unemployment rates. A higher minimum wage raises labor costs, forcing firms to raise prices. When consumers reduce their demand, firms must cutback their production and labor demand. Firms also might reduce their labor demand since it may now become cost effective to automate production. Minimum wage critics generally believe that this disemployment effect creates hardship for a large enough segment of the low-wage work force that it outweighs benefits received by those fortunate enough to keep their jobs.

Since many believe that black youth are the least productive workers, it follows that they should experience a disproportionate share of the layoffs which result. Summarizing this position, Baumol and Blinder (1979:510) state that minimum wage law "though apparently designed to protect low-skilled workers, is in fact a crippling impediment to any attempt to improve job opportunities for blacks."

Many economists believe that the minimum wage does not have a negative impact on black youth employment. First, these proponents (Cherry 1985) note that if the demand decline results in most workers experiencing either a modest decline in the hours of employment per week or weeks worked per year, they would still benefit; though they have less hours per year of work, this is more than offset by the higher hourly wage. A numerical example will illustrate these points.

Suppose, at the current minimum wage of $3.35/hour individuals are working fulltime year-round (2080 hours/year) so that they have yearly earnings of $6968. If the minimum wage was raised to $4/hour they would have a higher yearly income as long as they worked at least 1742 hours per year; the equivalent of slightly less than 44 weeks. Thus even if workers are laid-off, as long as their unemployment is less than two months they have both more income and more nonmarket time. Given the small labor demand elasticity most studies find and the high turnover in many low-wage jobs, this outcome is quite plausible. Indeed, even if individuals suffer somewhat greater unemployment, their situation would be improved if they value the gained nonmarket time more than the lost income.

Proponents also reject any notions that black youth are the least productive members of the low-wage work force. Interestingly, there is little evidence that black youth suffer disproportionately. Brown, Gilroy, and Kohn (1982) find that there are as many studies which indicate black youth experience a smaller disemployment effect than white youth as those which indicate that it is greater. They (1982:508) conclude that any contention that black youth are differentially affected "must rest on theoretical rather than empirical grounds."

LIBERAL VIEWS ON BLACK YOUTH UNEMPLOYMENT

Liberal explanations emphasize influences external to black youths: the overall strength of aggregate demand, labor market imbalances, and discriminatory barriers. According to Clark and Summers (1982:227): "The teenage unemployment problem is not the lack of desire to hold jobs, but the inability to find work." In a study of job advertisements, they found that for most low-wage jobs requiring no skills or previous experience, employers were swamped with applications. When they focused on the very worst jobs advertised in the Sunday paper, they found an average of fifteen to twenty responses within two days of the ad's placement.

During the 1970s, the job market for teenagers deteriorated for two reasons: a less robust economy and an overcrowding of youth and women in low-wage markets. Clark and Summers find that teenage employment is especially sensitive to the overall state of the economy. They estimate that for each one-point decrease in the prime-age male unemployment rate — a proxy for the general vitality of the economy — there would be a 4.5 percent increase in the teenage employment rate; for black teenagers the increase would be 6.3 percent. They (1982:226) note that between 1969 and 1976, when the aggregate unemployment rate rose from 3.6 percent to 7.7 percent, "The proportion of 16–19 year olds suffering more than six months unemployment rose fourfold. For black youths the same figure increased by almost six times."

During the 1970s, there was a dramatic increase in the labor force participation rates of teenagers and adult women. The result was an overcrowding of applicants in low-wage labor markets. Not surprisingly, real wages for low-wage workers declined. Dooley and Gottschalk (1985) find that the percentage of male workers earning low wages increased from 15.4 percent in 1969 to 21.0 percent in 1977. Watcher and Kim (1982) found that the earnings of male youth deteriorated even further since the ratio of youth-to-adult male earnings declined during this period. The decline was relatively greater for white youth who were able to maintain employment in the face of adverse labor market conditions by adjusting downward their wage demands. Freeman and Wise (1982:10) believe that the reduction in the gap between white and black youth wage rates "contributed to the deterioration in the black versus white [youth] employment."

Many investigators (Clark and Summers 1982) find that low-wage jobs are filled through personal contacts rather than through public advertising. Businesses will often hire by asking relatives, neighbors, or current employees to identify applicants. Using these informal networks lowers screening costs. Moreover, employers are more confident when relying on trusted recommendations than on an applicant pool generated by advertisements. Hiring through informal networks is advantageous to white youths since there are a disproportionate number of white-owned firms. This differential access to information is magnified by segregated housing, schooling, and social arrangements.

After World War II the large black migration to northern urban areas began. Previously, blacks lived in southern rural areas. Even when the farmwork done was minimal, they were considered employed. As a result of this "disguised" rural unemployment, simply by shifting from a rural to urban environment, the official measure of the black youth unemployment would increase. Indeed, John Cogan (1982) estimates that the entire growth in black youth unemployment rates between 1950 and 1970 can be explained by the decline in the number of agricultural jobs available to southern youth.

Many liberal economist contend that black employment is lower the further away firms located from black residential areas. Commuting costs — time and money — make it unrealistic for black youths to consider employment at firms which are distant from their homes. In this case, the movement of low-wage manufacturing and service sector jobs away from the central business district could explain the increasing employment difficulties innercity black youths have been experiencing.

RADICAL VIEWS ON BLACK YOUTH UNEMPLOYMENT

Radicals believe that liberal critiques of conservative views are extremely useful. These critiques undermine racial stereotypes and the view that internal inadequacies are responsible for low black youth employment rates. However, radicals believe that liberal explanations understate the importance of combatting discriminatory practices. Even when research (Clark and Summers 1982; Culp and Dunson 1986) document the consistent racist nature of employment practices, liberals refuse to emphasize anti-discrimination legislation. Since liberals believe racism is not in the interest of capitalists, they view these racist practices as anamolies and/or atavisms and feel more comfortable emphasizing other structural factors. In contrast, radicals believe that racism is the fundamental cause of black employment problems.

Radical and liberal differences are illustrated by their contrasting evaluations of training programs and the spatial mismatch theory. Liberals believe training programs are important and believe the suburbanization of employment opportunities has been responsible for increased black employment difficulties. Thus, when conservatives cite studies that training programs have had little impact on black earnings or that the spatial location of jobs has had little influence on black employment, liberals are quick to claim they are faulty. In contrast, radicals do not find these studies threatening since they tend to believe that without a fundamental attack on the racist hiring practices of firms, higher skill levels and/or lower commuting requirements will have little impact on black employment.

Radicals contend that racism persists because it serves the financial and political interests of capitalists. Racism enables capitalists to maintain an underemployed work force — an industrial reserve army. This group can be underpaid and overworked either directly or through subcontracting. They can be used as a threat against better-paid white workers. Radicals also believe that racism allows the government to reduce social spending by dividing the working class. It encourages white workers to blame blacks for inadequate living standards and inadequate public services.

Radicals believe that American capitalism required increased racism after World War II. Until the 1930s, European immigrants provided U.S. capitalism with an industrial reserve army. Their integration into American society created potential labor shortages. However, the movement of blacks out of agriculture in the post-World War II period provided capitalism with a new industrial reserve army.

Political considerations also impacted adversely on black workers (Cherry 1977). After World War II there was a concerted effort to purge communist influence from unions. Communists had gained considerable influence as a result of their leadership in union organizing and relief efforts during the Depression. After the Taft-Hartley Act made it illegal for communists to be union officials, many firms gave their workers generous contracts to convince them that they could win more with anti-communist than communist leadership.

These developments intensified racism in two ways. First, it was communists who had fought for multi-racial unity within the union movement. They convinced many white workers that through unity all workers gain. This made distinctions between the Congress of Industrial Organizations (CIO) and the American Federation of Labor (AFL) clear. With the elimination of communists, the new leadership convinced their white membership that there was more to be gained by uniting with the racist AFL than maintaining unity with black workers. Thus, the elimination of communists resulted in the weakening of racial unity within the union movement and the increased willingness of union leaders to adopt racist strategies (Fusfeld and Bates 1984).

Second, desiring to minimize the concessions given to unions, firms began to shift portions of production to the nonunion sector or move their production away from high-wage urban areas. While a modest segment of white unionized workers benefitted, these policies generated greater inequality among blue-collar workers. Though they gained access to manufacturing jobs, black workers dominated the expanding low-wage tier (Bonacich 1976).

National black–white income data disguised this intensification of racism. As long as blacks were moving out of agriculture, low-wage manufacturing employment was an improvement so that the national black–white income ratio rose modestly, However, Michael Reich (1981) has shown that within urban areas and within occupations, black–white income ratios were unchanged; this despite the dramatic improvements in the education and skills of black workers compared to their white counterparts.

Up until the 1970s, U.S. capitalism was the unchallenged world industrial power. If even then black workers had to run faster just to stay in place, it is not surprising that with increased international competition and worldwide economic stagnation, their position would deteriorate. With growing international competition, there are not enough markets for all so that excess industrial capacity will appear worldwide. As a result, racism becomes an important vehicle to rationalize growing unemployment. World competition made it too costly to provide decent social services. Again racism serves the needs of capitalists by convincing whites that blacks are responsible for the reduced quality of urban services. Finally, racism by splitting the working class made it easier for capitalists to cutback the wages of all workers and to attack unions. Thus, radicals contend that capitalism is responsible for the growth in racist attitudes and practices which, in turn, has been responsible for the persistence of black youth employment problems.

CONCLUDING REMARKS

This paper has demonstrated that conservative views rationalize the persistent employment problems of black youths by "blaming the victims." Liberal views are useful in combatting the conservative perspective but are inadequate: they highlight market imperfections and imply that with appropriate government policies problems can be eliminated. Radicals believe that only by eliminating racist practices can black youth employment problems be eliminated.

For most radicals, the major policy initiatives recommended are campaigns for full employment and stricter enforcement of anti-discrimination legislation. While these policies are popular, from my perspective, they are totally inadequate and potentially counterproductive, as long as they are predominately *electoral* strategies, emphasizing *federal government* initiatives. The "left" in this country only is able to influence national strategies when they rely on *local, nonlegislative* activities. Civil Rights legislation and moderations in U.S. military adventures occurred only after leftists had built successful grassroots movements that engaged in nonlegislative actions. Indeed, part of the reason that some politicians began espousing progressive agendas was an attempt to coopt these activities.

Not only are legislative strategies ineffective but in the attempt to curry favors from a broader legislative constituency compromises are made which undercut political clarity. Without being able to espouse clear values and explanation, it is impossible to convince large numbers to join left-wing movements. Eventually, the left-wing leadership of progressive movements is either isolated and/or compromised so that token legislation is sufficient to undermine the movements ability to sustain itself.

Given these dangers, a legislative strategy, attempting to pressure the federal government could still be justified if modest reforms were sufficient to reduce significantly the employment problems faced by black youths. However, modest reforms will only at best ameliorate the worst aspects of the problem; poverty, deprivation, and powerlessness will remain. Indeed, if racist attitudes and myths are not systematical confronted, the basis for reform reversals will be present and the gains shortlived. In particular, only if the white working class can be won to support anti-racist policies based on class interest, can fundamental change be brought about. Since the elite is well aware of the dangers they face from a united working-class movement, they will likely attempt to shape "reforms" in ways which provide the seeds of disunity.

Revolutionary leadership has the potential for overcoming many of the dangers reform movements face. First, it should have no illusion that this or that reform will be the panacea and thus not be as likely to be compromised or coopted by some legislative strategy. Second, it should realize that to maintain independent organizations which focus on local activities and local demands is the lifeblood of the movement. Third, it should be most sensitive to overcoming racist attitudes and myths even if this should have a short-term negative impact on the organizations' popularity and thus appear to endanger legislative victories. Fourth, and most importantly, revolutionary leadership provides the basis for a revolution which is the only possibility for ending racism. Capitalism is a system of economic inequality and inequality is inevitably justified by racism or other chauvanistic ideas. Those in power or those who attain privileges use racism to rationalize away the situation of the less privileged and less powerful. Only communism offers an alternative because communism does not require economic inequality to survive. While even communist movements can be compromised and undermined, they are the best hope for black youths and all of mankind.

REFERENCES

Allen, S.G. 1981. Compensation, Safety, and Absenteeism: Evidence from the Paper Industry. *Industrial and Labor Relations Review* 34:207-218.

Anderson, Elijah. 1980. Some Observations on Black Youth Unemployment. In, *Youth Employment and Public Policy*, Bernard Anderson and Isabel Sawhill (eds.). Englewood Cliffs, NJ: Prentice-Hall.

Ballen John and Richard Freeman. 1986. Transitions between Employment and Unemployment. In, Freeman and Holzer, pp. 23–74.

Baumol, William and Robert Blinder. 1979. *Economics*. New York: Harcourt, Brace.

Bonacich, Edna. 1976. Advanced Capitalism and Black/White Relations in the United States: A Split Labor Market Interpretation. *Journal of Sociology* 81:601–628.

Brown, C., C. Gilroy and A. Kohen. 1982. The Effects of the Minimum Wage on Employment and Unemployment. *Journal of Economic Literature* 20:487–528.

Cherry, Robert. 1977. Theories of Racism. In, *Problems in Political Economy*, David Gordon (ed.). pp. 170–183. Lexington, MA: Heath.

_____. 1985. Textbook Treatments of Minimum Wage Legislation. *Review of Black Political Economy* 13:25–38.

Clark, Kim and Lawrence Summers. 1982. The Dynamics of Youth Unemployment. In, Freeman and Wise, pp. 199–230.

Cogan, John. 1982. The Decline in Black Teenage Employment: 1950–70. *American Economics Review* 72:621–638.

Culp, Jerome and Bruce Dunson. 1986. Brothers of a Different Color: A Preliminary Look at Employment Treatment of White and Black Youth. In, Freeman and Holzer, pp. 233–260.

Datcher-Loury, Linda and Glen Loury. 1986. The Effects of Attitudes and Aspirations on the Labor Supply of Young Men. In, Freeman and Holzer, pp. 377–402.

Dooley, Martin and Peter Gottschalk. 1985. The Increasing Proportion of Men with Low Earnings in the United States. *Demography* 22:25–34.

Feldstein, Martin and David Ellwood. 1982. Teenage Unemployment: What Is the Problem?'' In, Freeman and Wise, pp. 17–34.

Ferguson, Ronald and Randall Filer. 1986. Do Better Jobs Make Better Workers? Absenteeism from Work Among Inner-City Black Youth. In, Freeman and Holzer, pp. 261–298.

Freeman, Richard. 1986a. Who Escapes? The Relation of Churchgoing and Other Background Factors to the Socioeconomic Performance of Black Youths from Inner-City Poverty Tracts. In, Freeman and Holzer, pp. 353–376.

_____. 1986b. The Relation of Criminal Activity to Black Youth Employment. Paper presented at ASSA Meetings, New Orleans.

_____ and Harry Holzer. 1986. *The Black Youth Employment Crisis*. Chicago: University of Chicago Press.

_____ and James Medoff. 1982. Why Does the Rate of Youth Labor Force Activity Differ across Surveys?'' In, Freeman and Wise, pp. 75–114.

_____ and David Wise. 1982a. *The Youth Labor Market Problem*. Chicago: University of Chicago Press.

_____ and David Wise. 1982b. The Youth Labor Market Problem: Its Nature, Causes, and Consequences. In, Freeman and Wise, pp. 3–20.

Fusfeld, Daniel and Timothy Bates. 1984. *Political Economy of the Urban Ghetto*. Carbondale IL: Southern Illinois University Press.

Holzer, Harry. 1986. Black Youth Nonemployment: Duration and Job Search. In, Freeman and Holzer, pp. 23–70.

Jackson, Peter and Edward Montgomery. 1986. Layoffs, Discharges, and Youth Unemployment. In, Freeman and Holzer, pp. 115–141.

Jencks, Christopher. 1987. Genes and Crime. *The NY Review of Books* 36(Feb 12):33–41.

Lerman, Robert. 1986. Do Welfare Programs Affect the Schooling and Work Patterns of Young Black Men? In, Freeman and Holzer, pp. 403–438.

Loury, Glenn. 1985. The Moral Quandary of the Black Community. *The Public Interest* 79:9–23.

Murray, Charles. 1984. *Losing Ground: American Social Policy 1950–1980*. New York: Basic Books.

Myers, Samuel. 1986. Comment. In, Freeman and Holzer, pp. 438–441.

Piore, Michael. 1979. *Birds of Passage*. Cambridge: Cambridge University Press.

Viscusi, Kip. 1986. Market Incentives for Criminal Behavior. In, Freeman and Holzer, pp. 301–346.

Wachter, Michael and Choongsoo Kim. 1982. Time Series Changes in Youth Joblessness. In, Freeman and Wise, pp. 155–185.

Williams, Walter. 1981. A Culprit is a Culprit. In, *The Fairmont Papers,* Bernard Anderson et al. (eds.). pp. 51–53. San Francisco: Institute for Contemporary Studies.

12

The Comparable Worth Debate: An Evaluation of the Issues

ELAINE SORENSEN

INTRODUCTION

The U.S. Civil Rights Commission Chairman, Clarence Pendelton, denounced the concept as "the looniest idea since 'Looney Tunes.' " President Reagan called it "a cockamamie idea. . . [that] would destroy the basis of free enterprise." These men were referring to a strategy for rectifying economic inequities confronting women and minorities known as equal pay for comparable worth. Despite this opposition, comparable worth has gained considerable momentum during the past few years. Nearly every state government has taken initiative on this issue and at least fifteen have increased salaries for workers in occupations that have an over-representation of women or minorities. Numerous labor unions, feminist organizations, and the Democratic Party have also endorsed the idea.

As popular support for comparable worth policies has grown, so has its opposition. Conservative opponents of comparable worth argue that a comparable worth policy would undermine the "free market" system of wage determination, a system which they believe is above reproach both logically and legally. On the other hand, some progressive persons argue against a comparable worth strategy. They contend that it is divisive, pitting blue-collar and minority workers against their female co-workers. Furthermore, it is argued that comparable worth proposals do not reduce inequality and may even exacerbate it by increasing the salaries of skilled workers more than unskilled workers.

This essay will first introduce the concept of comparable worth. It will then survey the general objections to the concept and analyze their shortcomings.

COMPARABLE WORTH AND WAGE DISCRIMINATION

Comparable worth policies seek to counteract the persistent wage inequities that women and minorities experience in the labor market. White women's earnings relative to white men's earnings have remained disturbingly rigid during the past thirty years. In 1986, white women employed full-time still earned $.63 for every dollar that white men earned, the same ratio as in 1956 (U.S. Census 1987). Although the earnings gap has improved slightly during this period for people of color, the earnings gap is greater for minority women than it is for white women (black women earn $.57 and Hispanic women earn $.53) and minority men still earn substantially less than white men (black men earn $.71 and Hispanic men earn $.65). Earnings increase with education for all workers, but women and minorities earn less than white men at every level of education.

For example, women with four years of college education earn less on average than men who have not completed high school (black men with four years of college education earn about the same as white men who have completed high school).

Severe occupational segregation by sex and race also characterize the U.S. labor force. Nearly one out of three white women and one out of four women of color are employed as clerical workers. Another one-fourth of the white female work force is employed in service work and two professional classifications; teaching and nursing. Minority women are also heavily concentrated in service work (21 percent) and many work as machine operators (14 percent). Men of color are highly concentrated in different occupations than women and white men. For example, two out of three black men are employed in blue-collar and service work, and only one out of six are employed as managers or professionals. Within blue-collar work, 70 percent work as laborers and operators. One-fourth of white men, on the other hand, are employed as managers and professionals, and another one-fifth are employed as craft workers.

Proponents of comparable worth policies argue that extensive occupational segregation in the labor force contributes to the sex- and race-based earnings disparities that persist in the U.S. labor market. It allows firms to pay lower wages to workers in jobs with an over-representation of women and minorities. These jobs become identified as "women's work" or "minority men's work," and simply because of these labels firms pay workers less than they would if these jobs employed white men. For example, in the state of Washington a comparable worth study found that the job of licensed practical nurse was held primarily by women and that the job of correctional officer was dominated by men. It also found that these two jobs were equivalent with respect to the amount of knowledge, mental demands, accountability, and working conditions associated with the two jobs. However, in 1983, the state of Washington paid an entry level licensed practical nurse $985 per month while paying the correctional officer $1358 per month.

Proponents of comparable worth posit that if a single employer pays jobs with an over-representation of women or minorities less than jobs with an over-representation of white men, one that cannot be supported by corresponding differences in the requirements of the job, then the employer is guilty of sex- and race-based wage discrimination. The purpose of a comparable worth policy is to eliminate this type of discrimination. After it is implemented, wages for jobs with an over-representation of women or minorities will reflect job responsibilities, unencumbered by sexually or racially biased notions. Thus, in the state of Washington a comparable worth strategy would increase the salary of the licensed practical nurse to that received by comparable male dominated occupations such as that of correctional officer.

THE COMPARABLE WORTH DEBATE

Conservative Arguments. Conservative opponents of comparable worth espouse three arguments against comparable worth policies all of which assume that the labor market is free and competitive: discrimination is not a major problem in today's labor market; the sex- and race-based earnings disparities are due to productivity differences between women (minorities) and men (whites); and jobs do not have intrinsic worth to a firm, their value is determined by supply and demand.

1. The Free Market Eliminates Discrimination

Conservative opponents of comparable worth argue that discrimination is not a principal factor contributing to the sex- and race-based earnings gaps. According to this view, a free market provides sufficient incentive to eliminate discrimination. In such a market, employers can not afford to discriminate against minority and female workers. If they did, an incentive would exist for some employer to hire them since discrimination would depress their market wage compared to that received by white men. With this cost advantage, the non-discriminating employer would outperform those who discriminate. Eventually, competitive forces would compel discriminating employers to discontinue such practices or lose their business, thus eliminating discrimination from the market.

Although in theory the free market ensures that employers do not discriminate, in fact, until the passage of the anti-discrimination laws of the early 1960s, the U.S. labor market was characterized by blatant discriminatory practices and institutions. Employers could pay women less than men for exactly the same work and they could refuse to hire blacks and other minorities, simply because of their race. These types of blatant discriminatory practices did not wither away under competitive pressures. Instead, legal prohibition was necessary to eliminate them. Thus, federal policies and court rulings have clearly reduced the discriminatory practices that are deeply imbedded in American labor markets. Unfortunately, however, these changes have not eliminated all types of discrimination. Proponents of comparable worth have identified yet another pervasive discriminatory pattern that causes workers in female or minority dominated jobs to receive less than they would if these jobs were dominated by white men. This form of discrimination deserves judicial and legislative attention, just as other forms have received.

2. Pay Gaps are Caused by Productivity and Labor Supply Differences

Conservative opponents of comparable worth argue that women and minorities have different supply characteristics than white men and these differences explain their low relative earnings. They claim that women expect to drop-out of the labor force while raising their children, and thus choose low paying occupations that do not impose severe wage penalties for discontinuous labor market behavior. They also select occupations that are close to home, have convenient hours, and do not require overtime, to accommodate their family responsibilities. These choices limit women's labor supply and reduce their earnings potential. Conservative opponents of comparable worth also claim that minorities receive less education and poorer quality education, on average, than whites. This limits the types of occupations available to minorities and thus reduces their relative earnings.

Empirical research, however, has repeatedly shown that less than half of the sex- and race-based earnings disparities can be accounted for by differences in productivity-related characteristics between women and minorities and white men. In other words, differences in labor force attachment between women and men and differences in education between minorities and whites do not explain most of the earnings gaps. Consequently, existing research shows that even if women and minority men had identical labor market behavior as white men, they would still earn considerably less than white men. Comparable worth proposals attempt to eliminate that portion of the pay gaps which is unaccounted for by productivity-related differences, and which would remain even if women and minority men had identical labor force behavior to white men's.

In addition, an explanation of the earnings gap between women (minorities) and men (whites) that focuses upon productivity differences ignores the dramatic changes that have taken place in the productivity characteristics of women and minorities over the past thirty years. Between 1955 and 1977, the work life expectancy of a 20 year old woman increased from 14.5 to 26 years. In contrast, the work life expectancy of a 20 year old man drifted down from 41 to 37 years (Smith 1982). Thus, the number of years that women work in the labor force has clearly increased relative to men. Women are also marrying later, having fewer children and heading more of their own households than 30 years ago. All of these changes suggest an increased attachment to the labor force among women and yet their relative earnings have not improved.

The educational attainment of black men has also dramatically increased during the past 25 years. In 1962, white men in the civilian labor force had completed an average of 12.1 years of education; black men had completed an average of 9.0 years. By 1980, this education gap had almost disappeared: white men's average educational attainment increased to 12.7 years and black men's increased to 12.3 years (U.S. Department of Labor 1982). Yet, black men working full-time still earn 71 percent as much as white men. Thus, the productivity characteristics of women and minorities have changed, yet their pay persistently lags behind that of white men.

3. *Different Jobs Can Not Be Compared*

Opponents of comparable worth have expressed concern over the comparisons of dissimilar jobs that are made by comparable worth proposals. Can the job of nurse be compared to that of a tree trimmer to assess the relative worth of these jobs? They contend that job evaluations, the method used by comparable worth proposals to compare different jobs, are not an objective measure of a job's worth; the only objective measure is the salary that an employer must pay to attract workers to the job. Such a salary is determined by competitive market forces of supply and demand, forces external to an individual firm.

Advocates of comparable worth argue that wages are not exclusively determined by market forces; other factors, such as discrimination, also play a role. Furthermore, market forces themselves reflect and reproduce discrimination. This allows employers to pay workers in jobs with an over-representation of women and minorities less than if those jobs were held by white men. Advocates of comparable worth need a technique to measure the extent to which salaries are discriminatorily depressed in jobs with an over-representation of women and minorities.

Most comparable worth proposals have used an a priori factor-point job evaluation plan to assess jobs, the most commonly used plan in the United States. It consists of a set of factors and weights which are expected to reflect the requirements of a job. The factors generally fall into four broad categories: skill, effort, responsibility, and working conditions. Weights are applied to each factor and indicate their relative importance. Once the weights and factors are chosen, a basic set of procedures are followed to evaluate jobs. First, questionnaires specifically designed for the factor-point plan are completed. Based upon this information, jobs are evaluated on each factor. Jobs are assigned a level of points that is commensurate with the amount of each factor required to perform the job. These factor scores are summed for each job to produce a total score, which are used to establish an internal ranking of jobs according to their worth to the firm.

Comparable worth proposals do not alter the basic procedures of a job evaluation plan; they use the same techniques that management has traditionally used to evaluate jobs. The differences between comparable worth proposals and management's traditional practices do not take place during the evaluation of jobs, but during the determination of wages.

Management uses job evaluation plans as an instrument in wage determination, but they typically limit its use to comparisons within so-called job families. Job families consist of jobs that have similar skill requirements or are performed in the same division of the firm. Wages from the external labor market are pegged to a few occupations within each job family. Management determines the occupational salaries of other jobs within each job family by comparing job evaluation scores to those of the few occupations with external wages. For example, suppose the prevailing wage for a clerk/typist is $1000 per month, then all jobs within the clerk/typist job family would be adjusted around that salary according to their job evaluation score in comparison to that of the clerk/typist. Thus, the prevailing wages of other occupations outside of the clerk/typist job family, such as janitor or truck driver, would not enter into the determination of wages for this job family.

Comparable worth studies use the results of a job evaluation to examine a firm's existing salary practices for all jobs, regardless of their job family. Rather than using external wages for certain occupations, they use the salaries received by jobs dominated by white men as their set of comparison occupations. Salary comparisons are made between jobs with an over-representation of women or minorities and jobs that are dominated by white men. If the former salaries are less than the latter and the jobs are deemed comparable according to the criteria established by the job evaluation plan, then a comparable worth policy would increase the salaries of jobs with an over-representation of women or minorities.

Opponents of comparable worth argue that job evaluations can not be used in this way. Yet, numerous jurisdictions have already conducted such studies. Unfortunately, opponents of comparable worth tend to think that job evaluations are only capable of fulfilling their original purpose, which was to justify and perpetuate the existing wage structure. Clearly, comparable worth proposals alter the existing wage structure, by eliminating sex- and race-based wage discrimination. However, they do so by applying the basic procedures used by management to evaluate jobs.

Progressive Arguments. The progressive concerns regarding comparable worth legislation have focused upon its possible divisive nature and its reinforcement of existing salary practices.

Comparable Worth Would Lower Male Wages. Some have feared that comparable worth will benefit women at the expense of men, hindering attempts to unify male and female workers. Yet, in no instance has comparable worth been introduced in a form which has resulted in wage cuts for male workers. It is generally accepted by the courts and Congress that the elimination of wage discrimination is best accomplished by increasing the wages of those discriminated against, not by decreasing the wages of those unaffected by discrimination. Federal legislation mandating a comparable worth study of

Federal pay practices (H.R. 5680-Oakar, 1984) specifically prohibited reducing anyone's pay because of this legislation. Similar prohibitions have been included in many state and local comparable worth proposals as well.

Employers may suggest lowering male salaries in particular jobs considered "overvalued" or they may suggest lower across-the-board increases for all workers in order to pay for higher wages in female dominated jobs. Advocates of comparable worth have consistently fought against these employer suggestions. For example, in May 1984, Donald Devine, then director of the federal Office of Personnel Management, held a private meeting of union officials representing federal employees and attempted to convince them that the wages of blue-collar workers would be lowered if a comparable worth bill before the House was enacted. The union officials were not convinced by Devine's arguments. They later testified before the Subcommittee on Compensation and Employee Benefits that unions were long familiar with employer "divide and conquer" tactics.

A policy of equal pay for comparable worth can be seen as a threat to those who are trying to maintain their *relative* wage or it can be seen as an egalitarian policy, one that can increase the likelihood that all workers receive a fair wage. As an egalitarian policy comparable worth can unite workers in their struggle with employers for decent wages for all workers. Advocates of comparable worth will most likely continue to fight against suggestions of lowering male wages to pay for comparable worth since this approach could undermine a general consensus for the policy.

Comparable Worth Will Decrease the Earnings of Minority Males. Some progressive and conservative opponents of comparable worth have argued that its implementation will decrease the earnings of men of color. This position was stated quite forcefully by Michael J. Horowitz, counsel to the director of the Office of Management and Budget, when he remarked that: "There is nothing that the Reagan Administration has done that holds as much long-term threat to the black community as comparable worth. The maintenance man will be paid less so the librarian can be paid more" (*New York Times*, 22 January, 1984).

This position ignores the wage discrimination that minority males experience due to race- and sex-based occupational segregation. Many public sector comparable worth studies have shown that a disproportionate number of minority males work in female or minority dominated jobs. Furthermore, they earn less than workers in comparable white male dominated jobs (NCPE 1987). A number of states, including New Jersey, New York, and Wisconsin, have already begun increasing the salaries of workers who are employed in minority or female dominated jobs. Clearly, additional research is needed in this area, but it would be rather surprising to find that occupational segregation by race does not contribute to the earnings disparities that minority workers face.

Comparable Worth Justifies Existing Wage Inequities. It is sometimes argued that comparable worth does not sufficiently challenge the present hierarchical wage structure. According to one opponent of comparable worth, "advocates of comparable worth don't want to achieve equality" (Cowley 1984:57). Instead, comparable worth will "enshrine" the existing earnings inequalities "by giving them the force of law" (Cowley 1984:57). Similar sentiments were echoed by a more sympathetic author when she stated that comparable worth "can have only a modest effect on the overall degree of inequality because it does not attack all forms of inequality" (Feldberg 1984:323). She later added that comparable worth "does not directly challenge the concept of a [wage] hierarchy; in fact, its insistence that jobs be evaluated implies a hierarchy" (Feldberg 1984:323).

Comparable worth proposals attack the existing hierarchical wage structure by arguing that it reflects wage discrimination against workers in female and minority dominated jobs and that this source of wage inequality should be eliminated. They do, however, accept a wage hierarchy as long as that hierarchy reflects job requirements and not the predominant sex or race of the worker in the occupation. In fact, job requirements are the criteria used to measure the extent to which female or minority dominated jobs are underpaid relative to comparable white male dominated jobs.

Some analysts argue that job requirements are the traditional criteria used by firms to justify wage inequity and thus its use by comparable worth proposals reinforces existing wage inequities. However, one of the most important findings of comparable worth studies is that employers have *not* applied this criteria uniformly to all occupations. Instead, they have applied a different set of standards for occupations with a disproportionate number of women or minorities than that used for occupations with a disproportionate number of white men.

Using job requirements to determine the extent of wage inequities does not imply that so-called unskilled female or minority dominated jobs will be unaffected by comparable worth proposals, in fact, quite the contrary. The largest disparities between current salaries and proposed comparable worth salaries typically occur among the lowest paid and supposedly unskilled female dominated occupations. For example, the occupational categories with the largest comparable worth pay disparities in the state of Washington were: telephone operator, laundry worker, nurse's assistant, general clerk, and secretary, three of which were the least skilled female dominated occupations examined.

It is true that comparable worth proposals would not cure all forms of inequality in U.S. society. However, they would reduce a serious source of earnings inequality in the United States, namely sex- and race-based wage discrimination against women and minorities. It would accomplish this by increasing the salaries of jobs with an over-representation of women or minorities, all of which tend to earn *less* than the average white male. For example, the highest paid female dominated job in the United States is the job of registered nurse and it pays less than the average salary received by white men. Thus, if the ideal is greater income equality, a comparable worth policy would certainly move the United States towards that goal.

CONCLUSION

The demand for comparable worth has emerged at an opportune moment. Many people have become increasingly aware of a disturbing trend towards greater inequality in the distribution of income in the United States. It is argued that the tax and budgets cuts under the Reagan Administration, as well as the relative decline of the smoke stack industries and the absolute rise in the service sector, have contributed to this trend. An increase in the poverty rate has also been noted. By 1986, 13.6 percent of the population lived in poverty, up from 11.4 percent in 1978. Women represent two-thirds of the poor adult population, while half of the families living in poverty are headed by women, the fastest growing type in the country. A comparable worth policy would increase the salaries of low paying traditionally female and minority dominated occupations within the service sector. Thus a comparable worth policy could alleviate the unfortunate trend toward greater income inequality.

REFERENCES

Cowley, Geoffrey. 1984. Comparable Worth: Another Terrible Idea. *Washington Monthly* 15:52–57.

Feldberg, Roslyn L. 1984. Comparable Worth: Toward Theory and Practice in the United States. *Signs: Journal of Women in Culture and Society* 10(2):311–328.

Gregory, R.G. and R.C. Duncan. 1981. Segmented Labor Market Theories and the Australian Experience of Equal Pay for Women. *Journal of Post Keynesian Economics* III(3):403–428.

National Committee on Pay Equity (NCPE). 1987. *Pay Equity: An Issue of Race, Ethnicity, and Sex*. Washington, D.C.: NCPE.

Smith, Shirley J. 1982. New Worklife Estimates Reflect Changing Profile of Labor Force. *Monthly Labor Review* (March):15–20.

Sorensen, Elaine. 1986. Implementing Comparable Worth: A Survey of Recent Job Evaluation Studies. *American Economic Review* 76(2):364–368.

Treiman, Donald J. and Heidi I. Hartmann (ed.). 1981. *Women, Work, and Wages: Equal Pay for Jobs of Equal Value*. Washington, D.C.: National Academy Press.

U.S. Bureau of the Census. 1987. Money Income and Poverty Status of Families and Persons in the United States: 1986. *Current Population Reports*. P-60 Series, No. 157. Washington, D.C.: U.S. Government Printing Office.

U.S. Department of Labor. 1982. *Employment and Training Report of the President*. Washington, D.C.: U.S. Government Printing Office.

13

Political Economy and Family Policy

JULIE MATTHAEI

The family plays a central role in the distribution of income and wealth in our society, reproducing class, race, and gender inequalities. This paper will: (1) present a radical and feminist analysis of the ''traditional'' family system, (2) discuss the recent breakdown of this system, (3) present a radical and feminist critique of the traditional family system, and (4) indicate social policies which would build a family system more consistent with the principles of equality, freedom, and social justice.

THE "NATURAL" FAMILY

The development of capitalism and wage labor in the nineteenth-century United States brought with them new familial institutions. The family continued to be patriarchal — ruled by the husband/father — but was less defined by and involved in commodity production, either as a family firm, or as a family enslaved to producing for others. The family emerged as an increasingly personal and feminine sphere, physically separate and distinct from the competitive and masculine economy (Matthaei 1982). Since, in the nineteenth century, ''scientific'' explanations of social life were replacing the former religious ones, the new familial institutions were viewed as ''natural,'' and stress was placed on their determination by biological similarities and differences. This ''natural'' family system has three, interconnected parts:[1]

1. *''Natural'' Marriage*. Marriage is seen as a union of naturally different and complementary beings: men/males and women/females (biological sex and social gender are equated). Men and women are believed to be instinctually heterosexual; those who form homosexual liaisons are viewed as unnatural and perverted.[2] Men are seen as natural bread-winners, competing in the economy, and women as natural homemakers, caring for their husbands and children in the home, and segregated into dead-end, low paid ''women's jobs.'' Forced into this sexual division of labor, men and women need one another to be socially complete, and in order to undertake the essential function of marriage, which is seen as . . .

2. *''Natural'' Parenting*. Parenting is seen as the biological production of offspring, a process in which adults pass on their identities and wealth to their children, to ''their own flesh and blood.'' Children are seen as the responsibility and property of their parents. Women/females are seen as naturally endowed with special maternal instincts which make them more qualified than men/males for parenting.

3. *''Natural'' Community*. Connected to the view of family life as natural is a white racist view of society which divides people into races and views whites as the biologically superior race. Whites rationalize their political and economic domination of people of color not only as natural but also as part of the ''white man's burden to civilize the

savages."[3] Races and white supremacy are perpetuated as social entities by the prohibition of racial intermarriage; by the passing down of wealth or poverty, language and culture to one's children; and by racially segregated institutions such as housing and job markets.

THE BREAKDOWN OF THE "NATURAL" FAMILY SYSTEM

In the last fifteen years, the "natural" family system has been breaking down and coming under increasing attack by feminists and others.

1) *Married women have entered the labor force and "men's jobs" in growing numbers, challenging the "natural" sexual division of labor*. Now over half of married women are in paid jobs at any one time. Women are demanding entry into the better-paid "men's jobs,", and pressing their husbands to do "women's work" in the home. The "natural" marriage union between a bread-winning husband and a homemaking wife has become the exception rather than the rule, characterizing only 29 percent of husband/wife couples in 1985 (U.S. Bureau of the Census 1985a).

2) *Married women's labor force participation has created a crisis in day care:* there is a severe shortage of day care facilities, especially affordable ones. In New York, for example, between 830,000 and 1.2 million preschool and school-age children vie for the fewer than 135,000 available licensed child care placements (Select Committee on Children 1987). The shortage of day care, combined with the absence of flexible jobs, forces parents to use make-shift arrangements: 2.1 million or 7 percent of 5–13 year olds whose mothers work outside the home are admittedly left unsupervised; actual numbers are much higher (Children's Defense Fund 1987).

3) *Growing numbers are not living in husband/wife families;* only 57 percent of all households include married couples. Adults are marrying later, spending more time living alone (23.4 percent of all households) or with friends or lovers. Homosexuality appears to be on the rise, and lesbians and gay men are coming out of the closet and demanding their rights. Marriages have become very unstable: divorce rates more than tripled between 1960 and 1982, more than doubling the number of female-headed households (1986 and 1987 Statistical Abstracts).

4) *"Natural" parenting is on the wane*. Divorces create "unnatural" female-headed households, most with dependent children. Unwed mothering has increased to comprise one in five births and over half of all births among blacks (1987 Statistical Abstract). Remarriages create "unnatural" families, with step-parents and -siblings. More "unnatural" is the trend for sterile couples, gays, and singles to obtain children through artificial insemination, surrogate mothers, and inter-country, inter-racial adoptions.

What do these trends mean? Members of the so-called Moral Majority interpret them as the breakdown of THE family; their solution, embodied in the Family Protection Act of the late 1970s and early 1980s, is to put the "natural" family back together: encourage marriage; discourage divorce, unwed mothering, homosexuality; and get married women out of men's jobs and back into the home. The radical perspective is the opposite; the "natural" family is only one of many possible family systems, a very oppressive and ineffective one at that, as the next section will show. Growing numbers are rejecting the "natural" family system, and trying to create alternative family structures. What society needs is a radical family policy to focus and facilitate this process of dismantling of the old family system and constructing a new and more liberated one.

THE RADICAL CRITIQUE OF THE "NATURAL" FAMILY

The radical critique of the "natural" family has many prongs. All of these are underlain by a common claim — the "natural" family is not natural, necessary or optimal, and a more adequate family system needs to be developed.

1. *The "natural" family system is not natural.* Biological differences in skin color or sex organs, and biological similarities between parent and child, do not necessitate a particular family form, or hierarchy and difference between the sexes and races. Past family systems have been very different from the "natural" family.[4] It is not nature but our society which is producing and reproducing the "natural" family, and its associated institutions of gender and race difference and inequality, through parenting practices, laws, labor market structures, and culture.

2. *The "natural" family system is classist and racist.* The conception of the "natural" family is generated by the dominant culture of upper-class, native-born whites, who then claim it applies to all. Since being a man means bread-winning and supporting a homebound homemaker and children, men without "family wage" jobs due to unemployment, class, or race discrimination are seen (and often see themselves) as less than manly. Black women, forced into the labor force to compensate for their husbands' lack of economic opportunity, are viewed as unfeminine, castrating "matriarchs," and the extended and chosen family system which blacks have developed to combat poverty and economic insecurity is condemned as deviant (Stack 1974). The inability of the poor to properly parent their children because of their meager resources is seen as a fault in their characters, and they are criticized for having children at all, as if the poor do not have a right to parent.

3. *The "natural" family system impoverishes female-headed households.* Women and children face high risks of poverty. Married women are to specialize in unpaid homemaking and mothering, complementing their husbands' bread-winning. Divorce or widowhood leaves women with little access to income, but with major if not full emotional and financial responsibility for the children.[5] "Women's jobs" do not pay enough to cover child care and keep female households with young children out of poverty. The present welfare system (Aid to Families with Dependent Children), structured to support the "natural" family system, does not even provide female-headed families with poverty-level income (see Amott in this collection). The result: the majority of black and Hispanic female-headed families (50 and 53 percent, respectively), and 27 percent of white female-headed families, are poor. Children are penalized the most: 54 percent of children in such families are poor (U.S. Bureau of the Census 1985a.).

4. *"Natural" marriage creates inequality between the sexes.* Since wives are relegated to unpaid housework and low-paid jobs, they are economically dependent upon their husbands. Fear of losing this financial support can force women into subservience to their husbands, and into staying in unsatisfying marriages. Indeed, some feminists see "natural" marriage as a struggle in which men have gained the upper hand by monopolizing the higher-paid jobs (Hartmann 1981). Whatever its origins, "natural" marriage is clearly unequal, making mutual love and respect difficult.

5. *"Natural" parenting is oppressive and unjust.* Along with financial responsibility, parents are given almost total power over children. Children have no rights, and no system through which they can complain about mistreatment or find alternative parents

(Rodham 1976). In a society where most men are under the power of bosses, and women under that of their husbands, parenting provides an arena where adults have total power and authority. It is easy to forget one's children's needs and use or abuse them to fill one's own needs. What results is not only an epidemic of child physical and sexual abuse,[6] but also the training of each child to accept and participate in hierarchical and authoritarian systems, from schools to workplaces to politics (Miller 1981).

6. *The "natural" family perpetuates inequality between families*. Inequality persists through the generations, because parents pass down their economic position to their children. Inheritance keeps ownership of the means of production in the hands of a few, mostly white, families.[7] Children born into higher-income families receive better nutrition, housing, health-care, and schooling than their poor counterparts, have the "insurance" of wealthy relatives to back them up and encourage risk-taking, and can expect to inherit wealth. On the other hand, 11 million children (one in five) must live without even the most basic goods and services (U.S. Bureau of the Census 1985a). This is not only unjust but also irrational: it is in society's interest to guarantee quality health care and education to its future workers and citizens.

7. *The "natural" family system discourages the formation of alternative families, while forcing many into unwanted "natural" families*. Its broad and virulent anti-gay discrimination — from education, employment, housing, and marriage laws to media images — makes it very difficult for people to love and share their lives with people of the same sex. It discriminates against couples who are unable to have children biologically by treating adoption and artificial insemination as "unnatural" and undesirable options. On the other hand, the "natural" family's equation of sex, reproduction, and marriage creates unwanted children by creating opposition to sex education, birth control for unmarried teens, and abortion. Forty percent of all births are mistimed or unwanted — for those under 24, a disastrous 53 percent — forcing millions of women into premature or unwanted motherhood and/or marriages (1987 Statistical Abstract).

CONCEPTUALIZING A SOCIAL FAMILY SYSTEM

The "natural" family system is inadequate, oppressive, and is coming apart at the seams. At the same time, all need the love, warmth, sharing and parenting which family relationships provide.[8] Hence, criticism is not enough; an alternative and better vision of family life needs to be delineated, along with a set of concrete policies to bring such a new family system into being.

The oppressiveness of the "natural" family system was accepted because its institutions were seen as natural and inevitable. Our new family system would be a consciously social one, its institutions developed through study, discussion, struggle and compromise, and continually criticized and improved so as to maximize freedom, equality, self fulfillment, democracy, and justice. Here are some of the central principles of such a system; while it may appear utopian, many are living out parts of this vision now.

Social Marriage. Marriage would become a symmetrical relationship between whole, equal, and socially independent human beings, each participating in a similar range of familial, economic and political activities.[9] Its basis would be mutual love of the other, i.e. liking of, respect for, and sexual attraction to the person the other is, as providing the reason for intimate sharing of lives and living spaces and, if desired, parenting. Couples would not be expected to stay together "for better or for worse . . . as long as ye both shall live"; nor would they need to, since each would have earnings.

Social Parenting. Parenting would be recognized as a quintessentially social activity which, by shaping our unconsciousnesses, bodies, and minds, shapes the future of our society. Society would ensure that each child is well cared for and educated, since the upbringing of children as physically and psychologically healthy, creative, educated, and socially-conscious citizens is essential both to society's well-being, and to our belief in equal opportunity. This would include providing children and their parents with economic and institutional support, as well as seeking out optimal parenting practices and educating prospective parents in them.

Social Community. Cultural and economic differences between groups of people would be acknowledged to be social rather than natural products. All human beings would be recognized as equally human citizens of the world, and a concept of basic human rights, both political and economic, developed. Intercultural marriages would be encouraged to further social understanding.

BRINGING THE SOCIAL FAMILY INTO BEING: A POLICY CHECK-LIST

Although the "natural" family system is in decline, the social family system cannot replace it unless there are many changes in our economic and social institutions. Here are some of the policies which will help bring about these changes; many are now in place in other countries.

1. *Policies Which Socialize Parenting*.

a) Policies which establish the right of all adults to choose when and if they wish to parent. Universal sex education and parenting training for adolescents, as well as access of all to free, safe, 100 percent effective birth control, abortions, and adoption placement are needed to make every child a wanted child. At the same time, society must recognize the right of those who are infertile, gay, or single to parent, and support the development of alternative modes of obtaining children from adoption to artificial insemination and in-vitro fertilization.[10] The right to parent must also be protected by programs to help low-income parents with the costs of child-rearing (see 1b). Finally, the right to parent must be seen as socially established, rather than inhering in the genetic connection between a parent and a child; parenting rights must be revocable if a parent neglects or abuses a child, and society should seek to prevent child abuse through an effective system of child advocates and parenting support and training.

b) Policies which ensure a basic, social inheritance for every child. The best way to ensure healthy and provided-for children is to ensure this health and income to all families through a system of national health insurance and a combination of anti-poverty measures, from full employment, to comparable worth, to a guaranteed annual income. In addition, since having children does increase a family's poverty risk, family allowances should be provided to parents according to need.[11] Furthermore, all children need to have access to high quality, free or sliding-scale education, from pre-school day care when their parents are at work, to elementary and secondary school and college. This "social inheritance" program would be paid for by high inheritance taxes and very progressive income and/or luxury taxes. Such taxes would, in themselves, help reduce the present gross inequalities of opportunity among children.[12]

c) Policies which socialize child-care costs: government- and business-subsidized day care. Making quality child-care available and affordable to all should be the joint financial responsibility of business and government, since it benefits both employers and society at large. A few trend-setting employers now provide child-care benefits to their workers, having found that these more than pay for themselves by decreasing worker absenteeism, increasing productivity, and attracting top workers (Blau and Ferber 1986). Current federal funding through Title 20 is woefully inadequate; many states are serving less than 30 percent of their eligible populations (Select Committee on Children 1987). One survey found that one-fourth of all full-time homemakers, and one-half of all single parents, were kept from employment and training programs by the unavailability of child-care (California Governor's Task Force on Child Care 1986). Again, Sweden provides the example to follow: government pays 90 percent of the child care costs of public day care centers, which are used by over half of children with employed mothers (Blau and Ferber 1986).

On the other hand, to permit parents with job commitments to spend more time with their children, especially their infants, a system of paid leaves from work without loss of one's job or seniority must be established. The United States does not even have laws guaranteeing prospective parents an unpaid leave when they have or adopt a child.[13] In a few states, women can use their temporary disability insurance to pay for 4 to 10 weeks of pregnancy/infant care leave (Kamerman et al. 1983). Again, Sweden is the model in this area, with: (1) paid, year-long parental leaves; (2) up to 60 days a year paid leave to care for sick children; and (3) the right for all full-time employed parents with children under eight to reduce their work weeks (with reduced pay) to 30 hours a week (Ginsberg 1983). Radicals have advocated a shorter work week without reduction in pay as a solution to unemployment and low productivity, for it would create more jobs, reduce unemployment, and increase output (Bowles, Gordon, and Weisskopf 1983); a consideration of the needs of parents makes such policies even more desirable. Other innovations which allow adults to combine work with parenting are flex-time and flex-place (working at home); the extension of health, pension, and other benefits to part-time workers; and the cafeteria benefit plan, which allows dual-career couples to eliminate doubly-covered benefits in favor of more of other benefits, such as leaves or child-care support (Kamerman and Hayes 1982; Farley 1983).

2. *Policies to Support Egalitarian, Symmetrical Marriages* (in which partners participate equally in parenting, housework, the labor force, and political life).[14]

a) Comparable worth, affirmative action, increased unionization. Comparable worth would increase the pay of women's jobs to that of men's jobs requiring comparable skill, effort, and responsibility (see Sorenson in this collection). Affirmative action encourages women to enter into traditionally masculine jobs. Women need to organize in unions to fight for the above, and for general wage increases: one platform is "solidarity wages," again practiced in Sweden, in which workers agree to take part of their wage increase to reduce inequalities among them. Together these policies would stop the segregation of women into low-paid, dead end, less-satisfying jobs, reduce women's economic dependence upon men, and encourage more similar work and family participation by the sexes.

b) Socialization of parenting (see 1 above) would support symmetrical marriage, for it would allow adults to combine parenting with labor force commitments, reducing the pressure to specialize as in ''natural'' marriage.

c) Social support for the formation of ''unnatural'' marriages and non-traditional households. This includes repealing sodomy laws and advocating legislation prohibiting discrimination against gay employment, housing, insurance, foster parenting, adoption, and other areas.[15] Gay relationships must be legitimized in marriage laws, to give spouses health insurance, pension, inheritance, and other benefits and rights enjoyed by heterosexual spouses.[16] The repeal of co-residence laws, which in many states prohibit the cohabitation of more than two unrelated adults, is needed to allow the formation of non-biologically-based extended families.

d) Individual rather than joint taxation of married couples. Our present income tax system is progressive and married couples are taxed on the basis of their combined incomes. This discourages wives from entering the labor force since, when a woman's earnings raise the household's tax bracket, much of her earnings are paid to the government in taxes.[17] Taxing adults individually (as is currently done in Sweden), rather than jointly, would, instead, encourage both members of a couple to participate in the labor force.

e) Policies to aid the casualties of the ''natural'' marriage system. Until the above changes are achieved, women and children will continue to face high poverty risks when they live in female-headed households. Many feminists advocate the strengthening of alimony and child-support laws; however, this both reinforces the ''natural'' marriage notion that husbands should be the main providers, and reproduces class and race inequality, because wives' and childrens' incomes depend on that of their husbands/fathers. Extensive welfare reform (see Amott in this collection), combined with the policies above, is a better solution.

3. *Policies to Create Social Community*. Labor market reforms (2a) must always aim at eliminating both race and sex segregation and discrimination. These, along with social inheritance policies, will go far in stopping the economic reproduction of racial inequality in the United States. The decline of ''natural'' parenting views of children as ''one's own flesh and blood'' will foster, and in turn be fostered by, the decline of conceptions of race, as both are replaced by a view of a human community reproduced through social parenting.

ACKNOWLEDGEMENTS

This paper has benefited from the research assistance of Jean Kendall, and from comments by Michele Naples of the URPE Crisis Reader Collective. It has been presented, in different forms, to the URPE Summer Conference, the Social Concept History Group, Marxist-Feminist I, and to groups at Vassar and Le Moyne Colleges, all of which provided helpful comments.

NOTES

1. Natural is in quotes because the ''natural'' family system is actually a social product.
2. In contrast, previous times viewed homosexual attractions as natural (and shared by all) but immoral and not to be acted on (Weeks 1979).

3. Similarly, whites in the Eugenics movement argued that poor whites had inferior genes, and worked to limit their reproduction (Gould 1981).
4. Among the Rangiroa, adopted children were given equal status and rights as biological offspring, and considered "one belly" (from the same mother) with one another and with their other siblings (Sahlins 1976). In the New England and Southern colonies, mothering among the wealthy was essentially biological, producing one's husband's children, who were then nursed and cared for by poor white or slave women. Mead (1935) found societies where men and women shared the early care of children. Many societies see polygamy as the norm for marriage; others have allowed females to live as men and take wives after having cross-sex dreams (Blackwood 1984). Among the ancient Greeks, the highest form of love for an adult man was homosexual love for a younger man.
5. In 1983, only 35 percent of mothers caring for their children with absent fathers received any child-support, and the average yearly payment was only $2,341; only 6 percent of separated or divorced women received any alimony (1987 Statistical Abstract).
6. The media has focused on child abuse by strangers — on day care scandals and missing children — whereas the vast majority of children are abused by their parents or relatives (Eliasoph 1986).
7. The wealthiest 2.4 percent of households owns 65 percent of the income-producing wealth (Edwards, Reich and Weisskopf 1986).
8. Some feminists and gays have taken an "anti-family" position, as if the "natural" family is the only family form (Barrett and McIntosh 1982); however they usually advocate some alternative, family-like institutions.
9. If this seems far-fetched, an October 1977 CBS-New York Times National Survey found that 50 percent of 30–44 year olds, and 67 percent of 18–29 year olds preferred a symmetrical marriage (of a man and woman who both had jobs, did housework, and cared for the children) over the traditional, complementary one.
10. Most doctors refuse to artificially inseminate single or lesbian women. The developing practice of surrogate mothering is very controversial among feminists and radicals. Since eggs can be fertilized outside of a womb, and embryos can be raised in incubators from the age of a few months, there are many other possibilities, including impregnating men, or even producing infants entirely outside of human bodies, as Marge Piercy (1976) and Shulamith Firestone (1970) have envisioned.
11. Sweden and France give housing allowances to parents (Kamerman and Kahn 1979); many European countries have national health insurance and family allowances. Swedish policy is to guarantee all citizens a minimum standard of living; in the United States, the needy only receive support through "entitlement" programs, which require certain qualifications (such as being a female household head with children) other than being poor, and which do not, in any event, raise incomes up to the poverty level.
12. See Chester (1982) for a review of Western thought on inheritance.
13. Kamerman and Kingston (in Kamerman and Hayes 1982) found that paid maternity leave was available to fewer than one-third of all employed women in 1978, and averaged only about six weeks of benefits.
14. Cuba encourages such marriages through its "Family Code," adopted in 1975 (Randall 1981); however, it still discriminates against gay couples.
15. Sodomy laws, which outlaw forms of "unnatural sex" (e.g. anal intercourse and oral/genital sex, either heterosexual or homosexual) still exist in many states, and were recently upheld by the Supreme Court, although they are seldom enforced. Many cities and a few states have passed gay rights legislation, and more and more employers have extended their non-discrimination policy to include sexual preference or orientation.

16. In June 1987, the Swedish Parliament approved a bill which gave gay couples the same rights as heterosexuals married by common law; it will allow couples to sign housing leases as couples, regulate the division of property after a break-up, and grant lovers the right to inherit property in the absence of a will (*Gay Community News,* June 14–20, 1987).
17. Even though the recent tax reform reduced the progressivity of the tax system, and a 1983 reform exempted 10 percent of the income of the lower-earning partner from taxation, the "marriage penalty" persists (Blau and Ferber 1986).

REFERENCES

Barrett, Michele and Mary McIntosh. 1982. *The Anti-Social Family*. London: New Left Books.

Blackwood, Evelyn. 1984. Sexuality and Gender in Certain Native Tribes: The Case of Cross-Gender Females. *Signs* 10(1):27–42.

Blau, Francine and Marianne Ferber. 1986. *The Economics of Women, Men, and Work*. Englewood Cliffs, NJ: Prentice-Hall.

Bowles, Samuel, David M. Gordon, and Thomas E. Weisskopf. 1983. *Beyond the Wasteland: A Democratic Alternative to Economic Decline*. New York: Anchor/Doubleday.

Chester, Ronald. 1982. *Inheritance, Wealth, and Society*. Bloomington: Indiana University Press.

Children's Defense Fund. 1987. Unpublished paper.

Edwards, Richard, Michael Reich, and Thomas Weisskopf. 1986. *The Capitalist System*. Third Edition. Englewood Cliffs, NJ: Prentice-Hall.

Eliasoph, Nina. 1986. Drive-In Mortality, Child Abuse, and the Media. *Socialist Review* No. 90, 16(6):7–31.

Farley, Jennie (ed.). 1983. *The Woman in Management*. New York: ILR Press.

Firestone, Shulamith. 1970. *The Dialectic of Sex*. New York: Morrow.

Ginsberg, Helen. 1983. *Full Employment and Public Policy: The United States and Sweden*. Lexington, MA: D.C. Heath and Co.

Gould, Steven J. 1981. *The Mismeasure of Man*. New York: Norton.

Hartmann, Heidi. 1981. The Unhappy Marriage of Marxism and Feminism. In, *Women and Revolution: A Discussion of the Unhappy Marriage of Marxism and Feminism,* Lydia Sargent (ed.). pp. 1–41. Boston: South End Press.

Kamerman, Sheila and Alfred Kahn. 1979. *Family Policy: Government and Families in Fourteen Countries*. New York: Columbia University Press.

_____ and Cheryl Hayes(eds.). 1982. *Families That Work: Children in a Changing World*. Washington: National Academy Press.

_____ et al. (eds.). 1983. *Maternity Policies and Working Women*. New York: Columbia University Press.

Matthaei, Julie. 1982. *An Economic History of Women in American: Women's Work, the Sexual Division of Labor, and the Development of Capitalism*. New York: Schocken Books.

Mead, Margaret. 1935. *Sex and Temperament in Three Primitive Societies*. New York: William Morrow and Co.

Miller, Alice. 1981. *The Drama of the Gifted Child*. Trans. by Ruth Ward. New York: Basic Books.

Piercy, Marge. 1976. *Woman on the Edge of Time*. New York: Fawcett.

Randall, Margaret. 1981. *Women in Cuba: Twenty Years Later*. New York: Smyrna Press.

Rodham, Hilary. 1976. Children under the Law. In, *Rethinking Childhood,* Arlene Skolnick (ed.). Boston: Little, Brown and Co.

Sahlins, Marshall. 1976. *The Use and Abuse of Biology: An Anthropological Critique of Sociobiology*. Ann Arbor: University of Michigan Press.
Select Committee on Children, Youth and Families, U.S. House of Representatives. 1987. Fact Sheet: Hearing on Child Care, Key to Employment in a Changing Economy. March 10.
Stack, Carol. 1974. *All Our Kin*. New York: Harper & Row.
U.S. Bureau of the Census, Current Population Reports. 1985a. Household and Family Characteristics: March 1985. Washington, D.C.
_____. 1985b. Money Income and Poverty Status of Families and Persons in the United States. Washington, D.C.
_____. 1986. 1987. Statistical Abstract of the United States. Washington, D.C.
Weeks, Jeffrey. 1979. *Coming Out: Homosexual Politics in Britain, from the Nineteenth Century to the Present*. London: Quartet Books.

PART FOUR

ORGANIZED LABOR

14

Expanding the Fight Against Shutdowns

DAN SWINNEY
and
JACK METZGAR

Unless an effective fight to save America's industrial base is mounted in the next few years, it is hard to exaggerate the bleak prospects facing unions, industrial communities and working people in general. Besides being devastating blows in themselves, plant closings and the threat of plant closings are a major means through which corporations are extracting concessions from both unions and communities, concessions which are dramatically reducing living standards and life expectations.

While only fundamental changes in national economic policy can reverse America's industrial decline, these changes are unlikely to come about unless there is a widespread movement of labor unions and community groups to shape their own destinies on the terrain of local economic development. There will be no constituency for the needed changes unless current policies are fought plant by plant, community by community.

This paper argues that, as the crisis of manufacturing has deepened, the labor-community fight against shutdowns has accumulated a rich mine of experience and insight upon which it is now possible to wage a series of more effective struggles, with far-reaching consequences. It argues that while fighting shutdowns on one front, labor must become much more deeply involved in local economic planning — in efforts to retain and create jobs in the community. This is not only essential for immediate objectives, but provides an opportunity for labor to mount an aggressive political and economic offensive in the broad public interest.

THE CRISIS OF MANUFACTURING

The mid-1980s provided one of the longest business-cycle expansions in postwar American history. Yet manufacturing, still the core of our economy, remained in crisis.

Well paying, largely unionized manufacturing jobs were the engine of America's postwar prosperity. From 1949 to 1969, goods-producing jobs grew by more than 33 percent — from about 15 million to about 20 million. During the 1970s, manufacturing as a whole was stagnant, failing to produce any significant job growth. Since 1980, there has been a net loss of more than 2 million manufacturing jobs.

Nor is the crisis of manufacturing a temporary phenomena — a "correction" or "restructuring" — that will soon end "naturally." Many companies and plants that have survived in reduced forms until now are in precarious condition. They will not survive the next economic downturn, no matter how moderate it is. Many will not survive until then. As many as one-third of the remaining industrial jobs are in jeopardy over the next ten years. Far from being near the end of the crisis, we are at its very beginning.

While certain areas of the country are hit much harder than others (more than half the total manufacturing job loss has been concentrated in six states — Illinois, Indiana, Ohio, Michigan, Pennsylvania and New York), the crisis directly threatens every local economy that has any substantial dependence on manufacturing. As *Business Week* documented (March 3, 1986), "the decline of manufacturing threatens the entire U.S. economy. . . as [the growing] service-sector jobs don't pack the punch of industrial jobs — in wages, innovation, and productivity. . . [and as] companies are abandoning manufacturing to bolster profits — quick fixes that foreshadow a national crisis."

Key postwar American institutions have not only failed to respond to this crisis, they are actively fueling it. Both corporations and financial institutions are deepening the crisis as they turn from productive investment to speculative manipulation of paper assets. While cheering this process on as the workings of a "free market," the Reagan Administration systematically dismantled much of the social, economic and physical infrastructure that had sustained the American economy since the New Deal.

Some state and local governments have been much more activist and creative, but all are struggling to make up for reductions in federal funding for a variety of services. Moreover, the federal government's *laissez-faire* philosophy has encouraged local politicians and business leaders to engage in destructive competitions to reduce their "social wage" and to provide increasingly expensive "incentives" to footloose corporations.

The American labor movement — a key player in building America's postwar prosperity — is particularly threatened. Assaulted on every front, unions are weaker now than at any time since the Wagner Act was passed in 1935. Manufacturing job loss saps key industrial unions of members, resources and political influence. This makes other unions, less directly affected by the crisis of manufacturing, vulnerable to corporate and government attacks on wages, standards and union power. Everywhere unions are faced with cruel dilemmas where jobs are pitted against wages and standards, as all spiral downwards and unions seem helpless to stop them.

Despite its apparent helplessness in situation after situation, labor's response to the crisis of manufacturing contains many positive elements for the future. In what follows we look at the possibilities for national intervention, and local-level efforts to fight shutdowns. Then, in a third section, we address labor's potential to shape local economic development.

LABOR'S NATIONAL PROGRAM

At the national level, organized Labor is nearly alone in advocating a radically new level of government intervention in economic life and is one of the most important defenders of the social welfare system against New Right and neoliberal attacks. The top leadership of the AFL-CIO, the Autoworkers, the Steelworkers, the Machinists and other unions have developed a national economic policy program which is virtually the only coherent and feasible alternative to the Right's program. Besides traditional labor advocacy of social welfare programs and stimulative fiscal and monetary policies, labor has been the chief and most consistent advocate of a national industrial policy focused on saving the manufacturing sector and its jobs.

A national industrial policy would establish a federal government mechanism to coordinate various forms of government subsidies to industries in trouble to get them back on their feet. It would also permit intervention to facilitate increased employment in new growth sectors by, for example, coordinating job training. It would involve regional and sectoral planning of a sort common in most other advanced industrial countries, but completely alien to United States reliance on "the free market." Through such a mechanism, government could intervene decisively in corporate decision-making. For instance, government subsidies could be conditioned on corporate agreement to specific investments which take into account the social impacts of investment and plant location decisions.

There are lots of different ways that this major new policy direction might work out in practice. As many people have pointed out, it could result in even tighter corporate control of the American economy and a new form of "corporate welfare" (e.g., tax breaks for poor corporations with no strings attached). But this is not the only possibility. A national industrial policy could provide a major vehicle for labor and industrial communities to shape corporate decision-making in the broad public interest. It could provide a whole new arena for the citizenry at large to affect its economic destiny — and the fates of hundreds of industrial communities across the country.

Which direction a national industrial policy might take in the future is highly dependent, in our view, on labor taking the lead now in expanding the fight against shutdowns toward major new initiatives in local and regional economic development. Only in this way will labor be able to build a constituency for an industrial policy approach to our economic problems. And only in this way will labor and industrial communities adequately prepare themselves to play an active and decisive role in shaping both the broad direction and the specific actions of an industrial policy program.

FIGHTING SHUTDOWNS

The fight against shutdowns had its birth in 1977 in Youngstown, Ohio, when a group of clergy spearheaded an effort of that community to take over and run a steel mill that was being closed by U.S. Steel. The Steelworkers national leadership was initially cool to that and subsequent efforts in Youngstown to stop the wave of plant closings there through worker and community ownership. But as the closing of steel mills continued to devastate formerly prosperous industrial communities, the union moved decisively toward the approach pioneered in Youngstown — contesting U.S. Steel's unmitigated right to close mills in Chicago and in Duquesne, Pennsylvania, in 1984 and experimenting with various forms of worker ownership since then.

In the 1980s community-based groups have formed permanent union-community coalitions to fight shutdowns on a systematic basis. The Tri-State Conference on Steel, with an active membership in Ohio, Pennsylvania and West Virginia, grew out of the Youngstown effort. In the Pittsburgh area, Tri-State led in the formation of the Steel Valley Authority, which is funded and run by a coalition of steel towns and is specifically chartered to take over abandoned facilities through eminent domain and set up worker-community owned firms that are democratically managed. (Eminent domain refers to the government's right to take private property for public use or for the public interest.)

The California Plant Closures Project in Oakland has been fighting shutdowns for nearly a decade, attracting increasing union and local government support, as has the Calumet Project for Industrial Jobs in northwest Indiana and the West Side Jobs Network in Chicago. One of the most successful of such groups is the Naugatuck Valley Project, a coalition of religious, Citizen Action and United Autoworkers leaders in Connecticut. In 1984 Naugatuck stopped a brass wire mill from being closed, engineering a worker buyout and forming Seymour Specialty Wire.

Even where there are not permanent coalitions, individual local unions have mobilized community support to challenge plant closings. United Electrical Workers (UE) Local 277 in New Bedford, Massachusetts, established model practice when it detected the early warning signs of a plant closing and began its fight several years before the closing would have occurred. Threatening to take over the local machine tool plant through eminent domain, the city of New Bedford forced Gulf and Western to sell the plant to an outside entrepreneur who made a commitment to abide by the union contract and to make the necessary investments to keep the plant viable.

Likewise, UAW Local 645 mounted an impressive community campaign to back up its threat to organize a boycott of General Motors products in the Los Angeles area if GM closed its assembly plant there. And UE Local 1154 at Stewart-Warner Corp. in Chicago spearheaded a community coalition that has put local political pressure on the company to stop disinvesting its Chicago plants. Though the ultimate outcome of each of these union-initiated efforts is still in doubt, in each instance the union began fighting the shutdown well before it was announced by the company and before the facilities had been stripped of their productive assets.

Against the magnitude of the crisis in manufacturing, these efforts of unions and labor-community coalitions may seem relatively insignificant. But they are not. A lot has been learned about how to fight back and what is needed to mount a broader offensive.

No longer do experienced coalitions merely decry the occurrence of a plant closing and protest against it. They actively seek alternatives based on sound business practices, contending with major corporations over the viability of existing facilities. In areas where anti-shutdown groups have been active, the educational value of public debate over the fate of a plant is incalculable: these campaigns have shattered the myth that corporations always know what they're doing. They have shown that there can be viable alternatives to corporate decisions, and have educated local public opinion on the difference between decisions based solely on private profit-maximizing criteria and those which include a social cost analysis.

A process of more effectively fighting shutdowns has been developed. It begins with what are now widely recognized as *early warning signs* of potential plant closings, with systems for monitoring local plants for these signs. Some of these signs include:

— changes in ownership or management instability.
— disinvestment, inadequate maintenance, no capital improvements.
— declining sales, loss of sales force, loss of major customers.
— sudden changes in management behavior (see LeRoy, Charpentier and Swinney 1986).

Research into specific plant closings has shown time and again that profitable plants are being closed — because they are *not profitable enough* for traditional entrepreneurs or investors, or because they are located in communities (often black or Latino) and mature industrial sectors that are being discarded in this period of deindustrialization.

Plants in distressed industrial communities close because of problems with succession — there simply isn't a son or daughter who wants to take over the old man's small manufacturing company. They close because they are mismanaged by owners who are used to the wide tolerance of an expanding economy and are unprepared to provide creative and innovative leadership under current conditions. Through early warning efforts these conditions can be identified at a time when something can be done which preserves jobs, economic stability and justice.

Of course, there are some plants that cannot be saved no matter how strenuous the effort — because of shrinking markets, dramatic changes in technology, or unbeatable foreign competition. Hence, the first step taken by a union or community coalition is a brief pre-feasibility analysis which identifies situations that cannot be salvaged and are not worth further risk, money or emotional energy. If there isn't a reasonable opportunity to retain jobs and capacity, leadership is earned by a firm "No Go" decision, and valuable resources are preserved for other opportunities.

The next stage for action around such an opportunity is a full feasibility analysis which looks at a company's markets, financial capacity, management resources, etc., to determine potential for and risk associated with further investment. In many cases, with a relatively small financial investment, unions and community leaders can obtain from local and state governments the kind of money and talent required to do a full feasibility analysis. Several pro-labor consulting groups — like the Industrial Cooperative Association, Locker Associates, and the Midwest Center for Labor Research — have pioneered in incorporating information and perspectives from the workers directly linked with a company. These shopfloor insights vastly improve the quality of the study and can also serve as an organizing tool, raising the expectations and confidence of the workers themselves.

If the feasibility study determines that a plant could be viable, the labor-community coalition, in alliance with local government, has a variety of options for intervention depending on what is required. Community or union pressure can be exerted to get the company to change debilitating management practices, investment strategies or the business plan. Local government and the development network can offer technical and financial assistance to facilitate these changes.

If these efforts don't work, local government can explore the possibility of using eminent domain to take a facility and sell it to a new owner who is willing to do what is required to make the plant viable. Just the threatened use of eminent domain has had an important impact on key struggles in Massachusetts, Pennsylvania and Illinois. Finally, the fight against shutdowns has opened up a wealth of possibilities for developing new and more democratic forms of ownership — including worker ownership, community ownership and hybrid forms of local entrepreneurship.

Most of the fights against shutdowns thus far have begun too late, after the plant is already down. Most of the feasibility studies have been negative, eminent domain has only been used as a threat, and worker ownership has been successful in only a handful of cases. But there now exists a clear methodology for doing better in the future. Beginning with an early warning system, through the feasibility process, the public intervention and the possibility of worker ownership — each stage relies on bringing workers' production insights and community interests into the process of business decision-making. Each stage educates workers and the local community about business and prepares them to intervene more effectively in the future.

COALITION BUILDING AND LOCAL ECONOMIC DEVELOPMENT

Even the best fight against a shutdown is inherently reactive, and the final result will be dependent on the economics of a single plant. But fighting shutdowns can be a first step toward broader labor participation in the whole range of local economic development activities.

Where unions have made a determined effort to fight plant closings, public officials have become increasingly sensitive to the problems of deindustrialization and more willing to challenge corporate decisions. When left to themselves, public officials will follow the lead of local business leaders, who very often advocate decreasing living standards to improve the "business climate." But when challenged with a labor-community coalition mobilized around a real alternative, politicians can often act in surprisingly supportive ways.

Similarly, local government economic development staff are often eager to work with labor-community coalitions who have real alternatives to present. Development staff's day-to-day work involves trying to come up with something that can stem the tide of economic decline in their communities, and they are often acutely aware that business-led efforts to improve the "business climate" lead to a dead-end in the long run.

Likewise, many staff of neighborhood development corporations have a background in community organizing, share the democratic values of the labor movement and are eager for the opportunity to work with unions. Even many local business people — particularly local merchants — can be mobilized around alternative business plans and new economic development approaches. The interests of locally-based business are often antithetical to those of absentee conglomerates who control the fates of so many local communities.

In distressed industrial communities, the reality is sinking in. Traditional approaches to economic development are widely perceived as inadequate to face the current crisis, and there is a growing void of political, economic and social leadership — a void which labor can and must fill. As ill-prepared as labor might seem at the moment, local business and political leaders are even less prepared. This is partly because they have not experienced the full brunt of the crisis as labor has, and because they are used to representing a narrower range of interests than labor inherently does.

Labor has no choice but to fill this void. As labor advances its short-range objectives to dramatically coalesce with the needs and interests of the broader community, it can regain and even surpass its previous strength and status in society. Leading the fight to save manufacturing industries and industrial communities can propel the labor movement into a position not only of effectively representing the interests of its dues-paying members, but in being the most effective force in representing the interests of the growing section of our society that is feeling the weight of the deepening crisis.

In the course of this struggle, new assumptions and objectives begin to emerge. Various clashes sharpen the exposure of classes and institutions and the values that guide their roles and influence in society. The need for dramatic changes in local and national policy is revealed in event after event on a local level. New forms of economic democracy become real and reasonable options, and the potential of a labor-managed market economy is suggested.

CONCLUSION

For labor to maximize its role in the immediate period ahead, it needs to re-hone its skills in the use of traditional tactics related to organizing, negotiations, strikes, boycotts and legislative initiatives. The capacity to fight effectively on many fronts gave labor what prestige and strength it has today and is a prerequisite for effective relations in new types of initiatives. The new relations that labor seeks need to be based on strength and mutual respect, not token representation on a committee or capitulation to powerful interests under the guise of "cooperation."

For these purposes, as well as for gaining broader economic leadership, labor must:
1. *Broaden its ties on the community level*. There is a growing network of organizations and leaders being pulled into the crisis with labor, including community organizations, churches, development organizations, local business organizations and local government. These contacts need to be built on the community level and require a high level of understanding on labor's side of why this contact is being built, what the issues are, and what the opportunities and pitfalls are. The labor movement needs to train its local leaders to engage in this type of liaison work and not rely solely on relationships established by national and state-level contacts.
2. *Continue to expand labor's experiments*. Creative efforts linked to economic development are just one part of the creative revival needed in the labor movement in all its different aspects of work. Because of the complexity and dangers of experiments in difficult times, it is necessary to be rigorous in our evaluation of these new initiatives. Labor needs to be determined to look closely at complex facts and issues; to encourage debate and evaluation; to have a willingness to acknowledge mistakes; and to be skilled in building unity within the labor movement and between labor and the broader community.

Specifically related to playing a leading role in local economic development, the labor movement needs to give concerted attention to new approaches that have emerged in the last few years:

a. *Early warning research and networks*. Union members are a vast untapped resource in identifying difficulties and opportunities in troubled industries. They are a resource for anyone interested in economic development. Unions, therefore, have the potential to be more comprehensive and factual than many traditional resources. In utilizing this capacity, the labor movement can more effectively target opportunities for intervention.

b. *Expand labor's role in management*. Unions need their own alternative corporate plans and aggressive campaigns against mismanagement and socially destructive business practices. Labor's interests in jobs inevitably stand in sharp contrast with those guided by the desire for the greatest profit in the shortest amount of time.

c. *Setting up unionized worker-owned firms*. Labor needs concrete examples of how capable workers are of establishing and managing companies. Through worker-owned firms, labor has a unique opportunity to demonstrate that socially conscious assumptions can guide the use of business and entrepreneurial skills. In these projects, labor necessarily needs technical and financial capacity. Working with local development organizations in worker-ownership efforts not only provides the opportunity to learn technical skills, but also educates development professionals about the role of labor and the advantages of democratically run enterprises.

d. *Developing labor's "capital strategies."* Labor can play a direct role in economic development through the vast financial resources it has direct and indirect control over, such as pension and insurance funds. These funds can provide tremendous leverage in economic development projects that are done on behalf of union members and their communities. As craft unions have provided funds for construction projects, industrial unions like the Steelworkers are contributing to the funds required for pre-feasibility and feasibility studies. This is money well spent. The use of union-controlled funds needs to be conceived of on a broader scale.

e. *Organize for government intervention on behalf of jobs, productive capacity, and the industrial community.* We cannot afford to cede the role of government to narrow anti-labor interests in the corporate community. Many examples of positive government intervention, particularly on the state and local levels, have emerged in the last decade. It's up to labor to strengthen its effort to define the terms for that intervention and to promote the interests and involvement of the local community.

REFERENCES

Bensman, David and Roberta Lynch. 1987. *Rusted Dreams: Hard Times in a Steel Community.* New York: McGraw-Hill.

Bluestone, Barry and Bennett Harrison. 1982 .*The Deindustrialization of America.* New York: Basic Books.

CNT. 1986. *Working Neighborhoods: Taking Charge of Your Local Economy.* Chicago: Center for Neighborhood Technology.

Cohen, Stephen S. and John Zysman. 1987. *Manufacturing Matters: The Myth of the Post-Industrial Economy.* New York: Basic Books.

Doherty, Barbara. nd. *The Struggle to Save Morse Cutting Tool.* Southeastern Massachusetts University Labor Education Center.

The Editors. 1986. *The Home Grown Economy: New Directions for Community Self-Reliance. Changing Work* magazine, Newton, MA. (Spring).

Kennedy, Donald (ed.). 1984. *Labor and Reindustrialization.* Pennsylvania State University Department of Labor Studies.

LeRoy, Greg, Elaine Charpentier and Dan Swinney, 1986. *Early Warning Manual Against Plant Closings.* Chicago: Midwest Center for Labor Research.

Lynd, Staughton. 1982. *The Fight Against Shutdowns.* San Pedro: Singlejack Books.

Mann, Eric. 1987. *Taking On General Motors: A Case Study of the Campaign to Keep GM Van Nuys Open.* Los Angeles: Institute for Industrial Relations, UCLA.

MCLR. 1986. *Labor Tackles the Local Economy: Reindustrialization from Below.* No. 9. Chicago: Midwest Center for Labor Research.

_____. 1987. *Mismanagement & What Unions Can Do About It.* No. 10. Chicago: Midwest Center for Labor Research.

15

Labor Givebacks or Labor Fightbacks

KIM MOODY

By the mid-1980s the symptoms of organized labor's ills had become so numerous and visible that even the Executive Council of the AFL-CIO thought them a proper subject for public discussion. The most obvious symptom was labor's decline as a proportion of the work force, from 23 percent in 1980 to 18 percent in 1985.

To diagnose and prescribe treatment for this ailment, in 1982 the AFL-CIO established the Committee on the Evolution of Work. Three years of discussion and deep thought produced a report entitled "The Changing Situation of Workers and Their Unions," which concluded that labor's weak pulse was due to the failure of labor law. It addressed the problem of a changing work force, but it contained no substantial criticism of labor's internal regime, its practice in collective bargaining or its politics. Its recommendations were entirely administrative and technical in nature. The closest thing to a strategic direction was the observation that unions seem to have better success with workers who are "better educated than the general population" and that public sector workers provide a source of union growth. Remarkably, the report completely ignored the question of concessionary bargaining and the consequent decline in union power. As a prescription for labor's ills, the report was more malpractice than cure.

Nineteen eighty-seven was the eighth year of concessionary bargaining. This trend emerged after the Chrysler bail-out of 1979–80. It has been reflected in the unbroken slide of average first-year wage increases in major collective bargaining agreements, from 11 percent in 1981 to 1.2 percent in 1986. By 1986 almost every major union in every industry had given some form of concessions. These have included not only straightforward wage cuts, but two-tier wage systems under which new hires receive a lower rate than current employees, lump-sum payments in lieu of rate increases (which creates a lower floor for the next bargaining round), and the wholesale dumping of work rules and conditions.

The AFL-CIO leadership and some of its academic allies have regarded concessionary bargaining as a temporary phenomenon linked primarily to ailing firms and recessionary economic conditions. For example, in their 1984 book, *What Do Unions Do?*, Richard Freedman and James Medoff, both consultants for the Committee on the Evolution of Work, stated: "Concessions are therefore found only in industries undergoing extreme economic problems." A 1985 Brookings Institution study by Daniel J. B. Mitchell, however, indicates that by 1984–85 concessions had hit every major industry in which bargaining occurs. Mitchell explicitly rejects the conventional economic explanations in favor of what he calls a "demonstration effect." That is, once healthy employers see others getting concessions, they too demand them.

Equally unconvincing is the argument that concessions were a product of recession or of foreign imports. Three years of recovery have brought no less pressure from employers. By the mid-1980s financially sound, profitable firms, such as General Motors, General Electric and AT&T, routinely demanded and received concessions from once powerful unions. It is plausible to link concessions to imports in industries such as auto, steel or textiles. But imports obviously play no role in trucking, airlines, railroads, grocery, meatpacking, hotels, finance, construction and a great many other industries without foreign competition.

Seeing economic cycles or trade policies as the root of an essentially temporary phenomenon is a comforting thesis for labor leaders accustomed to orderly bargaining through well-defined institutional arrangements. To see employer aggression as a permanent part of the landscape would require a complete break with their business-as-usual style of functioning.

The concessions trend results from the disintegration of the major institutional arrangements of the post-WW II social compact. Two decades of global capitalist crisis characterized by declining profit rates in the advanced industrial nations and the globalization of capital markets have led U.S. capitalists increasingly to seek investment opportunities elsewhere. In the process they have internationalized markets and intensified competition on a world scale. The subsequent decline of traditional industries and the pressures of competition, both domestic and international, have led employers to seek substantial reductions in labor costs. The labor peace of the social compact is no longer a priority for capital. To reduce labor costs throughout the economy a change in power relations was necessary.

For over a decade now the major employers have sought to undo those institutions that support labor's power at the bargaining table and in the political arena. The decline of the NLRB as a protector of labor's rights far precedes the Reagan era. One reason for the purposeful unraveling of the "social safety net" is to make it that much harder for workers to tell aggressive employers to "take this job and shove it."

Management's new aggressiveness means that pattern bargaining, the main technique by which unions have attempted to raise wages and benefits since 1945, now lies in a shambles. The hallmarks of pattern bargaining in the post-World War II era were the Big Three auto contracts, the Basic Steel Agreement, the rubber contracts, the National Master Freight Agreement, the major meatpacking contracts, and the Bituminous Coal Agreement. All of these have been undermined or undone in the past several years.

Meanwhile, the heads of the AFL-CIO remain enamored of their legislative focus, despite their failure to win a single major battle since labor law reform was defeated under Carter in 1978. While legislation could affect labor law enforcement or foreign imports, it can do little about naked employer aggression in industry itself. To confront that aggression would require confrontation on a scale not seen for decades. It would require a mobilization of union members and of other sectors of society with an interest in confronting corporate power. That includes unorganized workers, oppressed minority communities, the women's movement, peace and anti-intervention activities, and anti-apartheid activists, all of whom confront different aspects of American capital's late twentieth-century fight for global dominance.

Bureaucratic coalitions of some of the above named groups for legislative purposes are one thing; a disorderly alliance from below is something else. In the bureaucratic imagination such a confrontationist alliance would be seen as a pointless exercise in stirring up a hornet's nest. In the world of the labor bureaucracy, self-criticism and change are limited to questions of technique or administration. The endorsement of Walter Mondale in the primary is seen as a brilliant strategic innovation. The issuing of associate memberships, insurance policies, and credit cards — a proposal from the Committee on the Evolution of Work — is thought to address the question of organizing the unorganized. Indeed, the whole "debate" on labor's future might have remained mired in the jargon of electronic image polishing if a group of workers in Austin, Minnesota had not decided to take their fate and that of the workers in their industry into their own hands.

In 1984, the members of United Food and Commercial Workers Local P-9 rebelled against their International union's strategy of orderly retreat through concessionary agreements. The UFCW had reopened its contracts with the major old-line meatpackers in 1981–82 and granted them a three-year wage freeze. The logic was that low-wage, non-union companies were now operating in the meatpacking industry and capturing more and more of the market. The UFCW proposed to hold down their members' higher wages while attempting to organize the non-union firms and pull their wages up. The object was to preserve and extend pattern bargaining.

The problem was that the employers, both high and low-wage, didn't go along with this neat and orderly plan. Once they saw they could get concessions, they went for more — again and again. The union was broken at Armour and beaten at Iowa Beef (now IBP, Inc.), the leading low-wage company. The UFCW did not succeed in organizing some of the most aggressive new firms and was unable to pull the lower wages up. By late 1983, UFCW Packinghouse Division chief Lewie Anderson admitted to the *Wall Street Journal* that only about a third of the workers in the industry were still under the pattern. From January 1982, when the freeze was implemented, to January 1985, average wages in meatpacking plants plummeted from $9.19 to $7.93, according to the Bureau of Labor Statistics. Then in the summer of 1984, a year before most of its contracts expired, the UFCW agreed to reopen the Hormel contract and take a pay cut from $10.69 to $9.00 an hour. The company was asking for a larger pay cut, so the UFCW leadership imagines to this day that it accomplished something positive with the $1.69 give-back.

The new President of Local P-9, Jim Guyette, had opposed the UFCW's strategy of pre-emptive concessions from the start. P-9 members voted to reject the cut. The Hormel plant in Austin was new, having replaced an older one there, and was built to produce 50 percent of Hormel's total shipments. It was the most modern and efficient in the industry. Furthermore, Hormel was a highly profitable, growing concern. P-9's bargaining position was a rather good one. Guyette later expressed the thinking that underlay P-9's move at that time: "If the newest plant in the industry takes a cut in wages, then the other plants are going to say they can't compete. If the concessions are going to stop, then they are going to have to stop at the most profitable company with the newest plant."

Local P-9 developed a multi-faceted plan for dealing with Hormel. Ray Rogers and Ed Allen of Corporate Campaigns, Inc. were brought to Austin to lay out a plan of action. A campaign directed against Hormel and its leading financial partner, First Bank, was designed to get P-9's message out to the people of Austin, to meatpacking towns throughout the "Hog Belt," and to other meatpacking locals of the UFCW. The UFCW rejected this plan, so P-9 agreed to hire Rogers and Allen themselves. By the time the strike date came on August 17, 1985, P-9's struggle with Hormel was well known and had support. In a pamphlet put out in 1986, P-9 members described what the local and Corporate Campaigns had accomplished:

> Working together, New York City-based Corporate Campaign, Inc (CCI) and the members of P-9 have achieved a great deal since January of 1985. They have focused national media attention on the problems facing all packinghouse workers; broken down the barriers to communication that existed between workers at the many Hormel and FDL Foods plants; distributed well-researched literature dealing with the issues of give-backs and workplace health and safety to over 500,000 homes across the Midwest; mobilized support from over 3,000 unions and other organizations in every state in the country; generated legal assistance to fight for the workers' Constitutional rights and to defend them against the legal attacks of Hormel, the government and the UFCW leadership; and kept the P-9 rank and file moving as a constructive, non-violent force, rather than leaving them idle, isolated and frustrated.

The last point can hardly be stressed too much. Observers were struck by the constant state of membership mobilization and the mass democratic character of decision-making in Austin. At the heart of this mobilization was the Austin United Support Group. Formed by spouses of the P-9 members in October 1984, the Support Group involved hundreds of volunteers in its Austin-based support activities. Along with the local union, the Support Group operated out of the Austin Labor Center until the May 1986 trusteeship — then it moved down the street. A 24-hour strike kitchen provided hot meals. An emergency fund was established to help families in immediate need. The more long-run "Adopt-a-P-9-Family Fund" allowed local unions around the country to help a specific striking family. The Labor Center's walls became the canvas for mural art.

Thousands of unionists from around the country visited Austin for mass rallies. And all the while, P-9 members traveled the country with their message. They could be found not only at labor events, but at Central America and South Africa solidarity events. P-9ers supported embattled farmers in the upper Midwest and the farmers support them. Peace movement activists were brought to Austin to train P-9 members in non-violent direct action techniques. Rallies and fund-raisers were organized coast to coast. P-9 organized support within other UFCW meatpacking locals. In several locals the election of officers was fought over the question of support for P-9. By the end of 1986, over 3,000 local unions and labor organizations had contributed money to P-9. Anyone who was concerned about labor's general decline and its inability to mobilize support outside its own ranks could see that what was happening in Austin was an example for the rest of the labor movement.

The leadership of the UFCW and eventually of the AFL-CIO didn't see it that way. In their view, P-9 had broken from the Hormel chain and repudiated pattern bargaining. P-9 was accused of breaking solidarity and going it alone. UFCW President William Wynn called the strike a "suicide mission." In January 1986, shortly after the National Guard was called to Austin to escort scabs into the plant, UFCW Vice-President Lewie Anderson denounced P-9 and its strike on Ted Koppel's "Nightline." The attack became a national campaign. An issue of the "UFCW Leadership Update" attacking P-9 was approved by the AFL-CIO Executive Council and circulated nationally in February 1986.

The UFCW's attack on P-9 was significant more for what it revealed about the way top labor bureaucrats view the world than for what it said about P-9. The UFCW's 1984 strategy of concessions could not be justified with the usual argument used to sell concessions — save jobs by saving the company — since Hormel was a highly profitable firm. The UFCW's argument was thus the need to preserve pattern bargaining above all, as the basis of solidarity. The "Leadership Update" reminded the errant P-9 that the purpose of a national wage rate was to prevent the companies from playing local against local to win lower wages.

The pious little lecture on national wage rates and competition was pure hypocrisy, for the UFCW's strategy of preemptive concessions did the very opposite of what pattern bargaining was created for. That is, by granting first a wage freeze and then a wage cut to the high-wage firms in recognition of their competition problem, the union itself put wages into competition. It was inevitable, then, that the employers would move against any semblance of a pattern.

To UFCW officials, "solidarity" became a lifeless conception more akin to obedience than to workers actively supporting one another. The sort of mobilization conducted by P-9 was not even recognizable as solidarity to the UFCW leadership. UFCW Region 13 Director Joe Hansen remarked: "When Guyette talks about this solidarity shit it makes me want to puke."

For Lane Kirkland, P-9 was not a victim of corporate aggression, but one of the problems of the labor movement: locals and small unions running off and getting into fights they can't finish. The AFL-CIO Executive Council statement backing the UFCW states that: "Today's economic and political climate make it imperative that unions follow realistic bargaining strategies... not 'all-or-nothing' stances...." At the February Executive Council meeting, Kirkland indicated that the federation would no longer allow groups like P-9 and PATCO to drag labor into losing fights. He let it be known that one of the reforms coming down the pike would be to give the Executive Council the power to prevent strikes that it did not think could be won. Kirkland told the Council: "We must be part of the general staff at the inception, rather than the ambulance drivers at the bitter end." In other words, his means for dealing with employer aggression is to further rein in militant locals or unions through increased centralization of the AFL-CIO.

The UFCW has punished P-9 for its attempts to build active solidarity, to fight concessions, and to revive the combative spirit of industrial unionism in meatpacking. In May 1986, the UFCW declared P-9 to be in trusteeship. They subsequently imposed a contract that contained much of the language in the contract the company had imposed in the Fall of 1984. Its wage settlement put Austin Hormel workers one penny above where they had been in 1981 by September 1988. Furthermore, the Austin contract was four years long, putting that plant out of sync with the others in the Hormel chain.

Some of the P-9ers countered by founding the North American Meat Packers Union (NAMPU) and filed for a representation election with over 600 signatures. That election has been indefinitely delayed by the NLRB. NAMPU hoped to become a long-range alternative to the UFCW by winning over other dissatisfied packing locals to create a genuine industrial union of packinghouse workers (packing locals are currently submerged and relatively powerless within the UFCW, which since a 1979 merger has been dominated by officials from the former Retail Clerks union). NAMPU did get a representation at an Excell plant in Texas, but the odds were too great against the fledgling Austin-based union and it lost to the UFCW.

For coming up with this plan, NAMPU activists have been stigmatized as "dual unionists." This term, of course, sends even the boldest of radicals running for cover. It shouldn't. The CIO itself was nothing if not a bunch of dual unionists and labor splitters. Even the AFL, from which it split, was created in 1886 by craft unions that had split from the Knights of Labor. As we watch today's labor leaders stand slack-jawed before millions of unorganized workers, it is simply inconceivable that those millions will be organized without something new, dual, and audacious happening. Whether it comes from inside the "official" labor movement or from outside is anyone's guess. But the transformation of the labor movement may well require some new unions, both in new industries and in some old ones where the existing union has abdicated.

The defeat of the Austin strike at the hands of the UFCW International sent a clear message to employers throughout the meatpacking industry. In 1986–87, several firms sought a new round of concessions. Patrick Cudahy, John Morrell, and IBP all demanded deep wage cuts from the UFCW. The local's resisted and long strikes ensued. All of these strikes lasted several months (Morrell and Cudahy still going as of September 1987). The settlement at IBP was a disaster. It included a 32-month wage freeze and a two-tier wage set-up, under which workers hired after December 14, 1986 would make less than those hired before.

The struggle of P-9 against the concessionary retreat of the UFCW underlines some very real problems which are scarcely addressed in the official discussion of labor's future. Chief among these is the rise of competitive bargaining and "enterprise unionism." Enterprise unionists consciously try to bolster the competitive position of their own employer, through concessions or through various "non-adversarial" programs such as Quality of Work Life, participation on the board of directors, profit sharing, or simply by allowing wages, benefits, and working conditions to be bargained on a competitive basis. Enterprise consciousness, then, is the opposite of solidarity consciousness, an "each local for itself" mentality.

Lance Compa, a representative of the United Electrical Workers, has written: "It is the breakdown of industrial unionism and the introduction of enterprise unionism, not concessions in and of themselves, that pose the real threat to the labor movement." Compa is right about the breakdown of industrial unionism and the danger of enterprise unionism. He is wrong, however, when he calls P-9's action an example of enterprise unionism. More importantly, he misses the real point of the concessions trend of the past seven years. Concessions are not something "in and of themselves." They are an instrumental part of the decay of industrial unionism. The opening of contracts to grant concessions is an act that puts wages into competition no matter how compelling the circumstances that prompt them. It has been the willingness of so many International unions to grant concessions that has undermined pattern bargaining and encouraged enterprise unionism, not the resistance of brave individual locals to concessions.

It did not take long for the competitive logic of concessionary bargaining and non-adversarial enterprise unionism to move beyond mere concessions in the major pattern agreements, to their break-up. Indeed, 1986 saw the demise of the last two major pattern agreements — steel and telephone. The breakup of the Bell system was of course a factor in the collapse of the latter, but there was nothing to prevent the CWA from attempting to impose a standard wage and benefits pattern on the seven regional operating companies. Instead, it bargained first with AT&T within the framework of that company's needs, and afterwards separately with each of the operating companies and even with the individual state-level Bell companies. The result is no real pattern at all and the end of standard conditions in telephone.

The case of steel was a purer example of how concessions for competitive reasons led to the fragmentation of the pattern bargaining that used to characterize industrial unionism in the United States. The Basic Steel Agreement was one of the original CIO master contracts established in 1945–46. In 1983, the United Steelworkers granted the seven major producers in that agreement sizable concessions to improve their competitive position against foreign steelmakers. It did not take the domestic corporations long, however, to notice the competitive factors among themselves. In 1985 the steelmakers announced that they would no longer bargain as a group with the USWA. In 1986, the Steelworkers announced their strategy: to grant different contracts to each company based on the union's perception of each one's competitive position. It was the ultimate expression of putting wages into competition. The union bargained separately with each company and granted labor costs concessions ranging from $3.60 an hour at LTV to $.40 at Inland Steel. USX, the largest steelmaker, refused to go along with the union's assessment of its financial need (the union had offered it only a wage freeze, much less than Bethlehem and LTV received). The company locked its workers out for six months and achieved a disastrous settlement which had the union explicitly agree to the elimination of 1,346 jobs.

In other industries, such as trucking, coal, meatpacking, rubber and electrical, the union involved failed to organize new employers or run-away shops within their industry. In these cases, the union membership became a declining proportion of the work force and control of the labor market was lost as low wage companies put competitive pressure on unionized employers. With the exception of the United Mine Workers, the unions in these industries responded to these pressures by granting, reluctantly or willingly, concessions designed to improve the competitive position of their employers.

The rise of competitive bargaining didn't stop with the collapse of the major national patterns. By the end of 1986, it had also led to the demise of a number of regional patterns such as West Coast lumber, Southern and Western wood products, East and Gulf Coast longshore, among others. As soon as most of the patterns were eroded, bargaining rapidly devolved right down to the workplace/local union level. In the wake of separate bargaining in steel, for example, Armco bargained different wage levels at most of its plants.

In auto, the pattern had come unglued first when the Chrysler contract went out of sync with GM and Ford. But that was only the beginning. The 1984 contracts at GM and Ford opened the door to concessions at the local plant level, which introduced competitive norms within the companies. Whipsawing, the bidding by workers in one plant against those in another doing the same work, unfolded at General Motors from 1985. The 1987 UAW settlement at Ford, went even farther in institutionalizing plant level competitive bargaining and "team concept" (the latest wrinkle in Japanese-style labor management techniques) by forcing locals to come up with a plan for increased "operating efficiency" within six months of the signing of the contract. The pay-off, at Ford, was a job security program known as Guaranteed Employment Numbers (GEN) that was supposed to keep hourly employment at the same level for the life of the contract. In fact, GEN was full of holes and allowed the company to lay-off in the event of a sales slump. The real significance of the 1987 contract, however, was the stamp of approval the UAW leadership gave to competitive bargaining.

The economic basis for whipsawing was rooted in the twin phenomena of overcapacity and outsourcing. GM, which continued to produce about 70 percent of its components "in-house" (compared to about 40–50 percent for Ford and 30–35 percent for Chrysler), had too many plants producing the same components and/or cars to support its declining market share. Thus, with some plant closings inevitable, it was able to get the locals at different plants to "bid" against one another for the work. Ford, which had already trimmed its operations and reduced its work force drastically by the mid-1980s was able to use the threat of outsourcing, either to parts of its international production system or to outside domestic firms, to the same end. GM, which planned to build 11 plants in Mexico (bringing its Mexican total to 29), further positioned itself to continue whipsawing on an international scale. Thus, in the auto industry of the late 1980s, the competition faced by local unions at virtually any Big Three plant was global and open-ended. This situation could be repeated in any manufacturing industry.

Another trend illustrated in the P-9 events was the effect on bargaining of the growth of multi-jurisdictional or general unionism. During the 1980s more unions turned toward the recruitment of members from outside their traditional industrial base. Thus, the UAW, Steelworkers, the UFCW and most others began organizing or absorbing various groups of workers. In the case of the UFCW, this trend had meant that the meatpacking sector of the union, which joined with the Retail Clerks International Union in the 1979 merger that created the UFCW, increasingly took on the local, enterprise style of bargaining that had characterized the retail clerks approach. In other cases it usually meant that the new groups in the union found their concerns low on the organization's agenda.

Since very little new organizing of any kind occurred in the 1980s most of the trends away from industrial unionism has been accomplished through mergers or the absorption of a smaller organization. "The Changing Situation of Workers and Their Unions," provides a rudimentary set of guidelines for mergers that at least takes into account the economic logic of a proposed merger. But few unions paid much attention. At least half the mergers that occurred from 1979 through 1985 had no economic logic. Most unions that sought growth did so by picking up (and usually fighting over) public employee associations that were not yet affiliated to the AFL-CIO. This trend, too, was undermining the ability of any one union to standardize wages, benefits and conditions in a given industry. It dove-tailed all too well with the growth of competitive bargaining and enterprise unionism.

The industrial unionism of the 1930s embodied a strategy of mobilization and of an egalitarian standardization of the terms of employment. Today's increasingly diversified unions are building structures of demobilization and passivity and they have accepted the employers' own competitive imperative as the basis for bargaining practice. Unfortunately, a simple reorganization of the unions along current industrial lines is precluded by the entrenched interests that created the mess, the labor bureaucracy. It is also true that the industrial landscape is changing rapidly. The industries on which the CIO was based have receded, sometimes dramatically, and others have arisen. While some of these new industries are goods-producing, factory-based industries, many are service industries with no tradition of unionization. The relationship of an industrial union to the employers in its industry is further complicated by the rapid and apparently non-stop shift in corporate ownership. In any event, the restructuring of the American labor movement is unlikely at all without the emergence of two mutually reinforcing movements: a rank and file rebellion within the major unions and a genuine crusade to organize the unorganized.

There will be no fundamental change in the social balance of forces if the millions of low-wage workers are not organized. A significant proportion of the unorganized are women, blacks and Latins, whom all the surveys show to be more friendly to unionism than the average white male. This points to a style of organizing that is different from that generally practiced, one that emphasizes social issues as well as economics. The successful organization of clerical workers at Yale University is an example. There, comparable worth was a central issue in the organizing drive and contract negotiations. The Yale strike drew on the strengths of both active labor solidarity and of the women's movement. A modern version of the social unionism of the early CIO is needed.

The question of industrial unionism is also relevant to the organization of many new service-producing industries. Like the mass-production industries in which the CIO was based, today's service-producing industries embody the classic direction of capitalist organization. Increasingly, they are dominated by recognizable centers of capital, they employ vast numbers of low-wage semi-skilled labor, and they produce commodities for the market. This is exploited labor in the classic Marxist sense. The fact that the products produced by this labor are services (or in many cases hybrids of both goods and services, as in communications) in no way changes their natures as commodities. These workers are employed and exploited by capital and the very same tensions that produce unions wherever wage labor exists are at work. This, of course, does not make unionization inevitable, but it does make it possible.

Unfortunately, the labor bureaucracy is rendering this possibility more difficult each year. Its new commitment to competitive bargaining, general unionism and its defense of an unattractive bargaining record during the 1980s, make new organizing even more difficult. Workers do not need unions to negotiate wage cuts or freezes or to pit "teams" of workers against each other. Furthermore, the identification of the organizable as the "better educated" more "middle class" elements of the working class misses the real target. The vast majority of the new service-producing workers are poor and less educated than the professionals and craftsmen the AFL-CIO envisions as its own members. That is why they need unions and why the polls continue to show that the majority of them would like union representation. But the labor leadership, with only a handful of exceptions, seem content with their circle the wagons strategy and the pursuit of an ever narrower political agenda.

Unionization of low-paid industrial and service workers will have to go hand in hand with transformation of the existing unions and/or the formation of new ones. Changes on the scale required will have to come from the ranks. Rank and file rebellion as an organized force inside the major International unions has been scarce in the last few years. But what has taken shape is a growing grassroots resistance to concessions coupled with solidarity consciousness. P-9 was only the latest in a series of hard fought battles against employer aggression. There is genuine anger in the ranks of labor about the companies' incessant demands for give backs and union leaders' willingness to go along. Promises that jobs would be saved or conditions restored have turned out to be lies. The companies keep coming back for more in good times as in bad. We have seen strikes like the coal miners' battle with A. T. Massey, the copper miners' strike against Phelps-Dodge, steelworkers at Wheeling-Pittsburgh, cannery workers at Watsonville Canning in California and scores of others. Many of these strikes have lost or at best have only minimized concessions. But increasingly, as with P-9, the strikers have found willing support among other rank and file workers. In May 1984, when 400 workers at the A.P. Parts plant in Toledo struck, auto and other workers in that town surprised everyone by turning out in thousands to stop the scabs. During the coal miners' strike against Massey, miners from other firms and nearby steelworkers rushed in carloads to join massive sit-downs to stop scab coal deliveries. Support for the mostly Chicana and Mexicana strikers at Watsonville has also been strong.

The massive support for P-9 was the crest of this new wave in the ranks. It is by no means inevitable that this new militancy, which is still a marginal force, will gather enough steam or organize itself for the job of transforming today's bureaucratic unions into fighting organizations. But the return of the will to fight is the first best hope.

16

Women Workers, Feminism and the Labor Movement

RUTH MILKMAN

INTRODUCTION

Women's relationship to work and to the organized labor movement has changed dramatically in the postwar decades, and especially since the 1960s. The vast increases in female labor force participation which occurred in this period produced equally vast social and cultural shifts, transforming family relations as well as women's sense of "place" in the larger society. The growth of a mass feminist movement led to enormous changes in consciousness about gender — not only among movement participants but in the general population. While inequality between women and men has by no means been eliminated, the goal of equality has won popular legitimacy — above all, in the context of the labor market — and women's expectations of work have been heightened accordingly.

Within the labor movement, too, there have been important changes. In 1973, the AFL-CIO endorsed the Equal Rights Amendment. The following year, the Coalition of Labor Union Women (CLUW) held its founding conference, establishing an institutional base for women in the labor movement which the major unions gradually came to accept. In the years that followed, unions took up such "women's issues" as affirmative action, child care, equal pay for work of comparable worth, and parental leave. Female representation in labor leadership also grew significantly during the 1970s, especially at the local and regional levels. In 1980, CLUW president Joyce Miller became the first woman member of the AFL-CIO's Executive Council, followed in 1981 by Barbara Hutchinson of the American Federation of Government Employees, and in 1987 by Lenore Miller, President of the Retail, Wholesale and Department Store Union.[1]

Clearly, the rebirth of feminism did not leave organized labor unaffected. And yet, the impact of the contemporary women's movement on the labor movement has been surprisingly limited in a number of crucial respects. The recent gains in women's representation in union leadership, for example, are quite modest in relation to the substantial increases in female union membership which have occurred in recent years. As a 1980 CLUW study concluded: "With regard to some of the traditional measures of progress and equality — in particular, adequate representation at the power centers of institutions — women are absent from the agenda" of the labor movement.[2] This study also found that those unions which did seriously address "women's issues" tended to do so at the national level, and were often ineffective in reaching rank-and-file women in their local unions (Coalition of Labor Union Women 1980: 5, 18).

The continuing underrepresentation of women among unionized workers is another critical problem. In 1986 only 12.9 percent of the nation's employed women were union members, compared to 21.5 percent for men (U.S. Dept. of Labor 1987: 219).[3] To be sure, the gap has been far wider in past years. Because of the recent decline of union strength in some predominantly male manufacturing industries, and increases in labor's recruitment of members in the more heavily female service and public sectors, women today make up a greater proportion of union membership than ever before — 34 percent in 1986. Yet a significantly larger proportion of the total labor force is female — 46 percent in 1986 (U.S. Dept. of Labor 1987: 219).

Women's relationship to the labor movement has never been an easy one, and it would be unreasonable to expect all of the old difficulties suddenly to disappear in the wake of women's increased labor force participation or the feminist resurgence. Indeed, the period in which these developments occurred has been a particularly troubled one for organized labor. Unions have suffered severe membership losses and have become increasingly isolated from the larger society during these years. But if the dilemma of the unions' relationship to women is not entirely new or surprising, resolving it has never been more critical for the future of the labor movement than it is today. For the dramatic growth of female employment in recent decades directly correlates with the decline in union membership in that period. If the labor movement is to recover from those extensive losses, it must both organize among the vast numbers of unorganized women workers and improve its relations with those women who are already unionized.

WOMEN WORKERS AND UNIONIZATION: RECENT TRENDS

The expansion of the female labor force and the feminization of union membership in recent decades were linked to a larger transformation in the occupational structure as a whole. As economic growth shifted away from manufacturing and toward service and clerical employment, the historical concentration of organized labor in basic industry grew increasingly problematic. As early as the mid-1950s, the percentage of the work force represented by unions began to decline (U.S. Dept. of Labor 1980: 60). There was some new organizing during the postwar decades, but it failed to keep pace with the growth of the work force. In 1986, the latest year for which figures are available, union membership hit a postwar low of 17.5 percent of the labor force (U.S. Dept. of Labor 1987: 219).

Large numbers of women entered the ranks of organized labor over the postwar decades, and even with the vast expansion of the female labor force, the density of unionism among women has been maintained to a far greater extent than among men. At the same time as organized labor as a whole has declined in strength, it has become increasingly feminized. In 1956, women were 18.6 percent of all union members; by 1978, they comprised 24.2 percent of the total. When employee associations are also included in the figure, the proportion of women is even higher, rising from 23 percent in 1973 to 30 percent in 1980, and to 34 percent in 1986 (LeGrande 1980:9; U.S. Dept. of Labor 1980:62; Gifford 1982–83:1).[4] Indeed, in the 1970s, almost all of the growth in labor organization membership was made up of women workers.

This feminization of the labor movement was not the result of any special commitment to organizing women workers *as women*. Rather, it was the unintended consequence of a series of efforts to offset the general decline in membership by organizing particular occupational groups — at one stage, teachers; later, hospital workers; and most recently, public sector clerical and service workers — all of which happen to be predominantly female. Indeed, the composition of the organized female work force today is very different from the traditional base of the organized labor movement. By 1984, nearly half (46 percent) of the nation's 5.9 million women union members were in public sector employment, while another quarter (23 percent) were in either services or sales enterprises in the private sector. Less than a fifth (19 percent) were in manufacturing, labor's traditional stronghold (see Table 1).

Table 1
Women Members of Labor Organizations, Selected Industry Groups, 1984

	Number of Women Union Members (thousands)	Women Members as a Percent of:		Distribution of all Women Workers
Industry Group		Organized Women in all Industries	All Women Employed in this Industry	
Private sector[a]	3,187	54.4	9.5	81.7
Mining and Construction	21	0.4	4.1	1.3
Manufacturing	1,252	21.4	18.9	15.3
Transportation, Communications, and Public Utilities	479	8.2	32.1	3.4
Wholesale and Retail Trade	588	10.0	6.4	23.9
Finance, Insurance and Real Estate	77	1.3	2.2	8.2
Services	764	13.0	6.3	29.6
Government	2,676	45.6	33.1	18.3
ALL INDUSTRIES	5,863	100.0%	14.0	100.0%

[a]Includes agriculture, forestry and fisheries (not shown separately).

Sources: Columns 1, 2, and 3 are derived from data on annual averages for the year ended in September 1984 reported in Larry Adams, "Changing Employment Patterns of Organized Workers," *Monthly Labor Review*, vol. 108, no. 2 (February 1985), p. 29; column 4 is computed from data for September 1984 published in U.S. Department of Labor, Bureau of Labor Statistics, *Employment and Earnings*, vol. 32, no. 1 (January 1985), p. 93.

Unionism among women workers expanded quite unevenly, so that while some occupational categories (for example, teachers) are now highly organized, others — most importantly, private-sector clerical occupations — remain largely outside the labor movement. In the public sector, management opposition to unionization is generally less formidable than in comparable private sector workplaces, and frequently public employees are already organized in associations (without collective bargaining rights), so that unionization victories are often considerably easier to achieve than in private industry (Bell 1985). Consequently, many unions have rushed to organize public workers in order to boost membership levels — and dues — at a time when both are sorely needed.

Public sector unionism has been especially significant for women workers in the 1980s, with the emergence of union-led comparable worth campaigns in many state and local government settings (see Blum 1987). Partly as a result of these campaigns, unionization in the public sector has resulted in a significant narrowing of the gender gap in earnings in that sector (Freeman and Leonard 1985). In contrast to the dynamism of the public sector, however, there have been relatively few efforts to extend unionism to the millions of "pink collar" workers in such private industries as banking or insurance. Unionism among private-sector clericals remains very limited, and most of it involves clericals employed by manufacturing firms with organized blue-collar work forces (Wagner 1979).

The uneven pattern of female representation in the labor movement today validates the perspective on "organizability" which suggests that women workers are no more difficult to recruit into unions than their male counterparts, once a serious effort to organize them is undertaken. In this view, while some industries and occupations may be particularly difficult to unionize, this is not due to the gender of the workers involved, but rather to other factors. Perhaps the most convincing bit of evidence on this point is the fact that the labor organization with one of the largest female memberships today is the Teamsters' union (second only to the National Education Association). Despite its poor public image, the Teamsters' union has been unusually aggressive in the organizing field (and interestingly, its Director of Organizing, Vicki Saporta, is female), and has nearly half a million female members. Other unions with large numbers of women members are listed in Table 2.

The recruitment of women workers into unions is surely a necessary condition for effective representation of their special concerns within the labor movement, but it is not a sufficient condition. The large influx of female members into many important labor organizations in recent years has had little direct impact on the overall character of these unions or their institutional functioning, especially at the national level. Women's representation in top leadership positions, as Table 2 shows, is disproportionately small in relation to their membership in all the unions with large numbers of women, and in most cases the disparity, despite recent progress, remains vast. The general problem of distance between the concerns of rank and file workers and union leaders is especially severe in the case of women workers. Not only do male officials tend to resist female encroachment upon their leadership, but women themselves often have difficulty in viewing themselves as full participants in the male culture of the union's internal life. Unaccustomed to wielding power in the public sphere, and intimidated from the outset by the prospect of self-consciously maneuvering for power within an organization, women members often decline to enter the competition at all (Wertheimer and Nelson 1975).

More generally, the dominant cultural imagery of labor organization and of union power remains male and blue collar. Union leadership, and to some extent even union membership, has a long history as a male prerogative. During the major waves of unionization prior to the postwar era, women workers were a small minority of the work force in the crafts and industries that formed the cornerstone of the key organizing drives. Women were then seen (not entirely without reason) as temporary workers, marginal to the economy; and unions developed as essentially male institutions. Even in industries with large female work forces, like the textile and garment trades, or in periods when women had a relatively large presence within organized labor, like the World War II

Table 2
Female Membership and Leadership in Labor Organizations With 200,000 or More Women Members, 1978 and 1985.

Organization	Year	Women Members (thousands)	Women as % of All Members	Women Officers and Board Members	Women as % of All Officers & Board Members
National Education Association	1978	1,240	75	5	55
	1985	1,000	60	3	33
International Brotherhood of Teamsters	1978	481	25	0	0
	1985	485	26	0	0
United Food and Commercial Workers	1978	480	39	2	3
	1985	na	na	na	na
American Federation of State, County & Municipal Employees	1978	408	40	1	3
	1985	450	45	4	14
Service Employees International Union	1978	312	50	7	15
	1985	435	50	9	18
American Federation of Teachers	1978	300	60	8	25
	1985	366	60	11	32
Communication Workers of America	1978	259	51	0	0
	1985	338	52	1	6
International Brotherhood of Electrical Workers	1978	304	30	0	0
	1985	330	30	0	0
Amalgamated Clothing and Textile Workers' Union	1978	331	66	6	15
	1985	228	65	3	9
International Ladies' Garment Workers Union	1978	279	80	2	7
	1983	219	85	3	13
Hotel and Restaurant Employees	1978	181	42	1	4
	1985	200	50	2	8

Sources: 1978 data are from Coalition of Labor Union Women, Center for Education and Research, *Absent from the Agenda: A Report on the Role of Women in American Unions* (New York, mimeo, 1980), Tables 3 and 5; 1985 data are from Naomi Baden, "Developing an Agenda: Expanding the Role of Women in Unions," *Labor Studies Journal*, vol 10, no. 3 (Winter 1986), pp. 236, 238.

years, they seldom advanced to positions of real power in the unions.

In the 1950s and early 1960s, before the implications of the rise in female labor force participation were manifest, and before the resurgence of feminism, the labor movement maintained its traditional posture toward women workers. They were still seen as a marginal group, in need of special forms of protection, and not as full participants in union activity. Even as the two-worker family began to emerge as the norm in the inflationary era which began in the 1960s, many unionists clung to the old ideal of securing a "family wage" for their (male) members, and continued to view women workers along traditional lines. But ultimately, the changes which transformed women's roles and consciousness in the larger society also led to changes inside the labor movement.

FEMINISM AND UNIONISM IN THE 1970s

By the 1970s, when the process of female recruitment into unions had greatly enlarged the numbers of women in the labor movement, pressures began to build for change in the unions' traditional outlook toward women. Women's caucuses and women's committees emerged in a variety of unions, the numbers of women holding office in local unions grew, and more generally, there was an upsurge in female union activism, starting in the early 1970s (Foner 1980; Baden 1986). In addition, some new forms of organizing among women workers began to develop through initiatives originating outside the established unions, drawing on the consciousness-raising techniques and other innovations of the broader women's movement (Seifer and Wertheimer 1979).

This new activity was very much influenced by the rebirth of feminism in the 1960s and 1970s, but the linkage was indirect. The women union activists whose numbers grew in this period typically rejected any direct identification with the women's movement. They perceived it as a movement of and for professional women, on the one side, and affluent college students who rejected conventional family and cultural practices in favor of alternative lifestyles, on the other.[5] This was not an entirely inaccurate perception: the majority of feminist activists are college-educated women from middle-class families, although the actual composition of the movement is more diverse than mass media stereotypes tend to suggest (Carden 1974: 28-30).

Moreover, while in principle feminism offers collective solutions to gender inequality, in practice, there is a highly individualistic thrust to the U.S. women's movement. The slogan "sisterhood is powerful" notwithstanding, its primary emphasis often seems to be gaining more power for individual women within American society — and in the labor market — as it stands. This individualism is largely due to the fact that so many feminist activists can reasonably aspire — once sex discrimination is no longer a barrier — to professional occupations comparable to those held by men of their class. From a trade union or working-class women's perspective, the individualistic thrust of this "corporate feminism" reinforces the sense of distance engendered by the class composition of the movement (Ehrenreich 1981; Gordon 1983).

Nevertheless, it would be extremely misleading to presume that working-class women have not been influenced by the feminist resurgence. On the contrary, growing numbers of them readily endorse the movement's basic goals, a phenomenon perhaps best captured in the familiar disclaimer, "I'm not a women's libber, but . . ." More than any other feminist principle, the ideal of gender equality in the labor market has won enormous popular support (Seifer 1973; Social Research Inc. 1973; Rubin 1976:130–32). To be sure, structural change in the labor market has lagged far behind the attitudinal shifts. In general (and the only real exceptions here are the elite professions), despite the passage of anti-discrimination legislation, the vast majority of women workers remain in poorly paid, low status jobs (U.S. Dept. of Labor 1982; Rytina 1982; Beller 1984).

Perhaps the most important effect of the resurgence of feminism on women workers has been to raise their expectations. As women with newly heightened expectations of work are faced with unchanged, or even deteriorating job prospects, some of them have developed a distinctive new consciousness, particularly younger and college-educated women. Under certain conditions, this new consciousness expresses itself in what, for want of a better term, I will call trade union feminism.[6] The identification of feminism with middle-class professional women and with a politics of individualism has set limits on this kind of activity, but has by no means prevented its development.

Efforts to organize around women's issues within the unions, and the new campaigns to unionize unorganized women workers through special appeals to them "as women" have typically been initiated by women themselves, rather than by union leaders, although there are exceptions. Organized labor has become an important ally of the women's movement in many legislative and other public campaigns in recent years — for example, in the campaign for parental leave legislation. However, where its internal affairs are concerned, progress has been much slower. This is not only because of the historical character of trade unions as institutions of "male culture." In addition, the labor movement is dominated today, as it often has been in the past, by a siege mentality, and by a deeply rooted mistrust of any efforts to assert the special interests of a group within the membership. This mistrust is particularly intense if such efforts appear to be associated with a political ideology — feminism included (Kessler-Harris 1985).

The defensive stance of unions toward feminism has historical roots in the immediate postwar period. The broad attacks on labor during those years, combined with the specific effects of McCarthyism, led to a retreat from the agenda of "social unionism" that labor pursued in the 1930s and 1940s, while the economic prosperity of the 1950s facilitated a greater emphasis on wage and benefit gains over political challenges to the status quo. By the 1960s, organized labor was no longer at the dynamic center of oppositional politics in the United States, and defined its interests rather narrowly. Indeed, its posture toward the new social movements of the day — the antiwar and student movements, the environmental movement, as well as feminism — tended to be conservative or even hostile. And, despite the fact that organized labor stands to gain from developing special appeals to women workers, efforts along these lines were quite slow to emerge, and were at first met with defensiveness rather than ready support from union leaders.

In the 1970s, in spite of all the obstacles, the growing numbers of women in both the labor movement and the work force produced growing pressure for change. Union leaders could no longer ignore the growing efforts to assert the special interests of women as a group within the ranks. Gradually, the pressure began to yield results, amid growing indications that the heightened expectations of women workers had created some important new opportunities for organized labor. Surveys found that unorganized women have a greater interest in joining unions than unorganized men, for example (Kochan 1979: 25; Freeman and Medoff 1984: 29). And, perhaps more significantly, unions are currently winning representation elections in which women are the bulk of the work force, and those in which "women's issues" are emphasized, more often than other representation elections (Moore and Marsis 1983:30; Freeman and Leonard 1985:6). Creating a political space for women, historically a marginal problem for the labor movement, has now emerged as a central dilemma.

In this context, women's union leadership has grown significantly in recent years, especially at the local and regional levels (Baden 1980; Nelson 1987). The public sector unions, which have been particularly active on the comparable worth issue, show particularly striking gains in women's leadership. Thirty three percent of AFSCME's local presidents were female in 1982, for example, up from 25 percent several years earlier; and women hold 45 percent of all local union offices in AFSCME (Bell 1985: 288).

Another reflection of the changed position of women in the labor movement is the emergence of explicitly feminist trade union organizations. Among these, the two most successful are CLUW and 9 to 5. Although both are designed to improve the situation of women workers within the labor movement, their approaches to this project contrast sharply. While CLUW primarily directs its efforts toward securing more status and power for women within the established labor movement structure, 9 to 5 has sought instead to develop new organizational forms for women workers, which implicitly challenge the established traditions of the labor movement while simultaneously expanding the space for women within it. Each approach has advantages and disadvantages; together they illustrate the range of problems and possibilities facing feminists engaged in union activity.

CLUW AND WOMEN UNIONISTS

CLUW held its founding convention in Chicago in March 1974, where over 3,000 women from 58 different unions gathered. The Statement of Purpose adopted at this first convention outlined four basic goals for the organization: organizing unorganized women into unions; working within unions in support of affirmative action; involving more union women in political action and in legislative campaigns to improve the condition of women workers; and encouraging women to participate within their unions (*New York Times* 1974; Coalition of Labor Union Women 1974).

Membership in CLUW was limited to those who were already union members — a policy decision which was made in the planning meetings held prior to the founding convention. This membership policy reflected the new organization's origins: it was established by a group of women with extensive experience in the labor movement, who believed that in order for CLUW effectively to influence the unions, membership had to be limited in this way. Not only in its membership rules, but also in its internal organizational structure, CLUW placed itself squarely in the trade union tradition from the outset, with a full complement of elected officers and a standard committee structure (Sexton 1974; Troger 1975; Foner 1980:516–520).

The influence of the women's movement was also very much in evidence at CLUW's founding convention. "One result of this meeting," president-elect Olga Madar of the United Automobile Workers told the *New York Times,* "is that fewer and fewer union women will be saying 'we are not women's libbers.' By coming here, they have proved that they are" (*New York Times* 1974). And while criticism of union leadership was restrained, there was a visible determination to impress upon union men the seriousness of the project. As Myra Wolfgang of the Hotel and Restaurant Workers put it in a much-quoted exclamation: "We have a message for George Meany. We have a message for Leonard Woodcock. We have a message for Frank Fitzsimmons. You can tell them we didn't come to Chicago to swap recipes!" (*John Herling's Labor Letter* 1974).

In the decade since its founding, CLUW has grown into an 18,000 member organization with 75 local chapters (Nelson 1987:236). Its current president, Joyce Miller, sits on the AFL-CIO's Executive Council. CLUW is highly visible within the labor movement and has been effective in exerting pressure on the AFL-CIO regarding women's concerns. It also functions as a network of women union officials, who comprise its most active constituency. Under the aegis of its foundation-funded ''Empowerment Project,'' the organization developed programs specifically to enhance the leadership skills of women unionists. And locally, CLUW chapters have undertaken a wide range of issue-oriented activities, often in coalition with other labor and women's groups (Weiner 1983; *CLUW News,* various issues).

Although formally the organization remains committed to its original goal of organizing the unorganized, its sparse resources have set severe limits on CLUW's abilities to work effectively toward this goal. In 1982, together with the AFL-CIO's Industrial Union Department, it did launch a ''Women's Organizing Campaign'' in the Washington/Baltimore area, but this effort yielded little in the way of concrete results and was abandoned entirely after only two years (Moore and Marsis 1983; *Wall Street Journal* 1983, 1984). CLUW has been far more successful as a vehicle for promoting women's leadership among those who are already active in their unions, and this is, in practice, the main function of the organization. While rank-and-file women are frequently not even aware of CLUW's existence, women who have already become union activists see it as very beneficial (Sexton 1982:111).

CLUW's internal structure mirrors that of a typical union, and virtually all of its top officers are full-time union officials, so that it enjoys limited autonomy from the established union leadership. As one sympathetic critic observed: ''Its [CLUW's] leadership is well-respected, and it has a good track record with labor, but in my opinion about half the CLUW board should be rank and file. Maybe women from the ranks wouldn't worry about their jobs being jeopardized if they spoke out'' (quoted in Sexton 1982:117).

CLUW's approach to change presumes that the key difference between women and men is that women lack leadership skills, self-confidence, and therefore power. While taking account of the fact that women have ''family responsibilities'' that obstruct their union activity, CLUW does not view this as the basis for a critique of established organizational forms within the labor movement, but rather as an additional handicap which women must somehow overcome. As the CLUW slogan, ''A Woman's Place Is In Her Union'' implies, all the needs of women can be taken care of within the existing framework of trade unionism. The problem with unions is only that women do not have a large enough role in them; the solution is for women to equip themselves to compete more effectively, on the established terms, for leadership (for example, see *Daily Labor Report* 1981; and Coalition of Labor Union Women 1982).

Certainly, for those women pursuing full-time careers in the unions, CLUW's outlook and strategy have much to recommend them, and it is no accident that female union officials have become the organization's main constituency. Having more women in positions of leadership in the labor movement is important, and also CLUW's watchdog role vis-a-vis the AFL-CIO on women's issues makes a valuable contribution. But it is difficult to see how CLUW can effectively expand and overcome its isolation from the nation's women workers so long as its primary energies are consumed in the internal politics of the labor movement. The price of CLUW's success in winning ''insider'' status — and still quite a marginal insider status at that — has been very high indeed. And if the organization should ever step too far beyond the boundaries of what is acceptable to the labor movement's leadership, it will risk losing its hard-won legitimacy.

CLUW's limitations are largely self-imposed. It was founded by women trade union officials, and has remained faithful to their original vision of CLUW as an insiders' organization. While pressure from its broader constituency has pushed CLUW a bit more than its founders intended toward organizing the unorganized and rank-and-file educational work, it is not surprising that these have remained nominal goals rather than becoming the practical focus for the organization's energies. If the larger labor movement were revitalized, and rank-and-file activism there grew, CLUW too might develop into something more than a loyal opposition of women officials within organized labor. But any such initiative would have to come from outside of CLUW as it is presently structured.

THE "WORKING WOMEN'S MOVEMENT" AND SEIU DISTRICT 925

Sharply contrasting with CLUW in its relationship to the labor establishment is another major feminist effort to influence the established unions, 9 to 5, which originated as a project of a younger group of activists. In the early 1970s, young feminists with roots in the New Left formed several independent working women's organizations, primarily among previously unorganized office workers. The best known and most successful of these groups was 9 to 5. Founded in Boston in 1973, it is now a national organization with chapters in many localities. Similar groups sprang up in other major cities around the country in the same period (Tepperman 1976; Seifer and Wertheimer 1979; Goldberg 1983).

Initially, these new groups avoided any formal ties to the established unions. The organizers felt that their constituency, women office workers, could not be expected to identify directly with organized labor. Unions, after all, were popularly perceived as organizations of blue-collar workers, and culturally, as part of the male world. As Karen Nussbaum, a founder of the original Boston group who would later become 9 to 5's executive director put it: "When we started... 'union,' 'collective bargaining,' 'contract negotiations'—these words didn't mean anything to us. It wasn't like 'refrigerator' or 'electric light'—things that we had grown up with that were very familiar concepts. These were completely alien" (quoted in Tepperman 1976:92). Thus, rather than taking unionization as an immediate objective, the working women's movement concentrated at first on consciousness-raising and on public dramatizations of specific issues affecting women office workers. As other commentators have suggested, the groups essentially functioned as "pre-union" organizations (Lynch 1979; Koziara and Insley 1982).

However, 9 to 5 moved closer to the organized labor movement over time. It received a charter from the Service Employees' International Union (SEIU) in 1975, and then began organizing SEIU Local 925 in Boston. Shortly afterward, the SEIU and 9 to 5 entered into a similar arrangement in nearby Providence, Rhode Island (Seifer and Wertheimer 1979:179–80; Nussbaum 1980:152). Then, in March 1981, the national office of "Working Women" (9 to 5's name at the time) and the SEIU announced a much more ambitious joint undertaking. This was SEIU District 925, charged with unionizing unorganized women clerical workers all over the United States. The new district was a division of the SEIU, but drew its staff directly from 9 to 5, and had some autonomy within the union structure. In the words of SEIU president John Sweeney, the district was to be run "for women and by women who understand their problems" (*New York Times*

1981; Hill 1981). In 1987, after six years of organizing, District 925 represents 7,500 workers in bargaining units around the country. It maintains interlocking directorates with 9 to 5, which continues its former work outside the boundaries of the union, as a separate entity, and which claimed 13,000 members in 1987.[7]

There are a number of important contrasts between 9 to 5 and CLUW. The major practical focus of 9 to 5 is on consciousness-raising and organizing among unorganized women workers, and outside of its link to the SEIU it is not deeply involved in the trade union officialdom. More fundamentally, 9 to 5's strategy reflects an implicit critique of the assumption CLUW relies on — that once women are brought into the trade unions and accorded more power within the existing structure, their needs will be satisfied. 9 to 5 views the organizational forms traditionally associated with unionism as problematic for women, and draws instead on the innovative, relatively unstructured organizational forms developed in the women's liberation movement. Leadership roles are downplayed, for example, in order to encourage participatory democracy within the organization and in order to develop the confidence and skill of as many members as possible (Goldberg 1983: 45-47).

The focus of 9 to 5 on clerical workers is important in this regard. While CLUW's membership reflects the composition of the labor movement as presently constituted (which is quite different from the makeup of the female labor force), 9 to 5 defines its constituency as clerical workers, easily the largest occupational group among women workers, accounting for over one-third of the female labor force. And rather than limiting itself to unionization, 9 to 5 focuses on issues of special concern to women, such as equal opportunity, age discrimination, and the specific practices of banks and insurance companies toward their women employees. The group's overriding goal is to win "rights and respect" for office workers (Goldberg 1983: 33-37).

9 to 5's tactics also depart from those traditionally used in labor organizing. The consciousness-raising process developed by the women's movement is one model here; the organization has also developed several innovative ways of rallying support in highly visible public settings, as well as making very skillful use of the media. Rallies on National Secretaries Day, the introduction of the popular film *9 to 5*, and more recently, a widely publicized campaign focused on the health hazards of video display terminals, are among these efforts.

Unionization is also a goal of the organization, but is conceived of as a long and complex process, with particularly delicate aspects for women. In contrast to CLUW's focus on "empowerment," 9 to 5 rejects the traditional "macho" image of unionism, insisting that women workers, unaccustomed to viewing themselves as powerful, will be successfully unionized only if a different, more woman-oriented culture of unionism is developed. District 925 also strives for more rank-and-file participation and internal democracy than is typical of most unions today. In general, rather than trying to fit women into the existing organizational forms of unionism on an equal basis with men, 9 to 5 focuses on the ways in which women workers and their culture are different from male workers and male culture, and seeks to develop organizational forms both inside and outside the framework of unionism which take those differences seriously and respond directly to the special needs of women workers.[8]

As long as it remained a "pre-union," there were limits on 9 to 5's resources and on what it could offer to its constituency of female clericals. The District 925 linkage was intended to expand those resources without losing the conception of women as having special needs. It is an experiment without precedent in the United States labor movement: a union led by women, with roots in the women's movement, whose stated goal is to unionize the overwhelmingly female clerical work force with the backing of one of the nation's largest labor organizations. Yet it *is* very much an experiment, for both 9 to 5 and the SEIU. While careful to negotiate considerable automony for their operations, District 925's staff acknowledges that in order to retain (and hopefully expand) the SEIU's support, it needs to garner some quick results in the form of dues paying members. And that pressure makes District 925's focus quite similar to those of a number of other unions, such as AFSCME and CWA, which are actively engaged (sometimes in direct rivalry with one another) in public sector clerical organizing. Indeed, the bulk of District 925's organizing successes have been in the public sector. It is true that, unlike blue-collar organizing, public sector unionization has a demonstration effect relevant to private-sector clericals, as District 925 staffers point out.[9] But the public sector emphasis is obviously also a product of the constraints imposed by the SEIU, which operates in a fashion more akin to other unions than to 9 to 5's original vision.

The dilemma for 9 to 5, it seems, is how to preserve its distinctive vision and approach to organizing, now that it is encapsulated in the legal and institutional framework of mainstream trade unionism. Certainly its relationship with the SEIU has put the office workers' group in a position to go beyond simply consciousness raising and public media campaigns, supplying a vehicle through which it can begin to accumulate some real power. While its size remains modest, at the same time, a number of other unions have adapted District 925's tactics in their own clerical organizing drives, particularly in the public sector and in organizing clericals on university campuses.[10] As Naomi Baden points out: "If imitation is the highest form of flattery, the District [925] is well appreciated" (1986:245).

CONCLUSION

CLUW and 9 to 5 are but the most successful and visible products of the opening toward feminism within the labor movement to emerge in the 1970s. There also have been a range of specific efforts along these lines within individual unions, many of them locally based. And several unions have initiated campaigns around issues of particular concern to women workers — most recently, pay equity and parental leave. These developments have laid the groundwork of what could potentially develop into a far more extensive feminist mobilization within the unions. However, the wrenching downturn in union membership in the 1980s has not done much to encourage further progress. The labor movement is in its deepest crisis since the early 1930s, with steep membership losses and extensive "givebacks" in wages and benefits won in earlier years eroding union power. Although these problems have been concentrated in the manufacturing sector, where women's presence is in any case minimal, the entire labor movement has been thrown on the defensive, and the space which has opened up for women's concerns is in jeopardy. In the longer run, however, if the labor movement is revitalized, the feminization of union membership could become the basis for a full-scale alliance between the nation's women workers, with their own distinctive consciousness, and organized labor. In that context, the seeds planted with such difficulty by feminist trade unionists in the 1970s and 1980s may finally bear fruit.

ACKNOWLEDGEMENT

This is a revised and updated version of the author's article, "Women Workers, Feminism, and the Labor Movement Since the 1960s," originally published in *Women, Work and Protest: A Century of US Women's Labor History,* edited by Ruth Milkman (Boston and London: Routledge and Kegan Paul, 1985). Permission to reprint the article is gratefully acknowledged.

NOTES

1. Very little has been written about these developments. The most thorough single account, although now somewhat dated, is Foner (1980).
2. The representation of women in union leadership is an aspect of women's relationship to the labor movement which has received relatively extensive study. The most detailed (although now rather dated) analysis is Wertheimer and Nelson (1975). See also LeGrande (1980), U.S. Commission on Civil Rights (1982), Koziara and Pierson (1981), and Baden (1986).
3. These figures include members of labor unions and employee associations. Unless otherwise indicated, all figures on union membership in this article will include both.
4. The way in which the U.S. government collects data on labor organization membership has changed over the years. Initially, data was only collected on unions, and not for employee associations. In the early 1970s, data was collected on both types of organizational membership, separately. In 1981, at the beginning of the Reagan Administration, the government simply stopped collecting data on the subject. For 1981 and 1982, no data were collected at all. Starting in 1983, when the government resumed collecting data on union membership, this time as part of the Census Bureau's Current Population Survey, both unions and employee associations were included but no breakdown was made between the two.
5. Evidence on this point is fragmentary, but see Seifer (1976:247–248), Sexton (1982:109–111), and Fonow (1977:155–165) for illustrative examples.
6. Roberta Goldberg (1983) found that most of the women active in the chapter of Working Women that she studied in Baltimore were in their twenties and thirties. Younger women were also predominant in District 925's organizing at the Syracuse office of the Equitable Life Assurance Society, as Moberg (1983) notes. See also Ferree (1980), Sigel and Reynolds (1979–80), and Blum (1987).
7. These membership figures were obtained in telephone interviews with Denise Mitchell (Washington, D.C., December 3, 1987), representing District 925, and with Deborah Meyer (Cleveland, Ohio, November 30, 1987), representing 9 to 5.
8. For a discussion of the use of a similar notion of difference among feminist trade unionists in Italy, see Beccalli (1984).
9. Author's interview with Jackie Ruff, District 925's executive director, Washington D.C., June 17, 1983; telephone interview with Denise Mitchell, December 3, 1987.
10. Compare, for example, the District 925 campaign at the Syracuse office of the Equitable Life Assurance Society (see Milkman 1983) and the Hotel and Restaurant Workers' Union organizing drive at Yale University (see Ladd-Taylor 1985).

REFERENCES

Baden, Naomi. 1986. Developing an Agenda: Expanding the Role of Women in Unions. *Labor Studies Journal* 10(3):229–249.

Beccalli, Bianca. 1984. Women and Trade Unions in Italy. In, *Women and Trade Unions in Eleven Industrialized Countries,* Alice Cook, Val Lorwin and Arlene Kaplan Daniels (eds.). pp. 184–214. Philadelphia: Temple University Press.

Bell, Deborah E. 1985. Unionized Women in State and Local Government. In, *Women, Work and Protest: A Century of U.S. Women's Labor History,* Ruth Milkman (ed.). pp. 280–299. Boston: Routledge and Kegan Paul.

Beller, Andrea H. 1984. Trends in Occupational Segregation in Professional Occupations. In, *Sex Segregation in the Workplace: Trends, Explanations, Remedies,* Barbara F. Reskin (ed.). pp. 11–26. Washington, D.C.: National Academy Press.

Blum, Linda. 1987. *Re-evaluating Women's Work: The Significance of the Comparable Worth Movement.* Unpublished Ph.D. dissertation, Department of Sociology, University of California at Berkeley.

Carden, Maren Lockwood. 1974. *The New Feminist Movement.* New York: Russell Sage Foundation.

Coalition of Labor Union Women. 1974. *Statement of Purpose, Structure and Guidelines.* Pamphlet. Chicago.

——. 1980. *Absent from the Agenda: A Report on the Role of Women in American Unions.* Mimeo. New York: CLUW Center for Education and Research.

——. 1982. *Empowerment: A Handbook for Union Women.* Washington, D.C.: CLUW Center for Education and Research.

——. *CLUW News.* Various issues. New York.

Daily Labor Report. 1981. Union Organizers Exchange Ideas on Recruiting More Women Workers. Jan. 29, 1981, pp. A6-A8, D1-D4. Washington D.C.: Bureau of National Affairs.

Ehrenreich, Barbara. 1981. The Women's Movements: Feminist and Antifeminist. *Radical America* 15(1–2):93–101.

Ferree, Myra Marx. 1980. Working Class Feminism: A Consideration of the Consequences of Employment. *The Sociological Quarterly* 21:173–184.

Foner, Philip. 1980. *Women and the American Labor Movement from World War I to the Present.* New York: Free Press.

Fonow, Mary Margaret. 1977. *Women in Steel: A Case Study of the Participation of Women in a Trade Union.* Unpublished Ph.D. dissertation, Department of Sociology, Ohio State University.

Freeman, Richard B. and James L. Medoff. 1984. *What Do Unions Do?* New York: Basic Books.

—— and Jonathan S. Leonard. 1985. Union Maids: Unions and the Female Work Force. NBER Working Paper No. 1652. Cambridge: National Bureau of Economic Research.

Gifford, Courtney D. (ed.). 1982–83. *Directory of U.S. Labor Organizations, 1982–83 Edition.* Washington, D.C.: Bureau of National Affairs.

Goldberg, Roberta. 1983. *Organizing Women Office Workers: Dissatisfaction, Consciousness, and Action.* New York: Praeger.

Gordon, Suzanne. 1983. The New Corporate Feminism. *The Nation* 236:129, 143–147.

Hill, Ann. 1981. District 925: A New Union for Office Workers. *Socialist Review* 11(5):142–146.

John Herling's Labor Letter. 1974. (March 30 issue). Washington, D.C.

Kessler-Harris, Alice. 1985. Problems of Coalition-building: Women and Trade Unions in the 1920s. In, *Women, Work and Protest: A Century of U.S. Women's Labor History,* Ruth Milkman (ed.). pp. 110–138. Boston: Routledge and Kegan Paul.

Kochan, Thomas A. 1979. How American Workers View Labor Unions. *Monthly Labor Review* 102(4):22–31.

Koziara, Karen S. and David A. Pierson. 1981. The Lack of Female Union Leaders: A Look at Some Reasons. *Monthly Labor Review* 104(5):30–32.

_____ and Patrice J. Insley. 1982. Organizations of Working Women Can Pave the Way for Unions. *Monthly Labor Review* 105(6):53–54.

Ladd-Taylor, Molly. 1985. Women Workers and the Yale Strike. *Feminist Studies* 11(3):465–489.

LeGrande, Linda H. 1980. Women in Labor Organizations: Their Ranks Are Increasing. *Monthly Labor Review* 101(8):8–14.

Lynch, Roberta. 1979. Women in the Work Force. *The Progressive* 43(10):28–31.

Milkman, Ruth. 1983. Pink-Collar Unions: Breakthrough at the Equitable. *The Nation* 237 (Dec. 3):564–566.

Moberg, David. 1983. Clerks Outmaneuver Bosses. *In These Times* 7(March 30–April 5 issue):5.

Moore, Richard and Elizabeth Marsis. 1983. Will Unions Work for Women? *The Progressive* 47(8):28–30.

Nelson, Anne. 1987. Women in Unions. In, *The American Women, 1987–88: A Report in Depth*, Sara E. Rix (ed.). pp. 232–238. New York: W.W. Norton and Co.

New York Times. 1974. 3,000 Delegates at Chicago Meeting Organize a National Coalition of Labor Union Women. (March 25).

_____. 1981. Women's Group Set to Organize Office Workers. (March 4).

Nussbaum, Karen. 1980. Women Clerical Workers and Trade Unionism. (Interview). *Socialist Review* 10(1):151–159.

Rubin, Lillian B. 1976. *Worlds of Pain: Life in the Working-Class Family*. New York: Basic Books.

Rytina, Nancy F. 1982. Earnings of Men and Women: A Look at Specific Occupations. *Monthly Labor Review* 105(4):25–31.

Seifer, Nancy. 1973. *Absent from the Majority: Working Class Women in America*. New York: National Project on Ethnic America.

_____. (ed.). 1976. *Nobody Speaks for Me! Self-Portraits of American Working Class Women*. New York: Simon and Schuster.

_____ and Barbara Wertheimer. 1979. New Approaches to Collective Power: Four Working Women's Organizations. In, *Women Organizing: An Anthology*, Bernice Cummings and Victoria Schuck (eds.). pp. 152–183. Metuchen, NJ: Scarecrow Press.

Sexton, Patricia Cayo. 1974. Workers (Female) Arise. *Dissent* 21(3):380–395.

_____. 1982. *The New Nightingales: Hospital Workers, Unions, New Women's Issues*. New York: Enquiry Press.

Sigel, Roberta S. and John V. Reynolds. 1979–80. Generational Differences and the Women's Movement. *Political Science Quarterly* 94:635–648.

Social Research Inc. 1973. *Working-Class Women in a Changing World: A Review of Research Findings*. New York: McFadden-Bartell Corporation.

Tepperman, Jean. 1976. *Not Servants, Not Machines: Office Workers Speak Out*. Boston: Beacon Press.

Troger, AnneMarie. 1975. The Coalition of Labor Union Women: Strategic Hope, Tactical Despair. *Radical America* 9(6):85–110.

U.S. Commission on Civil Rights. 1982. *Nonreferral Unions and Equal Employment Opportunity*. Washington, D.C.

U.S. Department of Labor, Bureau of Labor Statistics. 1980. *Directory of National Unions and Employee Associations, 1979*. Bulletin 2079. Washington, D.C.

_____. 1982. *The Female-Male Earnings Gap: A Review of Employment and Earnings Issues*. Report 673. Washington, D.C.

_____. 1987. *Employment and Earnings* 34(1):219–222.

Wagner, David. 1979. Clerical Workers: How "Unorganizable" Are They? *Labor Center Review* 2(1):20–50.

Wall Street Journal. 1983. Labor Letter. (August 23):1.

_____. 1984. Labor Letter. (March 6):1.

Weiner, Elizabeth. 1983. Still Sticking to the Union. *In These Times* 7(March 30–April 5 issue):8–9, 15.

Wertheimer, Barbara M. and Anne H. Nelson. 1975. *Trade Union Women: A Study of Their Participation in New York City Locals*. New York: Praeger.

PART FIVE

SOCIAL POLICY ISSUES

17

Do Cities Have a Future?

PETER MARCUSE

CONTRASTING VIEWS OF URBAN DYNAMICS

Cities were done for, the conventional wisdom held fifteen years ago. Everyone who could afford a suburban house was getting one, businesses were moving out too. Central cities could no longer afford a decent level of services, many were on the edge of bankruptcy, congestion, pollution, crime, aging infrastructure; all spelled the end of cities as they used to be. Changes in consumer preferences and life-styles, facilitated by advances in technologies (the automobile above all), were producing a new form of "urban" life, megalopolitan perhaps more than urban. Short-sighted leadership in the old cities were not only failing to adapt, but by various subterfuges (such as borrowing to pay current expenses) signing the death-warrant of those cities. The dominance of the old cities was a thing of the past.

But everything is different today. The conventional wisdom has it that consumer preferences have changed again, that people like living in central cities once more, cities are "revitalizing," frugality has avoided fiscal crisis, the major cities, now global centers, will be where more and more of what's important in the world will be happening. What happened? Has something new, that could not be predicted, suddenly burst forth onto the scene?

I will suggest here that the conventional analysis is simply wrong. It turns by-products into causes, neglects underlying changes, views history short-sightedly, separates technical developments from relations among people, and misses the real dynamics of urban change. I will suggest here an alternate explanation, and argue that it more satisfactorily explains what has transpired and give more reliable guides to what may be expected in the future.

THE SPATIAL RESTRUCTURING OF CITIES

Cities are shaped by the necessities of production and power within the prevailing relationships among classes and groups, rather than by their leaders' search for the best configuration to promote the happiness of their residents, or by the multiple independent expressions of consumer preferences. They grew up around the economic and political activities that took place in them. In earlier periods, their raison d'etre was the market place, the fort, the palace, the harbor, the cathedral. Later, with industrialization, they developed around factories, with workers' housing clustered in walking distance of places of work. Those are the historic patterns. Their spatial reflection has until now been a centralized city, with most activity concentrated in the center and land uses getting less and less dense as one travels further and further from the center. For the same reasons, in the industrial period large cities tended to cluster near each other; so one had concentrated regional belts of urbanization along the East Coast of the United States, in the Birmingham-Manchester corridor in England, in the Ruhr Valley in Germany.

The twentieth century saw changes in these patterns, because of changes both in the ways production was carried out and in the relations among those who were involved in it. Marx spoke of the distinction between developments of the "forces of production" and the "relations of production," the first being essentially physical and technical, the second social. The classic Marxist formulation thus would summarize the present problems in cities as an outcome of the fact that the relations of production have not changed to adapt adequately to developments in the forces of production. To use more conventional terms, the motor of profit, which has produced the wealth (and the cities) we have today, is now inadequate to produce or distribute that wealth in accordance with the real needs of people, yet those who reap the profit are locked into its support.

The conventional explanation for how modern cities came to be as they are is quite different. It suggests that improvements in transportation technology, coupled with the independent expression of consumer preferences, were the causative factors, producing vastly greater metropolitan areas, suburbanization, and decentralization. At its most simplified, "the auto created the twentieth century city," goes the argument.

Marxists would suggest the causes for city growth go deeper. The possibilities of producing greater profits from larger, more highly organized factories initially created a demand for a vastly larger work force. The requirement of getting that work force to the factories produced, in response, advances in transportation technology — first railroads, then trolleys, then automobiles. Cities were shaped by the drive for profits and the demands that drive created, not by the possibilities created by independent and autonomous advances in technology. The steam engine and the automobile did not "cause" the growth of cities, but both were produced by the same underlying changes in the way production was carried out.[1]

The automobile did not "cause" the more recent decentralization and decline of cities, either. Nationally, decentralization came about because efficient production, particularly of heavy capital goods — steel, automobiles, machinery — could, by the first decades of the twentieth century, be better undertaken in large, single-story, space-consuming buildings, in which assembly lines and automatic movement of pieces of work and machinery were easier. So large amounts of land were needed; these were more available, and therefore cheaper, outside of cities than in them. At the same time, the growth of production in large units meant that factories could internalize the supply of many of their own needs: rather than depend on suppliers for repairs, for professional services, etc., each huge factory could afford to provide its own. So suburban and regionally scattered locations for industry made sense. And workers followed; again, with land being cheap and autos available, single-family homes in suburban tracts were an economical way for them to get housing.

THE RESTRUCTURING OF CLASS RELATIONS IN CITIES

But it was not only technical developments in the way production was carried out that led to the problems of older cities. It was also a different approach to the relations between workers and capital. In the nineteenth century employers paid workers as little as they possibly could, and worked them as many hours and as hard as they could get away with. Workers were poorly organized to fight on the new terms of the factory system. Nor was there any problem with selling what was produced; workers' demand did not have to be nurtured to provide a market either for necessities or for luxuries targeted to a different market. So the less workers got, the more profit capital made, and the faster the system grew.

With growth new problems emerged. For one, workers organized and struck for decent wages. Further, workers' buying power became important to sell what was being produced; expanded mass production of cheap goods required expanded mass markets, and too low wages would have a dampening effect on growth. So what has come be be known as the Fordist compromise was achieved: factory workers in the major industries were paid better, and could thus undergird a mass consumption of the goods being mass produced; they were therefore also willing to accede to the labor discipline necessary to keep those factories profitable, a result reflected in the postwar accords between unions and management.

Among what workers bought were single-family suburban homes. The spread of owner-occupied detached houses across the country-side was environmentally damaging and wasteful of natural resources, but very effective to produce contentment, a "stake in the system," a commitment to keep working and stop complaining, and at the same time to keep buying, keep consuming, keep the profits rolling in at the point of production. Landowners, builders and financiers could make money on it too. It was a form of housing that seemed to be ideal for everyone concerned.

Some workers, of course, continued to be paid very little, or to be unemployed or insecure, marginal. Without the rewards of mass consumption and a little plot of land in the suburbs to keep them willing to conform to the disciplines of production, other incentives were needed. Social agencies, philanthropic housing groups, and preachers made their contribution. More important, however, were discrimination and segregation, first against immigrants, then with far greater weight against blacks. Currently, Hispanics and "illegal" immigrants are feeling the effects of pressures for silence and obedient work at substandard pay. These exploited and oppressed groups perforce had to live in the cheapest housing, packed together in the older slums of central cities. Hence the ghettoes and slums that characterize most U.S. cities. And the industries that employed them also had to stay in the cities where their labor pool lived.

THE BREAKDOWN OF THE FORDIST COMPROMISE: THE OPPOSITION OF THE 1960s

These arrangements, while relatively stable in the 1950s, slowly became unstable as changes in the way production was organized began to change class relations.[2] Advancing technological development required less skilled work, reducing wages, and investment in capital goods replaced the need for labor, reducing employment growth. Many of the older "middle class": lower-level management, small shop-keepers, independent professionals, skilled factory workers, could be replaced by machines, their jobs "deskilled." At the bottom end, the need for unskilled workers remained, in the sweatshops and to service both production and consumption. At the same time, the role of other types of work increased: technically complex engineering, aggregation of financial resources, commercial exchanges, advertising and marketing, international business, and speculation in real estate to profit from all these changes. Professionals, with college educations and an unquestioning commitment to working and taking initiative to deal with new and unprogrammable, unquantifiable demands, were more and more needed. The results are visible in the statistics: as jobs are de-skilled and their wages reduced, and fewer workers needed, the number of the poor increase; as more technicians and professionals are needed, the number of the better-off increase; and the number in the middle declines (*Wall Street Journal* 1986).

The Fordist compromise that seemed so stable in the 1950s thus proved inadequate in the 1960s. The worst paid, and particularly the victims of racial oppression, refused to be content. The civil rights movement and the ghetto rebellions of the mid-sixties represented their unwillingness to tolerate second-class citizenship, either politically or economically. So the lower edge of the circle of compromise was broken.

So was the upper edge. The work that was required of the new professionals and technicians was difficult and burdensome, but hardly rewarding in a human sense. Its product was simply profit. The focus of all creative human energy on the pursuit of profit seemed to be more and more a waste, an irrational way to lead a life. So, many simply dropped out, became hippies, took jobs requiring efforts far below their potential. Others, with a more political orientation, went over into the opposition. They, and even more, their children, joined the New Left, fought in the War on Poverty (such as it was), demonstrated against the war in Vietnam, protested social injustice. Thus they came into a natural alliance with the Civil Rights movement and the revolt of the blacks and the poor.

These two breaks came together in the cities in the political events of the 1960s. (The ghetto rebellions were a response both to the spatial aspects and the reward structure of the Fordist compromise.) Spatially, the segregation of blacks in the ghettoes, and the spatial distinctions between the quality of housing and services there and in the suburbs, became intolerable to ghetto residents. Through the only weapon they had, social unrest, they made clear their dissatisfaction with the conditions that weighed down their lives. Many professional and technical workers, and particularly those "in training" in colleges and universities, similarly were dissatisfied with the conditions that hemmed in their futures. Those that did not drop out altogether formed the core of the middle class support that helped make the Civil Rights movement and the ghetto rebellions so audible a call for change in the nation's cities.

The establishment response was both "soft" and "hard." The War on Poverty was the soft response. It poured billions of dollars into social services and physical investment in physical (re-)construction. It supported the brief reemergence of government-subsidized housing as housing worth living in. It provided not only job training in conventional programs (often for future jobs that did not exist), but as importantly provided direct jobs for minority group members and community activists in administration and services, permitting them to develop skills, self-confidence, and claims to decent jobs on a permanent basis. So there was an upsurge in minority employment at almost all levels of government, even after the War on Poverty was officially over.

And over it soon was, to be replaced by the "hard" response to urban riots. As Nixon replaced Johnson in the White House, the use of armed force escalated as a reaction to ghetto unrest. "Rioters" were shot, and several killed, in Detroit and other cities. War on Poverty funds were curtailed; repression replaced concession as a response to protest. By the time Nixon's second term began, all seemed quiet on the urban front.

THE "URBAN FISCAL CRISIS"

The so-called "fiscal crisis of the cities" was the establishment's way of bringing about a new set of relations of production in the urban arena. The "fiscal crisis" permitted the final termination of the "soft" response to the ghetto uprisings. Under cover of the "crisis," social programs were curtailed, government employment reduced (which particularly, disadvantaged members of minority groups), and attention to the ghettoes diminished, all in the name of keeping cities out of bankruptcy. Alternative paths, of course, could have been pursued: cities were only in fiscal trouble to the extent that the establishment said they were. City governments could simply have raised local taxes, or the federal government could have collected more taxes nationally and allocated them to urban services, or reoriented other expenditures towards local governments, but none of these options was exercised. The fiscal crisis played much too neatly into the hands of capital, of the established political and economic leadership. In this sense, the crisis was fraudulent, a manipulated crisis that could have been avoided, but was not as the opportunities it provided for private business control over public actions became more and more apparent (Marcuse 1981).

The fiscal crisis of the cities was, to extend the Marxist term, a cleansing crisis. It cleared the way for a new compromise to reinforce existing relations of power and wealth, a new compromise based on new technical developments in the form and organization of production. It set the stage for the developments we now see in cities, the restructuring of space and the restructuring of class relations. The Period of Fiscal Crisis was Phase I of the new arrangement; the current Period of Gentrification is Phase II. The fiscal crisis put an end to the old arrangement, and began the new; gentrification represents the dominance of the new.

Spatially, the fiscal "crisis" brought about and made politically acceptable the abandonment of large sections of working-class housing in most major industrial cities. The working class that lived there was no longer needed. The new relations of production no longer paid them the wages necessary to maintain their housing while providing profit to landlords and interest to bankers. Nor was there any incentive for the state to keep them available for work by temporarily meeting their needs. Even the limited investment in the maintenance of the public facilities in such neighborhoods (streets, schools, parks, public safety, fire protection), was no longer functional for the capitalist state. With the defeat of the protests of the 1960s and under cover of the ideology of fiscal crisis, the state abandoned these former working-class areas. Some were simply no longer of interest (the South Bronx in New York, the Hough section of Cleveland, Watts in Los Angeles, for instance); others, as we shall see, were potentially desirable for other uses, and their cleaning out helped make those new uses possible (the lower East Side, Clinton and Chelsea in New York, south of Market in San Francisco). By promoting the idea of a fiscal crisis, the idea that the cities had no alternatives, that the money simply was not there to do otherwise, this wholesale abandonment was put through with only limited and ineffectual protest. Even many of those hurt most by it swallowed the fraudulent claim.

In class terms, the same fiscal crisis isolated and disarmed the increasing numbers of poor people, unskilled workers, blacks, members of minority groups, and poor women, whom the new system of production no longer needed, nor ever saw even a potential use for. The abandonment of housing and of households, of spaces in cities and sectors of classes, went hand in hand. A large reserve army of the unskilled unemployed was no longer seen as needed; services for them, the "safety net," the social investment in education and training, was redundant. People were abandoned with the buildings they lived in.

And people who were still needed, in the lower levels of the productive and administrative processes, were likewise put down under cover of the fiscal crisis. In the economy generally, real wages for factory workers fell for the first time since the Great Depression. At the city level, payrolls were slashed and the wages of those kept on were cut. The fiscal crisis was a wholesale attack on the level of pay of public employees, and a successful one: public employees' pay in most cities fell both absolutely and relatively in comparison to the private sector.

THE PERIOD OF GENTRIFICATION: SPATIAL AND CLASS CHANGES

Gentrification, the "revitalization" of working-class residential areas through physical up-grading with consequent displacement of lower-income households by upper income ones,[3] is both a spatial and a class phenomenon. The fraudulent fiscal crisis opened the door to new spatial, as well as class, relations in cities; gentrification is only part of the substance of, but a good symbol for, both the new relations.

With gentrification, areas close to the central business district, and areas with particular environmental amenities (waterfronts, views, parks) or a particularly desirable housing stock (brownstones, Victorian mansions) which had "filtered down" to working class or poor tenants, are reclaimed by upper middle-class professionals and technical workers and up-and-coming businessmen and women. The first wave of occupants does extensive renovation, sometimes themselves. At the same time, speculation is widespread, prices and rents sky-rocket, older residents are forced out either directly from buildings being renovated or indirectly because of escalating prices, and soon the area becomes Yuppie heaven. The process is the opposite of abandonment; abandonment creates both the push that forces some of those displaced by it (the more prosperous) to compete for housing in other older gentrifying neighborhoods, and the pull to new residents by forcing out poorer residents in areas that would otherwise be too difficult to gentrify (Marcuse 1985b, 1986).

These spatial changes are not simply a coincidental reshuffling of residential space, brought about by exogenous changes in tastes or changing demographic patterns, as the conventional wisdom would have them. They are directly linked to changes in the system of production, both in the forces of production and in the relations of production. The physical and technical changes in the way production is organized requires different uses of space in central cities, different types of persons to make it go, and different arrangements to make that type of person voluntarily contribute his or her labor to the process.

The new business needs for space are clear. The shiny skyscrapers characteristic of downtowns, even in such old manufacturing cities as Pittsburg, Detroit, and Cleveland, or old commercial centers like Boston, New York, and Philadelphia, or newer high-tech-oriented areas such as San Francisco or Houston, all witness the importance of office work (technical, professional, managerial and financial), in making the wheels of production continue to turn and the profits from it to continue to flow. Actual production may be undertaken by robots in the United States or Japan, or by under-paid and over-exploited workers in Haiti or Korea; but the chain of exchanges, of shipments and payments, of contracts and sales, of ownership and services, of marketing and distribution, must be integrated and kept moving. Such work is done in offices, particularly in the centers of finance and international trade, the global cities. Space is needed for it, over and above the available office space in downtown areas.

Downtown office space can expand vertically; hence the proliferation of skyscrapers throughout even mid-sized U.S. cities. But downtowns can also expand horizontally, if they can remove the older uses hemming them in. Gentrification is the residential aspect of that process; urban renewal was its predecessor; "revitalization" is its public relations name. The result is a spatial restructuring of the city to provide room for the new office uses, and their ancillary residential uses, that changes in the system of production have brought about.

Gentrification affects people as well as places. Changes in the system of production create gentrifiers, as well as gentrified neighborhoods.[4] The key group needing to be brought into voluntary compliance with the older system of production has been factory workers; Fordism is the name for that effort. Now it is the agreement of technical, professional, and managerial people to play their role that is crucial. Gentrification symbolizes the new accord. We may speak of the gentrification deal as being the contemporary version of the Fordist deal; the gentrification of class relations as being the broader societal pattern that has, as one aspect, the gentrification of space.

Thus, the gentrification deal has replaced the satisfactions of suburban living with the satisfactions of living in revitalized high-density urban areas as a way of guaranteeing social peace. It has produced the internalized support and participation in the prevailing system of the young professionals, technicians and managers now needed in increasing numbers. Suburban single-family homeownership had proven excellent at keeping a skilled working class content. Suburbanism required a substantial amount of time from its participants: in commuting, in mowing the lawn, in caring for the house and the children and driving to the public services and facilities any healthy and happy family needed and/or wanted. But for what was being asked of the new professionals, that arrangement is inappropriate. For them, quality of work counts more than quantity; fewer people, better trained and working compulsively, independently motivated and self-starting, are more useful than many people working just for pay and happy to get home at the end of the day. So the incentive structure has had to change.

Gentrification fits in neatly with the new patterns of work. Living close to work, commuting time — time taken from salaried or incentive-based work, hence not paid for hourly — is cut down. Providing more and more services and amenities for pay — everything from dining out to security services for each building, from private health spas to rooms for entertaining and custom interior design — makes high pay worth getting; having it all available right at hand means less time wasted procuring them, and more time available for work. Not having children to take care of means that women, as well as men, are freer to participate in "production," to put in as many hours as are necessary to keep the money flowing.

And of course social value systems have to conform to these new patterns. Consumption has to be seen as something desirable for its own sake. Impressing the neighbors, Veblen's conspicuous consumption, is only a step in the right direction. Delight has to be found in more and more expensive items and services, luxury for the sake of art, culture for the sake of spirituality, cooking for the sake of taste rather than appetite, dressing to display fashion and not beauty — and housing as a reflection of and contribution to the inner self, not as shelter or refuge. Thus the willingness of Yuppies to spend more and more on housing, to get locations that save time and make pleasure as well as work readily accessible, to get places that shore up identity, and that reveal who the occupant truly is. In a growing economy, the trend in this direction seems a permanently upward one; that makes expenditures on housing a good investment too; a double attraction to the new money-oriented class. Thus, gentrification, of housing and life-style, helps to integrate into the system those that 20 years earlier had criticized it most severely or threatened to drop out of it altogether. Those who became hippies or New Leftists yesterday have become Yuppies today. That is part of the gentrification deal.

Homelessness is the flip side of the gentrification deal: both the acceleration of homelessness and the way it is publicly dealt with. Gentrification accelerates homelessness; it "reclaims" for the new professionals what used to be housing of last resort for the marginal in the cities. At the same time, more and more are marginal as the need for occasional and unskilled work diminishes or is moved further from the central (and accessible) areas of cities. Gentrification, however, also requires that the homeless be removed, not only from homes in gentrifying areas, but also from the consciousness of the gentrifiers; they are a disturbing phenomenon, a reminder that all is not as it should be. Beyond that, homelessness exists because the housing system is working as it should, not because of some malfunction in it; that realization could be dangerous. Hence, hiding rather than housing the homeless becomes the order of the day (see Fabricant and Kelly in this volume).

Other aspects of current urban developments can only be mentioned here briefly. Real estate speculation, often made the villain of gentrification, is in fact more its agent than its cause. It may exacerbate the swings of the market, as it did before the Great Depression; more often, it will simply smooth them out, realizing, gradually, gains in value (or reflecting losses) that will occur in the future. On the public side, urban renewal programs are likewise more agent than cause; if the private pressures for it had not existed, it would not have occurred, and today much that was done under its public banner in the 1950s or 1960s can be done profitably with much less public investment. Nor is public housing a cause of urban spatial change; although its concentration and its neglect may have given rise to major problems, and although its signal successes[5] still hold much promise for the future, it plays much too small a role in the United States today to be more than a by-product of other forces.

Both racism and sexism have played major roles in structuring cities as they are today. Ghettoes created by private prejudice and public discrimination fit much too neatly into pervasive patterns of racism; the difficulties confronting women trying to find housing adequate to a range of needs ignored (when not condemned) by the housing supply system likewise reinforce a widely sexist urban pattern. Where factors of class, race, and gender come together, the extremes of benefit and of burden in cities are found. The current move towards privatization of public services and facilities is likely to aggravate precisely these distinctions. By asking residents to pay for maintenance of their own parks, by encouraging private schooling and garbage pick-up for profit and sale of subsidized housing to private owners, the Reagan Administration has accentuated the inequalities that income, race, and gender produce. For those towards the bottom of the ladder, the prospects produced by these patterns are not promising.

THE MOTOR OF CHANGE

No "conspiracy of the ruling class" has brought about what has been described here; but neither has it come to pass automatically. The process of societal change is a complicated one, in which general laws interact with individual choices to produce results predictable only in their very longest sweep. The gentrification model, for instance, seems neatly to meet the needs of the ruling class for spatial restructuring, shifting work skill requirements, and domestic political stability, at the same time permitting United States business interests to take advantage of the possibilities of the internationalization of operations. So the gentrification model is clearly functional for the U.S. ruling class. But no one person or small group meeting behind closed doors decided this was the way to go. Neither did it simply fall into place without human volition and struggle.

What happened, rather, was that different people acted, largely independently of each other, in directions that turned out (perhaps even sometimes to their surprise) to be very compatible. Later, seen with hindsight, that direction can be given a single label and understood to be part of a single model of change. Real estate developers, acting through the private market, found that business people were willing to pay high prices to locate downtown, and that residential uses nearby could likewise command good prices. Converting existing older working class housing seemed a profitable way to go, and so they did. Politicians, always happy to receive contributions from developers, found they could maximize their take by city policies fostering gentrification. National political leaders, seeing that the opposition to gentrification did not scare their business constituency nor pose a political threat to their own careers, ignored it. But there was opposition, and consequently struggle, and often that struggle put limits to how far the gentrification model could go. On the urban front, it involved struggles against displacement; on the work front, it involved struggles against foreign competition and the division of the international working class quest for a decent wage.

Nor were those in power united in the direction they wanted to go. In particular, in the urban aspects of the gentrification model, real estate interests came into conflict with businesses needing to use that real estate: developers' profits, after all, came out of the pockets initially of users of property. Owners of existing property had interests different from those of new developers; for existing owners, the less new directly competitive development the better, in many cases. Political leaders in different cities competed with each other for tax revenue and glory; business as a whole benefited, but just where the growth would take place was influenced to some degree by the competition among cities. Nationally, businesses with overseas operations had different interests from purely local ones, big business from small business, unionized from non-unionized, and high-tech from low-skilled. And these differences produced conflicts whose outcomes were not predictable in detail.

But, in general, the steps taken by various actors in the general direction of the gentrification model meshed with each other better than those going in any alternative direction, satisfied a wider array of more powerful interests, and had the most long-run potential for the most influential groups. Intellectuals, viewing the picture from a little distance, saw a pattern emerge, described it, applauded it or simply labeled it inevitable if it fit in with their own positions, and helped give it conscious form and ideological legitimacy — and, of course, a name. Whether the best of the analyses could have predicted just this outcome well before it happened is an open question, but clearly with hindsight the logic of events is clear. It is that logic, rather than any deliberate "plan" or any automatic "law," whose results we see about us today.

THE FUTURE OF CITIES

No logic can predict what the future of cities will be; what human beings do today and tomorrow, choosing among the options that history leaves open for them, will be decisive. The direction in which one group of persons and interests will try to go is clear: the gentrification deal is one that benefits capital, much of the present political leadership, and, at least in the short run, the upper segments of those who work for them. But they are not united in what they want, and internal conflicts, such as those referred to above, remain to be resolved.

Even more important, the existing political and economic leadership cannot run the country just the way they want; there is serious resistance from classes and groupings whose interests are not served by existing arrangements; from working people, poor people, members of minority groups, women, and those intellectually critical of the restrictions on their potentials created by a capitalist society. In the urban arena, anti-displacement activities, rent control battles, progressive city electoral results, and the movements for environmental quality and historic preservation all reflect political limits to the presently prevailing patterns of unbridled spatial change and its consequences. They all represent moments in the development of what have been called "urban social movements": movements involving masses of people, often engaging in quite radical direct political action and protest. The protest is in many ways akin to strikes and workers' action, but focused on issues of consumption rather than production. On the urban front, conflicts between residential and business interests emerge separately from more traditional class conflicts. In these newer conflicts, residents of various classes, colors and nationalities have interests in common that pit them jointly against representatives of business interests, even though some individuals stand on both sides of the divide.

So, opposition to more high-rise construction finds wealthy residents of the East Side of Manhattan on the same side as working-class communities in Brooklyn and minority neighborhoods in Harlem. Anti-displacement activities date back to the late 1940s and the early opposition to clearance in the name of redevelopment and renewal; such activities now often unify recent in-movers with old-time residents and solid middle-class residents with the homeless and the poor, in resisting new development at the expense of the old. Rent control, originally a movement led by tenants who were committed socialists, now has solid-middle class support; affluent as well as blue-collar residents see their interest in resisting the rise in real estate prices and rents. Home ownership, once an option for most, is now a possibility for fewer and fewer; only 22 percent of all households can afford to buy a new home today, and the prospects are perceived as getting worse, not better. Progressive local coalitions — in Burlington, Vermont, even under an explicitly socialist mayor — unite an unlikely coalition of environmentalists, senior citizens, tenants and rent control advocates, Yuppies and blacks and Hispanics, women's groups and unemployed youth; in Santa Monica, Berkeley, Ann Arbor, they have elected slates far to the left of the prevailing national stance. In Chicago, for the whole city, and in New York, for a number of local communities, a leadership is committed to growth only with equity and with adequate environmental, cultural, and historic protections. These developments suggest that the limits to gentrification will be political as well as economic.

What happens next will depend on how the conflicts among the various conflicting forces, among whom quite new alignments have been produced and others made possible by changes in the relations of production, are resolved. The short-range future looks as if the processes of spatial change presently under way will continue. The long-range future is not determined; the ingredients for a different path of progress are also there.

NOTES

1. The growth of many Third World cities, without benefit of cars or rails, to sizes exceeding those of the more "technologically advanced" cities, is further evidence, although other factors, including colonial international relations and changes in agricultural practices, need to be brought in to the explanation, in addition to changes in productive processes.
2. Just when the shift described below occurred is difficult to say exactly, since a number of factors came together to produce various components. Milestones may be taken to be: 1969, when producer services really took off (Sassen-Koob 1984) when manufacturing employment peaked (Rees 1986); or 1980, when the general trend to loss of population in older central cities reversed itself.
3. For a formal definition, see Marcuse (1985:198).
4. For the attention to gentrifiers as a separate phenomenon I am indebted to several writings of Damaris Rose.

REFERENCES

Alcaly, Roger E. and David Mermelstein. 1977. *The Fiscal Crisis of American Cities*. New York: Vintage.

Bratt, Rachel G., Chester Hartman, and Ann Meyerson. 1986. *Critical Perspectives on Housing*. Philadelphia: Temple University Press.

Castells, Manuel. 1983. *The City and the Grassroots*. Berkeley: University of California Press.

Fainstein, Norman and Susal Fainstein (eds.). 1982. *Urban Policy Under Capitalism*. Beverly Hills: Sage.

Foglesong, Richard E. 1986. *Planning the Capitalist City: The Colonial Era to the 1920's*. Princetion, NJ: Princeton University Press.

Marcuse, Peter. 1981. The Targeted Crisis: On the Ideology of the Urban Fiscal Crisis and Its Uses. *International Journal of Urban and Regional Research* 5(no. 3).

_____. 1985 Gentrification, Abandonment, and Displacement: Connections, Causes, and Policy Responses in New York City. *Journal of Urban and Contemporary Law* 28:198.

_____. 1986. The Beginning of Public Housing in New York. *Journal of Urban History* 12(No. 4)(August):353–380.

_____. Neutralizing Homelessness. 1988. *Socialist Review* 88(1):69–97.

Marx, Karl. (1849) 1935. *Wage Labor and Capital.* New York: International Publishers.

Mayer, Margit. 1988. Urban Social Movements in a Political Restructuring Context. *American Studies.*

Rees, John (ed.). 1986. *Technology, Regions, and Policy.* Totowa, NJ: Rowman and Littlefield.

Rose, Damaris. 1984. Rethinking Gentrification: Beyond the Uneven Development of Marxist Urban Theory. *Environment and Planning* 2(47).

Sassen-Koob, Saskia. 1984. The New Labor Division in Global Cities. In, *Cities in Transformation*, Michael P. Smith (ed.). Beverly Hills: Sage.

Shefter, Martin. 1987. *Political Crisis, Fiscal Crisis: The Collapse and Revival of New York City.* New York: Basic Books.

Tabb, William. 1982. *The Long Default.* New York: Monthly Review Press.

Wall Street Journal. 1986. U.S. Rich and Poor Increase in Numbers, Middle Loses Ground. (September, 22).

18

No Haven for Homeless in a Heartless Economy

MICHAEL FABRICANT
and
MICHAEL KELLY

Up to three million people now live without a home in the United States, mostly in our cities. In cities like New York, it is difficult to comprehend the scope of the homeless problem, with its more than 60,000 homeless riding the subways or seeking refuge in the train and bus stations at night.

Recently, a Chicago newspaper reported that fifty homeless people had been buried in the city's Potter's Field in January, after silently freezing to death. Charles Ford, the Director of Emergency Services said: "We have the feeling that the numbers are increasing... We are finding more and more people who live on the street involuntarily — young people, who in ordinary times would be able to find jobs, and more women and children."

Other cities of America's "heartland" have shared this experience. Detroit, with its massive unemployment, had over 27,000 homeless people in November 1984 — a 300 percent increase from 1982. The U.S. Conference of Mayors reported that up to 1,000 people were living in cars, trailers, tents, or campgrounds in Tulsa while another 200–300 people lived under city bridges.

In recent years, the temperate "Sunbelt" cities have been inundated with unemployed workers from the Northeast. Yet in Dallas, Phoenix and Los Angeles, for example, they have found few jobs, high rents, and a much lower level of entitlement to social services and income/maintenance than in their old homes.

The Union Rescue Mission of Los Angeles, the world's largest private mission, recently (for the first time in over 90 years) turned people away because all the 350 beds and 350 chairs were filled. Elsewhere, during the winter of 1983, Seattle turned away 4,000 families (roughly 16,000 people) who applied for shelter. And in Flagstaff, Arizona, many homeless families have been camping out in the National Forest which borders the city.

THE NEW VICTIMS

The homeless population has changed dramatically in appearance as well as quantity. Between 1945 and 1970 urban hobos, mostly older, alcoholic men, were the major skid row inhabitants. Since then, small but growing numbers of women have appeared. By the mid-1970s many younger black and Hispanic men, unemployed and lacking job skills, began using urban shelters and flophouses. Many had drug or alcohol problems. In New York City up to one-third of them were veterans, mostly of the Vietnam War.

At the same time, discharged mental patients became more prominent on the streets following deinstitutionalization. Those supporting this policy claimed that recent advances in psychopharmacology and treatment had now made community living feasible for institutionalized mental patients. New "wonder drugs," especially phenothiazines, were to supplant incarceration. Community-based treatment models became the new road towards "recovery" and social integration.

Deinstitutionalization, as it was employed, resulted more from fiscal than from therapeutic concerns. To begin with, the state mental hospital census doubled between 1950 and 1970. Housing and treating this influx required an incredible amount of money. Existing facilities were outdated and dilapidated. The unionization of state workers had further increased costs. According to one estimate, deinstitutionalization may have saved the state governments as much as $5.4 billion in expenditures between 1965 and 1974.

Meanwhile, the price paid in human misery has been monumental. Vital services, community supports and follow-up treatments were not adequately developed. Many of the 400,000 people discharged from mental hospitals between 1950 and 1980 were forced to fend for themselves. Temporarily, some maintained a marginal existence in low-income housing, but by the mid-1970s this too disappeared. Other than the street, the only alternatives left were adult homes or shelters. In these newly emerging "deviant ghettos," one finds neither compassion nor therapeutic treatments, but at best some form of repressive tolerance on the outer fringes of society.

The crisis, with its accompanying economic hardship, creates the need for increased mental health services among those most sorely afflicted. Yet, strict admission criteria have eliminated even this alternative for many.

The high rates of unemployment during the recession of 1980–1982 produced yet another wave of homeless people. Massive layoffs and plant closings produced situations where, in cities like Detroit, close to 20,000 workers per month lost their unemployment benefits. In 1983 Illinois had a 13.9 percent unemployment rate or 759,000 unemployed citizens, and also had the nation's highest rate of home foreclosures (1.6 percent). Shelters in Chicago, Detroit and elsewhere cited "the loss of a job" as a primary reason for homelessness.

The inability of younger blacks or Hispanics to enter the labor market has also contributed to the homelessness explosion. Their unemployment rate (over 50 percent) is the highest in the nation. Unable to find jobs or affordable housing, many young black and Hispanic men are crowded out of their family's apartment. In 1980, virtually no people under the age of twenty-one stayed in New York City municipal shelters. By 1985, they comprised 7 percent of the total shelter population. Recent estimates showed approximately 22,000 homeless youth in New York City, the largest subgroup of homeless.

Finally, homeless families are the newest and, perhaps, most frightening wave of homelessness. Headed mostly by women, living on AFDC, they represent the fastest growing group of homeless.

THE GOVERNMENT STRIKES BACK

To this grievous problem, the government response has sometimes been nightmarish. In Fort Lauderdale, a city councilman urged the spraying of trash with poison to cut off the "vermin's food supply." In Phoenix and in President Reagan's home city of Santa Barbara, anti-homeless ordinances prohibit sitting, sleeping or lying down in public areas such as parks, and consider trashbin refuse as public property. Hence, foraging for food is a criminal act. At the Federal level, a Department of Housing and Urban Development Survey concluded that there were but 200,000–300,000 homeless nationwide. Despite its numerous methodological flaws which considerably underestimate the problem, this survey has nonetheless been used to minimize government action. For example, HUD's recommendation against new, temporary shelters has seriously inhibited efforts for more significant change.

Obviously, the need for safe, decent shelter greatly outstrips the number of slots available. Recent estimates show only 330 shelter beds in Detroit, for a homeless population of 27,000. Chicago has approximately 1,000 beds for 20,000–25,000. In Connecticut, the second richest state, the less than 950 shelter beds far underserve its 10,000 homeless men, women and children. One shelter in Hartford turned away more than 3,500 applicants in a recent 12-month period.

Shelters also fail to meet the differing needs of homeless people. Alcoholics, the unemployed, the elderly and former mental patients are all lumped into one space. Sanitary conditions are often poor. Bathroom and shower facilities are woefully inadequate given the crowded conditions. Some municipal shelters, like the one in Washington, D.C., featured myriad abuses, including random beatings of homeless people by vicious security guards. Given these conditions, many homeless people have apparently "preferred the rats and the cold" to contending with the degradation of the public shelters.

In New York City, municipal shelters have repeatedly failed to meet basic health and safety standards. Overcrowding, unsanitary conditions and the menacing atmosphere of shelters discourage many of the most vulnerable homeless from seeking assistance. In effect, many elderly and mentally ill people hazard the street rather than risk a night at a shelter. Scores of homeless people in New York City reported violence in the public shelters. Two researchers noted that, "for most men we talked to, mention of the shelter conjured up . . . an ever present threat of violence. It is the violence which is the strongest deterrent to men who once there, vow never to return . . ." (Baxter and Hopper 1981:55).

The present growth in homelessness began during the 1970s which were also marked by the most acute economic crisis since the 1930s. The nation lost 30 million jobs during this period. By 1976 plant shutdowns had wiped out 39 percent of the jobs that existed in 1969, or an average of about 3.2 million jobs destroyed each year. While approximately 110 jobs were created for every 100 jobs that were destroyed, this ratio still represents a sharp reduction in job creation compared to the 1950s and 1960s. A striking increase in the unemployment rate also occurred, soaring from 5 percent in 1970 to approximately 10 percent in 1981.

These trends also helped depress wages for most workers. Those displaced from mill, auto or steel jobs were usually forced into lower paying, unstable work. The middle-level jobs represented by the old manufacturing line have rapidly disappeared, making job transition especially difficult for displaced workers. In effect, the educational and financial supports necessary to enable large numbers of displaced workers to move to jobs offering similar pay do not exist. And the overwhelming majority of new jobs are low paying and unstable. Consequently, at best, only a small fraction of displaced workers can be absorbed at the upper end of the wage pyramid.

UNDERCUTTING THE SOCIAL WAGE

The reduction of wages is not accidental but rather part of the dynamics of capitalism. This same process unfolded in earlier periods of economic crisis. As E. P. Thompson has noted:

> The first half of the 19th century must be seen as a period of chronic underemployment in which the skilled trades are like islands threatened on every side by technological innovation and by the inrush of unskilled or juvenile labor. . . In a number of trades. . . noted as both organized and highly paid in 1812 there was serious deterioration in the status and living conditions over the next 30 years (1963:243).

Declining living standards were also experienced by the unemployed during this period; and in 1834, the Doctrine of Less Eligibility was applied to the unemployed, keeping relief grants below the wages of the lowest paid laborer. Therefore, the wage reductions during this period coincided with lower relief grants. Substantial reductions in relief benefits between 1820 and 1840 placed many families below subsistence income levels.

These historic circumstances have contemporary parallels. This "social wage" (or welfare-state benefits), increasingly available to chronically unemployed and dislocated workers since 1930, has been redefined by the present economic crisis. The accompanying reduction in marketplace wages has led to today's intensified poverty and homelessness.

Recent reports by journalists, academics, advocates and the government underscore the dramatic reduction of entitlement benefits and services. Between 1980 and 1981 an intense drive emerged to make across-the-board cuts in all social welfare programs. Overall, cash welfare benefits declined by 17 percent. One million people were eliminated from Food Stamp coverage. Ninety percent of the working, AFDC families had their benefits reduced or eliminated. Finally, the value of general assistance payments has declined substantially. While these trends did not begin during Reagan's presidency, they have been dramatically intensified by this administration.

As cash benefits have eroded, both private and public sector housing investment decisions have also changed. The federal government effectively withdrew from the public housing market. In 1979 over 40,000 units of conventional public housing were completed. In 1985 only 5,000 units of conventional public housing were funded and the proposed budget for 1987 calls for a moratorium on all additions to the subsidized housing stock.

The central city renovations characterizing many U.S. cities have made matters worse. In New York, tax abatements gave incentives to convert low income housing to luxury apartment buildings. Between 1975 and 1981 approximately 35,000 units of low income housing were lost. New York City offers the most dramatic example of these market forces. Cities such as Chicago, Cleveland, Phoenix, Newark, San Francisco, and Denver also report substantial losses in their low-income housing stock to downtown renovation or luxury housing development. These trends partly respond to the changing economic structure which has allowed some elite professionals and entrepreneurs to benefit from a polarized job market which has hurt most workers. The increased demand for urban housing from relatively affluent people has pushed many low-income individuals and families out of the formal housing market.

The consequent increase in urban rents leaves poor people particularly vulnerable. Increasingly, general assistance and AFDC payments are simply insufficient to meet the new urban rent levels throughout the country. As has been noted: ". . . the amount of public assistance a recipient was allowed for rent — whether as a separate shelter allowance or as part of a flat grant, ranged from 20 percent to 60 percent of local fair market rent" (Harper and Hamberg 1984).

When basic rent allowances are insufficient to meet prevailing rents, then grants have more symbolic than real value. Entitlements that increasingly fail to meet basic survival needs (such as permanent housing) most dramatically indicate the growing inadequacy of today's "social wage."

DEVASTATING EFFECTS

The gap between benefits and prevailing rents has obvious consequences. Many cities report dramatic increases in eviction rates, disproportionately affecting low-income citizens. In New York City, where a half million eviction actions were initiated from a total stock of two million rental units, approximately half involved people receiving public assistance.

Many people have reacted by moving in with friends or relatives, thus increasing the density of their living space. In New York City alone over 230,000 families are doubled and trebled up. If but three percent of these families are made homeless this year the number of homeless families will nearly double.

As usual, women and people of color have been disproportionately affected. Because they are even less likely to have "primary sector" jobs, their wages are lower in the first place. And housing discrimination based on racism and on prejudice against single women with children predates the fiscal crisis. In New Jersey, for instance, the Division for Youth and Family Services frequently splits up families who apply for shelter, referring the children to foster care placement. Equally important, blacks and Hispanics may be victims of racially motivated violence within shelters or on the streets. In short, economic hard times and capitalist restructuring combine with social wage cuts to increase the plight of women and minorities and to further reduce their already inadequate options.

The diminution of options for the homeless is further reenforced by the imposition of work requirements in exchange for shelter. For instance, New York City has embarked on a "work experience" program whereby shelter residents perform 20 hours of work per week in return for $12.50. Residents who refuse to take part in this program are sent to "non work" shelters where it has been charged the conditions are inferior. Similarly, stringent work requirements are being imposed in municipalities throughout the country. These policies raise the spector of nineteenth-century type workhouses (which drove laborers to toil under horrible conditions for scant wages) being recreated in the late twentieth century.

Clearly, we have entered a period of economic resocialization. In effect, the whole labor force is being resocialized to new and lower wages while benefits are cut to show the poorest that an even more reduced living standard awaits them outside the marketplace or within the welfare system. Reductions in entitlement and spending have both freed resources for alternative investments and substantially diminished the living standard of the poor. These forces have combined to create a new subclass of poor; the homeless.

But for such shifts to succeed, entitlement recipients must also be resocialized. The welfare rights philosophy of the 1960s and 1970s which argued that all citizens are entitled to adequate living standards and affordable housing, is being replaced by an attitude that recreates nineteenth-century definitions of entitlement. Temporary shelters and soup lines for the homeless are replacing housing and an adequate food allowance as prevailing public policies. In effect, the state's legitimizing role is being reconstructed and translated into policies that reflect nineteenth-century structural and social relationships.

ROLLBACK IN WELFARE POLICY

During the economic crisis of the 1930s, the social wage or base entitlement of workers was redefined. In contrast to the erosion of benefits and economic rights in the current period, the Great Depression began an expansion of social insurance programs and a gradual increase in the social wage. Advances in defining economic entitlements continued, albeit gradually (as compared, for instance, to many Western European countries), during the postwar boom.

Many economists and historians have shown that the advance in the social wage during the 1930s was not an historic aberration. These improvements occurred because various groups of workers and/or citizens organized and pressed their demands for economic benefits. Social movements across a wide spectrum pressured the state to take a primary responsibility for assuring its citizens a certain minimum living standard, transcending church and private agencies that had been expected to assume this social function in the past. Between 1934 and 1936 this conflict peaked, and various reforms resulted which increased social insurance benefits and coverage. In effect, the intensified class conflict of this period forced both economic and wage concessions. The states also increased their investment in programs designed to help preserve social harmony.

The subsequent fifty-year expansion of the social wage has strengthened the position of many workers. Government benefits have cushioned many groups of workers from the market's instability. Unemployment insurance, disability benefits, AFDC and other entitlements have guaranteed those temporarily and chronically out of the labor force a minimum standard of living. During the 1970s, entitlement benefits, particularly unemployment insurance, even enabled many citizens to temporarily resist taking jobs for reduced wages. Part of the strategy necessary for workers to resist long-term wage reductions is to protect and expand the social wage benefits that have evolved during this period.

The homeless crisis reflects the unraveling of many of the advances of the last fifty years. Shelters and soup lines do not offer those presently or potentially homeless a basis for recreating their lives. At best these services only temporarily halt the physical, emotional and intellectual deterioration of the homeless person. If the needs of the homeless and chronically or temporarily unemployed are to be met, then economic entitlement must be expanded or advanced, not diminished. This expansion or redefinition must begin with the economic right of citizens to housing and a job at a livable wage. Jobs and housing must be pursued jointly and not separately: splitting the two will only further fragment individuals and groups, and thus make them more amenable to economic resocialization.

Obviously this kind of change will not automatically come from liberal policymakers or legislators. To the contrary, without forceful resistance there will be an ongoing, intensified drive to reduce the social wage. As in earlier historic periods, pressure must come from laborers, the unemployed and those most fundamentally affected by the economic crisis. Only such pressure can preserve and extend the present boundaries of the social wage.

As has already been suggested, social wage benefits are distributed through the welfare state. The scope, size and functions of the welfare state are intimately associated with the structure and trends in the larger political economy. Ian Gough and James O'Connor have noted that the welfare state performs two basic and often contradictory functions — legitimation and accumulation (O'Connor 1975; Gough 1979). Very simply, the legitimation functions of the welfare state are intended to maintain social harmony or legitimate the larger social system. Alternatively, the capital accumulation functions are intended to enhance the present and future productivity of labor and more directly contribute to the profitability of certain private sector industries.

In the area of housing, one legitimating function of the welfare state is the development of shelters for the homeless which appear to serve the needs of even the nation's poorest. Accumulation functions are met if the development of affordable and well maintained low-income housing positively affects the health of workers which in turn increases their productivity. Finally, Section 8 and other Federal legislation in the area of low-income housing directly support the accumulation process through subsidies to private developers.

These functional distinctions, however, are not as clean as they might initially appear. For instance, conflict(s) between legitimation and accumulation are embedded within each of these policies — shelter development, low-income housing creation and Federal subsidies to the private sector. Shelters are a relatively clean example of a legitimating service inasmuch as they give the appearance of addressing, if not resolving, the question of homelessness despite the persistence of the problem. Shelters, however, also aid the accumulation process by addressing the basic survival needs of some of the homeless and thus preserving at the most extreme margins a segment of this potential group of laborers. Just as importantly, the proliferation of shelters has a disciplining effect on the labor force and thus contributes to the accumulation process. This occurs because "the prospect of a degraded life on the dole serves to steal otherwise recalcitrant workers to the rigors of the laboring world, to stifle demands for higher wages or better working conditions and to cause those who do fall upon hard times to seek assistance elsewhere" (Hopper and Hamburg 1984:67). Some illustrations of similar conflicts in low-income housing policy and subsidies could also be developed.

Perhaps more important than the conflicts embedded in particular policies is that the tension between legitimation and accumulation is fundamental to the character and development of the entire welfare state. These conflicts are reflected in the level and direction of state expenditure. The appearance of a balance between these competing functions, however, has been disrupted during the past decade. For the first time in American history, a mature welfare state is confronted with a fiscal and economic crisis. The consequence has been an increased effort to redefine legitimating services or entitlements downward while concurrently supporting the accumulation process by disciplining the labor force and redirecting welfare state resources to the private sector. These trends have intensified the life circumstance of the poor and contributed to the expansion of homelessness.

We cannot develop, in the abstract, a blueprint of the many strategies for addressing homelessness, social wage reductions or, more generally, the economic crisis. Certain prerequisites have been identified: (1) developing critical linkages in campaigns between the interests of the working class (gentrification and sky-rocketing rents) and the poor (homelessness); (2) maximizing the opportunities for educating participants about the myths of deindustrialization, the housing crisis, etc.; and (3) heightening class tensions when surplus value is not appropriated to advance the interests of working class or poor people. Clearly, specific organizations must be created to actualize these strategic possibilities. Only then can a progressive, rational agenda emerge which will seriously address homelessness, and more fundamentally, the economic crisis.

ACKNOWLEDGEMENTS

We wish to acknowledge the substantial contributions of Steve Burghardt and Irwin Epstein. The editorial comments of the *Radical America* Collective on an earlier draft of this paper were also most instructive. A version was published in the *Resist Newsletter*.

REFERENCES

Baxter, Ellen and Kim Hooper. 1981. *Private Lives/Public Spaces: Homeless Adults on the Streets of New York City*. New York: Community Service Society.

Gough, Ian. 1979. *The Political Economy of the Welfare State*. London: Macmillan Press.

Hopper, Kim and Jill Hamberg. 1984. *The Making of America's Homeless from Skid Row to New Poor: 1945–1984*. New York: Community Service Society.

O'Connor, James. 1975. *The Fiscal Crisis of the State*. New York: St. Martin's Press.

Thompson, E. P. 1963. *The Making of the English Working Class*. New York: Pantheon.

FURTHER READING ON THE HOMELESS

Burghardt, Steven and Michael Fabricant. 1987. *Working Under the Safety Net*. Newbury Park: Sage Publishers.

Hartman, Chester. 1983. *American Housing Crisis: What Is to Be Done?* Boston: Routledge, Kegan and Paul.

Kasinetz, Philip. 1984. Gentrification and Homelessness: The Single Room Occupant and the Inner City Revival. *Urban Social Change Review* (Winter):9–14.

Salerno, Dan, Kim Hopper and Ellen Baxter. 1984. *Hardship in the Heartland. Homelessness in Eight U.S. Cities*. New York: Community Service Society.

Stern, Mark J. 1984. The Emergence of Homelessness as a Public Problem. *Social Service Review* (June):291–301.

19

The Struggle for Health

MEREDETH TURSHEN

INTRODUCTION

In the past decade a more inclusive definition of health and illness and a new understanding of the economic, social and political determinants of health and health care have emerged from research and action by the health left.[1] The old definition of ill health was based on medical explanations of how disease develops and a mechanical, biomedical model of disease. In the late nineteenth century, physicians used the germ theory to attribute diseases like smallpox to discrete, specific and external causal agents for processes that they thought were acute, self-limiting and short-lived (Powles 1973). The germ theory was never discarded; it is the basis for current research on a viral cause of cancer, for example. But most mainstream research today considers multiple causes, some of which are due to "life-style," implying it is the victim's choice of life-style that contributes to ill health. The new definition of health and illness emerging from Marxist analyses shifts attention to the socially important and historically specific question of why disease develops.

The new definition also switches to a holistic concept of health that considers the emotional as well as the physical aspects of illness (Conrad and Kern 1981). The health left recognizes that health and illness are products of the way society is organized and of the way subsistence and surplus are produced and distributed among society's members. Health and illness are products of the power relationships between producers and owners and between producers and distributors; they are also products of the way reproduction is organized (not only childbearing, but also childrearing). In other words, health and illness are socially produced.

This essay describes the broad scope of the political economy of health and lays out the issues that have been delineated and developed by the health left. Parts two and three set out a brief economic history of health policies in the United States and their consequences. The final section looks at proposed solutions to the health crisis.

THE POLITICAL ECONOMY OF HEALTH AND ILLNESS

A growing number of studies have demonstrated the dynamics of economic, social and political determinants of health and health care. They explain higher rates of disease and death among blacks (for example, the U.S. black male death rate is 34 percent higher than the white male rate and the black female rate is 45 percent higher than the white female rate) by showing the pervasive, negative impact of racism on health and on access to health services (Cooper et al. 1981). Many studies show the destructive health effects of poverty, as when unskilled manual workers are found to have a shorter life expectancy and experience more ill health than corporate executives (Townsend and Davidson 1982). The effects of sexism are evident in the poor health care received by women, including unnecessary operations like cesarian sections, hysterectomies and radical mastectomies (Ehrenreich and English 1973a, 1973b). Research on the multinational food industry explains the etiology of obesity and starvation.[2]

Accelerated exploitation of the labor force and associated stress correlate with high rates of heart disease, still the number one killer in America. Patients with these chronic conditions swamp hospital and insurance systems designed to handle surgery and acute episodes of disease. All of these studies demonstrate the dialectical relationship of health and illness to economic, social and political organization.

Socialist studies of health care analyze the unequal geographical distribution of medical services (e.g., there are fewer physicians in rural than urban areas except in ghettoes) and the unequal distribution among classes (the working class, poor and minorities have fewest services), as well as the paucity of preventive care. From an initial focus on muckraking accounts of scandals in the medical-industrial complex pioneered by the *HealthPac Bulletin* (Ehrenreich 1971; Kotelchuck 1976), the left turned to Marxist analyses of health care (Navarro 1986). The pharmaceutical industry, which makes excessive profits by overcharging (for example, in 1970 Hoffmann-La Roche sold valium to the British NHS at 400 times the cost, and in 1960 Schering's mark-up on a drug used in menopausal disorders was 7,079 percent) was deservedly singled out for particular investigation, both here and abroad (Muller 1982; McDonnell 1986). And family planning services, which have tricked or forced women into accepting sterilization, were exposed as frequently sexist, racist and imperialist attempts to control the growth of certain populations (Michaelson 1981).

The relation of occupational and environmental health hazards to industrial practices illustrates the need for a holistic approach to ill health. Many chronic health problems (e.g., cancer, asthma, bronchitis) are associated with pollution of the physical environment (toxic waste dumps, polluted air and water) by the petrochemical industry.

From the 1950s, with cheap oil expropriated from the Middle East, backed by an imperialist foreign policy and a pro-business domestic policy, the petroleum industry experienced an era of unexampled corporate prosperity. This fueled environmental deterioration and increased health hazards. The petroleum industry comprises eight branches — inorganic chemicals, dyes, and explosives; organic chemicals; fertilizers; plastics, rubbers, nuclear materials, vegetable and animal oils and fats; synthetic fibers and resins; pharmaceuticals and cosmetics; soaps, polishes, inks, matches, candles, and insecticides; and paints, varnishes, and lacquers. Together they account for most of the toxic wastes, noxious emissions, and hazardous occupational exposures associated with the precipitous rise in deaths from cancers (Epstein 1979).

The left progressed rapidly in analyzing industry's role in creating occupational and environmental health hazards, partly because trade unionists cooperated in these studies (Berman 1978; Gorz 1980; Chavkin 1984). Marxists looked at almost every aspect of work and the environment, from the health effects of the business cycle and shift work to occupational hazards for fertility and pregnancy and the health consequences of nuclear war. They showed that working conditions in the asbestos industry, cotton mills, and coal mines caused the respiratory diseases called white, brown and black lung, and that corporate owners knew and hid the health consequences of the work.

HEALTH MOVEMENTS AND HEALTH POLICIES

Once illness is lifted from the inevitability of biology or the victim-blaming ethic of individual responsibility, women and men can find the common origins of their illness. For example, company doctors regularly diagnosed asthma before miners realized that coal dust causes black lung disease. With a common cause identified, people can join together in combatting disease-producing environments (Freudenberg 1984). Although it is clear that health services do not and cannot produce health (at best, good medical care can relieve pain or restore a person to health), the fight for better, more humane and more accessible services is an integral part of progressive struggles (Sidel and Sidel 1984).

Many groups — blacks, women, communities — have organized in response to wretched living and working conditions and have been able to improve their health and health care. The Civil Rights movement obtained better living conditions for American blacks and consequently better health. In 1962 Rachel Carson published *Silent Spring* and set off a cannonade of demands for environmental rescue that still reverberates 25 years later. Strikes, student unrest and urban riots exerted pressure for change throughout the sixties (Piven and Cloward 1977).

Business and government responded with new legislation. In 1963, Congress adopted the first Clean Air Act and in 1965, a stronger Water Quality Act; Civil Rights legislation was passed in 1964; the 1969 Mine Safety Act was followed in 1970 by the Occupational Safety and Health Act (OSHA), the Environmental Policy Act (EPA) and the Toxic Substances Control Act (TOSCA). In 1965, at the height of the "Great Society," the American people won, not a national health service, which the British have enjoyed since 1948, not national health insurance, which has been on our national agenda since World War I, but Medicare and Medicaid. These two pieces of legislation were ostensibly designed to provide access to health care for the aged and indigent, but in fact became the gateway for the entry of private corporations into the health industry. Seemingly unlimited public revenues were made available to the private sector for more health services and products, new capital investment, and higher fees; public monies now fund about 40 percent of the direct costs of personal health care in the United States. Medical care, which had been in the hands of individual private practitioners and non-profit voluntary hospitals, passed to corporate conglomerates that own for-profit hospitals and employ doctors as salaried staff.

The steep 1973–75 recession heightened contradictions in the U.S. political economy. While the momentum for stronger clean air and clean water acts and for the enforcement of OSHA continued under the Carter Administration, corporations began to contest new regulations in court, as part of a wider plan to restore profits. With the election of Reagan in 1980, business sought to end government intervention (except in the defense sector) and to implement deregulation and a supply-side strategy that favored competition in a profit-making health care industry. Reagan's appointees brought a near halt to OSHA inspections, condoned sweetheart deals between industry and EPA, and sanctioned the despoliation of natural resources. The defeat of the Equal Rights Amendment and the weakening of the Civil Rights Commission undermined the ability of women and blacks to continue to improve their health conditions. Even before the balanced-budget Gramm-Rudman-Hollings bill was enacted in 1985, Congress accepted the dramatic cutbacks of health and welfare budgets proposed by David Stockman, the Administration's hatchet-man.

One of the most contested regulations — and one that illustrates the failure of cost-containment measures to challenge private control or the market system — is the billing of Medicare patients for hospital treatment on the basis of predetermined costs fixed for every illness or surgical procedure (called diagnostic related groups). The length of stay in hospital is no longer based on each individual patient's condition, and the result frequently is the premature discharge of very sick people. The reduction of Medicaid and the decline of public hospitals — processes that date back to the 1973–75 fiscal crisis of the cities — are features of the deliberate shrinkage of the public sector, which serves mainly the poor and minorities.

The corollary to public rollbacks is the expansion of the private market. In the new for-profit health care industry, national corporations purchase hospitals and run them like hotel chains, depriving communities of locally responsive institutions; non-hospital services are delivered in for-profit "emergicenters" and "urgicenters" located in suburban shopping malls, which offer no continuity of care. Health Maintenance Organizations (HMOs), originally nonprofit, prepaid group plans staffed by salaried physicians who emphasized prevention, are now profitmaking corporations (some HMOs are financed by insurance companies), aggressively competing for healthy, young, white patients who need less medical attention and avoiding the poor, the elderly, and patients with AIDS.

EFFECTS OF CONSERVATIVE POLICIES ON HEALTH AND HEALTH CARE

The first line of defense against ill health in a capitalist society is income-producing employment in a workplace that has a strong union to protect workers' health on the job and to negotiate benefits for them and their families. Conservative policies undermine that defense by promoting irresponsible corporate behavior. Among the specific consequences affecting health are: unfavorable wage rates, so that some full-time workers may live below the poverty line; negligible job creation, so that teenagers and dislocated older workers cannot find work; an assault on trade unions, which has eroded bargaining power; unhealthy and unsafe working conditions and increased air and water pollution, both of which are related to the unions' weakened position.

The second line of defense, when the first has failed, is a welfare state to supply life's essentials — the food, clothing, shelter, and medical care that the unemployed no longer have the income to purchase. By reversing 50 years of social legislation, the New Right's policies have exposed vulnerable members of society — the unemployed, children and the women who rear them on their own, the elderly, blacks and other minorities — to poverty, malnutrition and homelessness, as well as inadequate medical care.

The privatization of health care has severely limited access to medical services for the poor and minorities. One consequence is that sick people wait longer before seeking help; for some diseases like cancer, this delay can mean the difference between effective treatment and death. Death rates due to cancer are routinely higher among blacks, who get treatment later because the system does not facilitate their access to care. Another consequence is a lack of prenatal care for pregnant women resulting in higher death rates in childbirth. Deaths of black infants have been twice as frequent as deaths of white infants for most of this century; infant mortality is higher in the United States than in sixteen industrialized countries — a national disgrace. Currently, it is popular to blame high infant death rates on unmarried teenagers, but in fact the teenage pregancy rate is falling. What is rising is teenage unemployment, so that young people cannot afford to marry and support healthy families.

Thirty-five million Americans now lack health insurance; because insurance is a benefit of employment in the primary labor market, this number will climb to 65 or 70 million if the country experiences a serious economic recession. Will the health crisis combined with an economic crisis reopen the national debate on health care?

NEW OPPORTUNITIES PRESENTED BY THE CRISIS

The crisis appears to offer new opportunities for change in at least four areas, which are discussed in turn — how health care is financed, the type of care that women and children receive, the rights of workers to protect their health on the job, and the rights of communities to protect their environment.

National health insurance is a mechanism of payment (for example, a social security tax on employers) that would merely increase access to our inequitable and inadequate health care system. It was devised by Bismark in the aftermath of the 1848 uprisings to take the wind out of the sails of German socialism. In 1911, when British workers won it, national health insurance seemed a good idea. It was on the United States agenda in World War I, but was scuttled when health facilities were overwhelmed by a worldwide pandemic of influenza that took hundreds of thousands of lives in the United States alone. It was next considered in the 1930s as part of the New Deal, but President Roosevelt feared it would tip the scales of opposition to his program and he accepted instead the Blue Cross/Blue Shield insurance program that emphasized the role of voluntary (private, non-profit) hospitals. Truman tried again in 1948 and Carter in 1978 and some people think the next Democratic president will succeed in steering it through Congress. But perhaps this time AIDS, not influenza, will sideline national health insurance (see Arno, in this volume).

Because it is inferior to a national health service, national health insurance is not the left's choice; however, some people support it as the realistic alternative to our present system, claiming that a national health service has no chance of being adopted in the United States. Usually identified with Britain, nationalized health services treat 33 percent of the world's population in 14 countries. They are financed by taxation and employ salaried physicians and other health personnel in government-owned hospitals and health centers. A nationalized health system is not socialized medicine because it is controlled by physicians and bureaucrats, not by local communities. A bill for a U.S. national community health service was introduced in Congress by Ron Dellums in 1977.

Recently, voters in Massachusetts passed a non-binding referendum on a national health plan by two to one; they decided that only a national health plan can control costs rationally (Danielson and Mazer 1986). This could be the beginning of a state-by-state movement that will pressure Congress to reconsider the Dellums bill.

Another area of opportunity opened by the crisis is the type of care given to women and children. Here the women's health movement can continue to bring about change. The women's health movement has protected health or improved care along several dimensions ranging from abortion rights and protection against sterilization abuse to raised consciousness about the information women receive from physicians. It forced the withdrawal of dangerous drugs like DES and products like the Dalkon shield, and it pushed changes in hospital procedures (e.g., the acceptance of natural childbirth, partner present at delivery, breastfeeding, separation of biopsy from surgery for breast cancer). The movement drew attention to reproductive occupational hazards for women and men and challenged the overprescription of addictive drugs and the indiscriminate use of hormones in menopause. In ever greater numbers, women are training as physicians, midwives and physician's assistants; they have reappraised their role as nurses; and they have joined unions, striking for the right to do so when necessary.

In the 1990s, the women's health movement will tackle the problems of infertility, maternal and infant mortality and birth defects. Joining coalitions of blacks and other minorities to press for improved living and working conditions as well as greater access to medical care will result in better pregnancy outcomes.

A third area of opportunity related to the crisis is the protection of workers' health in which unions could play a stronger role. Ten years ago, the Oil Chemical and Atomic Workers Union started a coalition of unionists and environmentalists to campaign for legislation that would guarantee workers the right to know the hazardous nature of the materials they work with. Adopted first by the city of Philadelphia in 1981, right-to-know acts have been implemented in at least 13 states and 35 cities. However, such legislation falls short of giving workers the right to act, for example to shut down a dangerous operation. Right-to-act legislation can protect not only workers but also communities surrounding plants; the Bhopal disaster tragically demonstrated the community's need for such protection.

Community protection from environmental disaster is becoming a major preoccupation worldwide, and the crisis may provide the opening needed to effect change. The environmental movement has grown from a fringe protest to a national force for improved air and water quality. It has confronted major corporations and achieved significant reforms in national legislation and local enforcement. It has also survived corporate attempts to divide it from workers, a natural constituency, who were told that costly environmental controls would shut down plants and eliminate jobs. However, militant grass-roots efforts are fragmented and defensive, leading to piece-meal solutions, while national organizations like the Sierra Club are easily outspent and outmaneuvered by government and industry (Freudenberg 1984:250-257). To achieve the major demand on the environmental agenda for the 1990s — the right to participate in decision-making that affects our environment, including decisions made by private corporations — requires strong coalitions.

In the past decade coalitions have accomplished more than single-interest lobbies acting alone. Right-to-know legislation, cited above, is one example of union cooperation with environmentalists. The Massachusetts national health plan referendum was a victory for a coalition of the elderly, unions, progressive legislators, health reformers, and community organizations. Coalitions might help us to recoup our losses under the last administration and to continue pressing for a national health system, as well as to address the unresolved health problems of neglected groups like migrant laborers and Native Americans. Coalition-building offers the most promising way forward to a solution of the health crisis.

NOTES

1. When URPE published the special issue of the *RRPE* on the political economy of health in the spring of 1977, a handful of people were just beginning to explore health and health care in a Marxist perspective. That handful has grown to over 1000 members of the Socialist Caucus of the American Public Health Association; we have forged links with progressive health groups in Europe, Asia, Latin America, and Africa; and we have expanded our concerns to include women's health, occupational and environmental health, and human rights.
2. Burbach and Flynn (1980), Dinham and Hines (1983), Sen (1982), Silverstein (1984), for a full bibliography see Turshen (1982).

REFERENCES

Berman, Daniel M. 1978. *Death on the Job: Occupational Health and Safety Struggles in the United States*. New York: Monthly Review Press.

Burbach, Roger and Patricia Flynn. 1980. *Agribusiness in the Americas*. New York: Monthly Review Press.

Chavkin, Wendy (ed.). 1984. *Double Exposure: Women's Health Hazards on the Job and at Home*. New York: Monthly Review Press.

Conrad, Peter and Rochelle Kern (eds.). 1986. *The Sociology of Health and Illness: Critical Perspectives*. New York: St. Martin's Press.

Cooper, Richard et al. 1981. Racism, Society, and Disease: An Exploration of the Social and Biological Mechanisms of Differential Mortality. *International Journal of Health Services* 11(3):389-414.

Danielson, David and Arthur Mazer. 1986. The Massachusetts Referendum for a National Health Program. *Journal of Public Health Policy* 7(2):161–173.

de Beer, Cedric. 1986. *The South African Disease: Apartheid Health and Health Services*. Trenton: Africa World Press.

Dinham, Barbara and Colin Hines. 1983. *Agribusiness in Africa*. London: Earth Resources Research.

Doyal, Lesley. 1979. *The Political Economy of Health*. Boston: South End Press.

Ehrenreich, Barbara and John Ehrenreich (eds.). 1971. *The American Health Empire: Power, Profits and Politics*. New York: Vintage Books.

_____ and Deirdre English. 1973a. *Witches, Midwives, and Nurses: A History of Women Healers*. Old Westbury: The Feminist Press.

_____. 1973b. *Complaints and Disorders: The Sexual Politics of Sickness*. Old Westbury: The Feminist Press.

Epstein, Samuel S. 1979. *The Politics of Cancer*. New York: Doubleday.

Freudenberg, Nick. 1984. *Not in Our Backyards! Community Action for Health and the Environment*. New York: Monthly Review Press.

Gorz, André. 1980. *Ecology as Politics*. Vigderman, Patsy & Cloud.

Kotelchuck, David (ed.). 1976. *Prognosis Negative: Crisis in the Health Care System*. New York: Vintage Books.

McDonnell, Kathleen (ed.). 1986. *Adverse Effects: Women and the Pharmaceutical Industry*. Penang, Malaysia: International Organization of Comsumers Unions.

Michaelson, Karen L. (ed.). 1981. *And the Poor Get Children: Radical Perspectives on Population Dynamics*. New York: Monthly Review Press.

Minkler, Meredith and Carroll L. Estes (eds.). 1984. *Readings in the Political Economy of Aging*. Farmingdale, NY: Baywood Publishing Co.

Muller, Mike. 1982. *The Health of Nations: A North-South Investigation*. London: Faber and Faber.

Navarro, Vicente. 1986. *Crisis, Health and Medicine: A Social Critique*. New York: Tavistock Publications.

Navarro, Vicente (ed.). 1981. *Imperialism, Health and Medicine*. Farmingdale, NY: Baywood Publishing Co.

Piven, Frances Fox and Richard A. Cloward. 1977. *Poor People's Movements: Why They Succeed, How They Fail*. New York: Pantheon Books.

Powles, John. 1973. On the Limitations of Modern Medicine. *Science, Medicine and Man* 1(1):1-30.

Scull, Andrew. 1984. *Decarceration: Community Treatment and the Deviant—A Radical View*. New Brunswick: Rutgers University Press.

Sen, Amartya. 1982. *Poverty and Famines: An Essay on Entitlement and Deprivation*. Oxford: Clarendon Press.

Sidel, Victor W. and Ruth Sidel (eds.). 1984. *Reforming Medicine: Lessons of the Last Quarter Century*. New York: Pantheon Books.

Silverstein, Brett. 1984. *Fed Up! The Food Forces That Make You Fat, Sick and Poor*. Boston: South End Press.

Townsend, Peter and Nick Davidson (eds.). 1982. *Inequalities in Health: The Black Report*. New York: Penguin Books.

Turshen, Meredeth. 1982. "Health" and "Hunger." In, *Reading Lists in Radical Social Science*, M. Maier & D. Gilroys (eds.). pp. 173–179. New York: Monthly Review Press.

_____. 1984. *The Political Ecology of Disease in Tanzania*. New Brunswick: Rutgers University Press.

_____. 1988. *The Politics of Public Health*. New Brunswick: Rutgers University Press.

20

The AIDS Pandemic: A Public Health Failure

PETER S. ARNO
and
KARYN FEIDEN

INTRODUCTION

Since the first persons with Acquired Immune Deficiency Syndrome (AIDS) were identified in Los Angeles and New York City in 1981, the disastrous social, political, and economic consequences of the ever-worsening epidemic have become increasingly clear. The loss in human life has been staggering and the toll continues to rise. By 1991, AIDS will be among the top ten leading causes of death in the United States, far exceeding all other causes for people between the ages of 25 and 44.

AIDS has begun to lay bare the inherent contradictions in our health care system. The federal government's continuing failure to develop a coordinated national program to deal with the AIDS epidemic is a clear abdication of its responsibility to protect and defend the health of its citizens. Although federal funds are finally being pumped into scientific research, after unconscionable delays, strapped local governments continue to bear most of the costs for treating AIDS patients. Meanwhile, the private sector is scurrying to avoid new costs — insurance companies have sought to identify and disqualify individuals at risk for AIDS, while employers have turned to self-insurance at least partly to evade state insurance regulations and burdensome new cost obligations.

The AIDS epidemic has made one point abundantly clear: this nation has no coherent national health policy to cope with catastrophic illness. The result continues to be the wholesale abandonment of the poor, the unemployed and those too sick to maintain employment-related health benefits.

THE TRANSMISSION OF AIDS

Although there is no effective treatment currently available for AIDS and the development of a vaccine remains many years away, a great deal of biomedical progress has been made since serious scientific research got underway:

— The etiologic agent of AIDS, the human immunodeficiency virus (HIV), was discovered in 1983.

— A test for screening all donated blood and plasma for HIV antibodies was introduced in April 1985. Coupled with heat treatment of clotting-factor concentrates, the test has reduced the risk associated with transfused blood and blood products to an extremely low level.

— The three major routes of HIV transmission, which were all identified by 1983 — sexual transmission, inoculation of blood and perinatal transmission (between an infected mother and her infant during pregnancy or at birth) — remain the only ones demonstrated to be important. There is no evidence that AIDS is transmitted by casual contact (see Table 1).

Table 1
Transmission of HIV Infection

Known Routes of Transmission

I. Sexual
 - Homosexual, between men
 - Heterosexual, from men to women and women to men

II. Inoculation of blood
 - Transfusion of blood and blood products
 - Needle sharing among intravenous drug users
 - Needle stick, open wound, and mucous membrane exposure in health care workers
 - Injection with unsterilized needle

III. Perinatal
 - Intrauterine
 - Peripartum

Routes Investigated and Shown Not to be Involved in Transmission

I. Close personal contact
 - Household
 - Health care workers without exposure to blood

II. Insects

Source: Friedland and Klein (1987).

DEMOGRAPHICS

As of February 1, 1988, 52,256 persons have been diagnosed with AIDS in the United States; 29,206 (56 percent) of them have died (CDC 1988). Worldwide, more than 60,000 active cases have been reported in 126 countries. The Public Health Service (PHS) projects that by the end of 1991 there will have been a cumulative total of 270,000 AIDS diagnoses in the United States with more than 74,000 occurring in 1991 alone (PHS 1986). Another 3 million active new cases are likely to develop overseas within five years, according to the World Health Organization.

But the full dimensions of the AIDS pandemic still remain unknown. Human immunodeficiency virus is believed to infect between 1 and 1.5 million Americans and 5 to 10 million people throughout the world (generally, an infected person is or will become seropositive, meaning that the person has developed HIV antibodies). Although no one knows for certain how many of those now infected will eventually sicken and die, the PHS has projected that 20 to 30 percent will be diagnosed with AIDS within 5 years (PHS

1986). The Institute of Medicine/National Academy of Sciences report on AIDS (the IOM report) revised these figures upward. According to the report, "25 to 50 percent of seropositive persons will develop AIDS as defined by the CDC within 5 to 10 years of seroconversion, and a higher percentage cannot be ruled out on the basis of present studies" (IOM 1986:91).

By far the hardest-hit groups have been gay and bisexual men and intravenous (IV) drug users, who together comprise 90 percent of all reported cases. Minority groups have been disproportionately afflicted. According to the Centers for Disease Control (CDC 1987), reported AIDS cases divided along racial and ethnic lines as follows:

White	61%
Black	25%
Hispanic	14%
Other/Unknown	1%

Available data on the epidemiology of AIDS and projections over the next few years is summarized in Table 2.

Table 2
Projected Distribution of Adult AIDS Cases
U.S. by Patient Group
(1983, 1986 and 1991)

	1983		**1986**		**1991**	
Patient Group	%	**No.**	%	**No.**	%	**No.**
Homo/Bisexual Men	72.1	1929	72.6	11,300	70.0	51,100
Heterosexual IV Drug Abusers	18.2	486	17.3	2,700	16.4	12,000
Hemophilia	0.4	12	0.9	200	1.4	1,000
Transfusion Recipient	1.4	37	2.0	300	2.5	1,800
Other Heterosexuals	7.9	212	7.0	1,100	9.8	7,100
(Heterosexual contact)	(0.9	25)	(2.0	300)	(5.0	3,700)
(Born outside U.S.)	(3.7	98)	(1.3	200)	(0.3	200)
(Other)	(3.3	89)	(3.7	600)	(4.5	3,200)
TOTAL	100.0	2676	100.0	15,600	100.0	73,000

Source: Morgan and Curran (1986).

To date, the incidence of AIDS among heterosexuals has remained relatively small, but the epidemic's pattern in Africa, where homosexuality and IV drug use are thought to be relatively uncommon (Quinn, Mann, Curran and Piot 1986), indicates that sexually active heterosexuals are welcome hosts to the human immunodeficiency virus. As many African women as men are afflicted by AIDS (by contrast the male: female ratio in the United States is 13:1) and their age distribution suggests the course of a classic sexually transmitted disease.

Already evidence points to an alarming epidemiological shift in the United States. According to the CDC, just 2 percent of adult AIDS cases could be traced to heterosexual activity in 1986. By 1991, that figure is expected to swell to 5 percent, making it the fastest growing of any transmission category. The virus is currently believed to be creeping into the heterosexual community as a result of sexual contacts with infected IV drug users and their partners. Some public health experts in the United States have suggested that a window of one to two years exists to contain the epidemic among IV drug users before the spread to other heterosexuals becomes even more dramatic.

FEDERAL RESPONSE

Failure and indifference characterized the initial federal response to the AIDS epidemic, crippling early research and public health education efforts that might have slowed the epidemic's growth. From the beginning, two formidable barriers impeded the public health community's ability to respond appropriately to AIDS — the structural defects deeply imbedded in the American health care system and the ideological blinders worn by the Reagan Administration. In the normally staid editorial pages of *The New York Times,* a recent column was particularly critical of the Reagan Administration's response to AIDS:

> Historians will look back in amazement at the Reagan Administration's flaccid response during the first eight years of the epidemic's spread. They will ask how any President could fail to implement the most obvious public health measures, or tardily assign the making of national strategy to a quarreling commission with no recognizable expertise. They will wonder how his Cabinet members could be torpid spectators of the virus's spread, seeing it only as a pretext for impressing their own morals on others.
>
> But the wondering historians will find no answers. Mr. Reagan's refusal to lead, to take a personal interest in AIDS or set a policy and see it effectively conducted is beyond comprehension or excuse (*The New York Times* 1987).

Today, the killer disease has earned a prominent place on the nation's health agenda. Federal AIDS spending increased dramatically from $200,000 in 1982 to nearly $450 million in 1987 (see Table 3).

Table 3
Federal Funding on AIDS: U.S. Public Health Service (Fiscal Years 1981–1988)

	President's Budget Request	Earmarked in Congressional Appropriations and/or Actually Obligated
1981	0	$0.2
1982	0	5.6
1983	0	28.7
1984	$39.8	61.5
1985	60.5	109.2
1986	126.0	233.8
1987	203.4	(estimate) 447.4
1988	790.7	900.0*

*As of early November 1987, the federal FY 1988 AIDS budget is in a Congressional conference committee; appropriations in the $900 million range seem likely.

Source: Office of Technology Assessment (1985); U.S. Government Accounting Office (1987).

Nevertheless, questions about the government's early failure to safeguard the health of its citizens linger to haunt not only its victims and their families, but anyone committed to equitable, effective health care. Ideological, bureaucratic and fiscal constraints jammed the federal response during the first two years of the AIDS epidemic. The consequences of that delay are incalculable. What if the government had quickly recognized AIDS as a major health disaster and launched a well-coordinated, adequately funded plan of attack? What if money had been allocated for basic research and public education immediately? What if the disease's early victims had not been stigmatized gays or black and Hispanic drug users? Perhaps, then, the course of one of the most deadly epidemics of the twentieth century might have been different.

Why was the response to AIDS so lethargic? Racism and hostility to the gay community certainly provide part of the explanation. Racial minorities, primarily intravenous drug users, whose access to care has always been marginal, account for almost 40 percent of all reported AIDS cases. Although gays have substantially more political power, their lifestyle and sexual practices so offended influential right-wing ideologues that a trickle of AIDS cases became a flood before action was taken.

The AIDS epidemic occurred at a time when policymaking was dominated by a commitment to reduce the size and scope of federal social welfare programs, a coincidence with tragic consequences for public health. By treating AIDS as a series of state and local problems rather than a national public health disaster, the Reagan Administration insured a fragmented and inadequate response to one of the most devastating diseases in recent history. Two years were allowed to pass before it acknowledged that money had to be allocated specifically to AIDS. Then the Administration compounded a deadly mistake by withholding information from congressional committees seeking to determine the resource needs of Public Health Service researchers. Congress eventually earmarked $5.6 million in 1982, over a Presidential veto, but early surveillance, epidemiologic and laboratory research efforts had already been compromised (U.S. Congress 1983; 1985).

Since the early days of the epidemic public health officials have called for federal leadership and coordination of activities among different branches of government and the private sector in the fight against AIDS. It was not until June 1987 that President Reagan established a commission whose purpose is to advise the Chief Executive on the "medical, legal, ethical, social and economic impact of AIDS." Since its inception, however, the commission has been mired in controversy. It was widely criticized at the outset for the lack of expertise among the appointees. Reports of internal bickering and power struggles surfaced, eventually resulting in the dismissal of the executive staff director and later, the resignations of the chairman and vice-chairman of the commission. To date, the commission has been unable to begin the critical task so long neglected by the Reagan Administration: formulating a coherent national policy on AIDS.

ECONOMIC IMPACT

The economic repercussions of the AIDS epidemic, which are just beginning to be felt at the national level, are certain to spiral upwards in the next few years. A recent study estimated that the cost of hospitalization for AIDS patients hovered at $380 million in 1985 (Andrulis, Beers, Bentley and Gage 1987). By 1991, that figure is projected to range from $1.1 to $2 billion in *New York City* alone (Sullivan 1987). All told, economists project $8.5 billion in personal medical care costs in 1991 and many more times that amount in the loss to society of thousands of persons dying in the prime of their lives (Scitovsky and Rice 1987).

The need to care for a growing number of patients with expensive treatment demands has led to a widespread scrambling to avoid responsibility for costs. The federal government has shifted the burden to the state and local levels by denying disability benefits under Medicare. Pecuniary Medicaid policies have jeopardized the financial viability of public hospitals in many states. Meanwhile, the private insurance sector is moving to limit its financial liability by restricting eligibility through the use of AIDS antibody testing and other screening mechanisms. Private employers' efforts to control health care costs and the movement towards self-insurance have tended to reduce the cross-subsidies for providing indigent care.

With traditional payers turning their heads as the bill comes due, one vital question surfaces: who will pay the costs of AIDS? The look at financing trends presented here may raise as many concerns as it answers, but it also lays the groundwork for new approaches to health care financing.

THE PUBLIC SECTOR

The economic costs of AIDS, like the extent of patient care, is unevenly distributed among providers around the country. The hardest-hit cities — New York, San Francisco, and Los Angeles — currently account for 42 percent of the nation's total AIDS caseload and a concomitantly disproportionate share of costs. By 1991, however, according to the IOM report, 80 percent of the nation's cases are expected to fall outside the boundaries of New York City and San Francisco.

Many health care systems and municipal budgets, already strained to the breaking point, are likely to crack under the pressures of increasing need. Public hospitals are treating a disproportionate number of AIDS patients and in badly afflicted regions of the country they have been forced to reallocate resources by cutting back in other programmatic areas. Likewise, local governments that subsidize indigent care are finding their ability to provide other public services severely compromised. These problems are certain to intensify as the AIDS caseload rises around the country.

The two principal sources of payment for treating AIDS patients are private health insurance and Medicaid. The Andrulis study, while admittedly weighted heavily towards public hospitals, where care is more likely to be subsidized than in private voluntary hospitals, shows a striking distribution by payer source: 54 percent of the patients were covered by Medicaid while only 17 percent had private insurance.

Evidence further suggests that the proportion of AIDS patients covered by private insurance has declined over time and that payment responsibilities have shifted to the public sector, primarily through Medicaid. In San Francisco over the past five years, for example, a small but steady drop in the proportion of privately insured AIDS patients has been recorded with a concomitant increase in Medi-Cal (the Medicaid program in California) coverage (West Bay Hospital Conference 1984–1986). Similarly, the proportion of AIDS patients covered by Medi-Cal in the state of California jumped from 12 percent to 20 percent, between 1985 and 1986, which implies a drop in private insurance coverage (Kizer, Rodriguez and McHolland 1987).

As AIDS cases continue to spread outwards from the initially impacted cities, the threat to public hospitals grows in states with excessively stringent Medicaid eligibility criteria. In the South for example, only 15 percent of AIDS patients in public hospitals are covered by Medicaid, compared to 60 percent in the Northeast (Andrulis et al. 1987). As a result, levels of unreimbursed patient care are higher in the South than in any other region in the country.

Public hospitals clearly cannot increase their levels of care sufficiently to match the expected growth in the epidemic. If they continue to become the dumping grounds for inadequately insured and Medicaid-dependent patients, while the private voluntary and proprietary hospitals capture the bulk of AIDS cases with private insurance coverage, the financial condition of public hospitals will deteriorate further.

In an era when federal policy has shifted responsibility for domestic social problems to the local level, policymakers in Washington have assumed no meaningful role in the search for solutions to the fiscal challenges posed by AIDS. Indeed, the federal government has been unwilling even to offer AIDS patients preemptive qualification for Medicare disability benefits. Qualifying for Medicare as a disabled person requires a two-year waiting period, a ludicrous delay since more than 70 percent of AIDS patients die within their first two years of diagnosis. As a result, only two percent of AIDS patients have received Medicare payments. Proposals now pending before Congress would eliminate the two-year delay, significantly reducing the economic impact of AIDS on local governments, but legislation appears unlikely to pass in the near future.

THE PRIVATE SECTOR

Given the staggering costs of medical care, private health insurance is an important shield against poverty for many Americans who become seriously ill. But the AIDS epidemic tragically illustrates the chimera of employment-based coverage: those who are sick and in greatest need of insurance are least able to obtain it. One of the fundamental contradictions in our health care financing system is that as people become too sick or disabled to work, they lose their health coverage (assuming they ever had any) unless they can afford to pay their own premiums.

In the shadow of the AIDS epidemic, private health insurers have made no secret of their determination to reduce their financial vulnerability. To date they have already met with some success by raising premiums and screening out individuals perceived to be at high risk for AIDS. Ultimately, it is the industry's goal to deny coverage to those testing antibody positive on the grounds that they are at a much greater risk of becoming ill and dying from AIDS. According to its own nationwide survey, 91 percent of all queried insurance companies have said anyone who is antibody positive is uninsurable. Ninety-nine percent of the companies called anyone with ARC (AIDS-related complex) uninsurable (Health Insurance Association of America 1986).

The public health consequences of a policy permitting use of the antibody test as a screening mechanism for health insurance coverage could be disastrous. First, it is likely to drive high-risk groups further underground, making it harder to reach the very people who urgently need education and risk reduction strategies. Second, it sets a dangerous precedent for the use of other biotechnology-derived diagnostic and predictive medical testing. If insurance underwriters are able to crack open the door to advanced prognostic tests, patients at risk for heart disease, certain types of cancer, alcoholism, multiple schlerosis, etc. may ultimately be denied health insurance coverage.

Risk pooling is one of the more innovative health care financing techniques currently under discussion. At its best, it is a means of providing insurance, and therefore access to care for AIDS patients, antibody-positive individuals and others who are unable to obtain insurance coverage. Risk pools are generally state plans that provide health insurance coverage to individuals who have been turned down as bad (i.e., unprofitable) medical risks by private carriers. Insurance companies are mandated to contribute a small percentage of the premiums written in that state to a pool to defray its expenses.

State risk pools, however, are currently fraught with problems. High premiums, large co-payments and large deductibles limit their accessibility to the general population. Nationwide they enrolled only 21,000 people in 1986 and, despite high premiums, all but one of the pools lost money. As a result of the rapid growth of self-funded insurance plans, which are not required to contribute to high risk pools or pay state premium taxes, there is a shrinking financial base available to subsidize those losses. If high-risk pools are to play a significant role in providing access to health care, their financing base must be expanded to include self-insured businesses or wider tax-based revenues. Furthermore, the cost of policies needs to be lowered to affordable levels.

The movement towards self-insurance has serious implications not only for financing AIDS care, but for health care financing in general. Approximately 50 to 60 percent of the nation's covered labor force work for employers who are self-insured (Johnson and Higgins 1986; McDonnell, Guttenberg, Greenberg and Arnett 1987). It is the largest firms that are the most likely to self-insure: 85 percent of all firms with more than 40,000 employees and 70 percent of firms with 10,000 to 30,000 employees are self-insured (Johnson and Higgins 1986).

Because self-insured plans are virtually unregulated, employers may exclude from coverage any condition they choose. While there have only been a few scattered incidents of AIDS exclusion to date, growing costs may encourage employers to shift towards stricter underwriting practices, particularly pre-employment screening and disease-specific exclusion of benefits. Aside from the dangerous consequences of removing the bulk of group health insurance coverage from the purview of social regulation, the growth of self-insured plans reduces the cross-subsidization of health care by the private sector. As a result, the costs of indigent care are placed squarely on the backs of cities, counties and public hospitals.

CONCLUSION

If our current health care financing mechanisms are left unchanged, the AIDS epidemic will vividly demonstrate the tragic inequities of cost shifting. The ability of the insurance industry and private employers to limit their financial responsibilities in no way reduces the cost of AIDS treatment. It succeeds only in shifting those costs to someone else, most often the public sector. At the same time it aggravates the growing and severe problem of uninsured and uninsurable people in this country. If the federal government continues to abdicate responsibility, state and local governments will be squeezed by the need to make ever-larger contributions to Medicaid, indigent care programs, and faltering public hospitals.

Although the AIDS epidemic highlights tragic flaws in the health care system in this country, it also suggests new directions in which we can travel towards the goal of providing equitable, efficient health care. In some communities, innovative treatment models developed for AIDS are being studied for their lessons in treating patients with other catastrophic illnesses. Similarly, the calamity of AIDS should inspire new approaches to health care financing that will more fairly distribute the burden of caring for the sick. Nobody wants to bear the costs of this epidemic. But a progressive agenda for AIDS would help provide the political basis for cost sharing instead of cost shifting and allow us to begin at last to develop some form of guaranteed health insurance for all Americans.

REFERENCES

Andrulis, Dennis P., Virginia S. Beers, James D. Bentley and Larry S. Gage. 1987. The Impact of Medical Care for AIDS Patients on U.S. Public and Private Teaching Hospitals. *JAMA* 258:1343–1346.

Centers for Disease Control (CDC). 1988. *AIDS Weekly Surveillance Report*. United States AIDS Program, Center For Infectious Diseases.

Friedland, G. H. and R. S. Klein. 1987. Transmission of the Human Immunodeficiency Virus. *New England Journal of Medicine* 317(18):1125–1135.

Health Insurance Association of America. 1986. *Research and Statistical Bulletin* No. 4–86(August 22).

Institute of Medicine/National Academy of Sciences. 1986. *Confronting AIDS: Direction for Public Health, Health Care and Research*. Washington, D.C.: National Academy Press.

Johnson and Higgins. 1986. *Corporate Health Care Benefits Survey*. New York: Johnson and Higgins Health Group.

Kizer, K. W., J. Rodriguez and G. F. McHolland. 1987. *An Updated Quantitative Analysis of AIDS in California*. Sacramento: Dept. of Health Services.

McDonnell P., A. Guttenberg, L. Greenberg, R. H. Arnett. 1987. Self-insured Health Plans. *Health Care Financing Review* 8:1–15.

Morgan, W. M. and J. W. Curran. 1986. Acquired Immunodeficiency Syndrome: Current and Future Trends. *Public Health Reports* (September/October).

The New York Times. 1987. The Reagan AIDS Strategy in Ruins. Editorial (November 11).

Public Health Service. 1986. PHS Plans for Prevention and Control of AIDS and the AIDS Virus. *Public Health Reports* 101(July/August):341–348.

Quinn, T. C., J. M. Mann, J. W. Curran and P. Piot. 1986. AIDS in Africa: An Epidemiologic Paradigm. *Science* 234:955–963.

Scitovsky, Anne A. and Dorothy P. Rice. 1987. Estimates of the Direct and Indirect Costs of Acquired Immunodeficiency Syndrome in the United States, 1985, 1986, and 1991. *Public Health Reports* 102:5–17.

Sullivan, R. 1987. AIDS Cost for New York in '91 Put at $2 Billion by State Study. *The New York Times,* July 9:15.

U.S. Congress, House of Representatives, Subcommittee on Intergovernmental Relations and Human Resources of the Committee on Government Operations. 1983. *The Federal Response to AIDS,* Washington D.C.: U.S. Government Printing Office.

U.S. Congress, Office of Technology Assessment. 1985. *Review of the Public Health Service's Response to AIDS* (OTA-TM-H-24). Washington, D.C.: U.S. Government Printing Office.

U.S. General Accounting Office. 1987. *AIDS Prevention: Views on the Administration's Budget Proposals* (GAO-HRD-87-126BR). (August).

West Bay Hospital Conference. 1984–1986. *Monthly AIDS Hospital Utilization Reports*. San Mateo, CA.

21

The Political Economy of Military Spending

TOM RIDDELL

Throughout the 1980s the United States has experienced the most rapid expansion of military spending in its peacetime history. In the three decades from the late forties to the late seventies, the military spent $2 trillion to create a worldwide military establishment. In the seven years, from 1980 thorugh 1986, almost $1.5 trillion was spent to maintain and expand the conventional and nuclear forces of the United States. For Fiscal Years 1987 and 1988, Congress, responding to public opinion and continuing massive budget deficits, has started to slow down this remarkable buildup. Nevertheless, the Reagan five-year military plan calls for spending over $1.5 trillion between 1987 and 1991. Even a Democrat in the White House wouldn't reduce these projected budgets by much.

This massive buildup has renewed the debate over the economic dimensions of military spending. Why does the United States spend so much? Is military spending necessary for the operation of advanced capitalism? Are military priorities a root cause of the economic problems currently facing the United States? In fact, the answers to these questions are not simple and straightforward; military spending plays a contradictory role in the U.S. economy.

There are powerful economic forces that motivate higher levels of military spending. In the post-World War II period, four have been particularly important — the contribution of military spending to the overall level of demand for goods and services in the economy, the narrow economic interests of the military-industrial complex, the military foundations of the postwar Pax Americana, and the perceived political economic threat posed by the Soviet Union. At various periods, one or another of these factors may have been more important, but all of them play a continuing part in driving the world's largest military budget.

On the other hand, there are several possible adverse economic consequences of military spending. Military spending can be inflationary. It may not produce as many jobs as other forms of spending would. Military priorities may interfere with investment and economic growth. Finally, in the current period, the military buildup has contributed to the budget deficit problem.

MILITARY SPENDING AND AGGREGATE DEMAND

Military spending can be used to maintain the aggregate demand for goods and services in the economy and thereby avoid depressions. This role has become especially important in the post-World War II period. Prior to World War II, peacetime military spending was usually less than 1 percent of GNP. After a decade of depression in the 1930s, the unemployment rate was still above 10 percent when the United States entered the war. At the height of war spending in 1944, the unemployment rate was barely above

1 percent. Since the late 1940s, the national defense budget has ranged from 4 to 14 percent of GNP and the annual unemployment rate has never exceeded 10 percent.

Advanced capitalism has an inherent tendency toward depression; the system cannot maintain a level of demand for goods and services sufficient to ensure continuing economic growth. Consequently, the state must assume responsibility for spending to stimulate demand and to encourage growth. The ability to pursue this strategy of protecting the operation of capitalism was reinforced by the development of Keynesian economics in the 1930s and 1940s. The intensity of the Cold War in the immediate postwar period provided the convenient justification for a massive increase in military spending in the late 1940s and early 1950s. Continued high levels of military spending have helped to maintain the level of economic activity and to avoid a recurrence of the Great Depression of the 1930s. There has never been sufficient political support for massive spending for domestic programs to stimulate the economy and to support employment. Keynes himself said in 1940: "It is, it seems, politically impossible for a capitalist democracy to organize expenditure on the scale necessary to make the grand experiment which would prove my case — except in war conditions. . ." (Keynes 1940).

The recent military buildup provides an example where military spending has contributed to the growth of economic activity. In 1980, the national defense budget totaled $134 billion and accounted for 5.0 percent of GNP. By 1986, military spending had more than doubled to $273 billion and increased to 6.6 percent of GNP (Adams and Cain 1987). While the overall military budget increased at a rate of 7 percent annually in real terms (beyond the rate of inflation), the "investment" accounts (procurement, R&D, and construction) increased at an 11 percent clip (U.S. Congressional Budget Office 1987). At the beginning of the Reagan Presidency, this portion of the budget amounted to about a third of the total. But by the mid-1980s it had expanded to almost half the military budget as contracts to the corporate sector for weapons and research increased twice as fast as spending for personnel, operations, and maintenance. This weapons-led increase in military spending will put pressure on Congress to increase future military appropriations since the expansion of weapons systems requires larger budgets for operations and maintenance.

The stimulus to the corporate sector and industrial production from expanded weapons contracting was one of the most important contributors to the 2 percent annual growth rate of real GNP during the 1980s. From 1981 to 1984 industrial production in the defense and space industries increased by 9.5 percent per year while total industrial production rose only 3 percent annually. According to Nariman Behravesh, chief economist for U.S. studies at Wharton Econometrics: "Because defense increases have been focused on hardware, manufacturing has had a modest recovery. Defense spending increases probably provided the greatest momentum to growth in recent years" (*Business Week* 1985).

THE MILITARY-INDUSTRIAL COMPLEX

An additional economic factor sustaining military spending is the military-industrial complex. In his 1961 Farewell Address, President Eisenhower warned of "the conjunction of an immense Military Establishment and a large arms industry'' and that ''we must guard against the acquisition of unwarranted influence by the military-industrial complex.'' More recently, it has been labeled the ''iron triangle'' by defense analyst Gordon Adams (1981). It consists of groups, institutions and people that have vested economic interests in military priorities. In addition, they are in positions of political power to argue for and to decide on the level of the defense budget. The three ''sides of the triangle'' are literally linked by their common interest in promoting higher levels of military spending.

One side of the triangle is the military. The Pentagon employs one million civilians and two million people in the armed services. There are military bases and facilities in every state in the nation. To pursue military objectives and to protect their bureaucratic power, military personnel appear in public, before Congress, and within the administration to argue for an ongoing commitment to the military budget. Jobs, promotions, careers and incomes are at stake. The Army, Navy, Air Force and Marines even battle each other for control over programs and weapons systems. Interservice rivalry, in fact, is a major source of military duplication and excessive budgets.

A second side of the complex consists of the corporations that are involved in military contracting. Most of the major corporations in the United States are among the Pentagon's top contractors. Although more than 30,000 firms are prime contractors, the top 25 companies (including firms such as General Dynamics, McDonnell-Douglas, Lockheed, Rockwell, General Electric, Boeing, United Technologies, Raytheon, Westinghouse, IBM, RCA, Ford, General Motors, Exxon) every year get more than 50 percent of the business. The weapons industry is notoriously non-competitive — inefficiency, cost overruns, waste and corruption are rampant. Seven-thousand dollar coffee pots, $900 Allen wrenches, $700 toilet seats and $400 hammers, as well as government investigations of contract abuse by more than half of the Pentagon's top 100 contractors, contribute to the need for massive military budgets (Project on Military Procurement 1986). A 1985 Pentagon study found that profits as a percent of assets are substantially higher on military business (20.5 percent), than for commercial enterprise (13.3 percent) (Center for Defense Information 1987). The firms and their well-paid executives (on the average, their salaries are 20 percent higher than in the civilian sector of the economy) lobby for their own contracts as well as for a higher defense budget. They also have PACs (Political Action Committees) that contribute millions of dollars to congressional candidates.

The third leg of the triangle includes the politicians and the regions of the country that have become dependent on military largesse. Ten states receive almost two-thirds of the prime contract awards for military procurement. Throughout the 1980s, California has received between a fifth and a quarter of all of the contracting money spent by the Pentagon every year. In addition, ten states get more than half of the money spent on military bases and personnel (see Table 1). There are almost three million people in the private sector that work on military contracts. Consequently, some areas of the country become addicted to military spending — their jobs, incomes and tax bases are dependent on maintaining or expanding military budgets. Politicians are sensitive to the dependence and are protective of the supplier.

Table 1
State Distribution of Pentagon Funds, Fiscal Year 1986

Prime Contract Awards		Non-Procurement Expenditures	
State	**Percentage of Total**	**State**	**Percentage of Total**
California	20.4	California	15.3
Texas	8.0	Virginia	10.3
New York	7.3	Texas	7.6
Massachusetts	6.4	Florida	5.9
Florida	5.7	Georgia	3.7
Missouri	4.0	North Carolina	3.4
Connecticut	4.0	Maryland	3.2
Virginia	4.0	Washington	3.2
Ohio	3.8	Pennsylvania	2.9
Maryland	3.3	South Carolina	2.7
TOTAL	65.4	TOTAL	58.2

Source: Department of Defense, Directorate for Information Operations and Reports, "Prime Contract Awards by State and Region" provided by Alexis Cain at the Defense Budget Project, Washington, D.C.

INTERNATIONAL HEGEMONY

The objectives of U.S. foreign and military policy also require high levels of military spending. Capitalism has always been an international system. Economic growth and expansion are the lifeblood of profits. International access to markets, to raw materials, to investment opportunities and to cheap labor is an important option for most U.S. corporations. Imports and exports compared to GNP have both increased throughout the postwar period, reaching more than 20 percent by the mid-1980s. The United States is dependent on imports for more than 50 percent of its supplies of more than forty critical raw materials for industrial and military production. More than a quarter of U.S. corporate profits come from overseas operations.

Approximately half of the decline in economic activity in the initial years of the Great Depression resulted from the almost total elimination of international trade following the passage of the Smoot-Hawley tariff act and foreign protectionist retaliation. In the aftermath of World War II, Western planners were intent on avoiding a repetition of that experience. To that end, the United States took the lead in creating and dominating a stable international financial and economic system that would promote world trade. Given its unquestioned political, economic and military leadership at the conclusion of the war, it succeeded in creating a "free world" political economic system largely in its own image based on markets, private ownership, profit and restricting the power of workers around the world. An important foundation of this system has always been a worldwide military establishment, with 360 bases in over 40 countries around the world and with more than a third of its military personnel outside of the United States. The bottom line of the stability of the international economic and financial system and the dominance of the United States within it has always been the threat of, or the actual event of, military intervention with conventional or nuclear weapons. Wherever the leadership of the United States or one of its "free world" cohorts is threatened, U.S. military forces are ready to respond — in Vietnam from the 1950s to the 1970s; in South Korea, Lebanon, and Iran in the 1950s; in Central America throughout this century; in the Dominican Republic in 1965 and Grenada in 1983; and in the mid-East, northern Africa and the Persian Gulf in the 1980s. This global capability is expensive.

THE SOVIET ECONOMIC THREAT

Military spending is also motivated by a perceived Soviet political economic threat to the free world system. The existence of socialism in the Soviet Union suggests an alternative economic model to the growing number of independent nations in the world. As long as the United States dominates the international system and determines the rules, it can take advantage of its power. If countries begin to play by different rules and to establish their own independence, it challenges the control and influence of the United States and its multinationals. One response to this has been the arms race between the United States and the Soviet Union for global power. If Third World countries cross over to the Soviet side, U.S. policymakers fear the loss of access to markets, raw materials, investment opportunities and cheap labor. Consequently, in the postwar period, the United States has developed its ability to engage in direct and indirect military activities in the Third World in support of its client states and in opposition to most movements for national independence.

THE ECONOMIC EFFECTS OF MILITARY SPENDING

While this constellation of factors encourages continuing high levels of military spending, this use of resources can also produce a variety of negative impacts on the U.S. economy. In recent years, in fact, the peace movement and other critics of the defense budget have focused on the adverse economic effects of military spending.[1]

Increased military spending for a war or a peacetime buildup can be inflationary, but isn't necessarily so. Whether a military expansion produces inflation or not depends on the state of the economy, how it is financed, and monetary policy. For example, contrasting the Vietnam War buildup with the Reagan buildup is instructive. Between 1965 and 1968, military spending increased from 7.5 to 9.6 percent of GNP. The rate of inflation during this same period increased from just over 1 percent in the early 1960s to over 6 percent by the end of the decade. Inflation accelerated because the war expanded when the economy was at the peak of an expansion with low unemployment and little excess capacity. Markets were tight, and the extra demands of the war for labor and raw materials began to increase wages and prices at a faster rate. This increased demand in the economy was not balanced by a decrease in other forms of government spending because Lyndon Johnson was convinced that he could fight a war against poverty at home and a war against "communism" in Vietnam simultaneously. Johnson refused to increase taxes because he was afraid that the debate might force him to end his pursuit of both wars. At the same time, the rate of growth of the money supply accelerated to accommodate the increased federal budget deficit (as the Federal Reserve System lent money to the Treasury). The increase in the money supply made possible increased demands for labor and raw materials throughout the economy. These increased demands produced price increases. The result was a rapid acceleration in the rate of inflation that laid the groundwork for double digit inflation in the 1970s.

During the Reagan era, an increase in military spending from 5.0 to 6.6 percent of GNP has not produced increased inflation. In fact, the rate of inflation decreased from over 12 percent in 1980 to just over 1 percent in 1986. This buildup began at the moment that the United States was experiencing its worst recession in the post-Depression period; the increased military demand did not have to compete for labor and other resources with an expanding economy as it did in the Vietnam War. The buildup was not financed by tax increases, since the top priority of the first Reagan term was the 1981 tax cut; but in 1981–1983, the extra $100 billion of military spending was balanced by an equivalent decrease in non-military spending. Finally, in the early 1980s the Fed followed a tight monetary policy. Of course, if the economic recovery of the mid-1980s were to continue, along with the military buildup, looser monetary policy, and large deficits, then the rate of inflation might accelerate.

The effect of military spending on employment is somewhat complex. Some forms of military spending create fewer jobs than non-military spending. Weapons contracting, for example, requires skilled labor, technical scientific personnel, expensive raw materials, and lots of capital. So $1 billion of spending (1981 dollars) would create 21,000 jobs in guided missiles and 71,000 jobs in education. But there are some problems with this comparison. So many more education jobs can be created because teachers are not paid well and many work only part time. The contrast between weapons procurement and education, for example, also exaggerates the employment differential between defense and non-defense spending. A 1983 study by the Congressional Budget Office found that $10 billion of general defense spending (procurement, plus personnel, operations and maintenance, etc.) created 250,000 jobs and $10 billion of non-defense spending spread through the economy created the same number of jobs (U.S. Congressional Budget Office 1983).

Sometimes critics argue against military spending because it creates fewer jobs. But if military critics are honestly interested in full employment as a political objective, then overall economic policy is the appropriate focus, not simply military spending. If, however, full employment were pursued as a policy, shifting funding from some military programs to certain domestic programs could, in fact, creat more jobs. Barry Bluestone and John Havens in 1985 found that decreasing military procurement by $35 billion and reallocating those funds to programs for housing, transportation, infrastructure and education to "rebuild America" would create 250,000 new jobs (Bluestone and Havens 1985).

Perhaps the most pernicious economic effect of military spending is its association with factors that impede economic growth. Researchers have found inverse relationships between the portion of resources nations devote to the military and levels of investment, productivity growth rates, and civilian R&D. The larger the proportion of resources a society devotes to military spending the fewer resources there are for investment activities to expand the capacity to produce civilian goods and services. In the United States national defense purchases of goods and services actually exceed the value of net private domestic investment. In 1980, they were 7 percent larger and in 1985 they were 13 percent larger. More than one-third of all R&D money and a third of all scientists and engineers are involved in military activities. With increased spending for Star Wars research, this pattern will probably be accentuated. This allocation of resources limits the ability of a society to develop civilian goods and services, ultimately increasing the difficulties of competing in international markets against countries that have different priorities.

The most fundamental economic consequence of military spending is its effect on priorities, how a society uses the resources available to it. By spending money on the military, those funds are not available for other activities, for example, programs that might promote the quality of life and develop the resources and the people of a society for the future. These might include education, scientific research, recreation, environmental protection, care for the aged and the underprivileged, and so on. For example, Table 2 shows the effect Reagan's budgets have had on shifting the spending priorities of the federal government toward the military and away from social spending and other non-military programs.

Table 2
Composition of Federal Outlays, Percentage

	FY1980	FY1987
Military (National Defense, plus Veterans Benefits)	26	30
Social Spending	35	28
Social Security & Medicare	26	28
Net Interest	9	14
Other	5	1

Source: Center for Popular Economics, *A Field Guide to the U.S. Economy,* Pantheon Press, 1988.

Another clear way to capture the impact of the Reagan era's priorities is to examine the sources of the increased budget deficit from 1980 to 1986. The deficit increased from $74 billion and 2.7 percent of GNP to $221 billion and 5.2 percent of GNP. The extra 2.5 percent GNP share of the deficit comes from: an added 1.6 percent for the defense budget, an added 1.3 percent for interest on the debt, an added 0.6 percent from reduced revenues from the 1981 tax cut, and a *decreased* 1.0 percent share for non-defense spending categories in the budget (Center for Popular Economics 1988). The Reagan buildup has contributed to the massive budget deficit and to a reordering of priorities in the federal budget.

CONCLUSION

Military spending plays a somewhat contradictory role within American capitalism. While there are some adverse economic consequences associated with military priorities, there are also powerful economic factors motivating high levels of military spending. Mounting an effective political challenge to the military budget requires more than highlighting the negative economic effects that it may produce. It primarily involves raising fundamental questions about the priorities of the United States and its citizens. Should resources be allocated to nuclear and conventional weapons production to maintain aggregate demand and to support employment? Or should spending for housing, alternative energy, the elimination of poverty, and education be increased? Should military spending support a global presence to dominate the world for corporate exploitation, or should the United States develop an alternative foreign policy that relies more heavily on diplomacy to settle disputes and to protect national interests? Should priorities be determined by the military-industrial complex or the rest of us? Should research monies go toward Star Wars weapons or to develop new civilian products for the future and to enhance the ability to compete in international markets?

A movement to reduce military spending must be constructed from a coalition of peace and anti-intervention groups with organizations interested in full employment and other domestic programs. Such a movement necessarily involves challenging the foreign policy, major vested interests and the priorities of the nation.

ACKNOWLEDGEMENT

A previous, condensed version of this essay appeared in the September 1987 issue of *Dollars & Sense* magazine.

NOTE

1. A debate has emerged during the 1980s among critics of U.S. defense policy about the economic effects of military spending. Some argue that there are primarily adverse economic consequences (e.g., Melman 1974; DeGrasse 1983; Markusen 1986; Dumas 1986). Others have suggested that these arguments have been exaggerated and that military spending does not have unique macroeconomic impacts (e.g., Adams and Gold 1986, 1987). Still others have emphasized the economic contributions of military spending to American imperialism (e.g., Cypher 1981; Riddell 1982; Amott and Riddell 1984).

REFERENCES

Adams, Gordon. 1981. *The Iron Triangle: The Politics of Defense Contracting*. New York: Council on Economic Priorities.

Adams, Gordon and Stephen Alexis Cain. 1987. The FY 1988 Defense Budget: Preliminary Analysis. Washington, D.C.: Defense Budget Project.

Adams, Gordon and David Gold. 1986. Recasting the Military Spending Debate. *The Bulletin of the Atomic Scientists* (October):26–32.

_____. 1987. *Defense Spending and the Economy: Does the Defense Dollar Make a Difference?* Washington, D.C.: Defense Budget Project.

Amott, Teresa and Tom Riddell. 1984. The Freeze, Militarism, and the American Economy. *Socialist Review* 64(2):103–112.

Bluestone, Barry and John Havens. 1985. Reducing the Federal Deficit Fair and Square. Chestnut Hill, MA: Social Welfare Research Institute.

Business Week. 1985. Pentagon Spending Is the Economy's Biggest Gun (October 21).

Center for Defense Information. 1987. No Business Like War Business. *The Defense Monitor* 16(3).

Center for Popular Economics. 1988. *A Field Guide to the U.S. Economy*. Coordinated and written by Nancy Folbre. New York: Pantheon Press.

Cypher, James M. 1981. The Basic Economics of Rearming America. *Monthly Review* 33(6):11–27.

DeGrasse, Robert W., Jr., 1983. *Military Expansion, Economic Decline*. Armonk, NY: M. E. Sharpe.

Dumas, Lloyd J. 1986. The Military Burden on the Economy. *The Bulletin of the Atomic Scientist* (October):22–26.
Keynes, John Maynard. 1940. Editorial. *The New Republic* (July).
Markusen, Ann. 1986. The Militarized Economy. *World Policy Journal* (Summer):495–516.
Melman, Seymour. 1985. *The Permanent War Economy*. New York: Simon & Schuster.
Project on Military Procurement. 1986. Defense Procurement Information Papers. Washington, D.C.
Riddell, Tom. 1982. Militarism: The Other Side of Supply. *Economic Forum* (Summer):49–70.
U.S. Congressional Budget Office. 1983. *Defense Spending and the Economy*. Washington, D.C.: U.S. Government Printing Office.
_____. 1987. *An Analysis of the President's Budgetary Proposals for Fiscal Year 1988*. Washington, D.C.: U.S. Government Printing Office.

STATISTICAL APPENDIX

STATISTICAL APPENDIX

Compiled by Michele Naples, with Clara Graziano and Bai-bai Chen for the Editorial Collective

These statistical tables are based on official government statistics, and are subject to the same qualifications as standard measures (e.g., the unemployment rate represents only those who meet the official criteria to qualify as unemployed). We have attempted to update most of those included in the previous URPE crisis reader (1978), as well as providing new series. However, the data are not always strictly comparable with those of the 1978 reader. The abbreviations used in headings and to identify sources are listed at the end, as are footnotes to particular series and sources.

	Gross National Product		Corporate Sector				
	1	2	3	4	5	6	7
Years	B 1982 $	% C	After-tax corp profits B 1982 $	After-tax profit rate, mfg[1]	Corp debt/total debt, %	Corp liquidity ratio[2]	Bus failure rate[3]
1947	1066.7	−2.8	52.9	15.6		2.0	14.3
1948	1108.7	3.9	75.4	16.0		2.1	20.4
1949	1109.0	.0	75.7	11.6		2.2	34.4
1950	1203.7	8.5	71.1	15.4		2.0	34.3
1951	1328.2	10.3	68.9	12.1		1.9	30.7
1952	1380.0	3.9	71.0	10.3		1.9	28.7
1953	1435.3	4.0	67.2	10.5		1.9	33.2
1954	1416.2	−1.3	72.2	9.9		2.0	42.0
1955	1494.9	5.6	92.3	12.6		1.9	41.6
1956	1525.6	2.1	84.7	12.3		1.8	48.0
1957	1551.1	1.7	81.8	10.9		1.8	51.7
1958	1539.2	−.8	72.1	8.6		1.9	55.9
1959	1629.1	5.8	91.4	10.4	22.75	1.9	51.8
1960	1665.3	2.2	86.7	9.2	22.65	1.8	57.0
1961	1708.7	2.6	88.5	8.9	22.81	1.8	64.4
1962	1799.4	5.3	107.5	9.8	16.49	2.0	60.8
1963	1873.3	4.1	115.4	10.3	16.95	2.0	56.3
1964	1973.3	5.3	129.8	11.6	16.99	2.0	53.2
1965	2087.6	5.8	149.1	13.0	18.05	1.9	53.3
1966	2208.3	5.8	151.1	13.4	18.84	1.8	51.6
1967	2271.4	2.9	143.2	11.7	18.62	1.8	49.0
1968	2365.6	4.1	136.3	12.1	19.84	1.7	38.6
1969	2423.3	2.4	119.8	11.5	21.80	1.6	37.3
1970	2416.2	−.3	96.0	9.3	21.61	1.6	43.8
1971	2484.8	2.8	111.0	9.7	21.11	1.6	41.7
1972	2608.5	5.0	126.5	10.6	22.09	1.6	38.3
1973	2744.1	5.2	129.5	12.8	23.86	1.5	36.4
1974	2729.3	−.5	92.4	14.9	21.98	1.6	38.4
1975	2695.0	−1.3	112.5	11.6	20.11	1.7	42.6
1976	2826.7	4.9	128.4	13.9	19.92	1.7	34.8
1977	2958.6	4.7	151.3	14.2	19.90	1.6	28.4
1978	3115.2	5.3	157.5	15.0	21.10	1.6	23.9
1979	3192.4	2.5	142.6	16.4	22.70	1.5	27.8
1980	3187.1	−.2	107.8	13.9	22.81	1.5	42.1
1981	3248.8	1.9	113.6	13.6	22.67	1.5	61.3
1982	3166.0	−2.5	86.9	9.2	20.95	1.5	89.0
1983	3279.1	3.6	131.4	10.6	20.02	1.5	110.0
1984	3489.9	6.4	156.9	12.5	18.68	1.5	107.0
1985	3585.2	2.7	169.4	10.1			114.0
1986	3676.5	2.5	172.0				
	Source: ERP	Source: ERP	Source: ERP	Source: ERP	Source: ERP	Source: ERP	Source: ERP

	Corporate Sector					Financial Sector	
	8	9	10	11	12	13	14
Years	**Inventories/ sales, US Bus**	**Mfg inventories/ Bus inventories**	**Profits top 500 corps/total US, %**	**Sales top 500 corps/total US, %**	**Assets top 500 corps/total US, %**	**Prime interest rate**	**Fedl Reserve's holdings of US govt securities B $**
1947	3.22	48.9					22.6
1948	3.35	48.6					
1949	3.09	47.0				2.00	
1950	3.41	47.0				2.07	
1951	3.40	51.0				2.56	23.8
1952	3.23	51.6				3.00	24.7
1953	3.18	52.5				3.17	25.9
1954	3.08	51.0	43.2	55.1		3.05	24.9
1955	3.14	51.0	44.6	57.9	54.6	3.16	24.8
1956	3.24	52.2	48.3	56.7	58.4	3.77	24.9
1957	3.18	51.3	49.0	58.8	60.8	4.20	24.2
1958	3.02	50.8	44.8	57.9	60.5	3.83	26.3
1959	3.03	50.4	43.1	58.4	60.8	4.48	26.6
1960	2.99	50.1	43.4	59.2	61.0	4.82	27.4
1961	2.87	50.4	42.1	58.7	73.3	4.50	28.9
1962	2.84	50.8	39.3	58.8	73.1	4.50	30.8
1963	2.78	50.2	39.7	59.4	72.4	4.50	33.6
1964	2.78	50.3	40.4	60.1	73.5	4.50	37.0
1965	2.70	50.1	39.7	60.6	74.9	4.54	40.8
1966	2.85	51.3	41.7	60.0	77.5	5.63	44.3
1967	2.88	51.6	41.6	67.1	82.1	5.61	49.1
1968	2.82	51.5	47.1	64.1	84.7	6.30	52.9
1969	2.91	51.5	51.7	64.0	84.8	7.96	57.2
1970	2.89	50.6	53.8	65.5	87.8	7.91	62.1
1971	2.82	48.2	47.5	67.0	85.0	5.72	70.2
1972	2.75	47.1	47.3	65.6	81.1	5.25	69.9
1973	2.97	47.4	60.3	65.6	79.6	8.03	78.5
1974	3.45	49.0	87.4	78.6	85.5	10.81	80.5
1975	3.11	48.8	56.7	81.2	88.1	7.86	89.8
1976	3.14	48.4	61.0	80.7	89.1	6.84	97.0
1977	3.10	47.2	51.7	81.8	88.1	6.83	102.8
1978	3.12	46.3	54.1	81.4	86.1	9.06	109.6
1979	3.24	47.3	69.8	83.0	85.2	12.67	117.5
1980	3.26	47.4	87.9	86.3	88.6	15.27	121.3
1981	3.25	46.7	78.8	82.7	90.4	18.87	131.0
1982	3.02	45.7	70.7	82.0	91.3	14.86	139.3
1983	2.87	44.6	50.4	79.8	86.9	10.79	151.9
1984	2.88	44.3	50.7	75.3	86.7	12.04	160.9
1985	2.73	43.0	36.8	77.5		9.93	181.3
1986	2.60	41.8	33.0			8.33	186.5
	Source: ERP	Source: ERP	Source: *Fortune*, ERP	Source: ib	Source: ib	Source: ERP	Source: FB

	Bank Failures[4]		Government Sector				
				US Fedl Budget, B 1982 $[6]			
	15	16	17	18	19	20	21
Years	Number	Deposits held M $	US fedl govt spending B $[5]	Military	Net interest[7]	Transfers and social services[8]	Corp income taxes as % total fedl receipts
1947	1.5	0.663	34.5	318.2	110.8	189.9	21.59
1948	1.5	0.663	29.8	278.0	123.7	187.2	23.39
1949	1.5	0.663	38.8	303.8	128.0	193.3	29.72
1950	1.5	0.663	42.6	311.1	139.0	203.5	28.69
1951	3.4	11.663	45.5	564.0	143.4	184.9	29.71
1952	3.4	11.663	67.7	1122.9	151.3	179.5	34.63
1953	3.4	11.663	76.1	1306.4	170.5	174.6	32.84
1954	3.4	11.663	70.9	1235.7	170.2	178.6	32.76
1955	3.4	11.663	68.4	1106.9	175.1	192.1	29.67
1956	3.8	8.214	70.6	1144.3	192.4	214.0	30.77
1957	3.8	8.214	76.6	1262.0	212.6	231.0	30.00
1958	3.8	8.214	82.4	1313.8	228.4	260.9	29.28
1959	3.8	8.214	92.1	1413.9	233.2	300.8	25.49
1960	3.8	8.214	92.2	1411.9	286.3	303.5	27.64
1961	5.6	19.773	97.7	1478.3	253.0	905.3	22.20
1962	5.6	19.773	106.8	1630.0	265.4	962.4	20.59
1963	5.6	19.773	111.3	1693.1	298.6	1086.2	20.25
1964	5.6	19.773	118.5	1763.1	322.7	1147.3	20.85
1965	5.6	19.773	118.2	1675.7	350.1	1309.8	21.79
1966	2.5	8.842	134.5	1987.5	395.0	1536.0	22.98
1967	2.5	8.842	157.5	2515.9	451.9	1923.5	22.72
1968	2.5	8.842	178.1	3035.5	518.1	2299.4	18.65
1969	2.5	6.000	183.6	3233.0	628.5	2743.6	19.53
1970	1.0	15.000	195.6	3299.2	769.0	3602.7	16.94
1971	4.0	6.000	210.2	3365.9	870.3	4362.0	14.22
1972	2.0	57.000	230.7	3559.6	956.2	5286.2	15.42
1973	3.0	20.000	245.7	3689.8	1127.7	6336.8	15.57
1974	0.0	0.000	269.4	4200.2	1513.7	8446.3	14.58
1975	2.0	7.000	332.3	5073.2	1378.4	11120.4	14.55
1976	0.0	0.000	371.8	5655.0	1685.5	4455.9	13.89
1977	6.0	205.000	409.2	6544.3	2010.8	14923.4	15.44
1978	7.0	854.000	458.7	7544.5	2558.8	17548.4	15.00
1979	10.0	111.000	503.5	9144.5	3349.5	20988.3	14.18
1980	10.0	216.000	590.9	11483.4	4500.2	26754.4	12.43
1981	10.0	3826.000	678.2	14806.2	6461.0	33769.4	10.20
1982	42.0	9908.000	745.7	18530.8	8499.5	38868.0	7.97
1983	49.0	5459.000	808.3	21808.9	9327.5	44261.7	6.16
1984	80.0	2962.000	851.8	24537.9	11983.2	46617.2	8.54
1985	120.0	8059.000	946.3	28181.4	14431.5	52607.9	8.36
1986			989.8	31301.4	15568.5	55142.5	
	Source: SA	Source: SA	Source: ERP	Source: ERP	Source: ERP	Source: ERP	Source: ERP

	Government Sector			International Trade and Finance			
	22	23	24	25	26	27	28
Years	**Fedl surplus (+) or deficit (-) B 1982 $**[9]	**Fedl debt B 1982 $**	**Fedl debt/total debt nonfinancial sectors**	**Imports as % GNP**	**US direct investment abroad B 1982 $**	**Balance of payments on current account M $**	**% Fedl debt held by foreigners**
1947	18.1	1163	63.38	3.7		8992	0.16
1948	50.0			4.2		2417	
1949	2.6			4.2		873	
1950	−13.0			4.5		−1,840	
1951	24.3	1034	51.10	4.3		884	
1952	−5.9	1049	49.76	4.6		614	
1953	−25.1	1063	48.44	4.9		−1286	
1954	−4.6	1060	47.16	4.8		219	
1955	−11.0	1032	43.31	5.1		430	
1956	13.9	985	40.51	5.5		2730	
1957	11.7	945	38.48	5.7		4762	
1958	−9.4	953	37.43	6.0		784	
1959	42.1	957	43.22	6.3		−1282	4.13
1960	1.0	940	41.01	6.1	103.2	2824	4.48
1961	−10.6	950	39.51	6.0		3822	4.52
1962	−22.3	953	37.87	6.4		3387	5.03
1963	−14.8	957	36.12	6.2		4414	5.13
1964	−17.9	969	34.58	6.2		6823	5.24
1965	−4.1	951	32.44	6.5		5431	5.20
1966	−10.6	942	31.17	6.9		3031	4.34
1967	−24.0	960	30.38	7.1		2583	4.58
1968	−66.8	950	29.10	7.8	172.4	611	3.99
1969	8.0	925	27.89	8.2	178.4	399	3.04
1970	−6.7	927	27.59	8.6	186.2	2331	5.29
1971	−51.8	955	27.46	8.8	194.1	−1433	11.06
1972	−50.3	966	26.42	9.4	202.8	−5795	12.31
1973	−30.1	949	24.87	10.0	216.8	7140	11.96
1974	−11.3	912	23.89	9.8	204.1	1962	11.93
1975	−89.7	972	25.68	8.9	209.4	18116	11.53
1976	−116.8	1036	26.29	10.1	216.8	4207	11.95
1977	−79.6	1068	25.67	10.7	222.6	−14511	15.25
1978	−82.0	1093	24.87	10.9	225.3	−15427	17.46
1979	−51.1	1075	23.76	11.1	239.1	−991	14.72
1980	−86.1	1085	23.86	10.4	251.3	1873	13.94
1981	−83.9	1094	24.04	10.6	242.9	6339	13.28
1982	−127.9	1197	25.68	10.6	221.5	−9131	12.49
1983	−200.0	1358	27.08	11.2	199.4	−46604	11.79
1984	−171.7	1541	27.95	13.0	197.4	−106466	11.60
1985	−190.4	1745	28.71	13.1	208.7	−117677	11.03
1986	−192.8			14.2			
	Source: ERP	Source: FB, ERP	Source: FB, ERP	Source: ERP	Source: ERP	Source: ERP	Source: FB

	International Trade and Finance	Exchange Rate of the $[10]		Employment, Unemployment, Underemployment			Civilian U Rates by Race and Sex
	29	**30**	**31**	**32**	**33**	**34**	**35**
	Repatriated profits on US foreign investments M $	**nominal**	**real [Mar 1973 = 100]**	**Civilian U rate**	**Ave duration (weeks) each spell of U[11]**	**% LF experiencing U**	**Whites**
1947	1303.0						
1948	1553.0			3.8	8.6		3.5
1949	1615.0			5.9	10.0		5.6
1950	1839.0			5.3	12.1		4.9
1951	2154.0			3.3	9.7		3.1
1952	2120.0			3.0	8.4		2.8
1953	2215.0			2.9	8.0		2.7
1954	2555.0			5.5	11.8		5.0
1955	2817.0			4.4	13.0		3.9
1956	3100.0			4.1	11.3		3.6
1957	3263.0			4.3	10.5		3.8
1958	3287.0			6.8	13.9	17.9	6.1
1959	3586.0			5.5	14.4	15.3	4.8
1960	4616.0			5.5	12.8	17.2	4.9
1961	4998.0			6.7	15.6	18.4	6.0
1962	5619.0			5.5	14.7	18.2	4.9
1963	6157.0			5.7	14.0	16.7	5.0
1964	6823.0			5.2	13.3	16.2	4.6
1965	7436.0			4.5	11.8	14.1	4.1
1966	7526.0			3.8	10.4	13.0	3.3
1967	8021.0	120.0		3.8	8.7	12.9	3.4
1968	9368.0	122.1		3.6	8.4	12.4	3.2
1969	10912.0	122.4		3.5	7.8	12.5	3.1
1970	11746.0	121.1		4.9	8.6	15.3	4.5
1971	12706.0	117.8		5.9	11.3	16.3	5.4
1972	14764.0	109.1		5.6	12.0	15.5	5.0
1973	21808.0	99.1	98.8	4.9	10.0	14.3	4.3
1974	27587.0	101.4	99.2	5.6	9.8	17.9	5.0
1975	25351.0	98.5	93.9	8.5	14.2	20.2	7.8
1976	29286.0	105.6	97.3	7.7	15.8	19.1	7.0
1977	32587.0	103.3	93.1	7.1	14.3	17.9	6.2
1978	43465.0	92.4	84.2	6.1	11.9	15.9	5.2
1979	66700.0	88.1	83.2	5.8	10.8	15.8	5.1
1980	75936.0	87.4	84.8	7.1	11.9	18.1	6.3
1981	90056.0	102.9	100.8	7.6	13.7	19.5	6.7
1982		116.6	111.7	9.7	15.6	22.0	8.6
1983		125.3	117.3	9.6	20.0	19.6	8.4
1984		138.3	128.5	7.5	18.2	17.4	6.5
1985		143.2	132.0	7.2	15.6	16.7	6.2
1986		112.0	103.4	7.0	15.0		6.0
	Source: BS	Source: ERP	Source: ERP	Source: ERP	Source: HLS	Source: HLS, SA	Source: ETRP and MLR

Years	Civilian U Rates by Race and Sex			U Rates by Occupation [12]			
	36 **Blacks**	**37** **Women** **>=16**	**38** **Men** **>=16**	**39** **Professional, Technical**	**40** **Sales, Clerical**	**41** **Service workers**	**42** **Crafts**
1948	5.9	4.1	3.6				
1949	8.9	6.0	5.9				
1950	9.0	5.7	5.1				
1951	5.3	4.4	2.8				
1952	5.4	3.6	2.8				
1953	4.5	3.3	2.8				
1954	9.9	6.0	5.3				
1955	8.7	4.9	4.2				
1956	8.3	4.8	3.8				
1957	7.9	4.7	4.1				
1958	12.6	6.8	6.8	1.85	4.31	6.9	6.8
1959	10.7	5.9	5.2	1.15	3.73	6.1	5.3
1960	10.2	5.9	5.4	1.20	3.80	5.8	5.3
1961	12.4	7.2	6.4	1.48	4.69	7.2	6.3
1962	10.9	6.2	5.2	1.26	4.09	6.2	5.1
1963	10.8	6.5	5.2	1.30	4.09	6.1	4.8
1964	9.6	6.2	4.6	1.22	3.64	6.0	4.1
1965	8.1	5.5	4.0	1.02	3.33	5.3	3.6
1966	7.3	4.8	3.2	0.91	2.87	4.6	2.8
1967	7.4	5.2	3.1	0.89	3.13	4.5	2.5
1968	6.7	4.8	2.9	0.89	2.95	4.4	2.4
1969	6.4	4.7	2.8	0.91	2.97	4.2	2.2
1970	8.2	5.9	4.4	1.36	4.05	5.3	3.8
1971	9.9	6.9	5.3	1.86	4.67	6.3	4.8
1972	10.0	6.6	5.0	1.68	4.59	6.3	4.3
1973	8.9	6.0	4.2	1.46	4.06	5.8	3.7
1974	9.9	6.7	4.9	1.68	4.49	6.3	4.4
1975	13.9	9.3	7.9	2.48	6.39	8.6	8.3
1976	13.1	8.6	7.1	2.53	6.14	8.8	6.9
1977	13.1	8.2	6.3	2.34	5.74	8.2	5.7
1978	11.9	7.2	5.3	1.92	4.69	7.5	4.7
1979	11.3	6.8	5.1	1.83	4.49	7.2	4.5
1980	13.2	7.4	6.9	1.98	5.07	7.9	6.6
1981	15.6	7.9	7.4	2.24	5.42	8.9	7.5
1982	18.9	9.4	9.9	2.74	6.64	10.6	10.2
1983	19.5	9.2	9.9	2.68	5.44	9.6	8.4
1984	15.9	7.6	7.4	2.35	4.74	8.5	6.6
1985	15.1	7.4	7.0	2.12	4.36	8.9	7.2
1986	14.5	7.1	6.9	2.21	3.99	8.0	6.7
	Source: ib	Source: HLS, MLR, SA	Source: ib	Source: HLS, E&F	Source: ib	Source: ib	Source: ib

	U Rates by Occupation[12]				LF Participation Rates		
	43	44	45	46	47	48	49
Years	Operatives	Nonfarm laborers	Farmers, farmworkers	Layoffs /100 Employees	Civilian LF	Women	Married women husband present
1947				1.0	59350		
1948				1.3	60621	32.7	22.0
1949				2.4	61286	33.1	22.5
1950				1.1	62208	33.9	23.8
1951				1.2	62017	34.6	25.2
1952				1.1	62138	34.7	25.3
1953				1.3	63015	34.4	26.3
1954				1.9	63643	34.6	26.6
1955				1.2	65023	35.7	27.7
1956				1.5	66552	36.9	29.0
1957				1.7	66929	36.9	29.6
1958	11.0	15.1	3.2	2.3	67639	37.1	30.2
1959	7.6	12.6	2.6	1.6	68369	37.1	30.9
1960	8.0	12.6	2.7	2.4	69628	37.7	30.5
1961	9.6	14.7	2.8	2.2	70459	38.1	32.7
1962	7.5	12.5	2.3	2.0	70614	37.9	32.7
1963	7.5	12.4	3.0	1.8	71833	38.3	33.7
1964	6.6	10.8	3.1	1.7	73091	38.7	34.4
1965	5.5	8.6	2.6	1.4	74455	39.3	34.7
1966	4.4	7.4	2.2	1.2	75770	40.3	35.4
1967	5.0	7.6	2.3	1.4	77347	41.1	36.8
1968	4.5	7.2	2.1	1.2	78737	41.6	38.3
1969	4.4	6.7	1.9	1.2	80734	42.7	39.6
1970	7.1	9.5	2.6	1.8	82771	43.3	40.8
1971	8.3	10.8	2.6	1.6	84382	43.4	40.8
1972	7.0	10.3	2.7	1.1	87034	43.9	41.5
1973	5.7	8.5	2.6	0.9	89429	44.7	42.2
1974	7.5	10.1	2.6	1.5	91949	45.7	43.1
1975	13.2	15.6	3.6	2.1	93775	46.3	44.4
1976	10.1	13.7	4.5	1.3	96158	47.3	45.1
1977	8.9	12.1	4.7	1.1	99009	48.4	46.6
1978	7.5	10.8	3.9	0.9	102251	50.0	47.5
1979	7.8	10.9	3.9	1.1	104962	50.9	49.3
1980	11.4	14.6	4.6	1.7	106940	51.5	50.1
1981	11.4	14.7	5.3	1.6	108670	52.1	51.0
1982	16.2	18.5	6.5		110204	52.6	51.2
1983	11.9	15.8	12.0		111550	52.9	51.8
1984	10.3	15.3	11.8		113544	53.6	52.8
1985	9.9	12.8	9.4		115461	54.5	54.2
1986	9.7	13.7	9.1		117834	55.3	54.6
	Source: ib	Source: ib	Source: ib	Source: E&E	Source: ERP	Source: ERP	Source: HLS

	LF Participation Rates		The Price Level and Inflation				Productivity Output/hour Nonfarm Bus
	50	**51**	**52**	**53**	**54**	**55**	**56**
Years	**Married women with children under 6**	**Women as % of N**	**GNP deflator**	**Consumer price index (CPI)**	**Energy price index**	**Rate of inflation (of CPI)**	**All Employees**
1947		28.1	22.1	69.9		14.4	51.6
1948	10.8	28.5	23.6	72.1		7.8	53.1
1949	11.0	29.0	23.5	71.4		−1.0	54.3
1950	11.9	29.4	23.9	72.1		1.0	57.7
1951	14.0	30.3	25.1	77.8		7.9	59.6
1952	13.9	30.8	25.5	79.5		2.2	60.9
1953	15.5	30.6	25.9	80.1		0.8	62.3
1954	14.9	30.8	26.3	80.5		0.5	63.2
1955	16.2	31.4	27.2	80.2		0.4	65.0
1956	15.9	32.0	28.1	81.4		1.5	64.9
1957	17.0	32.3	29.1	84.3	90.1	3.6	66.2
1958	18.2	32.7	29.7	86.6	90.3	2.7	67.9
1959	18.7	32.7	30.4	87.3	91.8	0.8	70.1
1960	18.6	33.3	30.9	88.7	94.2	1.6	70.9
1961	20.0	33.6	31.2	89.6	94.4	1.0	73.1
1962	21.3	33.8	31.9	90.6	94.7	1.1	75.5
1963	22.5	34.1	32.4	91.7	95.0	1.2	78.2
1964	22.7	34.4	32.9	92.9	94.6	1.3	81.3
1965	23.2	34.8	33.8	94.5	96.3	1.7	83.3
1966	24.2	35.6	35.0	97.2	97.8	2.9	85.1
1967	26.5	36.2	35.9	100.0	100.0	2.9	87.0
1968	27.6	36.6	37.7	104.2	101.5	4.2	89.3
1969	28.5	37.3	39.8	109.8	104.2	5.4	88.9
1970	30.3	37.7	42.0	116.3	107.0	5.9	89.1
1971	29.6	37.8	44.4	121.3	111.2	4.3	91.8
1972	30.1	38.0	46.5	125.3	114.3	3.3	94.7
1973	32.7	38.5	49.5	133.1	123.5	6.2	96.4
1974	34.4	38.9	54.0	147.7	159.7	11.0	94.3
1975	36.7	39.6	59.3	161.2	176.6	9.1	96.0
1976	37.5	40.1	63.1	170.5	189.3	5.8	98.5
1977	39.4	40.5	67.3	181.5	207.3	6.5	100.0
1978	41.7	41.2	72.2	195.4	220.4	7.7	100.8
1979	43.3	41.7	78.6	217.4	275.9	11.3	99.2
1980	45.1	42.4	85.7	246.8	361.1	13.5	98.8
1981	47.8	42.8	94.0	272.4	410.0	10.4	99.8
1982	48.7	43.5	100.0	289.1	416.1	6.1	99.2
1983	49.9	43.7	103.9	298.4	419.3	3.2	102.6
1984	51.8	43.7	107.9	311.1	423.6	4.3	104.3
1985	53.4	44.1	111.5	322.2	426.5	3.6	104.8
1986	53.8	44.4	114.5	328.4	370.3	1.9	105.5
	Source: HLS	Source: ERP	Source: ERP	Source: ERP	Source: ERP	Source: ERP	Source: ERP, BLS, BS, E&E, MLR, SCB

Years	Productivity: Output/hour: Nonfarm Bus: 57 Nonsupervisory employees	Productivity: Output/hour: Mfg: 58 All employees	Productivity: Output/hour: Mfg: 59 Production workers	Productivity: Rate of Growth (C log): Nonfarm Bus: 60 All employees	Productivity: Rate of Growth (C log): Nonfarm Bus: 61 Nonsupervisory employees	Productivity: Rate of Growth (C log): Mfg: 62 All employees	Productivity: Rate of Growth (C log): Mfg: 63 Production workers
1947	51.7	36.5	31.4				
1948	53.4	38.1	33.1	0.02866	0.03263	0.04330	0.05348
1949	55.3	39.5	35.0	0.02235	0.03539	0.03625	0.05517
1950	58.0	42.4	37.1	0.06073	0.04645	0.07097	0.05815
1951	59.2	42.5	37.4	0.03240	0.02146	0.00103	0.00808
1952	60.5	43.5	38.9	0.02158	0.02049	0.02500	0.03948
1953	62.0	45.1	40.4	0.02273	0.02538	0.03554	0.03935
1954	64.0	46.2	42.4	0.01434	0.03155	0.02430	0.04816
1955	65.3	49.3	44.9	0.02808	0.01974	0.06375	0.05606
1956	65.8	50.6	46.6	−0.00154	0.00860	0.02615	0.03771
1957	67.4	51.9	48.7	0.01983	0.02382	0.02682	0.04472
1958	70.2	52.5	50.5	0.02536	0.04011	0.01163	0.03598
1959	71.7	55.5	52.7	0.03189	0.02121	0.05407	0.04269
1960	72.8	56.9	54.7	0.01135	0.01558	0.02511	0.03740
1961	75.3	58.5	57.0	0.03056	0.03376	0.02853	0.04035
1962	77.3	61.1	59.2	0.03230	0.02594	0.04276	0.03769
1963	79.5	64.0	62.2	0.03514	0.02777	0.04728	0.04965
1964	82.6	67.1	64.9	0.03888	0.03902	0.04627	0.04346
1965	84.2	70.4	67.6	0.02430	0.01827	0.04868	0.04045
1966	85.4	72.0	69.0	0.02138	0.01420	0.02192	0.02036
1967	87.2	73.6	71.7	0.02208	0.02135	0.02202	0.03801
1968	89.1	76.2	74.4	0.02609	0.02154	0.03576	0.03782
1969	88.4	78.2	76.6	−0.00449	−0.00770	0.02561	0.02828
1970	88.9	79.0	78.5	0.00225	0.00594	0.00934	0.02441
1971	91.9	83.2	82.4	0.02985	0.03270	0.05282	0.04921
1972	94.1	88.5	86.5	0.03110	0.02329	0.06081	0.04847
1973	95.8	91.1	88.7	0.01779	0.01825	0.02959	0.02473
1974	94.0	91.3	90.1	−0.02203	−0.01915	0.00162	0.01564
1975	96.2	90.9	92.2	0.01787	0.02276	−0.00429	0.02331
1976	98.2	95.6	95.7	0.02571	0.02108	0.05020	0.03737
1977	100.0	100.0	100.0	0.01511	0.01817	0.04547	0.04370
1978	101.0	102.6	102.5	0.00797	0.01035	0.02584	0.02461
1979	99.5	104.5	104.9	−0.01600	−0.01581	0.01809	0.02281
1980	99.5	106.1	109.2	−0.00404	0.00068	0.01534	0.04082
1981	100.5	108.8	112.8	0.01007	0.00974	0.02493	0.03226
1982	100.7	109.7	117.5	−0.00603	0.00160	0.00862	0.04037
1983	104.1	118.1	124.9	0.03370	0.03381	0.07348	0.06176
1984	105.5	124.8	130.3	0.01643	0.01326	0.05525	0.04194
1985	105.4	128.8	135.8	0.00478	−0.00135	0.03130	0.04142
1986		132.9	140.1	0.00666		0.03169	0.03127
	Source: ib	Source: ib	Source: ib	Source: ib	Source: ib	Source: ib	Source: ib

		Strikes		Income Distribution		Ave Gross Hourly Earnings, Private Non-farm	
	64	65	66	67	68	69	70
Years	Industrial accident rate[13]	Number of work stoppages[14]	Workers involved in strikes[15]	Wages and salaries as % of national income	Spendable hourly earnings, nonsupervisory workers 1977 $[16]	Current $	1977 $
1947	18.8	3693	2170	66.2		1.13	58.5
1948	17.2	3419	1960	64.2	2.83	1.22	58.9
1949	14.5	3606	3030	66.0	2.98	1.27	62.3
1950	14.7	4843	2410	64.8	3.07	1.33	64.0
1951	15.5	4737	2220	65.5	3.03	1.45	63.6
1952	14.3	5117	3540	67.3	3.07	1.52	65.5
1953	13.4	5091	2400	68.6	3.23	1.61	68.7
1954	11.9	3468	1530	68.4	3.30	1.65	70.5
1955	12.1	4320	2650	67.2	3.43	1.71	73.3
1956	12.0	3825	1900	68.7	3.55	1.80	75.9
1957	11.4	3673	1390	69.2	3.58	1.89	76.9
1958	11.4	3694	2060	69.3	3.60	1.95	78.0
1959	12.4	3708	1880	68.7	3.67	2.02	80.0
1960	12.0	3333	1320	69.8	3.72	2.09	81.4
1961	11.8	3367	1450	69.6	3.76	2.14	83.0
1962	11.9	3614	1230	69.2	3.85	2.22	85.0
1963	11.9	3362	941	69.1	3.87	2.28	86.3
1964	12.3	3655	1640	69.0	4.01	2.36	87.5
1965	12.8	3963	1550	68.3	4.14	2.46	89.0
1966	13.6	4405	1960	69.0	4.13	2.56	90.3
1967	14.0	4595	2870	70.2	4.18	2.68	92.2
1968	14.0	5045	2649	71.0	4.22	2.85	94.0
1969	14.8	5700	2481	72.5	4.22	3.04	95.0
1970	15.2	5716	3305	74.3	4.25	3.23	95.7
1971	15.5	5138	3280	73.4	4.37	3.45	98.3
1972	15.9	5010	1714	73.1	4.54	3.70	101.2
1973	17.0	5353	2251	72.4	4.48	3.94	101.1
1974	17.6	6074	2778	74.1	4.31	4.24	98.3
1975	17.0	5031	1746	73.6	4.26	4.53	97.6
1976	18.1	5648	2420	72.7	4.34	4.86	99.0
1977	19.3	5506	2040	72.7	4.43	5.25	100.0
1978	21.2	4230	1623	72.3	4.40	5.69	100.5
1979	22.3	4827	1727	72.8	4.26	6.16	97.4
1980	20.4	3885	1366	74.3	4.03	6.66	93.5
1981	19.2	2568	1081	74.0	3.93	7.25	92.6
1982	16.6	96	656	75.7	3.97	7.68	93.4
1983	16.2	81	909	74.3	4.03	8.02	94.9
1984	17.7	62	376	73.0	4.03	8.32	94.6
1985	17.3	54	324	73.5	3.92	8.57	94.1
1986		69	533	73.8		8.76	94.9
	Source: N&G, MLR	Source: HLS	Source: ib	Source: ERP	Source: BGW	Source: ERP	Source: ERP

Median Family Incomes by Race and by Marital and N Status

Years	71 All black families	72 All married-couple families (All Married-couple Families)	73 Wife in paid labor force (All Married-couple Families)	74 Wife not in paid labor force (All Married-couple Families)	75 All female-headed families	76 Males (Unrelated Individuals)	77 Females (Unrelated Individuals)
1947	1614.0	3109.0			2172.0	1349.0	792.0
1948	1768.0	3272.0			2064.0	1244.0	861.0
1949	1650.0	3195.0			2103.0	1437.0	856.0
1950	1869.0	3446.0			1922.0	1539.0	846.0
1951	2032.0	3837.0	4631.0	3634.0	2220.0	1909.0	917.0
1952	2338.0	4061.0	4900.0	3812.0	2235.0	2002.0	1019.0
1953	2461.0	4371.0	5405.0	4117.0	2455.0	2177.0	972.0
1954	2410.0	4333.0	5336.0	4051.0	2294.0	1696.0	966.0
1955	2549.0	4599.0	5622.0	4326.0	2471.0	1831.0	1054.0
1956	2628.0	4973.0	5957.0	4645.0	2754.0	1980.0	1160.0
1957	2764.0	5157.0	6141.0	4833.0	2763.0	2102.0	1264.0
1958	2711.0	5315.0	6214.0	4983.0	2741.0	2114.0	1268.0
1959	2917.0	5662.0	6705.0	5317.0	2764.0	2118.0	1318.0
1960	3233.0	5873.0	6900.0	5520.0	2968.0	2480.0	1377.0
1961	3191.0	6037.0	7188.0	5592.0	2993.0	2638.0	1407.0
1962	3330.0	6263.0	7461.0	5764.0	3131.0	2351.0	1461.0
1963	3465.0	6593.0	7789.0	6039.0	3211.0	2424.0	1476.0
1964	3839.0	6932.0	8170.0	6338.0	3458.0	2965.0	1555.0
1965	3994.0	7330.0	8633.0	6706.0	3535.0	3194.0	1767.0
1966	4691.0	7944.0	9279.0	7256.0	4074.0	3181.0	1908.0
1967	5094.0	8398.0	9917.0	7570.0	4269.0	3514.0	1917.0
1968	5590.0	9144.0	10686.0	8215.0	4477.0	4086.0	2239.0
1969	6190.0	10001.0	11629.0	8879.0	4822.0	4134.0	2397.0
1970	6279.0	10516.0	12276.0	9304.0	5093.0	4540.0	2483.0
1971	6440.0	10990.0	12853.0	9744.0	5114.0	4627.0	2688.0
1972	6864.0	11903.0	13897.0	10556.0	5342.0	5000.0	2858.0
1973	7269.0	13028.0	15237.0	11418.0	5797.0	5657.0	3300.0
1974	8006.0	13847.0	16461.0	12082.0	6413.0	5998.0	3493.0
1975	8779.0	14867.0	17237.0	12752.0	6844.0	6612.0	3978.0
1976*	9242.0	16203.0	18731.0	13931.0	7211.0	7217.0	4318.0
1977	9563.0	17616.0	20268.0	15063.0	7765.0	7831.0	4840.0
1978	10879.0	19300.0	22100.0	16200.0	8500.0	8900.0	5500.0
1979	11574.0	21500.0	25000.0	17800.0	9900.0	10200.0	6000.0
1980	12674.0	23141.0	26879.0	18972.0	10408.0	10939.0	6668.0
1981	13266.0	25065.0	29247.0	20325.0	10960.0	11848.0	7370.0
1982	13598.0	26019.0	30342.0	21299.0	11484.0	12470.0	8058.0
1983	14561.0	27286.0	32107.0	21890.0	11789.0	12888.0	8863.0
1984	15432.0	29612.0	34668.0	23582.0	12803.0	13566.0	9501.0
1985	16786.0		36431.0	24556.0	13660.0		
	Source: HS, SA	Source: ERP, CPR, SA	Source: ib	Source: ib	Source: ib	Source: ERP, CPR, SA	Source: ib

	Income Distribution				Households Earning > $35,000 (1983 $) 1967 on [or Families > $35,711 (1983 $) before 1967]	
	78	**79**	**80**	**81**	**82**	**83**
Years	**% Persons below poverty level**	**% Blacks below poverty**	**% Hispanics below poverty**	**% Poor who are white**	**% All[17]**	**% Black[18]**
1951					4.6	0.5
1952					5.1	0.8
1953					6.3	1.1
1954					6.6	1.1
1955					7.2	0.9
1956					8.7	1.3
1957					8.2	1.2
1958					9.0	2.1
1959	22.4	55.1		72.15	10.8	2.1
1960	22.2			70.93	12.0	3.9
1961	21.9			70.38	13.1	4.3
1962	21.0			69.05	13.9	3.8
1963	19.5			69.27	15.1	4.3
1964	19.0			69.22	16.6	5.7
1965	17.3			67.79	18.0	5.9
1966	14.7	41.8		72.98	20.3	7.3
1967	14.2			68.36	17.0	5.9
1968	12.8			68.51	18.6	7.0
1969	12.1	32.2		69.29	20.0	7.5
1970	12.6	33.5		68.90	19.7	8.3
1971	12.5	32.5		69.56	19.6	7.5
1972	11.9	33.3		66.24	21.8	9.3
1973	11.1	31.4		65.91	22.6	9.5
1974	11.2	30.3		67.33	25.5	10.9
1975	12.3	31.3	26.9	68.73	23.8	10.6
1976	11.8	31.1	24.7	66.80	25.3	11.5
1977	11.6	31.3	22.4	66.40	25.9	11.6
1978	11.4	30.6	21.6	66.53	27.2	13.4
1979	11.7	31.0	21.8	65.90	26.8	12.7
1980	13.0	32.5	25.7	67.24	24.3	11.2
1981	14.0	34.2	26.5	67.92	23.3	10.1
1982	15.0	35.6	29.9	68.31	23.3	9.5
1983	15.2	35.7	28.0	67.99	24.3	11.1
1984	14.4	33.8	28.4	68.25		
1985	14.0	31.3	29.0	69.18		
	Source: CPR, SA	Source: ib	Source: ib	Source: ib	Source: CPR	Source: CPR

	Family Status						
Years	**84** % Women 14 and over, never married	**85** % Women 18 and over, never married	**86** % Women 14 and over, married	**87** % Women 18 and over, married	**88** % Women 14 and over, divorced	**89** % Women 18 and over, divorced	**90** % Families with 3 or more children
1950	19.6		66.1		2.2		14.1
1951	19.1		66.5		2.1		
1952	19.1		66.6		2.3		
1953	18.3		66.9		2.3		
1954	18.5		67.0		2.3		
1955	18.2		66.9		2.3		17.5
1956	18.2		66.7		2.4		
1957	18.6		66.6		2.3		19.1
1958	18.8		66.0		2.3		19.5
1959	18.7		66.3		2.4		20.0
1960	19.0	11.8	65.9	71.3	2.6	2.9	20.5
1961	19.4		65.3		2.8		20.8
1962	19.6		65.3		2.7		21.4
1963	20.0		64.9		2.8		22.2
1964	20.3		64.4		3.0		22.3
1965	20.7	12.4	63.7	70.5	3.1	3.3	21.9
1966	20.9		63.7		3.1		21.6
1967	20.9		63.2		3.2		21.3
1968	21.7		62.6		3.2		21.2
1969	21.8	13.5	62.3	68.9	3.3	3.7	20.7
1970		13.7		68.5		3.9	20.3
1971		14.1		68.1		4.0	19.7
1972		13.8		68.5		4.3	18.8
1973		13.9		68.1		4.5	17.6
1974	22.5	14.3	61.1	67.6	4.4	4.9	16.9
1975		11.0		66.7		5.3	16.2
1976		11.5		66.2		5.7	15.6
1977		12.2		65.3		6.2	14.7
1978		13.0		64.2		6.6	13.8
1979		13.6		63.5		6.6	13.0
1980		14.3		63.0		7.1	11.9
1981		14.8		62.4		7.6	11.5
1982		15.3		61.9		8.0	10.9
1983		16.0		61.4		7.9	10.6
1984		16.4		60.8		8.3	10.4
1985		16.4		60.4		8.7	10.2
	Source: SA	Source: ib	Source: ib	Source: ib	Source: ib	Source: ib	Source: ib

ABBREVIATIONS IN HEADINGS

Ave	average
B	billions
Bus	business
C	change from previous period
Corp	corporations, corporate
Fedl	federal
ib	*Ibid.*, same as previous column of data
LF	labor force
M	millions
Mfg	manufacturing
N	employment
O	output
Tr	trillions
U	unemployment
$	dollars
%	percent

NOTES

1. Profit rate is on stockholders' equity, mfg corps. The data series after 1973 is not strictly comparable with earlier data. The figure for the old series in the fourth quarter of 1973 was 13.4, for the new series 14.3.
2. This is current assets/current liabilities.
3. Rate is per 10,000 US corps.
4. The data for 1947–1969 are based on totals published for the periods 1947–50, 1951–55, 1956–60, 1961–65, 1966–68, which have been evenly divided among the respective years to give yearly estimates.
5. The figure for the transition quarter between 1976 and 1977 was $96.0 billion.
6. Price index used is GNP deflator.
7. Includes interest 1947–74, net interest 1974–86.
8. Includes education, veterans' benefits, health, labor and welfare. Income security included only from 1961 forward.
9. The figure for the transition quarter 1976–77 was -23.3
10. This is the multilateral trade-weighted value of the US dollar.
11. Since one person may have more than one spell of unemployment in any year, this understates the ave duration of unemployment experienced per person.
12. Data from 1983 on are not strictly comparable with earlier data.
13. Rate is lost-workday accidents per 500 full-time equivalent workers.
14. Data for 1982–86 only include strikes involving > = 1000 workers; in 1981 there were 145 such strikes.
15. Data for 1982–86 only include strikes involving > = 1000 workers; in 1981 there were 729 such strikers.
16. Hourly wage and/or salary income plus benefits (e.g., health insurance) minus personal income taxes and Social Security taxes.
17. The % all families over $35,722 (1983 $) in 1967 was 22.2.
18. The % black families over $35,722 (1983 $) in 1967 was 9.6.

ABBREVIATIONS AND SOURCES

BGW — Bowles, Samuel, Gordon, David, and Weisskopf, Thomas. 1982. A Continuous Series on 'Real Spendable Hourly Earnings.' New York: Economics Institute of the Center for Democratic Alternatives; and their unpublished data.

BLS — US Dept of Labor (DOL), Bureau of Labor Statistics (BLS). 1986. *Employment, Hours, and Earnings, United States, 1909–84,* Bulletin 1312–12. Washington, DC: US Government Printing Office (GPO).

BS — US Dept of Commerce (DOC). Various years. *Business Statistics*. Washington, DC: US GPO.

CPR — US DOC, Bureau of the Census (BOC). Various years. *Current Population Report*. Washington, DC: US GPO.

ERP — US Council of Economic Advisors. 1987. *Economic Report of the President*. Washington, DC: US GPO.

ETRP — US Office of the President. Various years. *Employment and Training Report of the President*. Washington, DC: US GPO.

E&E — US DOL, BLS. Various months. *Employment and Earnings*. Washington, DC: US GPO.

FB — US Federal Reserve Board. Various months. *Bulletin*. Washington, DC: US GPO.

HLS — US DOL, BLS. 1985. *Handbook of Labor Statistics*. Washington, DC: US GPO.

HS — US DOC, BOC. 1975. *Historical Statistics of the United States*. Washington, DC: US GPO.

MLR — US DOL, BLS. Various months. *Monthly Labor Review*. Washington, DC: US GPO.

N&G — Naples, Michele I. and Gordon, David M. 1981. The Industrial Accident Rate: Creating a Consistent Time Series. New York: Institute for Labor Education and Research.

SA — US DOC, BOC. Various years. *Statistical Abstract*. Washington, DC: US GPO.

SCB — US DOC, Bureau of Economic Analysis. Various months. *Survey of Current Business*. Washington, DC: GPO.

LIST OF CONTRIBUTORS

LIST OF CONTRIBUTORS

Teresa Amott teaches economics at the University of Massachusetts in Boston, is a member of the *Dollars and Sense* collective, and is active in the Economic Literacy Project of Women for Economic Justice, a multiracial women's advocacy group.

Peter Arno is associated with Baruch College, Mt. Sinai Medical School, City University of New York.

Rhon Baiman teaches economics at Mount Ida College in Newton, Massachusetts and is a Ph.D. candidate in economics at the New School for Social Research. He is active in URPE and in the Democratic Socialists of America (DSA).

Robert Cherry is Associate Professor of Economics at Brooklyn College. His article is an abbreviated version of a chapter from his forthcoming book, *Discrimination: Its Economic Impact on Blacks, Women, and Jews.*

Michael Fabricant is Associate Professor at Hunter College in New York and is on the board of the National Coalition for the Homeless. He has written on housing and homelessness and is the author of *Working Under The Safety Net: Empowerment, Service Work and Advocacy in the 1980's.*

Karyn Feiden is a freelance writer living in New York City.

Diane Flaherty is Associate Professor of Economics at the University of Massachusetts — Amherst, and is staff economist for the Center for Popular Economics.

David M. Gordon teaches economics in the Graduate Faculty of the New School for Social Research and directs the Center for Democratic Alternatives in New York City. Among his publications, he is co-author of *Beyond the Waste Land: A Democratic Alternative to Economic Decline* and *Segmented Work, Divided Workers: The Historical Transformation of Labor in the United States.*

Michael Kelly is a social worker and supervisor of the Apartment Project of the Bowery Residents' Committee in New York.

Peter Marcuse is Professor of Urban Planning at Columbia University. He was president of the Los Angeles City Planning Commission, and is new chair of The Housing Committee of Community Board 9 in Manhattan.

Julie Matthaei teaches economics at Wellesley College, and with the Economic Literacy Project of Women for Economic Justice of Boston. She is author of *An Economic History of Women in America*, and is at work on a book entitled *Beyond Sex and Blood: Economy, Family, and the Breakdown of the "Natural" Family.*

Jack Metzgar teaches at Roosevelt University in Chicago and is editor of MCLR's semi-annual journal *Labor Research Review.*

Ruth Milkman is Associate Professor of Sociology at the City University of New York Graduate Center and at Queens College. She serves on the editorial boards of *Feminist Studies* and *Politics & Society*. Her articles on women, work and unions in the past and present have appeared in many books and periodicals. She is the editor of *Women, Work and Protest: A Century of Women's Labor History* (Routledge and Kegan Paul, 1985) and author of *Gender at Work: The Dynamics of Job Segregation by Sex during World War II*.

Kim Moody is a staff writer for *Labor Notes* and a member of Local 22 of the Newspaper Guild. His forthcoming book, *An Injury To All: The Decline of Organized Labor in America,* will be published by Verso in 1988.

Michele Naples is Assistant Professor of Economics and Women's Studies at Rutgers University. She has researched the postwar history of industrial conflict in the United States, and its empirical relationship to productivity growth. She has twiced served on the URPE steering committee.

Marilyn Power is an Associate Professor of Economics at St. Olaf College.

Michael Reich teaches economics at the University of California, Berkeley. He is the author of *Racial Inequality: A Political Economic Approach*.

Tom Riddell teaches economics at Smith College and is on the staff of the Center for Popular Economics.

Sam Rosenberg is Associate Professor of Economics at Roosevelt University. He is on the Board of Directors of the Midwest Center for Labor Research.

Saskia Sassen is Associate Professor, Graduate School of Architecture and Planning, Columbia University.

Elaine Sorensen is Assistant Professor of Economics at the University of Massachusetts, Amherst. The subject of comparable worth has been the focus of her research for many years. She is currently on leave from the University and working at The Urban Institute, where she is the Principal Investigator of a two-year study on the economics of a comparable worth policy.

Dan Swinney is a former United Steelworkers local union officer who is now Executive Director of the Midwest Center for Labor Research (MCLR).

Chris Tilly is a doctoral candidate in the departments of Economics and Urban Studies and Planning at M.I.T., and a member of the editorial collective of *Dollars and Sense* magazine. He has been active in labor, community, and student organizing over the last 15 years.

Meredeth Turshen, a political scientist who teaches public health at Rutgers University, has been affiliated with URPE since 1975. She has written two books and published many articles about international health, workers' health and women's health.

THE UNION FOR RADICAL POLITICAL ECONOMICS

The Union for Radical Political Economics (URPE) is an interdisciplinary association devoted to the study, development, and application of political economic analysis to social problems.

Founded in 1968, URPE has sought to present a continuing critique of the capitalist system and of all forms of exploitation and oppression while helping to construct a progressive social policy and create socialist alternatives.

Through its publications, conferences, informal study groups, and other projects, URPE provides a forum for education and debate in which divergent and often conflicting interpretations can be critically evaluated.

URPE's Members

URPE members, both in the United States and abroad, come from a wide range of academic disciplines, theoretical traditions, and political activities. We work and study in universities and other educational institutions, community organizations, trade unions, non-profit groups, and other progressive institutions. Many view URPE as a haven for careful, dispassionate, non-sectarian discussion of often charged or controversial theoretical and political issues.

Publications

URPE publishes an informal quarterly newsletter on its activities and the quarterly journal, *Review of Radical Political Economics (RRPE)*. The *RRPE* presents articles on radical political economic theory and applied analysis from a variety of theoretical traditions — including Marxism, institutionalism, post-Keynesianism, and feminism. Special issues of the *RRPE* have included five on women on the economy and single issues on energy, imperialism, regional economic development, and value theory.

Other educational materials published by URPE include *Reading Lists in the Radical Social Sciences,* jointly published with Monthly Review and MARHO and periodically updated; *U.S. Capitalism in Crisi,* and *Crisis in the Public Sector* (jointly with Monthly Review). URPE has also published a variety of shorter pamphlets for use in teaching and research.

Conferences

URPE holds two national conferences every year.

The summer conference is held at a low-cost camp and is intended to provide an informal setting in which URPE members and other interested friends and family can discuss academic and political work, join in organizational business, and socialize.

A second, more formal academic conference is held each winter as part of the annual meetings of the Allied Social Sciences Association, the umbrella gathering for professional economists, where we present critiques of mainstream economics and discuss radical alternatives.

Regional groups and special caucuses also occasionally sponsor other events, often in cooperation with allied groups. Some sample conference topics in recent years have been energy, the rise of the right, the political economy of the Third world, race and class, Rainbow Coalition politics in New York, and political economics for progressive journalists.

Other Activities

URPE members also occasionally organize around special academic and political interests or goals — working on conferences, through study groups, around curriculum development, or to develop special topics.

One important activity is the long-standing Women's Caucus, which publishes a newsletter for URPE women and those interested in Class and Gender studies.

The quarterly URPE newsletter provides information on various working groups and special activities within URPE and other similiar organizations.

How to Join

A new one-year membership with four-issue subscriptions to the *RRPE* and the URPE *Newsletter* as well as a discount on the summer conference is $20 (or $10 without the *RRPE*). We hope you'll complete and mail the attached form and join URPE today. For further information contact the URPE Natinal Office at the address listed on the order form.